OBSERVING YOUNG CHILDREN
TRANSFORMING EARLY LEARNING THROUGH REFLECTIVE PRACTICE

FIFTH EDITION

D1305932

KRISTINE FENNING

*Humber Institute of Technology
and Advanced Learning*

SALLY WYLIE

NELSON
EDUCATION

NELSON
EDUCATION

Observing Young Children: Transforming Early Learning through Reflective Practice, Fifth Edition

By Kristine Fenning and Sally Wylie

Vice President, Product and Partnership Solutions
Anne Williams

Publisher:
Lenore Taylor-Atkins

Marketing Manager:
Terry Fedorkiw

Content Development Manager:
Liisa Kelly

Photo Researcher and Permissions Coordinator:
Karen Hunter

Senior Production Project Manager:
Natalia Denesiuk Harris

Production Service:
MPS Limited

Copy Editor:
Marcia Gallego

Proofreader:
MPS Limited

Indexer:
Judy Davis

Design Director:
Ken Phipps

Managing Designer:
Franca Amore

Interior Design:
Cathy Mayer

Cover Design:
Cathy Mayer

Cover Image:
Cultura/Aurelie and Morgan David De Lossy

Compositor:
MPS Limited

Library and Archives Canada Cataloguing in Publication Data

Wylie, Sally, author
    Observing young children : transforming early learning through reflective practice / Kristine Fenning (Humber College Institute of Technology and Advanced Learning), Sally Wylie. — Fifth edition.

Revision of: Wylie, Sally. Observing young children.
Includes bibliographical references and index.
ISBN 978-0-17-658077-3 (paperback)

    1. Observation (Educational method). 2. Early childhood education. 3. Child development. I. Fenning, Kristine, author I. Title.

LB1139.3.C3W94 2015   372.21
C2015-904662-9

ISBN-13: 978-0-17-658077-3
ISBN-10: 0-17-658077-8

I begin my dedication of this fifth edition with a thank-you to my amazing family. I am blessed to be able to pause, reflect, and appreciate who they are and enjoy the beauty of each moment with them. They instill a passion in me every day. I am forever grateful to Sally Wylie, my mentor, friend, confidante, and inspirational educator-leader who has led me down many wonderful paths, one of which is this amazing text. I am proud to carry on what Sally has so wonderfully begun. To my Humber family: I am fortunate to have your support as I follow my writing passions. The Humber ECE team and department continue to be leading edge, and I am grateful to be amid such greatness. I am also thankful to be supported by the amazing leadership of Lisa Teskey and Jason Powell, who empower me in so many ways. To our early childhood students, professional educators, children, and families in the community: I look forward to continuing to collaborate and co-educate with you in order to co-transform and give back to our community, for you are our leaders of the future.

Kristine Fenning

I dedicate my last edition of this text to the students of early childhood education and educators practising in our profession, knowing you will be the recipients of much random joy, the nurturers of the next generation, and the memory-makers for children and their families. I also dedicate this edition to my family and friends, without whose support I would not have completed the five editions. But most of all, I dedicate this edition to my grandchildren, through whose wondrous eyes I continually see life's delights anew. I leave further editions of this text in the most capable, dedicated, and worthy hands of my friend, colleague, co-editor, and visionary, Kristine Fenning.

Sally Wylie

BRIEF CONTENTS

Foreword xv

Preface xvii

About the Authors xxx

Acknowledgments xxxii

PART 1 WHAT IS OBSERVATION? 1

CHAPTER 1 AN INTRODUCTION TO OBSERVATION 3

CHAPTER 2 PREPARING TO OBSERVE 43

CHAPTER 3 LEARNING TO DOCUMENT THE ACTIVITY OF CHILDREN 87

PART 2 HOW IS OBSERVATION DOCUMENTED? 133

CHAPTER 4 OBSERVING AND RECORDING UNANTICIPATED BEHAVIOURS 135

CHAPTER 5 OBSERVING AND RECORDING TARGETED BEHAVIOURS 189

PART 3 THROUGH THE LENS OF REFLECTIVE, TRANSFORMATIVE PRACTICES 235

CHAPTER 6 INFORMING PEDAGOGICAL PRACTICE THROUGH THE LENS OF REFLECTION 237

CHAPTER 7 INFORMING PRACTICE THROUGH THE LENS OF EARLY IDENTIFICATION 287

CHAPTER 8 REFLECTIVE AND TRANSFORMATIVE: OBSERVER AS LEADER 333

Glossary 371

References 388

Index 412

CONTENTS

Foreword xv
Preface xvii
  Observing Young Children: The Fifth Edition xviii
  Structural Organization of the Fifth Edition xx
  Changes to the Fifth Edition xxii
  Special Pedagogy to Support Learning xxvii
About the Authors xxx
Acknowledgments xxxii

PART 1 WHAT IS OBSERVATION? 1

CHAPTER 1 AN INTRODUCTION TO OBSERVATION 3

  Focus Questions 5
Observation and Appreciation 5
  Observation and Appreciative Inquiry 6
Why Is Observation Important? 9
  Why Observe Children? 9
    Reasons for Observing Young Children 9
Observation and the Responsive, Inclusive Educator 14
The Essential Partnership 16
  Family Centredness 17
  Relationships with Families 17
  Family Diversity 18
  Culture and Transformation 19
Observations of Children during Play 22
Framing What Has Been Observed 26
  Principles of Development 28
  Areas of Child Development 30
  Rates of Development 32
  Norms and Developmental Guidelines 32
Observation and Pedagogical Documentation 33
  The Special Role of Observation in Different Philosophies 38
Observation in Research: A Brief Historical Perspective 39
Observation in Research: A Current Perspective 40
Summary 41

CHAPTER 2 PREPARING TO OBSERVE 43

Overview 44
    Focus Questions 44
Two Levels of Observation 44
    Personal Level 44
    Professional Level 45
Defining a Systematic Process of Observation 46
    The Process of Watching and Listening to Children 48
The Cycle of Observation 49
Variations of the Cycle of Observation 52
    The Cycle of Observation as an Interactive Process 54
        Inquiry: A Vital Part of the Cycle of Observation 57
        Pedagogical Questions 58
    Questions of Self-Reflection 59
Asking the Questions: Why, How, Who, When, Where, and What 61
    Why Observe Children? 61
    Other Reasons for Observing Young Children 62
    How to Observe Children 66
        Spectator Mode 66
        Participatory Mode 66
    Whom Will You Observe? 68
    When to Observe 68
    Where to Conduct Observations 69
    What to Observe 69
Challenges to Effective Observation 70
    The Time Challenge 70
    Other Challenges 71
    Problem Solving and Teamwork 72
The Rights of Children 75
Code of Ethics 76
    Code of Ethics and Standards of Practice 76
    Ethics and the Observation Process 79
        Observation and Identity 80
    Ethics, Pedagogical Documentation, and the Observer 82
Consent and Confidentiality 83
    Office Files 85
    Getting Permission for Observations 85
Summary 86

CHAPTER 3 LEARNING TO DOCUMENT THE ACTIVITY OF CHILDREN 87

Overview 88
    Focus Questions 89
Getting Started 90
    Increasing Accessibility: Sharing Responsibility for Observing
        and Documenting 90
    Learning to Record and Understand What We Are Observing 92
    The Documenting Process 92
    Observer Guidelines in the Community 93
The Role of the Observer and Language Usage 98
    Adapting Your Communication Style in Early Childhood 98
    Using Descriptive Language 99
    Developing Vocabulary 101
    Semantics and Pragmatics 101
Learning to Document 103
    Documenting Observations: A Unique Style of Writing 103
    Lecture Note Taking versus Recording Observations 103
    Rough Notes and Rewriting: Reproducing Thoughts 104
    Writing with Confidence 106
    Translation and Documentation 106
    Self-Evaluation 108
Examining Three Basic Concepts in the Observation Process 110
    Searching for a Definition of Behaviour 110
    Internal Conditions 112
    Characteristics 113
    The Three Concepts: How Are They the Same/Different? 113
    Characteristics and Labels 114
    Variables Affecting Behaviour: Changes in Environment, Situations, or Time 116
    Areas of Child Development/Domains 118
Understanding and Interpreting Observations 121
    What Are Interpretations? 121
    Variations within Interpretations 123
Forms of Bias in Our Observations 124
    Ensuring the Presence of Ethics in Our Observation Practices 124
    Being Aware of Bias 124
    Forms of Bias 127
    Bias and Perceptions 129

Portfolios 130
What Is a Portfolio? 130
What Is the Purpose of Developing a Portfolio? 130
What Is in a Portfolio? 131
Summary 131

PART 2 HOW IS OBSERVATION DOCUMENTED? 133

The Main Categories 133

CHAPTER 4 OBSERVING AND RECORDING UNANTICIPATED BEHAVIOURS 135

Overview 136
Focus Questions 138
Anecdotal Records 138
Purpose and Unique Feature 138
Format of Anecdotal Records 139
Anecdotal Interpretations 142
Interpreting Expanded Observations 145
Interpretations as an Evaluative Function 146
Adapting Anecdotal Records 146
Combinations and Adaptations 148
Perceptions and Cultural Inferences 149
Running Records 151
Purpose and Unique Feature 151
Format of Running Records 151
Diaries: A Type of Record Similar to Running Records 155
ABC Analysis 155
Purpose and Unique Feature 155
ABC Analysis and the Behaviourists 156
Format of ABC Analysis 157
Adapting ABC Analysis 158
ABC Analysis and Curriculum Development 159
Photographs 161
Purpose and Unique Feature 162
Format of Photographs 163
Pictorial Combinations: Photographs and Text 164
Visual Communication and Children with Extra Support Needs 165
Photographs and Other Documentation Methods 165
Photographs and Documentation Panels 166

Photographs and Pedagogical Documentation: Reflections
and Considerations 166
Ethics and Photo Documentation: Ethical Dilemma or Not? 168
Audio/Digital Voice and Sound Recordings 169
Purpose and Unique Feature 170
Format of Audio/Digital Recordings 170
Audio/Digital Voice Recordings and Children's Portfolios 172
Video Recording 172
Purpose and Unique Feature 172
Format of Video Documentation 176
Video Recording with a Specific Purpose: Socioemotional Development 177
Is Video Recording an Effective Method? 178
Learning Stories 179
Purpose and Unique Feature 180
Format of the Learning Story Narrative 182
Section One: Capturing and Developing the Story 182
Section Two: Reflecting upon and Interpreting the Learning That
Took Place 183
Section Three: Discussing Next Steps, Future Opportunities, and Extensions
of Learning 183
Technology-Enabled Learning Story Formats 185
Summary 186

CHAPTER 5 OBSERVING AND RECORDING TARGETED BEHAVIOURS 189

Overview 190
Focus Questions 191
Making Decisions 192
What Could Be Other Considerations? 192
Frequency versus Duration 193
Designing an Observational Tool 194
Checklists 195
Purpose and Unique Feature 195
Format of Checklists 196
Developmental Sequence of Skills 198
Knowledge of Children within the Group 199
Knowledge of Children within the Context of Their Environment 200
Making Checklists User-Friendly 200

Prepared/Commercial Checklist Examples 201
    Adapting Checklists 203
    Interpreting and Reflecting upon Information from Checklists 204
Rating Scales 205
    Purpose and Unique Feature 205
    Format of Rating Scales 205
    Commercial Examples of Rating Scales 206
    Rating Scales in Early Childhood 207
    Adapting Rating Scales 207
    Rating Scale Design Considerations 208
    Interpretation of Information from Rating Scales 208
Behaviour Tallying and Charting 209
    Purpose and Unique Feature 209
    Behaviour Tallying 210
    Format of Behaviour Tallying 210
    Using a Conventional Graph 212
    Textbook/Internet Examples 213
    Interpreting Observations, Charts, and Graphs 213
    Examples of Behaviour Tallying Adaptations 214
Participation Charts 215
    Purpose and Unique Feature 215
    Format of Participation Charts 216
    Adapting Participation Charts 217
    Interpreting and Reflecting upon Participation Chart
        Information 219
Profiles 220
    Purpose and Unique Feature 220
    Format of Profiles 221
    Adapting Profiles 222
    Reflecting upon Profiles 226
Pictorial Representations 227
    Pictorial Representation with a Global Focus 229
Sociograms 229
    Sociogram Variations: Ecomaps 230
Mapping 232
Summary 234

PART 3 THROUGH THE LENS OF REFLECTIVE, TRANSFORMATIVE PRACTICES 235

CHAPTER 6 INFORMING PEDAGOGICAL PRACTICE THROUGH THE LENS OF REFLECTION 237

Overview 237
    Focus Questions 238
Appreciative Inquiry Revisited 239
    Finding a Pedagogical Framework 240
Reflective and Transformative: Revisiting the Cycle of Observation 242
    Variations of the Cycle of Observation 242
    The Cycle of Observation as Community Building 246
    Joining the Cycle: A Community Response 248
    The Cycle of Observation: A Transformational Process 249
    Collaboration and Co-Inquiry 250
    Mutual Education 251
The Reflective Educator: Responding to and Sustaining the Observation Cycle 253
    A Focus on Reflection 253
    Creating Time for Documentation and Reflection 254
    Reflection, Appreciation, and Inquiry 255
Webbing: A Multipurpose Tool 258
    Webbing and Emergent Documentation 260
    "Thinking and Wondering" in Pedagogical Documentation 260
Portfolios and E-Portfolios: An Important Part of the Cycle of Observation 262
    What Constitutes an Artifact? 263
    Portfolio Preparation, Stages, and Content 264
    Roles of the Educator, Child, and Family 268
    Roles of the Supervisor, Director, or Principal 270
    Portfolio and Authentic Assessment: Types and Forms 271
        Display or Showcase Portfolios 272
        Working/Developmental Portfolios 272
        Assessment Portfolios 275
        E-Portfolios/Digital Portfolios 275
    Portfolios and Accessibility 278
        E-Portfolios and Voice-to-Text Programs 278
    Portfolios: Supporting Children's Metacognition 280

Portfolios and Professional Standards, Frameworks, and Documents 282
Summary 284

CHAPTER 7 INFORMING PRACTICE THROUGH THE LENS OF EARLY IDENTIFICATION 287
Overview 287
    Focus Questions 288
The Cycle of Observation and Early Intervention 288
Beginning with Observation 291
    Creating an Observational Plan 292
    What Are Early Intervention and Early Identification? 293
    Early Intervention and Identification: Where Does the Process Begin? 293
    Theories Underpinning the Early Intervention and Identification Process 296
    Understanding Early Identification as a System 297
    The Role of the Resource Professional 299
    Early Intervention, Identification, and Interprofessional Education 301
Children's Health and Well-Being 302
    Reporting Child Abuse 302
    Family-Centred Approach and Early Intervention 304
    Foundations of Family Centredness: Building Relationships 307
    Early Identification and Intervention: Sharing Personal and Sensitive
        Information 307
    Family-Centred Conversations: Finding the Right Time 310
Special Needs: A Multifaceted Term 312
Teams: Collaborating and Creating 313
Assessment 315
    Three Stages of Assessment 318
    Assessment Tool Terms or Jargon 319
    Who Administers Assessments? 322
    Screening Tools 322
        Commonly Used Screening Tools in Canada 323
    Functional Assessment Tools: How Are They Initiated? 324
    The Role of the Early Childhood Professional in the Assessment Process 324
        What Is an Individualized Plan? 325
    Individualized Strategies and Programs 326
    Observation and Assessment: Informing Adaptations 328
    Evaluation: Summative and Formative 328
Summary 332

CHAPTER 8 REFLECTIVE AND TRANSFORMATIVE: OBSERVER AS LEADER 333

Overview 333
    Focus Questions 334
The Environment Defined 335
    Responsive Relationships and the Socioemotional/Psychological Tone of
        an Environment 335
    The Physical Environment 339
    Early Childhood Frameworks and Environmental Assessments: Beginning with
        a Question 345
        Environmental Assessment Tools and Measures 347
    Environmental Assessment: Stakeholder Contributions 349
    Environmental Assessment, Pedagogy, and Context: Voices of Children and
        Adults 354
Community Capacity Building: Educating and Preparing for Future Early
        Childhood Observers 354
    Interprofessional Collaboration 355
    The Observer as Pedagogical Leader 357
    Observer as Mentor: The Important Role of Mentorship 360
    Observer as Lifelong Learner: The Importance of Professional Development 361
Pedagogical Documentation and Educator E-Portfolios 363
    E-Portfolio Design and Considerations 364
    Observer as Researcher 364
        The Educator-Observer: Longitudinal Studies and Ethnographic
        Research 365
    Observation and Pedagogical Documentation Trends 366
        Blogs 367
        Wikis 368
        Twitter 369
        Instagram 370

Summary 370

Glossary 371

References 388

Index 412

FOREWORD

The idea that observation is crucial to understanding diverse populations is hardly new to the early childhood community. Yet, to simply say that it is important to our practice understates its unparalleled significance to our work. From daily health and safety checks to determining potential foci for program planning, the employment of a critical eye has become the very foundation of all that we do! Consequently, learning how to observe in a systematic way is the cornerstone of programs for prospective early childhood educators. While these formative years of training cultivate a variety of skills, early childhood preparatory programs are especially committed to laying the groundwork for a professional journey that routinely incites the power of observation to facilitate a deeper awareness of the children and families we serve.

Although purposeful observation is a long-standing tradition in the field, its continued use in many early childhood settings should not be restricted to determining children's play interests and identifying and supporting related developmental milestones. While these functions are important to our work, they operate in tandem to tell but one part of a multifaceted story, a narrative rich with possibilities that can be illuminated only through the integration of a repertoire of observation-based strategies that make all aspects of a child's thinking visible (Wien, 2013). Researchers refer to this process as *pedagogical documentation* and argue that its transformative potential resides in its insistence upon seeing beyond development to capitalize on the complexity and diversity of teachable moments. Where conventional approaches to observing produce accounts of significant events that validate the perspective of the educator, pedagogical documentation celebrates countless ways of being, thinking, and doing and draws children, families, and educators together as co-constructors of knowledge. Together, they become capable, competent, curious, and critical thinkers (Ontario Ministry of Education, 2014) whose mutual collaboration generates innumerable theories to help make sense of the world. In this way, pedagogical documentation emerges as a mechanism for unmasking a tale otherwise constrained by conventional approaches to observation, which tend toward chronicling a series of seemingly random, isolated events without probing deeper to expose the common thread that binds them. In light of this limitation, the use of pedagogical documentation has gained increasing momentum in recent years. It is a shift that has transformed early childhood practitioners into pedagogical storytellers, whose partnerships with children, families, and colleagues produce inquiry-based learning journeys that honour the perspectives of all parties (Yu, 2008).

I'm proud to have been a member of the early childhood profession for nearly 15 years, an experience that has given me first-hand knowledge of the value of pedagogical documentation to transforming practice, primarily through my work as an early childhood program supervisor with a large urban institution. As our approach to planning revolved around children's emerging interests, conducting observations that captured these was our highest priority. Most staff became adept at doing so and routinely crafted experiences that were logically connected to the developmental continuum. After years of approaching curriculum design in this way, planning for emerging interests became second nature. So, too, was the ability to apply developmental rationale to all pedagogical decisions. Despite this aptitude, however, I sensed we were somehow missing the bigger picture—that significant pieces of learning stories were being silenced through engagement with a process for planning that positioned the educator as the expert.

As I continued at that time to grapple with this sense of unease, I happened upon an article on pedagogical documentation in a graduate course I was taking (Seitz, 2008). Of the numerous claims made, it was the authors' link between pedagogical documentation and the rights of individual learners that most resonated with me, especially when much of my own writing and research was committed to social justice issues. And so it came to be that learning stories were introduced to the programs I supervised, forging necessary links between multiple observations composed of details contributed by educators, children, and families alike. Suddenly voices once silenced by traditional curriculum practices were heard, generating questions for exploration and related hypotheses that reflected multiple perspectives and produced a depth of investigation our programs had never before seen. And just as that article suggested, this profound shift in process seemed to benefit, in particular, children and families from marginalized groups. In fact, collaborative inquiry and its subsequent chronicling built bridges across difference and partnerships in practice through which educators, children, and families became co-authors of learning stories with no finite ending, tales that could be told and retold in a continuous cycle of collaborative meaning-making. For populations who'd grown accustomed to alienation from mainstream educational practices, pedagogical documentation's valuing of a plurality of ideas and voices ushered in a new way of thinking and doing within our organization—a process through which what it meant to be an educator and a learner was necessarily disrupted, leaving no one member of our learning community profoundly unchanged. Never underestimate the power of observation!

Ryan Campbell, R.E.C.E., B.A. (ECE), M.A. (ECS), Ph.D.(c)
Professor, Humber College Early Childhood Education

PREFACE

The primary focus of this text is to promote observation and encourage pedagogically sound observational practices. Through observation and the creation of pedagogical documentation, we learn about, appreciate, and make visible the daily experiences of children: their dizzy play, their ability to create, their curiosity, how they understand their world, their capacity for wonder, and how, over time, they grow and change. Change happens to those who observe and document as well, and that is another exciting focus of the fifth edition of this text, *Observing Young Children: Transforming Early Learning through Reflective Practice.* Through the lens of appreciative inquiry and the cycle of observation, we invite you to create a new space in your mind where you can develop transformative ways of teaching and learning with children, families, the early childhood profession, your own community, and the global village.

This text provides a comprehensive investigation of the topic of observation and pedagogical documentation for students, educators, administrators, parents, and consulting professionals or clinicians (such as resource professionals, speech pathologists, occupational therapists, or physiotherapists) who are involved with young children. It is particularly relevant for educators of infants, toddlers, and preschoolers; children in junior or senior kindergarten; and children who are in private home daycare, after-school programs, elementary school, and other settings.

Throughout this text, the process of observation and pedagogical documentation of children is examined, along with the aspects of practice that support and influence the dimensions of an early learning environment. Through appreciative inquiry and reflection, professionals and families are brought together to form collaborative learning communities where mutual education takes place. Inquiry forms the basis for this process, asking questions such as, "What elements compose quality, responsiveness, and inclusiveness in early learning communities or environments?" and "How will self-reflection be valued or promoted within the day?" This investigative and reflective process can be truly transformational as it takes us to new places of thought and practice. Seeing new possibilities that can transform any practice is exciting and rewarding, especially knowing that through a new lens, the observer is able to better perceive the children's learning, a newcomer family's experiences, or the ways that community resources can build capacity and provide for enriched experiences for children and their families.

As students and professionals of early childhood education, you will explore and discover the world of children with this text and learn about families and communities. You will be amazed, surprised, and rewarded, for this journey and career is both a deeply personal and a professional process. We hope that, by studying and applying the content of these chapters and the online site, you will find a meaningful way to tell your own story, as well as the stories of children and families. We invite you to join in Chapter 1 and stay with us as the dialogue continues into the last chapter, where we explore the important role of observer as leader and mentor, as well as new directions of observation and pedagogical documentation involving technology and social media.

We are excited about your journey as you develop your observation skills and your sensitivities and abilities to document the world of children, portraying their experiences as meaningfully as you can. Once this process has begun, it leads to a lifelong pursuit of learning.

OBSERVING YOUNG CHILDREN: THE FIFTH EDITION

The fifth edition of *Observing Young Children: Transforming Early Learning through Reflective Practice* has been updated to reflect the changes occurring in the early childhood profession, such as the growing synthesis between early childhood programs and the role of public education. Benefiting from the global reach of innovative educational practices, the early childhood community in Canada has seen significant shifts and begun new ways of observing and documenting children's thinking and expression. We, the authors, have changed as well, deepening our beliefs in responsive, inclusive practices that reflect what is meaningful in children's lives and in the lives of their families and communities. Observation is still at the centre of our inclusive and responsive practice, reflecting who we are, what we believe, and how we reveal this to ourselves and others. How observation informs practice through appreciative inquiry is reflected in subjects such as family-centred practice, team relationships, capacity building, the environment, early intervention, and early identification.

Observing and documenting children's learning, growth, and experiences is a responsibility as well as a joyous practice. To support your learning, in this text you will find ideas, examples, guidance, strategies, and adaptations that are current and relevant, and that will be of benefit to you now and in the future. Many of the chapters have exhibits and links to various frameworks across Canada and internationally (including the Ontario Early Learning Framework, *How Does Learning Happen?*), enabling educators to draw connections between observing and pedagogical documentation with links to practice. You will note that some of the chapters are about skill building and have an informational focus, while other chapters explore philosophical practices such as the ethics of observation, concepts of mutual education, and the inclusive concept of environment.

For the seasoned educator, some of the content will be familiar, yet the appreciative inquiry approach and cycle of observation may give you a flexible and inspiring framework for creating or continuing to build sound observation and pedagogical documentation practices that engage all educators, children, families, and communities.

Part 1 focuses on observation in a broad sense, examining one of the most complex educational practices in the field of early childhood. Observation plays more than a vital role—it is the substance of all pedagogical documentation. It is still the primary means of acquiring the knowledge we have about children and all aspects of our professional practice. It is also in this portion of the text that we introduce the observer to the rights of children and the important ethical considerations we must reflect upon as we prepare pedagogical documentation.

Our current professional practice requires educators to be innovative, creative, and co-constructive in their approach. The documentation, presented primarily in Part 2, serves to demonstrate that with a wide variety of choices, observers can gather information that supports a holistic portrayal of any child. Premised on a pedagogical approach to documentation, these chapters highlight the importance of children, families, and educators co-observing, co-documenting, and making visible the voices of all in the learning environment. Each method in this text includes the practice and approach of appreciative inquiry and facilitates the use of inquiry, reflection, and interpretation within a team approach. Explored in depth are current and trending documentation methods, all of which can be technologically produced, prepared, accessed, and shared. Furthermore, these methods support choice and discussion; they can be adapted to support any philosophy or practice; and when these methods are combined or used alongside traditional observation or assessment methods, educators are better equipped to support transformation of their practices no matter where they are in the world.

Part 3 continues with the topic of pedagogical documentation, introducing curriculum and portfolio development (e-portfolios and hard-copy portfolios), as well as examining early intervention and early identification. New directions in social media and technology conclude this section, giving educators, families, children, and administrators a potentially new forum for co-documenting and making sense of what we see and hear, as well as for co-educating, co-constructing, and co-planning. Administrators of early childhood programs who are working to develop responsive, inclusive programs will find expert advice and innovative ideas as they consider the best possibilities in collaboration with their learning community for their centre, school, or agency.

This fifth edition emphasizes the links between observation and appreciative inquiry; observation and pedagogical documentation; responsive, inclusive practice and the cycle of observation; diversity within communities and capacity building; early identification/early intervention and professional relationships; and personal beliefs/values and the development of meaningful curriculum and environment. Using the cycle of observation, each link is examined to illustrate how observation may begin like a stone dropped in the water—beginning with the observation of a child, which sends ripples out in all directions to reach the community and even global shores.

STRUCTURAL ORGANIZATION OF THE FIFTH EDITION

The structural organization of the text remains the same as in previous editions. **Parts 1, 2,** and **3** serve to organize content into three main parts.

Part 1. Observation reveals how children see their world, what they think about it, how they use the things that are in it, and whom they trust, play with, and want to be around. Observation is setting-independent, serving no one particular philosophy, and is used by educators the world over. Observation is still the most important investigative methodology we have to discover how young children grow and develop.

Part 1 is divided into three chapters. Chapter 1 begins with a discussion of observation and appreciative inquiry and illustrates why observation is important in all aspects of education, regardless of pedagogy and philosophy. Play, family, diversity, and culture are examined as a context for observation, along with a look at the role of the educator in responsive, inclusive practice. Chapter 1 briefly examines areas of child development, rates of development, and developmental guidelines and principles. It includes the topic of observation in research, both historical and current perspectives. The chapter provides a foundation from which further learning can be pursued, linking current practice to all aspects of the observation process.

In Chapter 2, one of the most important concepts is introduced—one that you will see throughout the entire text—the cycle of observation. The basic questions of observation—who, what, how, when, where, and why—are also explored. Topics related to the observation process, such as occupational standards and challenges to effective observation, are investigated. This chapter is also about getting ready to begin the actual process of observation and relevant concepts to reflect upon, such as the rights of children, the Code of Ethics, and confidentiality—concepts and ideas that will lay the foundation for ensuing chapters.

Chapter 3 is about pedagogical documentation. In this chapter, you will learn the influence that bias and judgment have upon the observation and documentation process. An expanded section on bias will assist you with exploring the very real world of perception, values, and bias and their impact on your development as a professional. Expanded significantly in this chapter is the interpretation process. Chapter 3 will explain how different documentation methodologies require us to approach interpretations in different ways.

Another area thoroughly examined in this chapter is the actual writing process, with concrete, practical examples, guidelines, and suggestions. Few texts in the field of early childhood provide relevant information on the unique writing process that is pedagogical documentation. Even fewer texts address the concerns of mature students who have been away from school or those of newcomer students from other countries. This chapter will support their development as observers and writers of observations.

Part 2 introduces two major categories of documentation methods and is composed of two chapters illustrating a wide variety of ways in which to document and interpret the growth, learning, and experiences of young children. Chapter 4 speaks to the narrative, open style of pedagogical documentation, such as the anecdotal record, photographs and text, learning stories, audio recordings, and video recordings. The closed types of records illustrated in Chapter 5 include those that target specific behaviours, such as the checklist, or track the social play of a child, such as the participation chart.

Part 2 is the most pragmatic section in the text, as it provides numerous practical, current, and popular ways of gathering, documenting, and making visible the learning of children. We have tried to encompass a wide spectrum of documentation, from a basic checklist to examples of pedagogical documentation embraced and practised in schools and early childhood centres across Canada and around the globe. We do not promote one type of record above others; rather, we propose a variety of choices so that reflection may prompt an inquiry, new questions, a discussion, or, after reflection, the adoption of new pedagogical documentation methodologies that support and reflect the children and families in one's learning community.

The text and the online site provide numerous methods for documenting the experiences of young children, the interactions and relationships of adults and children, and the environment. The examples found in these two chapters can be used with different age groups, as well as with populations of children who may require adaptations or extra supports. An advantages/disadvantages chart of the methods is included in MindTap to allow for quick comparison.

The comprehensive exhibit examples in these chapters and online illustrate real student work that exemplifies the notion that through observation, students can construct their own meaningful documentation. We hope these examples will encourage you as you begin your journey as a student-observer.

The purpose of **Part 3** is to look through the lens of the cycle of observation to reflect and see new possibilities, creating a new space in your mind that can transform what you see and believe. Part 3 is about reflective practice—a key concept fundamental to observation, particularly when living in a society that is ever-changing, with research and practices that constantly evolve and reframe our thinking. Change invited us to create this fifth edition, where the vibrant process of investigating, learning, and reflecting continues to encourage dialogue, sharing, and discovery of innovative ways to observe and document the lives of children.

In Part 3, we explore how our beliefs and practices around observation are reflected in day-to-day interactions, families, communities, and the global village. With the immediacy of social media and the Internet, it is no wonder that we look not only to our own neighbourhoods but also outward to others for their philosophy and practices regarding children and families. Guided by responsive, inclusive practices, educators look to models and their principles, goals, and core values to reaffirm, discover, and reflect. Exploring alternative methods that assist us in creating the most useful, meaningful ways of sharing the learning and development of children is necessary.

CHANGES TO THE FIFTH EDITION

This text is the fifth edition of *Observing Young Children: Transforming Early Learning through Reflective Practice*. The first edition was published in 1999, the second in 2004, the third in 2009, and the fourth in 2012. Major changes in each edition reflect the changes in the field of early childhood, our knowledge base, legislation, and society, and an overall transformation of the pedagogy of education and play.

The general changes to each chapter are as follows:

- An overview is presented at the start of each chapter.
- Focus questions at the beginning of each chapter are included to prompt inquiry and discussion of key topics in the chapter.
- A summary is provided at the end of each chapter.

- Key terms are highlighted in each chapter and a glossary of these terms is provided at the end of the text.
- Each chapter incorporates exhibits designed to highlight a concept or provide a specific example of chapter material.
- The new colourful design with outstanding colour photos and print makes this edition visually interesting and engaging.
- An Advantages/Disadvantages section for each of the observational methods in Chapters 4 and 5 has been included in MindTap to allow readers to determine which best suits their purpose for observing.

CHAPTER 1

Chapter 1 begins Part 1 and has been revised to include new research, topics, terminology, exhibits, and concepts that reflect current and leading-edge early learning observational practices. Chapter 1 begins with the image of a child and details why this focus is all-important in the process of observation.

In this edition, the relationship between observation and appreciative inquiry is explored in depth to look for the "possibilities" where the voices of children can be heard. Inspired by sociocultural theory, inquiry-based thinking forms the catalyst for learning and pedagogical documentation. Reasons to observe are covered as in previous editions, but references to new inquiries, such as ethnographic research, illustrate the changing methodologies used to capture not only information but also the relationships of information and what that means. The content in Part 1 speaks to the educator as part of a responsible early learning community and highlights the importance of understanding the complex nature of the observational process. Using a responsive and inclusive lens for observation, this chapter strengthens the reflective practices of today's educators and further emphasizes the role of the educator as a partner in a broader early learning community.

CHAPTER 2

In this chapter, the key concept of the cycle of observation is introduced and explored in further detail than in previous editions, connecting this content to all chapters throughout the text. The observation cycle includes children, families, educators, the environment, the community, and much more. This concept is not new, but how it is used to support the main themes of this text is new and visionary; it is the primary vehicle for reflection and inquiry. New to this chapter are the deeply explored topics of the rights of children and ethical issues in observation and pedagogical documentation, and how these topics relate to the observer and the ethical and confidential process of observing and documenting the experiences of children. Chapter 2 has also been revised with new research, exhibits, photos, and examples.

CHAPTER 3

Chapter 3 separates this text on observation from all others as it clearly addresses the complicated task of writing, documenting what is seen or heard. As writing observations in the field of early childhood offers its own set of challenges, this chapter clearly addresses those challenges and the often-asked question, "How do I write this?" It tackles some of the main issues of writing: lack of confidence, writing when you have been out of school for some time and are returning as a mature student, and writing as an English-language learner. Writing observations in early childhood settings offers its own set of challenges, whether it is with the use of electronic devices or pen and paper. Student examples in the text demonstrate what is possible while providing strategies and ideas. The Chapter 3 focus on skill development is supported by dozens of closed-captioned videos featuring a wide range of age groups from the online Instructor's Manual. This chapter also explores the topic of bias, cautioning students to document their observations in such a way that represents children fairly and equitably. Chapter 3 also includes new photos, key terms, exhibits, and topics.

CHAPTER 4

Chapter 4 begins Part 2, introducing observational narrative methods that are open-ended, flexible, and focused on capturing the spontaneous learning and experiences of young children. In this edition, this chapter has been expanded to include methods that favour the practices of responsive, emergent, or play-based curriculum, focusing on the spontaneous learning opportunities in the early childhood setting. The choice we make reflects the inquiry. Creation of the documentation and subsequent revisiting by the educator and/or families and children shape what is important. These observational tools form one of the major groupings that can be represented in a child's portfolio. This chapter helps answer the question, "What are the advantages of the visual alternatives to print-dependent methods used to document the activity of children?" Using these observational methods offers ways to discover what is new about children, uncover what had been previously unknown, or begin to develop information about a story or project. Technology plays a role in the way we document the experiences of young children, and this chapter, along with Chapter 8, illustrates with examples the changing nature of observation.

Pedagogical documentation allows students to see their own learning through their observations, which gives them another benchmark for their success besides tests and assignments. Students and instructors are again privy to resources and links for this chapter online. Chapter 4 also contains new research, photos, examples, and exhibits.

CHAPTER 5

Chapter 5 offers many types of methods that target behaviours or experiences seen by educators as a means to learn specific information about a child or situation. In this edition, Chapter 5 examines these methods more clearly and in more detail, explaining why they are useful and giving examples that are meaningful for an educator. These methods have been streamlined with new content and examples that more thoroughly explain their possible adaptations. These observational methods are presented to invoke discussion and reflection regarding how educators might use them to inform their practice. For Chapters 4 and 5, a chart listing each documentation method's advantages and disadvantages is provided in MindTap.

CHAPTER 6

Chapter 6 is the first chapter of the last section: Part 3. Chapter 6 has been completely revised since the last edition. This chapter asks and answers the question, "How do we determine a framework in which to organize our pedagogical documentation, and how do we share that information?" Chapter 6 is the application of previous chapters. This chapter takes a broad look at how the cycle of observation opens the door to the mutual education of educators, families, and the community through reflection, inquiry, and appreciation. New research, exhibits, and content highlight how reflection and observation build self-awareness in educators, how mutual education between children and adults facilitates "possibility" thinking, and the importance of building our own pedagogy of observation and documentation. Chapter 6 prompts the reader to use a number of responsive and inclusive perspectives when observing young children, looking beyond the traditional developmental lens to consider many other approaches, such as those of sociocultural and psychological influences. Approximately half of this chapter is devoted to the development of portfolios. The investigation of portfolios reveals a comprehensive look into relevant subtopics such as e-portfolios, stages and content of portfolios, how to link documentation and information to professional standards and frameworks, and the various types and forms of portfolios. In addition, resources online provide examples, research, and related topics.

CHAPTER 7

Chapter 7 connects the learning from previous chapters and describes how early identification and early intervention transform practice with the cycle of observation. This chapter explores the complex process of both topics, starting with family-centred practice, interprofessional education, assessment tools, individual planning for a child with special needs, and the terminology associated with the individualized planning process.

Chapter 7 affirms the notion that observation is integral to everything we do as educators, especially when it involves children and families who need extra supports and services. In this edition, we realized that involvement in the observation cycle takes us beyond the corridors of early childhood settings and schools out into the community, both local and global; it causes us to step out to look back in and be involved in appreciative inquiry that involves assessment, teams, collaboration, and mutual education. The cycle of observation leads to discussion of referrals, adjustments and adaptations, environmental design, and the ways that children and families can draw assistance from the knowledge and skills of educators and the community. Integral to this chapter are further resources and examples provided online.

CHAPTER 8

Chapter 8, more than any other chapter in this text, introduces new terms, exhibits, and content. College and university instructors will be pleased to see this content included in the fifth edition. This chapter begins with an exploration of the role of environment as co-educator and co–play partner with children. Understanding that a quality environment is much more than just the physical attributes of a space is important; educators must observe a number of environmental aspects, including relationships and the psychological tone of the space, to understand its role and interactions with children.

Chapter 8 carefully weaves together all previous chapters in this text; the role of the educator has transformed so significantly that it is important to challenge our current professional paradigms of practice. Opportunities are vast for educators to take on the role of leader and mentor in evolving observational practices to reflect both pedagogical documentation methodologies and the necessary components within the cycle of observation that is discussed throughout this text. Examples are available online of educator leaders in the profession who are innovative in social media documentation methods in order to function in a co-education role with children and families.

Chapter 8 also explores trends in social media documentation, as there is much to learn about this social media technology, its ability to include the voices of children and families in real-time learning experiences, and its ability to make children's learning visible. To be a transformational observer, it is important to maintain currency in one's knowledge and skills regarding observation and documentation. Participation in ongoing professional development and communities of practice is important for educators, as is the documentation of one's own growth and development in a portfolio as an educator. Researcher and lifelong learner, participant in ongoing professional development, and contributor to community capacity-building are all-important roles that educators must assume to further support and promote innovative observational practices.

SPECIAL PEDAGOGY TO SUPPORT LEARNING

INSTRUCTOR'S RESOURCES

These online instructor's resources provide password-protected content for use by any instructor, and are especially helpful to part-time instructors or instructors new to this course material. Included in the resources for each chapter are expected content such as a test bank of informal and formal assessment items, Microsoft® PowerPoint® presentation slides, and an instructor's guide that contains key concepts, engagement strategies, reflective questions, internet and video exercises, and annotated lists of recommended resources, such as articles, texts, videos, and websites. The instructor's manual also includes sections on student motivation and challenges to learning, engagement strategies, and reflections on teaching.

The **Nelson Education Teaching Advantage (NETA)** program delivers research-based instructor resources that promote student engagement and higher-order thinking to enable the success of Canadian students and educators. Be sure to visit Nelson Education's **Inspired Instruction** website at http://www.nelson.com/inspired/ to find out more about NETA.

The following instructor resources have been created for *Observing Young Children,* Fifth Edition. Access these ultimate tools for customizing lectures and presentations at http://www.nelson.com/instructor.

NETA Test Bank

This resource was written by Kristine Fenning and Sally Wylie. It includes approximately 40 multiple-choice questions written according to NETA guidelines for effective question construction. Also included are more than 40 short answer and 80 essay questions that, together, cover the full scope of the text.

NETA PowerPoint

PowerPoint lecture slides for every chapter have been created by Kristine Fenning and Sally Wylie. There is an average of 18 slides per chapter, many featuring key figures, tables, and photographs from *Observing Young Children*. NETA principles of clear design and engaging content have been incorporated throughout, making it simple for instructors to customize the deck for their courses.

NETA Instructor's Guide

The Instructor's Guide to accompany *Observing Young Children*, Fifth Edition, has been prepared by Kristine Fenning and Sally Wylie. This manual is organized by chapter and contains sample lesson plans, learning objectives, suggested classroom activities, and a resource integration guide to give instructors the support they need to engage their students within the classroom.

As with the text, the Instructor's Guide represents a complete update of previous instructor manuals for this text. A key highlight or added value is that while students are using documents available online, instructors are able to access their own resources that connect to students' understanding of content explored within their text and online. This coordinated approach to learning and teaching offers a rich hybrid experience of research, examples, and content for all involved.

Day One Slides

Day One—Prof InClass is a PowerPoint presentation that instructors can customize to orient students to the class and their text at the beginning of the course.

MindTap

Offering personalized paths of dynamic assignments and applications, MindTap is a digital learning solution that turns cookie-cutter into cutting-edge, apathy into engagement, and memorizers into higher-level thinkers. MindTap enables students to analyze and apply chapter concepts within relevant assignments, and allows instructors to measure skills and promote better outcomes with ease. A fully online learning solution, MindTap combines all student learning tools—readings, multimedia, activities, and assessments—into a single Learning Path that guides the student through the curriculum. Instructors personalize the experience by customizing the presentation of these learning tools to their students, even seamlessly introducing their own content into the Learning Path.

MindTap for *Observing Young Children*, Fifth Edition, includes two sets of closed-captioned videos:

- Observation videos of children alone or in small groups are extremely valuable for instructors in the classroom and useful for students who do not otherwise have access to groups of children for observation. Question sets are provided with these videos.
- Video testimonials enhance the audio/visual experience for students by enlisting leading professionals in the early childhood profession and external community to examine and discuss key concepts from each chapter.

All the videos within MindTap function well as visual resources to assist students with the application of their learning and understanding of text material as well as providing opportunities for direct application of observation and writing skills.

STUDENT ANCILLARIES

MindTap
Stay organized and efficient with MindTap—a single destination with all the course material and study aids you need to succeed. Built-in apps leverage social media and the latest learning technology. For example,

- ReadSpeaker will read the text to you.
- Flashcards are pre-populated to provide you with a jump start for review—or you can create your own.
- You can highlight text and make notes in your MindTap Reader. Your notes will flow into Evernote, the electronic notebook app that you can access anywhere when it's time to study for the exam.
- Self-quizzing allows you to assess your understanding.

Visit http://www.nelson.com/student to start using MindTap. Enter the Online Access Code from the card included with your text. If a code card is not provided, you can purchase instant access at NELSONbrain.com.

ABOUT THE AUTHORS

Kristine Fenning is a program coordinator and early childhood professor with the Early Childhood Education program at Humber Institute of Technology and Advanced Learning. Kristine has an extensive background in adult education, community college, resource consultation, and early childhood education. Kristine's vitality and passion for early childhood has led her to fulfill a number of roles in her 24 years in the profession, including early childhood educator, resource teacher, resource consultant, and training coordinator. Kristine has presented various topics at conferences in both Canada and the United States and has authored and published other articles and documents pertaining to cohort-based learning, academic integrity, inclusion, and supervisory leadership. In collaboration with Toronto Children's Services and Humber College Child Care Centres/Humber ITAL, Kristine was a co-developer and co-originator of the professional development system now in place for early childhood educators, resource consultants, supervisors, and directors in Toronto. Her passions are teamwork, educational advocacy, inclusion, observation and pedagogical documentation, assessment, the role of technology in observation, and resource consultation. Kristine continues to be a member of a number of projects involving community partnerships, collaborative learning, and inclusion. She is a proud wife and mother of two beautiful daughters, who continue to teach her and empower her to make a difference in the lives of others.

Sally Wylie has been in the field of early childhood for three decades as an early childhood educator, resource teacher and elementary school teacher, program advisor for the Ontario Ministry of Children and Youth Services, and college/university professor. She has this to say about the topic of observation: "After 30-plus years in the early childhood education profession, observation is still one of my greatest interests and passions. I believe strongly that there is no test that could ever take the place of an educator with keen observation skills and the ability to communicate to others what is discovered." Sally has partnered with Humber Institute of Technology and Advanced Learning for a videoconferencing project with the Regional Training and Resource Centre in Early Childhood Care and Education for Asia in Singapore, and given workshops in Singapore on the topic of developing portfolios. Sally has co-presented at the National Association for the Education of Young Children in Canada and the United States, and collaborated with the Government of Ontario and TFO, Ontario's French-language educational authority, to produce a bilingual website for supervisors. She has published and co-published many articles. Sally finished her formal teaching career with Charles Sturt University–Ontario in the Bachelor of Early Childhood Studies Program, but has remained an active early childhood consultant with various early learning centres in northern Ontario. She is married and has three wonderful adult children and six grandchildren. Sally is currently writing fictional stories for young children.

ACKNOWLEDGMENTS

We would like to thank the following people for their contributions to this text; we continue to appreciate that it takes a community to write a text. To these individuals, we offer our appreciation of their gift of time and expertise and their willingness to share their experiences with the readers of this book. Thanks also to the parents and children who shared their faces with us in photographs and videos.

We would like to thank our families, without whose support this text would never have been possible. It was with their support and encouragement that we were able to advance our writing journey forward once again with this fifth edition.

We also wish to thank our colleagues and friends, whose encouragement has meant so much. Without support, it is difficult to persevere and complete a project, and we take this space to acknowledge those whose support has been much appreciated.

A special thanks to Ryan Campbell for his contribution to the foreword of this text. Ryan's commitment to the early childhood profession, in particular his work with diverse populations, is amazing. We wish to also thank the individuals, agencies, and organizations who gave permission for their contributions to be used in this text.

To students embarking on their career as early childhood professionals: this book is not only about you, but is written for you. To current early childhood professionals: we are excited about the many possibilities that this text can offer to your important roles and work with pedagogical documentation, leadership, research, and mentoring. Thank you for all that you do.

Our appreciation is extended to the diligent staff of the editorial and production departments at Nelson Education, whose expertise and organization kept everything on track throughout the entire process. We wish to thank Lenore Taylor-Atkins, publisher, for her expertise, cooperation, and generous support of this edition; Liisa Kelly, content development manager, for her unwavering patience; Terry Fedorkiw, marketing manager; Natalia Denesiuk Harris, senior production project manager; Joanne McNeil, manufacturing manager; Marcia Gallego, copy editor; and Lynn McLeod, project manager, rights acquisition and policy, as well as all the members of the production team at Nelson for their many contributions to the success of this fifth edition.

WHAT IS OBSERVATION?

Observation is the most important investigative methodology we have to discover how young children grow and develop. It has been the primary means of acquiring the knowledge we currently have about children today. Observation reveals how children see their world, what they think about it, how they utilize the things that are in it, and whom they trust, play with, and want to be around.

Whether you are a professional or student in early childhood, you occupy an important place in the lives of young children, and if you are lucky enough to work directly with them, you will be invited into their world: to see it, hear it, experience their thoughts and feelings, and be able to document all those observations. You will discover that conducting observations is not only a highly personal learning experience and a shared journey of discovery, but also a primary responsibility of an educator.

Part 1 is divided into three chapters. Chapter 1 introduces us to observation and appreciative inquiry and why observation is so important in all aspects of education regardless of philosophy. Observation is the foundation for everything we do in any early childhood setting, and examining the reasons for observation has to be a primary focus in this chapter. We begin our discussion of observation with the wonderful privilege and opportunity we have as professionals in early childhood to engage in dialogue with children, to watch and listen to their smiles and joys of discovery, and to marvel at the mysteriousness and uniqueness of childhood. Observation takes us into the realm of children. It is the only tool available to educators of young children if they wish to learn, understand, and wonder, and yet observation itself cannot be defined in such a simplistic way or this entire book would be reduced to a few pages. From the act of observing a child, it is important to recognize the numerous threads woven into the observation fabric: the role of the educator, the child, and the family, as well as documentation, culture and diversity, philosophy, pedagogy, early identification, and technology—to name a few. As you continue to discover and uncover the possibilities that observation offers, we hope you will come to appreciate observation as we do.

Chapter 1 not only examines the importance of acquainting yourself with areas of child development, rates of development, and developmental guidelines and principles, but also discusses the importance of observation in research, both from a historical and current perspective, so as to enable the observer to pursue further learning practices relating to this important aspect of professional practice.

Chapter 2 is a practical chapter that defines observation as a systematic process. This process includes engaging in inquiry, a cycle of observation, and the respectful pedagogical documentation of a child's expression during play. This chapter introduces the pragmatic preparation required for the observation of young children. The chapter continues with the significant questions of observation, such as how, when, who, and where you will observe. This chapter is about getting ready to begin the process of observation and what to consider, such as "How do I go about observing young children?" The discussion of the importance of consent and confidentiality, the rights of children, and the Code of Ethics highlights the considerations necessary before observing young children.

Chapter 3 is about getting started with the actual process of observing, documenting, and interpreting and reflecting on the learning experiences of young children. This chapter examines how language usage, combined with observation skills, produces knowledge about young children. We also learn about the importance of understanding how bias influences how and what we document and the important considerations we need to make when engaging in the observational process. As we interpret what we see and hear, we begin to understand our role in creating a culturally responsive environment and how our role is interwoven with those of the children and their families. We then begin as educators to appreciate the role of the family and its cultural influence on a child's development.

Chapter 3 is about writing and pedagogical documentation. Another area thoroughly examined is the process of documenting observations with examples, guidelines, and suggestions to assist in the actual process. In this chapter, the focus is on learning what to write and finding the appropriate ways to say it.

Few texts in the field of early childhood provide concrete information on the writing process, and even fewer address the concerns of mature students who have been away from school or those of new students from other countries. This chapter will support not only educators currently practising in the profession but also beginning observers and writers of documentation.

CHAPTER 1

AN INTRODUCTION TO OBSERVATION

Judy Barranco/iStockphoto.com

We are you! We are the student in class, the new graduate, the seasoned, experienced educator, the consultant, the professor of early childhood, the educator in the room of busy toddlers or questioning kindergarteners.

We represent a willingness to ask questions, inquire, and then listen. We are willing to transform curriculum, environment, and practices when we see there is a better way.

We are global in our approach, examining philosophies and practices in other countries. We learn from children, each other, our instructors, the Internet, journals, ebooks, textbooks, and countless other ways.

We observe through a variety of lenses: sociocultural, responsive education, emergent curriculum, developmentally appropriate practice, Reggio Emilia, and other philosophies and practices so we can learn and understand.

We learn no matter what our role: student, educator, community partner, or professor. We recognize that everyone coming to this expansive topic of observation will bring their own set of values, perspectives, and expectations. We hope this text will fulfill those expectations, change your perspective, and embrace the values of a responsive, inclusive educator whose passion is learning and understanding the lives of young children.

We invite others to share our perspective, adopt our philosophy of observation and pedagogical documentation, and accept our invitation to join in the journey of *Observing Young Children: Transforming Early Learning Through Reflective Practice*.

We are not constrained by a specific philosophy; observation is setting-independent. One of the things we strive for is creating access to the world of observation. Creating a supportive environment that encourages observation, values the process, and appreciates the discoveries made about young children, their families, environments, and cultures is our passion. We hope it becomes yours.

We hope that as you journey through your personal discoveries, challenges, and rewards, you, too, will include others, laugh, learn, and question. Welcome to observation!

The focus of Chapter 1 builds upon this image of the child and is primarily an introduction to the purpose and value of observation in the early childhood profession. However, as you will discover, observation is an invitation into understanding what we see and hear and is embedded in everything that we do. Knowledge of different methodologies is not sufficient in itself as observation is also a value, a philosophy, an attitude, a skill, and ultimately an important responsibility. Observation is interesting in that it belongs to all who work with children and their families; it is part of all cultures and performs basically the same function in all program or school philosophies: uncovering what we know about children.

In this chapter, you will discover and examine the role observation has played and continues to play in uncovering the world of children in any early childhood setting in Canada and the world. You will learn about a few of the many theories guiding early childhood observation practices, such as sociocultural theory, pedagogical documentation principles, and developmental guidelines and principles to frame and give meaning to observations.

1. What is the purpose and importance of observation, and how does it contribute to the quality of professional practice and early childhood settings?
2. What do we mean by an "appreciative inquiry" approach, and what is its relationship to observation?
3. Why is observation an integral part of any program or philosophy that involves educating and caring for young children?
4. What are the qualities that define a responsive and inclusive educator? What role does reflection play in developing these qualities?
5. How does observation and pedagogical documentation capture a child's thinking and feelings, and why is that important?
6. Why is it important to understand culture, diversity, and societal change?

OBSERVATION AND APPRECIATION

It is through observation that educators are afforded the opportunity to learn from, with, and about young children. From our observations, we can begin to appreciate the important role that educators play in documenting the learning, thinking, and inquiry of children, as well as the significance of making children's learning visible. It is through observation, interpretation, reflection, and evaluation that we gain insights into how children learn, the effects of socialization and culture on the child's personality and behaviour, how the environment influences behaviour and learning, and much more.

This book posits that to be an attuned, responsive, and inclusive observer, it is necessary to view children through an appreciative inquiry approach, seeing them as competent, able, intuitive investigators and inquirers, capable of co-constructing new learning and confident in their ability to question new experiences.

For many years, early childhood professionals have created their image of a child based on various developmental theories, as they are seen as a measurable way in which to understand what children are learning. We challenge the educator to broaden the scope of how children are seen by going beyond the constraints of one particular theory to view them, instead, in a responsive, inclusive, and holistic way encompassing a variety of theories to inform what is known and understood about how children learn, some of which are introduced in this chapter.

Listening attentively to what children are saying and being able to follow up with questions that uncover the child's level of understanding are essential skills in implementing a negotiated learning approach to curriculum. Both skills take practice. An image of the child who is competent and full of ideas is central to listening attentively to what children say. When teachers expect children to say interesting things and to contribute ideas, they will be much more likely to pay attention to what children have to say. When children know that their ideas are appreciated, they will be more willing to share them. (Fraser, 2011, pp. 187–188)

Educators could follow this example by employing a variety of theories to add meaning to their observations and documentation. Both adults and children deserve to be viewed as diverse human beings full of possibility, who are capable of contributing new knowledge to their world and who are appreciated for their uniqueness.

EXHIBIT 1.1   OBSERVATION AND APPRECIATION

What children do in their early years is truly wonderful. To fully appreciate all that they are doing and learning, early childhood teachers need tools for observing children directly and obtaining parents' observations of their child. I prefer to talk about appreciation, rather than assessment, for the following reasons: to appreciate means to value or admire. Appreciation also means being fully aware of something (or someone) with a heightened perception and understanding of that person or thing.

The early childhood teacher stands at the centre of the appreciation process. Her observations are critical because they are based on getting to know each child and appreciating the child's development in relation to her knowledge of young children's development.

–Dr. Harold Ireton

Source: Dr. Harold Ireton

OBSERVATION AND APPRECIATIVE INQUIRY

Inquiry/study

Appreciative inquiry is at the heart of observation and documentation. This inquiry-based process empowers the voices of educators, children, and families to create a curriculum that is meaningful to everyone, for it holds significance in their lives. Appreciative inquiry also encourages the co-construction and sharing of ideas and experiences between educators, children, families, and even community members.

The appreciative inquiry approach highlights the importance of open-mindedness and objectivity, curiosity, and inclusivity in observation. Essentially, it asks the observer to demonstrate respect, appreciation, and positive regard for children in every aspect of the observation process. Why does that child do what she does, and what makes that child unique?

The Ontario Ministry of Education document entitled *Think, Feel, Act: Lessons from Research about Young Children* (2013) is an appropriate example of appreciative inquiry thinking. This document suggests that educators reflect upon the following questions every day in their professional practice:

- What questions do I have about children in my program? What do I want to investigate further?
- What view of the child is portrayed in my current practices of documenting?
- What else can I document beyond children's developmental skills?
- How can others contribute to my interpretations and expand on the story my documentation tells? ("Reflect," para. 1)*

Take a moment to appreciate the inquisitive nature of these questions. Reflect on their meaning to you.

Inquiry into the connections a child makes in his learning requires educators to move outside the thinking of curriculum as something educators "create" or "do." Being alert to daily occurrences, playroom experiences, and children's interests are just some of the considerations of **emergent** or **play-based curriculum**. Exploring the answers to those queries gives direction and meaning, and that ultimately drives the curriculum, which is co-created with and experienced by the children, families, and educators. Through keen observation, an educator sees the connections that the child is making on a daily basis. The documentation of those connections can take educators completely outside the usual realms of curriculum thinking. In order to engage in this process, educators need to be prepared for these discoveries. This personal and professional "preparedness" will be examined closely in subsequent chapters in Part 1 and in detail in Chapter 6.

Appreciative inquiry expects early childhood professionals to be systematic, collaborative, and equitable in their approach; it is a give-and-take process, whereby both the educator and the child experience the teaching and learning roles in order to learn from one another. This process allows for the sharing of knowledge and discovery between adults as well as between adults and children.

This process further prompts early childhood professionals to consider a number of contextual factors that affect children's learning, such as development,

*Ontario Ministry of Education. *Think, Feel, Act: Lessons from Research about Young Children* (2014). Copyright Queen's Printer for Ontario, 2013.

Kristine Fenning

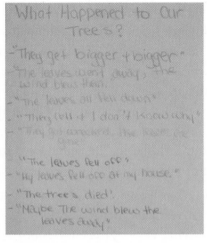

What Happened to Our
Trees?

- "They get bigger + bigger"
- "The leaves went away. The
  wind blew them."
- "The leaves all fell down"
- "They fell + I don't know why"
- "They got wrecked. The leaves are
  gone."

- "The leaves fell off"
- "My leaves fell off at my house."
- "The trees died".
- "Maybe The wind blew the
  leaves away"

Kristine Fenning

temperament, relationships, culture, environment, ability, family diversity, language, gender, philosophy and values, and quality. Each of these factors and others cause us to stop, look, listen, and inquire; observing young children must consider not only the child and her or his immediate learning environment but also much more. When we observe, as educators did at the Bruce Peninsula Family Centre, we open ourselves to possibilities. Take a moment to review the questions the children asked shown next to the photo of the tree. These questions demonstrate their inquiry process. When a child asked questions about the wind, and another child shared her observations about what the wind did with the leaves at her house, it began a journey of investigation: Where do the leaves go? What happened to our trees?

Appreciative inquiry has an impact on what we observe, how we interpret and reflect upon what we see and hear, and, finally, how we respond. Engaging in an appreciative inquiry approach when observing and recording requires effort, but the results are worth it. These sound inquiry practices help educators to develop positive working relationships with parents and co-workers. Educators familiar with this approach recognize that it is comforting for parents to know that their child's progress is noted, documented, and valued. This approach allows children to experience satisfaction and empowerment when listened to and gives them the opportunity to query, contribute to, and reflect upon their own learning. The wealth of information gained from observation holds significance because it broadens perspectives of all who are involved, it informs and transforms all aspects of our practice, and it is unique to every early childhood program. The role of appreciative inquirer must not be taken lightly.

WHY IS OBSERVATION IMPORTANT?

Observation is the most important investigative tool we have to discover the world of young children. This statement, although true, does not have the same power in its meaning as the short story that follows:

> A toddler (who loves butterflies) runs across the room, tips over a plastic bin, and scatters the toys on the floor. He flips the bin upside down and jams his index finger on the bottom of the bin, repeating intensely his word for butterfly, "Littlelittlelittlelittle." The educator sits down next to Isaac, looking and listening. She suddenly exclaims, "Take a look at this! The criss-crossing plastic on the bottom of the plastic bin has the shape of a butterfly! Good for you, Isaac, you found butterfly!" Isaac looks pleased and now wants to show everyone in the room.

This story is about discovering a toddler's learning and the role of observation; it is also about the sensitive observation of a responsive educator. Observing young children and recording their behaviour are considered essential practice in every early childhood setting. Along with telling Isaac's story, observation shows us something about him and his educator, who listened, observed, saw the butterfly in the design of the bin's plastic bottom, and responded to his delight. Welcome to this exciting process of discovery!

WHY OBSERVE CHILDREN?

What will be your reasons for observing? Make a short list of reasons why you would observe children. Are your reasons similar to those given below?

REASONS FOR OBSERVING YOUNG CHILDREN

Why do early childhood teachers want to observe? Why are observations so important? Making the connections between what we observe and understand is key. Let us begin by highlighting some of the main reasons for observation.

- *To observe children's growth and development.* Educators know that each child demonstrates specific interests, styles of learning, personality, knowledge, and skills. They know that children develop at different rates in their own way. They understand that documentation of Ahmed's questions, for example, is important. When Ahmed asked why snow has to be cold, this question indicates a keen interest in nature, a curiosity, and a desire to learn. Alternatively, an educator may note Kate's reluctance to sit on the carpet with other children. What are the reasons why Kate seems to shy away from this social activity?

Jaren Jai Wicklund/Shutterstock

Wiarton Kids' Den/Sally Wylie

- *To support early intervention.* Importantly, educators observe children to proactively monitor the developmental progress of children in their care and to support children who may be experiencing challenges. Careful observation of young children is extremely crucial in identifying children who may need assistance, resources, or services from their community. Being aware of the role of early intervention is a focus of Chapter 7.

- *To observe daily interactions between children and adults and between children and children.* Daily interactions are at the heart of any early childhood setting. Whether the interactions take place during the routines of the day, during play, or during quiet, one-to-one downtime, the building of social experiences and learning about and expressing emotions are crucial to the development of trust and attachment. Educators observe the children in their care to get a sense of each child faces challenge, demonstrates resilience, or shows caring toward others. They want to see who typically plays alone and which children engage in play with others. They also note the children who are able to relate to and bond with adults other than their family members. They keep track of the growing relationships and socialization between children for a variety of reasons; one of the most critical reasons is to share information with parents.

- *To observe the group as a whole.* There are many reasons why educators monitor the interactions of their group of children. They need to watch the group to make sure that a child is not being bullied or is not becoming too consistently aggressive with

Ilike/Shutterstock

others. Seasoned teachers will tell you that the dynamics of a group change over time, especially when a new child arrives or an old friend leaves the group. They may want to discover where the children are spending most of their time. Educators watch for and listen to the ebb and flow of the group's activity; it tells them when the group is working well together or when hints of discord or unrest exist within the social experience.

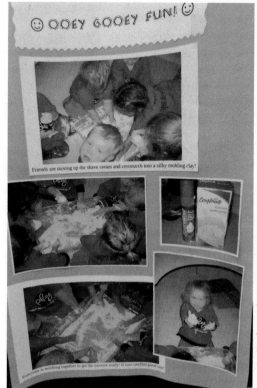

Bruce Peninsula Family Centre/Sally Wylie

- *To determine how children play with certain materials or equipment.* Educators are ever vigilant to what children say and do when they are playing, as well as how they invent new ways to play with ordinary objects. This information tells them about how children learn, what they understand, and how they feel about the materials and equipment in the room. Educators also pay attention to how children use creative or sensory materials. Some children love to plunge elbow-deep into sand or water, yet other children will hold on to the very tip of a container so as not to touch the sand or water. Responsive educators can use these opportunities to learn more about what the child feels about gooey or squishy materials. It is a good time to investigate this predisposition. The behaviour of children while manipulating materials or playing with materials reveals a great deal about their personalities.

- *To discover the variability of skills or temperament within each child.* When young children are acquiring new skills, knowledge, and ways of figuring things out, you will see a wide range of competence during the learning process. In a question-and-answer format in the article "Reflections on Documentation," Reggio Emilia pedagogista Dr. Tiziana Filippini reports that

> running was quite an interesting pattern that the children used. They could have chosen something else, but they found running to provoke a series of compelling questions: What is the shape of running? What is its directionality? Some children are running in circles, others are

running back and forth. The teachers began to wonder: What is at the heart of the children's experience of running? Perhaps it is about the impermanence of the activity. Running has a shape but you cannot see it because when you stop running, it is done; it is ephemeral. The children feel the physicality of running because they get red in the face, exhausted, sweaty, etc. But when they finish, nothing remains of what they did. In thinking about the shape of running, the teachers began to puzzle about its visibility and invisibility. Within this inquiry, documentation serves as the process through which the teachers and the children recognize the experience and attempt to interpret and make sense of it. (Turner & Wilson, 2010, p. 7)*

Children also display a wide variety of subtle differences from one time frame to another. Children can demonstrate variability in their personal behaviour even hourly or daily! This is all the more reason to keep an open mind about the discoveries that unfold in any setting with young children. Just when you think Rebecca is mastering getting on and off low equipment or chairs independently and with ease, she surprises you by falling repeatedly while trying to climb over the sandbox ledge. Similarly, children react differently to different people, welcoming some with smiles and rejecting others by walking away. One day, the child says, "You can play," and another day, "No, you can't be here."

© Woogies1/Dreamstime.com

- *To involve parents in the process of discovery.* As partners and co-educators of their child's learning journey, parents want to know how their child is doing, what friendships they might have, how they feel throughout the day, and how well they are developing, among other things. As experts of their children, parents have vested interest in educator observations, and will have observations of their own to share in the process. "Parents who have become child observers get really excited about what they are discovering. As they share their findings with the teacher and the teacher responds by sharing observations with the parent, their relationship changes dramatically. They become true partners in education and care" (Beaty, 2006, p. 425).

*Turner, T., & Gray Wilson, D. (2010). "Reflections on documentation: A discussion with thought leaders from Reggio Emilia." *Theory into Practice, 49*, 5–13, p. 7. Reprinted by permission of the publisher, Taylor & Francis Ltd.

- *To observe who is happy and having fun and who is sad, upset, lonesome, or frustrated.* What our image is of a child influences our expectations. When educators are asked to describe their image of a toddler, certain traits are identified with that age group. In the absence of knowledge of a particular toddler, an educator might have framed certain expected behaviour, and yet, once an in-depth understanding of that child is experienced, those "toddler characteristics" may not apply. If we perceive that a child is unhappy, our feelings or an image of what a child should be like is affected; we don't want the child to be sad. How many other influences or perceptions create our image of a child? How does it influence what we observe and how we respond?

    The view of what a child is and ought to be has deep roots in the culture, society, and family values of the people involved. Because we live in a multicultural society, and the people we work with come from many different backgrounds, the images we hold of children will reflect this diversity. (Fraser, 2012, p. 35)

- *To create pedagogy that supports the child, family, and community.* Pedagogy means the methods and practice of teaching. In other words, pedagogy is what you do as an educator of young children. This narrow definition actually is broad in its scope, casting light on an almost infinite array of teaching and learning possibilities. A pedagogical framework represents the ideas or core principles educators have that focus the practices within that framework. Every province and territory in Canada develops its own documents stating its pedagogical beliefs.

- *To observe the environment and make adaptations to it.* The environment plays an important educational role in the lives of young children. Understanding how children interact with the environment and with one another, as well as how the environment influences the behaviour of young children, is an important role for the educator-observer. It is imperative that educators observe the context of the environment, integrating this knowledge with input from families, children, and their community to co-prepare an environment that is responsive and inclusive of all learner needs, interests, and abilities. Over time, and with collaborative input from everyone, patterns may emerge informing educators that certain changes may need to be made to the environment. Please visit our extensive discussion in Chapter 8 as we connect our observations and pedagogical documentation to environmental design.

There is much to be said about documentation throughout this text, and much of it will be found in Chapters 6, 7, and 8, where the application of observations and pedagogical documentation are explored. Historically and in educational environments, documentation has been seen as the "end game"—what we compile at the end of our observations. Yet, we see the value of documentation as a process—a means to learn, explore, and appreciate. Opening up possibilities with ongoing documentation supports appreciative inquiry. While observing and documenting, we can co-learn with the children while we investigate "in real time." Pat Tarr (2011) describes the process of documentation this way:

> The act of pedagogical documentation becomes a dialogue. The process of pedagogical documentation involves returning to the children, their images and their words to gather their insights, their confirmation, or their disagreement, in a shared dialogue so that the children's interest can be supported. (p. 13)

Maloch and Horsey (2013) echo this sentiment:

> We hope that our students are inquirers—who make use of texts in purposeful ways to accomplish their own ends and answer their own questions—rather than "doers" of school tasks. That is, as they leave classrooms and schools, we hope for children to feel inspired to follow their own lines of inquiry, to move into and through the world as wonderers and learners. If the tools we offer in the classroom are grounded only in classroom tasks of focused inquiry but not embedded in a community focused on inquiring, children may leave our classrooms having learned fact, but not living as learners. (p. 485)

Developing documentation, then, is about observing and recording authentic experiences as they occur with the intent of discovery, as well as creating curriculum and methods of sharing that information with educators, families, and communities. Whether the medium is a website such as Pinterest, an app, an online journal, print, or the notes of other educators, learning through observation and documentation continues the early childhood tradition.

OBSERVATION AND THE RESPONSIVE, INCLUSIVE EDUCATOR

All human beings have the desire to feel included; it is one of our most basic needs. In the early childhood field, an educator is often viewed as **responsive** and **inclusive** by having a strong sense of self-awareness; an attitude of positivity, caring, and acceptance that permeates all aspects of practice; and an obvious respect for the individuality and uniqueness of self, children, families, and team. This requires creating an emotional climate whereby all children trust and "feel" as if they belong, that they are accepted, and that they are valued. **Inclusion** can be defined in many ways; however, this particular text takes an approach that inclusion functions as an attitude, a process, and a concept and is not restricted to children with special needs, but instead encompasses all children regardless of culture, class, appearance, beliefs, lifestyle, sexuality, gender, age, family composition, religion, or language. An inclusive environment has many benefits for children, for it is within this type of environment that

> children grasp ideas more easily and more effectively and maintain their interest in school when they have an educational program that enables them to connect their learning to their own lives and the world around them. The program should emphasize the interconnected learning that occurs when children are exposed to real-life situations and activities in the classroom, home, school, and neighbourhood. (Ontario Ministry of Education, 2010–2011, p. 16)

Responsive educators can then be seen as those who consider, respect, and appreciate "all children's strengths, abilities, and interests. They value and build on children's strengths, skills and knowledge to ensure their motivation and engagement in learning." It involves attentively observing and developing curriculum/planning that responds to and reflects "children's expertise, cultural traditions and ways of knowing, [and] the multiple languages spoken by some children" (Australian Government, Department of Education, Employment and Workplace Relations, 2009, p. 14; see also Pelo, 2006).

Responsive, inclusive educators build relationships with all members of an early learning centre or community and include every aspect of each child and family in all aspects of their practice. Being inclusive and responsive is a lifelong process, skill, and goal involving constant dynamic change and **disequilibrium** as educators continue to integrate and scaffold their new learning.

Part of this new learning and inclusive/responsive approach involves engaging in an ongoing process of reflection, a process synonymous with appreciative inquiry. Schön (1983), a well-known author on the reflection process, consistently refers to paying attention as "hearing" or "seeing" what is before you. For our purposes, this would refer to hearing and watching what students say or do in the context of learning, essentially paralleling the observation process.

It is through observing, reflecting, and documenting that experiences are validated, shared, and open for interpretation and collaboration from all those involved (Chorney, 2006; Paige-Smith & Craft, 2007). Furthermore, "reflective practice is a form of ongoing learning that involves engaging with questions of philosophy, ethics, and practice. Its intention is to gather information and gain insights that support, inform and enrich decision-making about children's learning" or other elements of teaching or learning and then reflect on the changes necessary to improve practice (Australian Government, Department of Education, Employment and Workplace Relations, 2009, p. 13). As we examine further in subsequent chapters, this inquiry-based process "encourages educators to challenge their own assumptions and beliefs about early childhood education and practices" (McFarland, Saunders, & Allen, 2009, p. 506) and promotes dialogue with other professionals about the most meaningful ways to support children (O'Connor & Diggins, 2002; Pelo, 2006). Throughout this text, you will note continuous reference to responsive and inclusive practice. There is much to be learned about how to be responsive and inclusive in our professional practice.

THE ESSENTIAL PARTNERSHIP

The best interests of the children bring families and educators into an essential personal and professional partnership. Sharing information from observations with parents is about creating, supporting, and nurturing relationships. These relationships are founded on a **reciprocal** learning process. Educators, like many other professionals, maintain a sensitive balance between providing a **quality** care service and responding within an emotional and personal relationship. Parents entrust their child to the educator's care, and the educators accept that responsibility with an attitude of mutual respect, trust, and confidence as noted in Exhibit 1.2.

> Showing respect means that programs and early childhood educators are **child-sensitive**, that is, they notice that children are unique, acknowledge this as important, and use this knowledge as a significant basis in planning the total program. "Respect" may be a more descriptive term than the frequently used "child-centred," which may seem rather one-sided or totally indulgent toward children. Respect demands responsiveness. (Gestwicki & Bertrand, 2008, p. 78)

EXHIBIT 1.2	CO-CONSTRUCTORS OF KNOWLEDGE

Educators and families can become the "co-constructors of knowledge in partnership with the child, and with each other. As such, they should find new rhythms with which to be teacher and learner, parent and learner. Through their collaboration and respective perspectives, they can have a deeper understanding of the thinking child, and of the ways in which each child is a co-constructor of knowledge.

'These partnerships, not easily achieved, have to be founded on trust and confidence.'"

—*Amilia Gambetti*

Source: Courtesy of Child Care Information Exchange.

FAMILY CENTREDNESS

Family is a child's world, and as educators it is important to understand the value of family in children's learning. Throughout this text we place the family and child at the heart of what we do; they have much to offer. Family centredness can be defined as

> a set of values, skills, behaviours and knowledge that recognises the central role of families in children's lives. It is sometimes described as working in partnership or collaboration. It involves professionals and families working together to support children's learning and development. Early childhood professionals who engage in family-centred practice respect the uniqueness of every person and family. They share their professional expertise and knowledge with families and at the same time regard families' expertise as valid, significant and valuable. (Kennedy & Stonehouse, 2012, p. 3)

RELATIONSHIPS WITH FAMILIES

When a child first begins a program, the sharing of information begins. The child's family is the first observer of the child; the family has much to share. Educators want to know from the parents what they can learn about the child and the family. The interest shown communicates respect and a willingness to learn and understand. Parents, in turn, want to know about the setting, the teachers, the program, and the policies. These initial exchanges and other daily practices strengthen bonds of trust and support.

In the article entitled "Partnerships in Learning: Linking Early Childhood Services, Families and Schools for Optimal Development," the concept of scaffolding is explored (Ashton et al., 2008). In this context, the term is used to describe the process of achieving understanding and congruence between the values and practices of home and school. Using Lev Vygotsky's and Jerome Bruner's ideas to support this concept, Ashton et al. suggest that open discourse between parties benefits the children. "Many children make successful adjustments to the perceived dissonance between home and school. Dialogue constructed within relationships built on common values, practices and understandings is likely to be most beneficial to the greatest number of children" (Ashton et al., 2008, p. 10). The willingness to engage in the sharing of ideas to best support the child "fosters learning from the very earliest years … and an interrelated ecological system" (Sheridan, 2004, p. 11). Misunderstandings or the inability to communicate or understand each other's belief system can "lead to compromised relationships between educators and parents, to false assumptions about families' aspirations for their children, and to both parties holding erroneous feelings" (Ashton et al., 2008, p. 11). The article clearly supports the practice of dialogue between home and school prior to the child beginning the program to support the transition to school and continued communication with all team members to ensure a positive experience and a constructive network of communication for all concerned.

> Gaining knowledge about children from multiple perspectives helps educators ensure that programs also value the unique and diverse characteristics of the children's families and the communities in which they live. It's not a "one-size-fits-all" approach. In particular, programs should be reflective of the cultural and linguistic backgrounds of the children and families they serve, including those from First Nations, Métis, Inuit and francophone communities. (Ontario Ministry of Education, 2014, p. 18)

Truly, the early years are the most opportune time for children and their families to experience acceptance outside the home and to develop respect for the diversity that exists within early learning and care settings in Canada today. Whether rural or urban, each setting reflects a **microcosm** of the community it serves. In that community, children thrive with opportunities for learning. Here is where children, staff, and family relationships grow, becoming more aware daily of one another's expectations, values, feelings, and priorities:

> Within any community setting …, children learn what is expected of them and what to expect from others through the cultural messages passed on from parents, grandparents, and other significant adults. These messages shape a child's understanding of everything from touch, positioning of one's body, what is regarded as mannerly, and how one thinks, senses time, and perceives space to beliefs about what is important and how to set immediate and lifelong goals. The ideal is for families and caregivers to be involved in a joint process that ensures that children thrive within their respective cultures. In the process, children may become bicultural. It is important, however, to assure that becoming competent in another culture adds to what a child already has and does not replace the cultural traditions of the family or origin. (Capone, Oren, & Neisworth, 2004, pp. xi, xii)

FAMILY DIVERSITY

Every family is a complex unit that is rich in diversity. Awareness of the diversity of family structures, ethnic backgrounds, and linguistic and cultural differences of the greater society means that early childhood educators are always challenged to create and respond to new ways of communicating with children and their families:

> In serving culturally diverse early learning and care families and communities, keep in mind that not all parents share the same ideas about how, where and when they should be involved in their children's schooling. Parents may also face barriers, such as limited time or limited proficiency in English. On the other hand, they, and their ethnocultural communities, may represent substantial resources that schools can draw on to assist English language learners and to enrich the cultural environment for everyone in the school. (Ontario Ministry of Education, 2005, p. 44)

A child's family and culture influence all facets of a child's life. Acknowledging this fact is an important step in the exchange of learning between educators and families. Sharing information with parents is about a commitment to

- listening to and valuing the families of each child
- recognizing that parents may have another point of view regarding their child
- working to create an open, meaningful, reciprocal learning process

The awareness that each child is unique in herself or himself contributes to an interest in the child and the family. When educators understand what families are trying to accomplish with their children, they can look for ways to support them.

Today, many children are cared for by one parent, grandparent(s), or extended family members. The child may be picked up and dropped off by a designated friend or relative. Throughout most of this text, the terms "family" and "parent" are used interchangeably. This reflects the reality that parents may not always be the primary caregivers as they struggle to balance other roles and responsibilities outside the family. This thought is echoed in many texts, in early childhood settings around the world, and in the views of various professionals: as the world changes, so does the configuration of the child's home life.

CULTURE AND TRANSFORMATION

Over the years, we have witnessed changes in the child-care profession in Canada. Some of the changes have been

- cultural and linguistic diversity in children and their families, particularly in urban areas
- increased numbers of newcomer families to Canada

- restructuring and administrative reorganization within organizations and government
- new directives from provincial or territorial governments

Why is it important to note change? Change in society reflects a **transformation** of ideas and practice. **Social construct theories** suggest that this transformation focuses on social interactions, collaborative learning, dialogue, and honouring the perspectives of others: transformative ways of knowing, seeing, and understanding. In early childhood, transformation means a shift or altering of concepts and ideas regarding relationships in early childhood centres, the framework of developing curriculum, and daily practices; it means that materials used will be in collaboration between educators, children, their families, and the community. Transformation speaks to diverse possibilities of doing things, or critically thinking of the new ways things could be done, which involves meaningful collaboration. Recognizing change in order to respond appropriately and act conscionably is one of the foremost responsibilities of an educator today.

EXHIBIT 1.3	FOSTERING A SENSE OF BELONGING

"Opportunities to engage with people, places, and the natural world in the local environment help children, families, educators, and communities build connections, learn and discover, and make contributions to the world around them. It fosters a sense of belonging to the local community, the natural environment, and the larger universe of living things. As well, communities benefit from the rich experiences they have in learning about, with, and from children."

Source: Ontario Ministry of Education. (2014). *How does learning happen? Ontario's pedagogy for the early years*, p. 19. Retrieved from http://www.edu.gov.on.ca/childcare/HowLearningHappens.pdf

How are the values of an urban or rural early childhood/learning centre demonstrated? Whose voices are heard? What ways of knowing or seeing would be included in an early childhood setting in the Atlantic provinces, Saskatchewan, or British Columbia? What about Quebec, Nunavut, or Manitoba? How would the ideas and values of each community be reflected in its philosophy and practices and, by extension, documented through observation? As referenced in Exhibit 1.3, the community plays a key role, fostering a sense of belonging for children and families.

"Based on the available Canadian research and the provincial curriculum frameworks that have been recently developed, it does appear that respecting diversity and working towards social inclusion are already part of the early childhood education culture in Canada; in fact, it is the early childhood community that seems to most recognize this potential of the early years."

Source: Martha Friendly and Nina Prabhu. (2010, January). *Can early childhood education and care help keep Canada's promise of respect for diversity?* (Occasional Paper No. 23), p. 24. Retrieved from http://www.childcarecanada.org/sites/default/files/crru_op23_diversity.pdf

Acceptance is a value that is part of Canada's diverse society. In child care, we must constantly ask ourselves if, through our attitudes and practices, we are creating a responsive atmosphere to meet the needs of our diverse communities. For the most part, we are familiar with the obvious ways educators demonstrate their acknowledgment of new cultures in the playroom. Examples include culturally inclusive books, music, food, games, artifacts, examples of festive dress, posters, and words of greeting and comfort in many languages.

In the article entitled "Respecting Culture in Our Schools and Classrooms," Pearson (2006) uses the image of an iceberg to reflect the idea that some cultural indicators are visible at the tip, whereas a vast number are hidden below the surface (see Exhibit 1.5). How often have we noted and looked for examples of "the hidden iceberg"—the part under the surface? Do we acknowledge others' concepts of tempo of work, notions of leadership, concepts of beauty, approaches to problem solving, incentives to work? If we do acknowledge different perspectives, such as those noted under the iceberg's surface, how is that demonstrated in early learning and care settings?

One of the main reasons to investigate change is to gain new insights. From new insights, we can begin to appreciate anew the influences on children and their families and understand their perspectives. In the article "Meeting the Needs of Refugee Families" (2007), Freire says, "The immigrant child when he leaves his country has been part of a plan.... The youngster has had the possibility to dispose of his/her belongings, to say goodbye, to think of what type of precious things that he may want to bring like his toys for example or books" (p. 1). Understanding the reality of just one child should give us pause for reflection. From the knowledge of this child's experiences, we may be better able to provide a program more responsive to the interests, strengths, and needs of the child and her or his family. Based on

EXHIBIT 1.5   **THE CULTURAL ICEBERG**

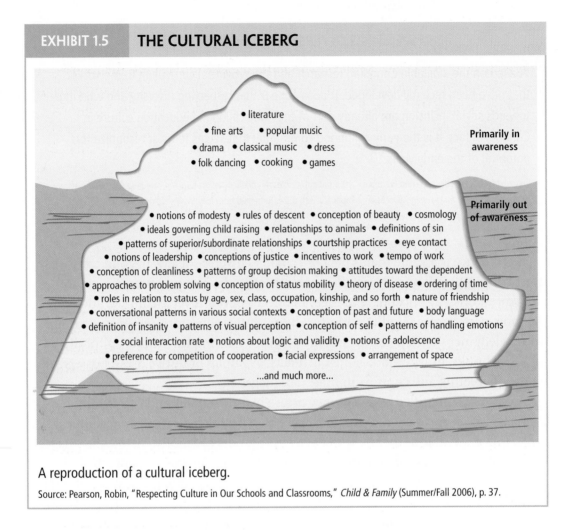

- literature
- fine arts   • popular music
- drama   • classical music   • dress
- folk dancing   • cooking   • games

Primarily in awareness

Primarily out of awareness

- notions of modesty   • rules of descent   • conception of beauty   • cosmology
- ideals governing child raising   • relationships to animals   • definitions of sin
- patterns of superior/subordinate relationships   • courtship practices   • eye contact
- notions of leadership   • conceptions of justice   • incentives to work   • tempo of work
- conception of cleanliness   • patterns of group decision making   • attitudes toward the dependent
- approaches to problem solving   • conception of status mobility   • theory of disease   • ordering of time
- roles in relation to status by age, sex, class, occupation, kinship, and so forth   • nature of friendship
- conversational patterns in various social contexts   • conception of past and future   • body language
- definition of insanity   • patterns of visual perception   • conception of self   • patterns of handling emotions
- social interaction rate   • notions about logic and validity   • notions of adolescence
- preference for competition of cooperation   • facial expressions   • arrangement of space

...and much more...

A reproduction of a cultural iceberg.

Source: Pearson, Robin, "Respecting Culture in Our Schools and Classrooms," *Child & Family* (Summer/Fall 2006), p. 37.

our observations and an appreciation of their experiences, networking in the community and taking the role of an **advocate** for needed family resources or services become part of our educator's role.

When the care and education of young children are viewed as a collective of relationships, we can all become collaborators in creating a better world. Observation is the foundation upon which opportunities can be built with windows for new perspectives.

OBSERVATIONS OF CHILDREN DURING PLAY

The work and beliefs regarding play of Friedrich Froebel (1887/2005), known as "the father of modern kindergarten," provide one example of how play has been well documented in various theoretical and philosophical approaches and literature for many years and how its role in children's learning has been gaining increased recognition from researchers and early learning professionals alike. Play is a personal and intrinsic process. Play is what children do to please and express themselves. It has often been said that play is the work of children. Play is a time of ordering, inventing, imagining, pretending, and discovering! Children structure their own vision of the world and their roles within it. In play, children demonstrate what they know how to do, what they understand, and what they want to master and learn.

For both children and adults, play nourishes the emotional and intellectual brain; it scaffolds new learning and experiences, it builds connections with others, and it facilitates discovery of meaning from the world. "Looked at as something common to the whole of humankind, play takes on still greater significance. Every culture it seems, has some unique forms of play, and most cultures seem to share some fundamental types of games and play" (Carlisle, 2009. p. xi). There is no question that play holds a unique meaning for every individual and is a common universal experience held by people all over the world regardless of ability, gender, race, culture, language, or other form of diversity. "Play is paradoxical—it is serious and non-serious, real and not real, apparently purposeless and yet essential to development. Play is resilient; there is increasing evidence that play deprivation has a damaging impact on development" (Hewes, 2006, p. 2). Children have the right and the opportunity to learn through play in quality early learning environments, with the nurturing and caring relationships and opportunities necessary to facilitate their growth in ways that support them individually (Canadian Heritage, 2009; Hewes, 2006; Ontario Ministry of Education, 2010–2011; Pascal, 2009).

Documentation from observing children's play is about communication, translating or interpreting their feelings and ideas, learning from them, and assisting them with their quest to understand. Observations uncover the amazing thought processes of children, the creative discoveries of how they see the world, and the wonder-filled ways in which they convey their feelings about life. When educators listen, watch, and record children's play in an area such as a dramatic play centre, they may observe them with their dress-up clothes and hear their comments about the shoes or where they are going. From their dialogue, mannerisms, and interactions, they tell us about their home life, dreams, and frustrations. In turn, educators can expand these experiences by talking with the children, asking questions, listening to their answers, or prompting new ideas.

For example, one morning, when Seth and Alexis set up their action figures in the construction area, they incorporated three large stuffed animals. One of the animals was a dog, and Seth said that was the "God-dog" because he was the biggest.

Seth put him on top of the highest shelf so that "God-dog" could survey the figures on the floor. The conversation went like this:

Educator: Will God-dog be coming down on the floor?

Seth: Yes, he will come down later when we have the castle finished.

Alexis, who had been stacking wooden blocks, looked up and replied, "No, Seth, he can't ever come down or he'll die."

Seth stood silently for a few minutes and then sat down, crossing his legs.

Educator: Do you and Alexis have to think about this some more?

Alexis: I think he can't come down.

Educator: What do you think, Seth?

Seth: Well, he can't come down now because we haven't started the battle. When the warriors start dying, he can come down. Then he can come down and get them.

Documenting the play of children is about looking and listening. As in the Seth and Alexis example, there are times to become part of the dialogue and times to be a spectator. "To be a good observer you have to suspend judgements … the idea is to learn the deeper meaning of what you are seeing. Observation combined with communication helps you seek out other perspectives. The best way to communicate is to develop dialoguing skills.… A dialogue is a form of communication used to gather information, learn from it, and discover new ideas" (Gonzalez-Mena, 2008, p. 4). "Children begin to communicate ideas and questions while they are experimenting and investigating by describing materials they used, indicating a problem they might have had, or beginning to listen to their peers or offer suggestions to them" (Ontario Ministry of Education, 2010–2011, p. 16).

Documenting the play of children is also about taking note of your own attitude concerning play because it will shape what you "think" you see and hear. In addition to other's perspectives, take the time to look at play through a number of different lenses: culturally, philosophically, developmentally, and socially. Each lens holds significant implications for our practice, in our observations, interpretations, and reflections; in the relationships we create; and in how we talk and share information with families and teams, as well as for the types of responsive and inclusive actions we take in our design of early learning environments and planning for young children.

Observations can be used as feedback to children about their interactions with one another. This practice of narrating what a child is doing, such as, "Are you feeling sad because Bridget took your Lego pieces, Josie?" helps children understand how they feel, how others may be feeling, or why certain events happened. Perhaps your feedback will help a child put into words what he or she is trying to express. If so, those observations will facilitate the child's social and emotional development. How does that make you feel?

If, while painting, a child looks up at the flickering of a fluorescent light and asks, "Miss Lisa, is there lightning in there?" it is a good teaching/learning opportunity for both of you. These spontaneous "teachable" moments contribute to the overall understanding of this child. What have we learned from just this one sentence? This child demonstrates understanding of weather phenomena, and he or she can speak in sentences using questions. The educator can use this opportunity to ask questions of the child to find out what he or she knows about lightning or probe how the child drew the conclusion that the flickering could be in the light. "Learning to explain represents an important part of children's discourse learning and gives them experience with how to construct an understanding of events and phenomena" (Gjems, 2011, p. 501).

Documenting an observation such as this one is also an excellent sharing opportunity with the child's family. These casual, spontaneous indicators of a child's thinking and character are some of the most important observations you can make and share. These kinds of ongoing documentations of even a brief discussion provide vital information for educators and families.

Parents miss out on these moments while they are at work or school, and the child's day, therefore, is partly invisible to the parents. Your observations can make those parts of the day visible to the parents and can make the child's thought process tangible to them. In this way, it's not just the products, such as paintings or colourings, that go home with the parents, but also the documentation of the process, including how the the work was done or what thoughts helped to create the artwork.

Observations can also be shared with other children. For example, if two children are playing in the sandbox outside and appear to be having difficulty sharing the toys, you could join them and tell them what you have observed: "Marva and LeAnne, I saw both of you trying to fill your pails with sand from the same spot. Both of you were digging, and it looked like you were getting in each other's way. Is that what I saw? What can you do to help each other?" This example also highlights how play is the platform for inquiry and exploration.

In group settings, children hit and hug, yell and whisper; they learn to include and deal with exclusion. They struggle with conforming to other people's ideas and priorities while trying to express their own. Observations about these everyday occurrences are made even more significant when documented. Noting whom a child seems to like and how she investigates a new toy is important. So, too, is listening to and documenting the evolution of a child's story while he is painting. These are relevant occurrences. "Did Siat have a good day today?" This is not a

rhetorical question but a real question that can persist in a parent's mind. An educator can assist parents by sharing their observations and documentation. When this is done, not only has information been shared, but the parent has also been listened to and has listened to the teacher—back and forth, to and from, and with—every day. Slowly, an essential relationship develops to the benefit of all concerned.

When documented and shared, these occurrences uncover or disclose something unique about that child. When shared with parents or families, they bring forth a family response and then, possibly, encourage them to share their observations. A treasured bond of communication has begun.

FRAMING WHAT HAS BEEN OBSERVED

Relating what you know about each child in your group to child development of that age group is also important in your role as educator-observer. Having an idea of the norms and developmental guidelines for most children of a certain age will help answer a question such as, "Is that normal for a three-year-old?" Framing your answers within the context of child development and knowledge of principles of development, norms, and rates of development will be helpful to you when sharing information with parents.

Changes in behaviour indicate that growth and development are (or are not) taking place, and parents need to know daily not only what the changes have been, but also why or what that reveals. In these conversations, discussions could take place concerning individual variations in a child's behaviour. The reasons for observing in an infant room, for example, would be primarily to share daily information with the families. Infants cannot tell the parents or caregivers how they felt during the day, what excited them, or why they weren't hungry, so the role of observation in these settings is extremely important. Significant changes occur quickly in these early months of life. Children will exhibit behaviour and skills in different ways throughout their developmental journey, and it is important to be aware of and understand that. Take the following situation for example:

> Rachel, a 14-month-old infant, was a curious baby who enjoyed moving herself around the infant room to grasp at the toys available on the shelves and to seek comfort from the teachers. She began crawling at 10 months and began pulling to stand at 11 months. However, instead of moving from crawling to walking, Rachel would scoot her bum backwards and forwards by bending her knees and using her feet to propel herself in the direction where she needed to go. When prompted by her teachers and parents to walk, Rachel would cry and sit down on the floor. This happened repeatedly until one day at home time, her mother shared her concerns with the educators about Rachel's resistance to walking. While in discussion, the team explored how all children develop and grow at different rates and noted that Rachel had found "her" way to move around and assert her independence. Hinging on Rachel's interests, together her parents and room teachers tried a new approach. Instead of having all the materials she enjoyed at a level requiring her to simply sit on the floor, they decided to place her favourite musical materials on the wall in front of mirrors, which required her to pull to stand and to practise her balancing. For Rachel, the new discovery of her favourite toys on the wall became a pleasurable time for her while standing, and within four weeks' time, Rachel was standing independently and beginning to take steps!

Infant educators strive to create a nurturing environment for them based on their observations of what the infants enjoy, how they thrive, and generally how they are developing. Reflecting upon their observations of each child in the group encourages educators to find new ways to facilitate infant interactions and relationships, expand curriculum possibilities, or transform their notions of their role.

Educators observe to learn about each child. Discovering the uniqueness of each child is one of the greatest joys and challengers of every educator. Sharing that information with families includes them and provides the connectedness between the child, the parent, and the educator. Rooting those observations to the principles of development; areas, rates, and sequence of child development; and guidelines of a child's physical, emotional, and intellectual growth provides valuable knowledge for parents.

Wiarton Kid's Den/Sally Wylie

PRINCIPLES OF DEVELOPMENT

The principles of development are beliefs about how children grow and develop. "To include everyone, early childhood settings must encourage healthy dialogue about the principles and shared beliefs that relate to inclusion, diversity, and equity" (Ontario Ministry of Children and Youth Services, Best Start Expert Panel on Early Learning, 2007, p. 11). Some principles have been founded on decades of child studies and/or have resulted from a base of research, observation, and discourse. One such example is *Early Learning for Every Child Today: A Framework for Ontario Early Childhood Settings* (ELECT; Ontario Ministry of Children and Youth Services, Best Start Expert Panel on Early Learning, 2007). This framework, introduced in 2007, was intended to further promote quality early childhood pedagogy in Ontario. Now also referred to as the Ontario Early Learning Framework, ELECT includes a continuum of development for children from birth to age eight. Seven years later, *How Does Learning Happen? Ontario's Pedagogy for the Early Years* was introduced, building on the learning that took place since the publication of ELECT, and capturing the critical importance of relationships and the foundations of "Belonging, Engagement, Expression and Well Being." The *How Does Learning Happen?* document builds on and works collaboratively with the principles of ELECT. Those principles from the ELECT framework are as follows:

1. Early child development sets the foundation for lifelong learning, behaviour and health.
2. Partnerships with families and communities strengthen the ability of early childhood settings to meet the needs of young children.

3. Respect for diversity, equity and inclusion are prerequisites for honouring children's rights, optimal development and learning.

4. A planned curriculum supports early learning.

5. Play is a means to early learning that capitalizes on children's natural curiosity and exuberance.

6. Knowledgeable, responsive early childhood professionals are essential. (Ontario Ministry of Education, 2014, p. 10)*

The National Association for the Education of Young Children (NAEYC) offers 12 principles, and an example of some of these principles can be found in Exhibit 1.6.

EXHIBIT 1.6 **12 PRINCIPLES OF CHILD DEVELOPMENT AND LEARNING**

1. All areas of development and learning are important.
2. Learning and development follow sequences.
3. Development and learning proceed at varying rates.
4. Development and learning result from an interaction of maturation and experience.
5. Early experiences have profound effects on development and learning.
6. Development proceeds toward greater complexity, self-regulation, and symbolic or representational capacities.
7. Children develop best when they have secure relationships.
8. Development and learning occur in and are influenced by multiple social and cultural contexts.
9. Children learn in a variety of ways.
10. Play is an important vehicle for developing self-regulation and promoting language, cognition, and social competence.
11. Development and learning advance when children are challenged.
12. Children's experiences shape their motivation and approaches to learning.

For more information about core considerations in developmentally appropriate practice, the 12 principles, and guidelines for effective teaching, see NAEYC, 2009.

Source: "Twelve Principles of Child Development" taken from *Developmentally Appropriate Practice in Early Childhood Programs Serving Children from Birth through Age 8*, http://www.naeyc.org/dap/12-principles-of-child-development. The National Association for the Education of Young Children (NAEYC).

---

*Ontario Ministry of Education. *Early Learning for Every Child Today (ELECT): A framework for Ontario early childhood settings*. (2014), p. 38. Copyright Queen's Printer for Ontario 2007. Used with permission.

Organizations will often highlight their guiding principles, stating how these principles guide their practices as an organization or how a particular educational program will be shaped, such as the child-care expansion initiatives developed by the Province of Quebec. Quebec offers the closest example of a publicly funded child-care system in Canada.

Governments may also illustrate the principles that guide the curriculum for all areas of the country, such as those developed by the Ministry of Education in New Zealand. *Te Whāriki* is the New Zealand Ministry of Education's framework for early learning. The curriculum policy statement emphasizes the learning partnerships between parents, children, and teachers. The four guiding principles of *Te Whāriki* emphasize holistic, culturally mediated learning:

- the curriculum should reflect the holistic development of children
- the empowerment of the child should be a key factor (Maori principle)
- family and community links should be strengthened
- children learn through responsive and reciprocal relationships (New Zealand Ministry of Education, 1996)*

When examining the principles of New Zealand's framework and the principles from the NAEYC and Ontario, what becomes apparent is their similarities, but also their differences. What similarities would you expect to find? What might some of their differences be? What other inquiries might you make about these three documents?

AREAS OF CHILD DEVELOPMENT

Areas of development represent groupings of similar, related behaviours, skills, growth, or attitudes that typically occur in a predictable pattern. For example, the fine motor developmental area includes such skills as **pincer grasp**, **palmar grasp**, **dexterity**, and coordination of fingers. How these groupings are determined and how and why they are organized depends on a variety of factors, and the discussion of those variations goes well beyond the scope of this text. Some examples of the many ways areas of development can be described are noted in Exhibit 1.7.

These examples are only a few of the many variations that describe the areas or **domains** of child development. Referring to them as domains or sectors or developmental areas means essentially the same thing. Adopting any one of the terms does not mean that one is more right than the other; the terminology is just different.

The reasons for a particular terminology are embedded in the philosophy or practices of that philosophy, and these will also vary from country to country. Be prepared for these distinctions as you progress with your academic courses. As a

*New Zealand Ministry of Education, 1996, p. 138.

EXHIBIT 1.7	VARIATIONS OF THE TERM "AREAS OF DEVELOPMENT"

Areas of Development

Gross motor	Fine motor	Speech and language
Cognitive	Self-help	Social-emotional

Domains or PIES

Physical growth	Intellectual development
Emotional and social progress	

Developmental Domains

Cognitive development	Language development	Perceptual development
Social and emotional development	Motor development	

Source: Courtesy of Sally Wylie.

professional educator, you will be expected to be aware of the jargon and terminology associated with your professional field of study.

When reflecting on your documentation, the areas of child development can be a **guide** or framework to interpret or give meaning to what you have just observed. For example, if you observed three-year-old Jamal in the construction centre, you would want to document what you observed in some meaningful way (see Exhibit 1.8). As

EXHIBIT 1.8	JAMAL'S DEVELOPMENT

Gross Motor

- Lifts big blocks with both hands
- Squats in front of the shelf

Cognitive

- Rebuilds blocks when they fall
- Builds a "garage" and pretends he is a race car driver

Fine Motor

- Pushes cars under bridge
- Lines up six cars in a row

Socioemotional

- Plays with blocks for 20 min.
- Shares blocks with peers

Self-Help

- Gets blocks off shelf
- Asks peer for some cars

Speech and Language

- Talks to self while playing
- Makes various car sounds

Source: Courtesy of Sally Wylie.

you will discover in subsequent chapters, there are a myriad of possible ways to document the activity of young children. However, if you choose to do so, you can organize your observations under the headings of each developmental area in order to discern the kinds of skills and knowledge Jamal showed you through his experience with materials in the construction centre.

RATES OF DEVELOPMENT

Children not only go through phases of what they like to do, but they also develop according to their own rate of development. For example, one toddler in a group may be pointing at things and imitating sounds but has a vocabulary of only 20 words, and yet another toddler in the same group may be labelling objects and using abbreviated sentences and have a vocabulary of over 50 words. Each child develops at his or her own rate. This variance in behaviours can be attributed to a wide variety of factors, such as experience, temperament, expectations of family and culture, and environment.

NORMS AND DEVELOPMENTAL GUIDELINES

The Ages and Stages maturational approach to child development was popularized by Arnold Gesell some 50 years ago. He believed that all children mature through certain sequential developmental ages and stages. "Arnold Gesell made detailed observations of growth and development. He outlined **norms** for physical development. Gesell felt that the first six years of life were the most important for physical development. His normative approach gained great popular acceptance" (Read, Gardner, & Mahler, 1993, p. 183).

The mention of this Ages and Stages approach in this text is included as an important **caveat**. Why? Because even Gesell was quite concerned that people would see norms or age expectations as necessary milestones rather than guidelines. He voiced apprehension about his developmental guidelines being seen as some kind of strict set of behaviours to be achieved at or before a certain time. That caveat is instructive even today as parents often want to know if their child is "normal."

Using any developmental or sequential approach or guidelines can be helpful in explaining behaviour, but they should not be a prescription. Any sequential approach or areas of development should be used only as a guide. All children develop at their own rate and learn about the world through their unique family, friends, culture, and child-care environment. Children five years of age may play the piano, dance, play soccer or chess, or have the sensitivity and perception of someone far older in years. Other five-year-olds may not demonstrate any of the skills mentioned, but those children may be able to ride a horse bareback or catch a fish independently. For a particular culture, that may be the norm. Observing children is part of appreciative inquiry, asking questions such as, "What are the expectations of the parents and their culture? How restrictive or permissive are the parents? What do families value in their children? What traits are encouraged or discouraged?" Whose perspective is revealed when observing and making assumptions about a child's development? We all bring different viewpoints to the table, as noted by Gordon and Browne (2007):

> Teachers bring to the partnership another point of view. As child development professionals, they see the child in relation to normal milestones and appropriate behaviours. They notice how each child plays with other children in the group—what seems to challenge Mickey and when Ramon is likely to fall apart. Unlike parents, teachers see individual children from a perspective that is balanced by the numerous other children they have taught. They observe how the child behaves with a variety of adults, sensing children's ability to trust other adults through interactions with them at school. When parents need help for themselves or for their child, teachers become resources. (p. 273)

Expect a diversity of skills and knowledge within a group of children. Knowledge and understanding of how children grow and develop will help parents further appreciate their child's own unique personality and abilities.

OBSERVATION AND PEDAGOGICAL DOCUMENTATION

For many years, educators have been conducting informal observations of young children and collecting **artifacts** that represent their learning. Using their knowledge of development, educators then interpret the knowledge and skills they have seen, incorporating the perspectives of the parent(s) to understand the strengths and skills of a child to be developed, to aid curriculum planning by knowing which materials and experiences to plan for children, and to understand the impact of the environment on children. This was often a one-directional approach, placing responsibility for gathering this information solely on the educator. Pedagogical documentation recognizes that the above approach still has merit, but it challenges the educator to make observation, documentation, and interpretation/reflection a shared experience for the child, the parent/guardian, and the educator.

Inspired by sociocultural theory, inquiry-based thinking and learning, and the **Reggio Emilia** philosophy, the pedagogical documentation approach applies to any philosophy of any setting in any part of the world. It is a process, an approach, a framework, and an ongoing cycle rooted in making observation and documentation a responsibility and experience of all learners within a classroom. Learners in this case would be broadly defined to include the parents or guardians, the educator(s), and the child, each playing a role in co-educating, co-learning, co-observing and documenting, and co-interpreting. Including the voices of the child and family is necessary for they have much to teach us and have many thoughts to share with us about the world and how they learn.

> Pedagogical documentation is grounded in a "pedagogy of listening"—that is, listening with all of your senses (Rinaldi, 2006), through collecting visual data (photographs, videotapes), audio data, and written notes for the purpose of understanding children's thinking in order to plan educational experiences for them, and as a reflective process for educators to understand their own role in the teaching/learning dialogue.... The intent is not to identify where children are at in the developmental process, and where they might be seen as deficit, but to remove those lenses that tend to blind educators from seeing the unique ways in which children construct their understanding of the world and ways in which they are actors in creating culture (Dahlberg et al., 1999/2007; Tarr, 2010; Tarr, 2011). (Tarr, 2011, p. 13)

If we revisit the concepts of responsiveness, inclusion, and appreciative inquiry, it is easy to see the connection these concepts have to pedagogical documentation. We need to use multiple views and lenses to appreciate and understand what it is that we are seeing and hearing, and that there is no child or individual who learns and develops in exactly the same way. It is about watching and observing with an open mind, with no preconceived ideas or judgments about what we presume to know and simply listening to, watching, and documenting the experiences of children, of families, and of educators.

In this approach to observing and documenting, we also follow naturally the lead of the child and use a variety of observation methods to capture meaningful information and moments in time that reflect the how, what, when, where, and why of children's learning in their own unique and individual ways. This documentation, as will be discussed in Chapters 4, 5, and 6, reflects some of the many ways to capture thinking, as listed in Exhibit 1.9. Depending upon who the observer is and the purpose of the observation, each method can offer meaningful information to aid further inquiry, new **provocations**, and new learning possibilities.

According to the Ontario Ministry of Education (2012), pedagogical documentation "transforms understanding of teaching and learning in five strategic

EXHIBIT 1.9 **WAYS TO CAPTURE THINKING**

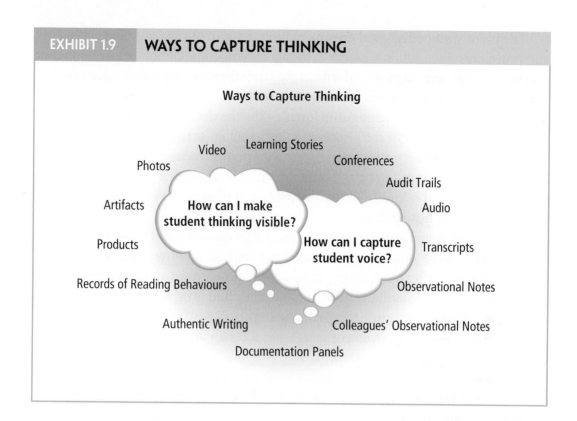

Ways to Capture Thinking

EXHIBIT 1.10 **PEDAGOGICAL DOCUMENTATION: TRANSFORMING TEACHING AND LEARNING**

1. Creates Shared Understanding
2. Celebrates the Rights of Individual Learners
3. Recognizes Students' Ownership of Their Learning
4. Actualizes Shared Accountability
5. Provides Voice in Learning for Everyone

Source: Ontario Ministry of Education. *Pedagogical Documentation: Leading Learning in the Early Years and Beyond.* Ontario Capacity Building Series: K-2. Secretariat Special Edition #30. Copyright Queen's Printer for Ontario, 2012.

ways" (p. 2; see Exhibit 1.10). These strategies authentically embrace the concepts of diversity, rights, shared understanding, ownership and accountability, and the voices of all in the observation and documentation process.

The premise of pedagogical documentation fits with the cycle of observation and process, as discussed in Chapter 2. Pedagogical documentation is a never-ending process of observing, inquiring, documenting, interpreting and reflecting, evaluating, and responding to new learning. A core element is also the collaborative sharing of perspectives, teaching, and learning (by the child, family, and educator), as well as interpretation of the information gathered, so as to promote responsiveness, inclusivity, and appreciation of others' viewpoints. Pedagogical documentation protects us from the need to be assessment focused and allows a process to evolve that is authentic and respectful of individuality and diversity. Everyone has and deserves a voice in this process.

Pedagogical documentation also proposes that access to and engagement with observation tools be a daily occurrence, so as to engage children, families, and educators in documenting the learning of all within a classroom and to make learning visible. When this role is shared, the image of the child is broadened, our knowledge and understanding grow together, and experiences of others benefit all. See Chapter 2 for more on the topic of increasing accessibility to observation and documentation within the classroom.

Pedagogical documentation and observation are key foundations of an inquiry-based practice. We have said previously, but it bears repeating, that observation is the most fundamental, universal, setting-independent way of learning about young children. Combine observation with pedagogical documentation and appreciative inquiry, and you have the ingredients for a creative, meaningful, and dynamic model that could be applied in virtually any early childhood setting.

What gives pedagogical documentation meaning? The inquiry reflected in the intention. If the inquiry or idea is authentic and reflective of the children, their families, the staff, and the community, it will be meaningful. Using observation as a lens into the world of others gives a voice to all involved and creates pedagogical documentation, which is education in its broadest sense.

"*Curriculum* is what 'we' include in the environment and embedded in children's experiences. *Pedagogy* refers to how we deliberately cultivate children's development (National Research Council, 2001). It is education in its broadest sense (Moss, 2004)."

Source: Gestwicki, C., & Bertrand. J. (2008). *The essentials of early childhood education (3rd Canadian ed.).* Toronto, ON: Thomson Nelson, p. 38.

When pedagogical documentation is used effectively, it slows down the process of making things meaningful by adding the educator's reflection about what was observed, asking others about their interpretations, talking to the children about the observed process, and then maybe documenting that whole process, and not just the observation with a personal interpretation. This process forces educators to really look at what they've seen a thousand times, whether it is a child getting dressed to go outside or a child washing hands. Embedded in these seemingly normal events are problems being solved, questions being asked, and basic concepts being explored. An example of a watchful eye has captured just this kind of event shown in Exhibit 1.11.

EXHIBIT 1.11 **LEARNING STORY**

"I arrived home from my walk last night and was greeted by this most perfect arrangement at the front door. 'Who did this?' I asked. Well it seems that Ash was asked to put his shoes away and took the opportunity to tidy up all the shoes lying in the entrance-way. I would like to think that this has something to do with a propensity toward tidiness and orderliness. Mmmmm, maybe it has more to do with his ever-increasing preoccupation with matching and lining things up. Has he busied himself with things like this at the centre?"

Ian Nolan/Getty Images

Source: Reproduced by permission of SAGE Publications, London, Los Angeles, New Delhi and Singapore, from Jocelyn Nana, Carr, M., and Lee, W. "Learning Story 4.1". *Learning Stories: Constructing Learner Identities in Early Education*. Sage Publications: Thousand Oaks, California, p. 67.

Pedagogical documentation examines what was just observed throughout the day, during any part of the day. Educators consider the questions of the child and other adults, and then reflect on what was uncovered. With pedagogical documentation, educators need to be responsive and inclusive good listeners and keen observers. Of course, they'll also need to be organized to quickly take advantage of those spontaneous learning experiences.

Pedagogical documentation is more than recording a specific skill or how a child enjoyed an activity. It is more than evaluating a particular curriculum objective to determine accomplishment.

THE SPECIAL ROLE OF OBSERVATION IN DIFFERENT PHILOSOPHIES

Within Canada and other countries, different philosophies are practised in the early childhood profession. These philosophies, in turn, are reflected in the **best practices**, curriculum, and policies of each program. What is embedded in every philosophy is observation; it is **generic** in nature and independent of setting.

Observations do not represent a particular philosophy; they instead reflect a philosophy and practice of inquiry. Our practices should be governed by a philosophy of what we believe about all aspects of our role, including but not limited to children, our views about childhood itself, our image of what an educator could be, and our values regarding relationships, families, partnerships, mentoring, sharing, and learning, including the willingness to change and transform as we continue to learn and discover. This text supports unequivocally the notion that there is more than one way to observe, document, and reflect upon the activity of young children. The tremendous variety of child-care experiences across Canada necessitates this flexible approach, as noted in Pence's keynote address at a national conference in Calgary, Alberta, in Exhibit 1.12.

EXHIBIT 1.12	CHILDHOOD IS A SOCIAL CONSTRUCTION

Pence proposed that "childhood is a social construction—it varies over time and it varies across cultures and contexts. And as different peoples and parents around the world work to create appropriate care for their children, they do this differently—not just because the materials, environments and technologies are different, but because their understanding of children, who they are and what they can do, are different. And because of these inherent differences, when we speak of 'quality care' there can be no single definition of what this thing called quality is, that there can be no single instrument or single method that captures it."

Source: Pence, Allan, "Seeking the Other 99 Languages of ECE: A Keynote Address by Alan Pence." *Interaction* 20.3 (Fall 2006). Alan Pence, Professor, School of Children and Youth, University of Victoria.

Observation and documentation will take on more of a dominant role in some philosophies or practices than others. For example, settings that adopt a **High/Scope** approach will use observations very differently from a centre that primarily uses a theme-based curriculum. The documentation developed from observations in a Reggio Emilia centre will again be substantially different from the ways observations are used in a **Montessori school** or centre that has developed an **eclectic approach** to its early learning framework.

The influence of theories such as Howard Gardner's theory of multiple intelligence, Daniel Goldman's theory of **emotional intelligence**, and Jerome Kagan's research on personality types has made professionals in the field more aware of the need to pay particular attention to children's learning styles. Theories such as these influence program philosophies, the development of curriculum, teaching strategies, and documentation methods. Most crucial, however, is the development of an educator's beliefs and willingness to learn from the children. This willingness requires a commitment to observe on a daily basis. What is *your* image of a child? How do you believe children learn and develop? Do you think what you believe will influence what you see?

In a **pluralistic**, democratic society, educators of young children know they have valuable opportunities to promote social interactions and chances for social learning. Regardless of the philosophy or setting, discovering the uniqueness of each child is the greatest joy and challenge of every educator. Observation skills are the key to unlocking those discoveries. Having inclusive, responsive educators who are aware of each child in the group is essential to achieving an atmosphere of trust, acceptance, and caring.

OBSERVATION IN RESEARCH: A BRIEF HISTORICAL PERSPECTIVE

When you are in an early childhood setting, look around at the environment and how the educators interact with the children and families. Almost everything will have been inspired by one or more philosophies. Philosophies are based on decades of theoretical discussions and research, and observation has played a key historical role, just as it does today.

From a historical perspective, two famous theorists who are often associated with unique observations are Jean Marc-Gasparad Itard and Jean Piaget. Both lived during very different times: Itard in the 1800s and Piaget in the 1900s. These men observed and documented behaviour for different reasons, but both, with their descriptive observations, contributed individually to the study of how children learn and develop.

With the growing industrialization of the Western world in the 19th and 20th centuries, people changed how they lived, worked, and viewed the education of children, setting the scene for the behaviourists. The rise in the popularity of science and sociology prompted researchers and theorists to embrace response, conditioning, and measurement. This scientific thinking was reflected in models and terms of defining behaviour. It concerned itself with explaining and measuring behaviour, turning away from the earlier concepts of Piaget and the **introspection** of Sigmund Freud, believing them to represent unscientific methods of determining behaviour.

In the mid-1900s, John B. Watson and B.F. Skinner posited that a conditioning process might be the answer to explaining all behaviour. Their assumption was that all behaviour is the result of environmental learning. If behaviours were rewarded, they would likely be repeated. Negative reinforcements, such as taking away a privilege, were seen to deter certain behaviours. Much of their work has influenced how we define the behaviours we observe today.

The behaviourists changed how we see, measure, and define behaviour. In this text, the definition of "behaviour" is partially based on the scientific work of the behaviourist school. Are the behaviourist theories of learning, then, the underlying philosophy of this text? The answer is "No." However, this text defines behaviour in ways that permit the observer to describe in a clear manner the experiences of young children, thereby allowing educators to interpret and reflect upon and give value to those observations. This text acknowledges the role of observation in all methods and philosophies but lays the groundwork for all those possibilities in a clear definition of observation.

The Child Study Movement established in the United States began to use observation for developing their child-related disciplines. Some of the most famous theorists from that tradition were John Dewey, Lewis Terman, and Arnold Gesell, in the period from the late 1800s to the early to mid-1900s. The theorists just mentioned shaped the early discourse of what learning is and what it is to learn.

OBSERVATION IN RESEARCH: A CURRENT PERSPECTIVE

Formal observation has been a valuable tool in establishing the difference between popular thinking and legitimate investigation. In a clinical research model, observation is used as a means of collecting data for a specialized topic of study that may clarify our understanding of children, views of play, or best practices for early identification and diagnosis.

Formal settings are settings in which the environment is constructed for a specific purpose, such as testing or a research study. Formal observation methods are conducted by professionals with extensive training and education, such as child psychologists, professors, psychiatrists, or researchers in educational positions.

Research into theory and practice can be found in professional journals and e-journals. Articles in professional journals are important in raising awareness of issues for discussion, such as the environment, diversity, inclusion, and professional development.

Government-funded initiatives such as the Canadian Council on Learning's *State of Learning in Canada* report (2010), foundations, and/or international programs regarding children and their care and development are backed by extensive research. This research can be in executive summary form, studies complete with methodology, projected outcomes, and time frames; they can also be found online in reports, pamphlets, and books or presented on a website.

Informal settings are the settings that are familiar, natural, and known to the child, such as daycare, before- and after-school programs, preschool programs, nursery school, full-day kindergarten, or private home care. The primary focus of observation represented in this text is about those observations made in these early learning and care settings.

A current example of research being done in an informal setting is **ethnographic research**. This research relies on observation and other tools such as **video diaries** and/or photographs. This type of research is similar perhaps to **longitudinal studies** in that it falls under the broad umbrella of **qualitative research**, which means that the research or outcomes from one study are not applied to any other studies. The intent of this research is not only to gather information but also to reflect what that information means and how it might be helpful in a **holistic** understanding or explanation of the culture and environment that is being studied. Fundamental to this type of research is the natural, real-world setting in which it takes place. The aim is to gather insights; examine how things are done; take into account the feelings and ideas of everyone concerned, including the children; and reflect and share the research results.

Research topics explored in formal settings have typically been seen as separate from those of less rigorous investigations of informal settings. Dr. Lilian G. Katz (2005), a professor emerita of early childhood education at the University of Illinois, addressed the notion of a two-tier system of observation, questioning the lack of communication between researchers in formal settings and the findings of educators in informal settings. It appears that Dr. Katz would like to see more dialogue between the two groups and more sharing of findings. Perhaps educators need to be more aware of and proactive about seeking new theories and research, and those specialists who conduct research in more controlled settings need to take some cues from educators "on the floor" concerning what research topics would be worth further detailed investigation.

SUMMARY *see, think, use, whom*

Observation reveals how children see their world, what they think about it, how they use the things that are in it, and whom they trust, play with, and want to be around. Through daily observation and interactions, educators appreciate not only the individual differences and unique personalities of each child but also the marvel of childhood. It is through observation and reflection that we gain insights into the effects of socialization and culture on a child's personality and behaviour.

In this chapter, we examined how important the relationship is between educators and children, parents and educators, and families and the community, and how when they all work together, they form a learning community. Listening to their voices contributes to a philosophy of transformation, which holds at its centre the practice of appreciative inquiry. From this approach, responsive, inclusive observers view children as competent, able, intuitive investigators, capable of co-constructing new learning and making meaningful choices in their play experiences.

In this chapter, we focused on the question "Why observe?" as it is the most basic question of our inquiry. Through inquiry and reflection, professionals, children, and their families are brought to a place of learning, understanding, and discovery. This discovery process is vital to becoming a responsive, inclusive educator who is open to new possibilities, who reflects upon the ideas and feelings of others, and who interacts in a responsive and inclusive manner.

Also in this chapter is the role that observations have played in the development of child-related philosophies and practices. Whether it is within the context of clinical research or informal early learning and care settings, observation is the foundation for what we learn about children.

CHAPTER 2

PREPARING TO OBSERVE

Vasilyev Alexandr/Shutterstock.com

Welcome to Chapter 2! This chapter builds upon the foundational concepts introduced in Chapter 1, but where to now? To begin our observational journey, we first need to find a map. Why a map? Maps are most useful when you're not sure where to start, where you're going, where something is, or how to get through the construction. Let's see if we can help navigate through the important and relevant topics in this chapter by sketching out a bit of a road map. Chapter 2 tackles some serious topics and introduces the cycle of observation, noting its importance to the observational process and laying the foundation for further discussions and exploration in subsequent chapters. Let's begin to chart new territory, making new observational discoveries!

OVERVIEW

This chapter not only builds on the question of why we engage in observation but also navigates the observational map, asking the classic questions of who, what, when, where, and how as they pertain to the observation process. Concepts are introduced in this chapter that are fundamental to answering those questions. Understanding these key concepts will lay the foundation for the ensuing chapters and prepare you to conduct meaningful observations and pedagogical documentation. This chapter explores the practical, day-to-day considerations of observation, such as how to record what is seen and heard in meaningful ways. You will also be introduced to the related topics of consent and confidentiality, the rights of children, and the Code of Ethics and Standards of Practice, and become familiar with documentation in office files and permissions. Fundamental to the observation and documentation process is the cycle of observation, which begins in this chapter and is followed throughout the text. This chapter introduces the pragmatic reality of starting the observation and documentation process.

FOCUS QUESTIONS

1. What impact does the consideration of consent and confidentiality have on the observer and his or her pedagogical documentation?
2. In what ways do the Code of Ethics and Standards of Practice relate to the observation of young children and pedagogical documentation?
3. Why is it important to think through the initial decisions of what, why, when, where, and how to observe?
4. Why are the procedures for obtaining consent from parents important in the field of early childhood education? Why are the rights of children noted in this chapter?

TWO LEVELS OF OBSERVATION

When observing young children, two levels of observation are occurring: personal and professional. Determining the differences between the two levels of observation is central to understanding the role of the professional educator.

PERSONAL LEVEL

The personal level refers to your present abilities as an observer. These skills have been enhanced by your years of education, your past and present jobs and interests, and your family and friends. Like the observation detailed in Exhibit 2.1, watching

EXHIBIT 2.1

EXHIBIT 2.1   THE ROLE OF OBSERVATION IN EARLY CHILDHOOD DEVELOPMENT

"I once sat by a window looking out across the street at a man who was acting very strange. I could see him only from the waist up, but that was enough for me to know he was making extraordinary gestures and facial expressions. I opened the window so I could hear his words. I was even more mystified. The words coming out of his mouth were in a language I didn't understand, and they sounded very strange indeed. I watched this man for some time, trying to figure out what he was doing walking back and forth on the sidewalk making weird gestures and sounds. I had decided he was crazy and had begun to feel afraid when finally I stood up and saw the whole picture. There at the man's heels was a dog. Immediately everything made sense. Aha, he's training a dog, I said to myself. I would have figured it out sooner if this man had been of my culture and used the command facial expressions, gestures, and, especially, the words I was familiar with. I learned two lessons from this experience: (1) You have to see the whole picture to understand. (2) It's important to know the meanings attached to the behavior."

Source: Gonzalez Mena, Janet, *Diversity in Early Care and Education: Honoring Differences,* 5th edition (New York: McGraw-Hill, 2008), p. 31.

the behaviour of others to make sense of what we are seeing and hearing is something that we do naturally every day, in many different contexts. Through those observation skills, you have developed your own ideas, opinions, and values. In turn, these lifelong experiences have created certain expectations. Before you began your studies, you probably wondered about what your classes and experiences with children would be like.

PROFESSIONAL LEVEL

You do not have to attend college or university to be able to tell someone what you saw a child do on the playground. However, in order to *frame your observations* in the context of human growth, development, culture, environment, and experiences and then *appropriately interpret* their significance to others, you *do* need formal education and mentoring. These skills represent the second level of observation: the professional level.

Central to your role as an educator-observer will be the development of observation skills. These skills, along with your understanding of how children grow and develop, will enhance your reflective practice and give you a solid foundation as you develop your career. Observation and planning are also linked closely together, as indicated by Catapano (2005):

> Two areas of knowledge must be well-established in the teachers' daily practice. First, they must understand child development and relate what they see in their classroom to what they plan for the children. They must understand what children do in their explorations and why. Next they must be child watchers, using observations to inform planning and practice as a regular part of their classroom structure. (p. 262)

DEFINING A SYSTEMATIC PROCESS OF OBSERVATION

Observation suggests that a person observes, watches, and sees the immediate environment primarily through the sense of sight. Yet observation is really a generic term for using all the senses, including hearing, smell, touch, and taste. When asked for our observations on a bakery, for example, we will probably comment on more than just what we see: we will remark on the wonderful aroma upon entering the bakery and certainly describe the tastes! Observation relies heavily on hearing as the sounds accompanying what is observed often take on great importance. Can you think of instances or situations when sound was the most important aspect of that experience? Tennis players say that the "plop" sound of the ball on the court or on an opponent's racket is as important to hear as it is for the player to see the ball or how the other player played the ball.

Educators will tell you that their observations are much more than that. Since young children communicate much of what they think and feel through their bodies, educators have to develop the expertise to "read" behaviours, that is, interpret what children are communicating through their behaviour or actions and the sounds they make, reflect upon their intent and purpose, and then convey that information to others.

Observation is a systematic process of watching and listening to children and recording their behaviour in a meaningful way for shared use. Observation, then, is a systematic process. A process is an ongoing series of events that has already started but has not yet finished. It proceeds in time, usually changing as it evolves. The process of observing can refer to the actual observation you are making on a specific child at a certain time, or it can refer to the entire lifelong practice of observation. This idea will be further solidified as we explore educator development in subsequent chapters. In those chapters, we will explore the evolution of reflective practice and the honing of one's skills, and come to see just how integral these are to the process of observing young children as the observations themselves. When developing observation skills, learning with, about, and among others always takes place along the way, even for an experienced educator, as in Exhibit 2.2.

EXHIBIT 2.2　　LEARNING ABOUT JERIMIAH

An experienced educator for five years now, today in my classroom, I experienced something for the first time. I had never really taken the time to see the world through a child's eyes, to allow the child to communicate to me through his actions the decision making that was taking place. Let me explain.

Two months ago, we had a new preschooler by the name of Jerimiah. Jerimiah had no siblings, and both he and his family were new to Canada within the last six months. Our centre was the first place of contact for this family. As Jerimiah began to settle into our program, I began to notice that Jerimiah played on his own most of the time, humming and talking to himself in a very low tone as he interacted with materials in the room. Two weeks after starting our program Jerimiah began pushing other children as they crossed his path, or at times he would be observed running up to a child to push him down. Educators at first were seeing only the visible behaviour of "pushing," and often were only responding by stopping him to tell him "no pushing." At the time, we were missing the key communication of what Jerimiah was trying to tell us.

With his parents, we agreed to begin observing and documenting Jerimiah's play and movements within the room. We took the time to listen and then interpret what we were seeing, and we were amazed by what we learned. We discovered that Jerimiah frequently gravitated toward materials in the classroom that could topple over. We saw musical instruments on shelves pushed to produce sound as they fell on the floor. We saw a child excited by his decisions and the sounds of these materials as they fell. We learned that he would smile when a child fell and began crying. Why was this information so important? Taking the time to view Jerimiah as a competent learner in the room was the key to seeing beyond the perceived "negative behaviour" constantly discussed and identified by the educators in the centre. Jerimiah was communicating his fascination with sound and movement. He wasn't meaning to hurt others—their tears and response to him were what he was fascinated with. He was focusing on the connection between when he pushed and the reaction he got—cause and effect. Making this important realization

(Continued)

prompted our team to rethink how we view children. We were caught up in the "behaviour" and we weren't listening. Once we determined what his behaviour and actions were communicating, we were able to respond with learning experiences that allowed him to engage with cause-and-effect actions in a more appropriate way. By doing this, the pushing of children stopped and peers began initiating interactions with him. Our children also began a new inquiry into sound and movement with Jerimiah leading our learning journey!

Source: Courtesy of Kristine Fenning.

As observers, what have we learned from Jerimiah's educator? What were some of the words used? Listening, interpreting, seeing, competent learner, cause and effect, documenting, reflecting, experiencing, inquiry, and, of course, observing. These words are those used by a reflective educator who viewed Jerimiah in a new way, engaging actively with the child and family and colleagues to uncover why Jerimiah was pushing other children.

It is a useful example of the kinds of interactions, problem solving, and communication that are practised by responsive educators within an inclusive learning environment. This begins our inquiry into the process of watching and listening to children.

THE PROCESS OF WATCHING AND LISTENING TO CHILDREN

People generally think that watching or observing young children is a passive activity. It is not. Why? The educator in the room is responsible for the children and their well-being. He or she plays a very active role, being totally engaged with the children throughout the day while constantly observing their individual and group behaviour.

Children communicate using their bodies to express themselves: a frown, a finger curling a strand of hair, shoulders

Wiarton Kid's Den/Sally Wylie

shrugging, and a loud, long sigh. Listening to children means being in tune with them—being open and sensitive to their actions, feelings, and ideas.

Listening is one of the most important aspects of observation; it means that the adult attends to the child and, by doing so, demonstrates value and respect for the child's voice. Listening gains a broader perspective, as shown in Exhibit 2.3. As Wilson (2014) reminds us, "*active listening* makes those around us feel appreciated, interesting, and respected. Ordinary conversations emerge on a deeper level, as do our relationships. Listening with intent may in fact reduce misunderstandings and we always learn more when we listen more than we talk" (p. 232).

EXHIBIT 2.3	VISIBLE LISTENING

"'Through careful listening, [teachers] are better able to spontaneously support and challenge a child to extend his thinking' (Gandini & Kaminsky, 2004, p. 9). Documentation is seen as "visible listening.... To ensure listening and being listened to is one of the primary tasks of documentation … as well as to ensure that the group and each individual child has the pos sibility to observe themselves from an external point of view while they are learning (Rinaldi, 2001). Your attention sends a message to a child that what they do has value and meaning."

Source: Browne, Kathryn Williams and Ann Miles Gordon, (2009) *To Teach Well: An Early Childhood Practicum Guide*, Pearson, NJ, p. 72.

THE CYCLE OF OBSERVATION

A **cycle of observation**, or **observation cycle**, begins with observations upon enrolment. Orienting a family to observation and the purpose of documentation is an important conversation. The conversations with the family and their views of their child is the ideal starting point. From there, the educators in the room would begin to observe and document the daily activity of the child to get a sense of what he or she likes to do, whom the child likes, and key information about the child's habits, personality, skills, and interests. As can be seen in Exhibit 2.4, educators may or may not have a specific purpose in mind for observing. Being a responsive observer means that it is important to listen to children and observe the spontaneity of their play, and this means that perhaps the purpose is simply just to watch, document, and learn. Observing a new child in the group is of particular interest to a responsive and reflective educator; there is so much to learn.

| EXHIBIT 2.4 | THE LENS OF OBSERVATION IN A HOLISTIC APPROACH |

When beginning the observation process, you may not have a specific purpose in mind or may not be sure of a focus. Often when we form new questions or areas of inquiry, we are led to different types of observations, and thus we become more holistic in our approach. Where do you begin? Perhaps you might be wondering about …

- What makes a particular child interesting. What about that child's communication? Does the child talk to both adults and children or express self with facial expressions and body language? What about infants? In what ways would an infant use body motion to communicate?

- How a child or group of children interact socially. Play-based observation yields the most amazing discoveries of children, from infants to children in kindergarten. Would the social play of infants be different from that of preschoolers? Is the social development of children from different cultures obvious during play?

- The subject of spirituality and young children. To understand how this might be captured through observation, check online for articles on the subject of spirituality and children. Query various early childhood philosophies, and you will find that the spirituality of children is a main consideration in documents such as *Belonging, Being and Becoming: The Early Years Framework for Australia* (Australian Government, Department of Education, Employment and Workplace Relations for the Council of Australian Governments, 2009).

- A child's attachment to his educators and caregivers or perhaps to his or her peers. Play-based groupings of children offer opportunities to examine play partners, relationships, and attachments. How are attachments formed? How do friendships develop? How do children deal with antagonistic peers? When a new child joins the group, how are those patterns of play changed? In Chapter 5, types of records, such as mapping, sociograms, or eco-maps, are investigated; these types of records have been specifically designed to track the social context of a child both at home and at a school or centre.

- A child who is new to the centre and/or country. What might you learn about the child's culture, language, and beliefs? Add to that exciting opportunities to learn about a new culture and language, find out about community resources for the family, and develop a relationship with the parents.

- A child who might benefit from extra support or who might be struggling in an aspect of her or his development. Perhaps the parents have approached you for help because they are concerned about their child. All children may have a time in their developmental pathway when they need some type of support due to the challenges they may be facing, behaviourally, developmentally, or for reasons beyond themselves. Through observation, you can find out which current abilities this child has, which skills require further development, and perhaps even which influences are affecting the child's overall progress. Chapter 7 will introduce us to the various types of professionals who may join the team to assist in supporting a child with diagnosed or undiagnosed special needs within the early childhood setting.

Whether observing a new child, a group of children at play, a child challenged by some aspect of his or her development, or monitoring an individual's development over time, engaging in the ongoing cycle of observation can be a truly wondrous and exciting learning journey for all involved. For children, parents, educators, and professionals, this cyclical process invites their perspectives so as to provide insight and to derive meaning from what they see and hear. As seen in Exhibit 2.5 and discussed in almost all subsequent chapters, there is no single entry point in this cycle. The observer may begin at any point of the cycle because observation occurs all the time in any philosophy. The *cycle of observation* includes components such as

- an initial inquiry, question, or wonder
- observation and pedagogical documentation
- interpretation and evaluation
- drawing connections and making learning visible
- co-construction of responsive and inclusive actions/plans
- collaboration from all team members throughout the cycle
- active reflection throughout

In Exhibit 2.5, note how the cycle supports observation, making the process truly transformative and meaningful with the participation of those involved.

Active reflection occurs throughout the cycle as it engages educators, families, and children in inquiry-based thinking and further observation, leading to discoveries that promote self-awareness, the improvement of professional practice, and experiences that promote learning for all who are involved. Another outcome that may be a result of the observation cycle is the pursuit of further assessment concerning a child, as explored in Chapter 7, or the environment, which is the focus of Chapter 8.

EXHIBIT 2.5   THE CYCLE OF OBSERVATION

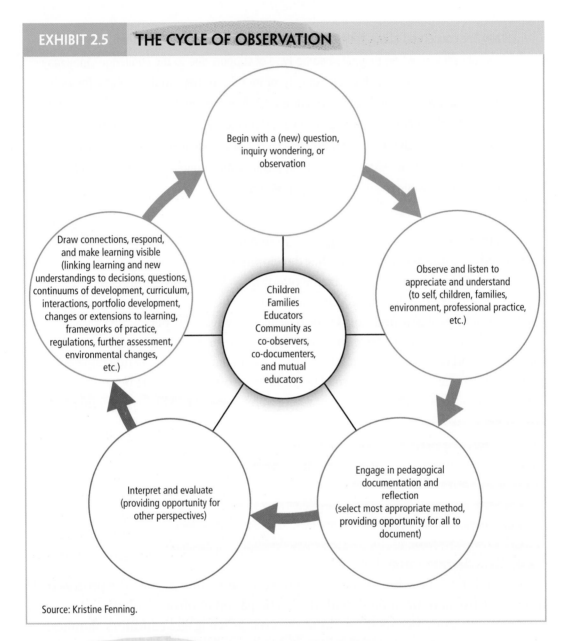

Source: Kristine Fenning.

VARIATIONS OF THE CYCLE OF OBSERVATION

How a cycle of observation is represented varies depending on philosophy and practices, the focus of the program and age groupings, parent involvement, community demographics, and other factors. In Carol Gestwicki's (2011) cycle of planning (Exhibit 2.6), she advises that it "allows teachers to use the three sources of knowledge to make developmentally appropriate decisions: (1) knowledge of age-related characteristics;

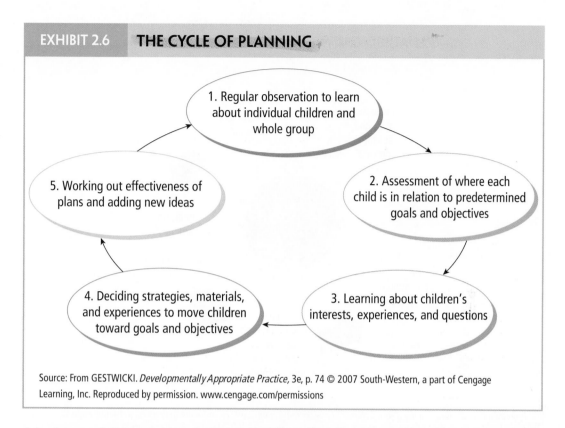

| EXHIBIT 2.6 | THE CYCLE OF PLANNING |

1. Regular observation to learn about individual children and whole group

2. Assessment of where each child is in relation to predetermined goals and objectives

3. Learning about children's interests, experiences, and questions

4. Deciding strategies, materials, and experiences to move children toward goals and objectives

5. Working out effectiveness of plans and adding new ideas

Source: From GESTWICKI. *Developmentally Appropriate Practice,* 3e, p. 74 © 2007 South-Western, a part of Cengage Learning, Inc. Reproduced by permission. www.cengage.com/permissions

(2) of strengths, interests and needs of individual children; and (3) knowledge of social and cultural contexts in which children live to ensure that learning experiences are both meaningful and relevant" (p. 74). Planning that is based on observations and adaptations made to the curriculum creates a responsive climate in the playroom.

Observation cycles, such as the one found in Exhibit 2.7, are based on observing and recording ordinary moments. This early learning cycle is based on a play-based model and uses a cyclical process that is similar to yet different from the Gestwicki cycle of planning found in Exhibit 2.6. The British Columbia Early Learning Framework includes

> the process of pedagogical narration [which] involves observing and recording ordinary moments, reflecting on what you have observed, sharing your description with others, collectively building new meanings from what you have learned so as to make children's learning visible, linking what you have learned to the Framework, and incorporating your learning into your planning process. (British Columbia Ministry of Education, 2009, p. 14)[*]

[*]*Understanding the British Columbia Early Learning Framework: From Theory to Practice,* p. 14. Copyright © Province of British Columbia. All rights reserved. Reproduced with permission of the Province of British Columbia.

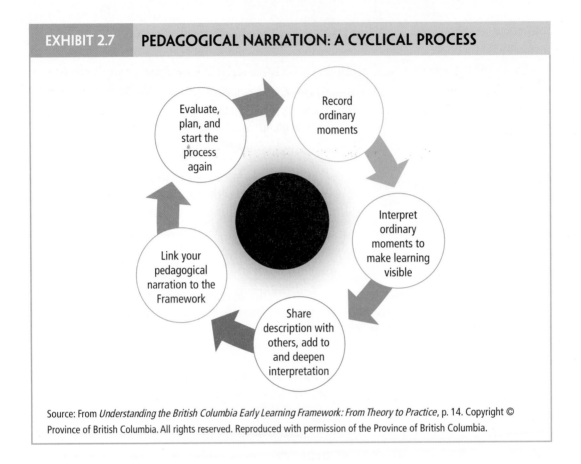

EXHIBIT 2.7   PEDAGOGICAL NARRATION: A CYCLICAL PROCESS

Record ordinary moments

Interpret ordinary moments to make learning visible

Share description with others, add to and deepen interpretation

Link your pedagogical narration to the Framework

Evaluate, plan, and start the process again

Another example of an existing observation cycle is the model and process used for documenting the progress of a child with special needs: initial observations, assessment, an individual plan with goals and strategies, implementation, and evaluation. This model and process is discussed in more detail in Chapter 7.

THE CYCLE OF OBSERVATION AS AN INTERACTIVE PROCESS

The cycle of observation, as we see it, is not a structured, prescriptive formula for teachers to direct their observation, planning, and reporting process. Rather, the cycle of observation is first and foremost an interactive process involving a team of others: parents, community professionals, educators, and children. It involves gathering multiple perspectives.

As with observation itself, the cycle of observation is also setting-independent and is an essential part of all inquiry. It is ongoing and **self-rectifying**, meaning that it is a vibrant process that provides an approach without a set time frame and prescribed outcomes.

Diagram 2.1 gives a visual of the key words representing essential ingredients of the observation cycle. In the diagram you'll note the interplay between the key words representing an equitable exchange rather than a hierarchy of who/what is most important.

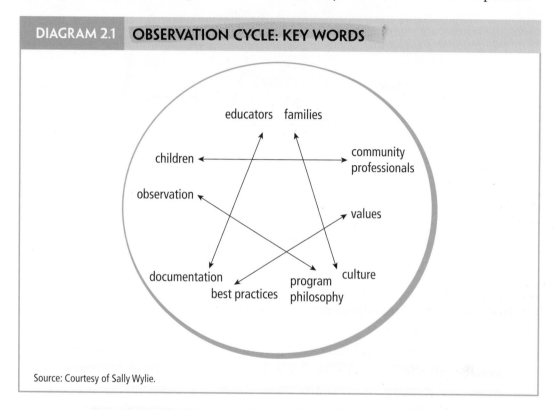

DIAGRAM 2.1 **OBSERVATION CYCLE: KEY WORDS**

Source: Courtesy of Sally Wylie.

The words in Diagram 2.1 combined with the guiding words in Diagram 2.2 illustrate the dynamic nature of the cycle of observation.

For example, when guiding words such as *perception* and *inquiry* refer to children and community professionals, it could mean that children have inquired about what people do in the community. Perhaps some of these professionals in the community loom larger than life, such as a firefighter or police officer. Having the children meet these professionals in their

Dan Holm/Shutterstock

DIAGRAM 2.2   OBSERVATION CYCLE: GUIDING WORDS

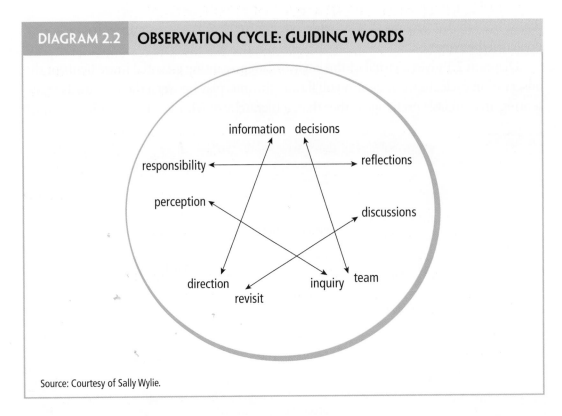

information   decisions

responsibility   reflections

perception

discussions

direction

revisit

inquiry   team

Source: Courtesy of Sally Wylie.

environment provides an opportunity for inquiry from both points of view. Observations from that real-life interchange form a basis for curriculum, talking points in the community, and inter-relationships, to name but a few possibilities.

This reflective process is transforming rather than conforming; the team (whoever that may be) creates and directs the process. As the team experiences the discussion, the team members form the direction for and purpose of their efforts using guiding words such as those found in Diagram 2.2. This process then could prompt discussions from the educators, who revisit the event with further documentation.

If the decision is to represent publicly what was learned, then a different decision will be made, and those involved will construct what that representation will look like. Will the documentation be presented as a documentation panel, a binder set up in the foyer, an article in the school newsletter, or a PowerPoint presentation to inform the board of directors, parents, and municipality? How will information be conveyed or transmitted?

Other decisions can be made, such as inquiring if the children wish to revisit their work of the previous week. If so, the work will be revisited and reflected upon, and perhaps thoughts will be added before further discussions take place or decisions are made. Please visit Chapters 6 and 7, where the topic of the observation cycle is discussed again.

INQUIRY: A VITAL PART OF THE CYCLE OF OBSERVATION

Inquiry is the vital thread from the beginning and throughout the observation cycle. As the cycle evolves, it will include questions that invite reflection and evaluation. This appreciative inquiry approach, involving reflective observation and an interactive, ongoing process, is a positive framework of informed, responsive, and inclusive practice and the central theme of this text.

Inquiry begins the cycle and maintains its momentum. The most important action a team can engage in is the process of inquiry: questioning. For example, before documentation begins, fundamental questions should be asked of those involved:

- What type of environment (social, emotional, cognitive, physical) do we wish to create with children and their families?
- What behaviours or values must I demonstrate to create or maintain this environment?
- How are children involved in the creation of their environment?
- What are our beliefs and values about learning? Children? Families?
- How will the documentation reveal our learning?
- What kinds of questions will our documentation reveal?
- How will self-reflection be valued or promoted within the day?

The discussions involving these kinds of questions prompt everyone to listen to others and examine the beliefs of others and themselves. Once educators begin to ask, listen, revisit, challenge, and reflect, divergent ideas emerge that move the group from where it was to where group members would like to be—a new space. This process is not necessarily easy, but whatever the perceived challenges might be, the will to problem-solve and construct creates a positive, responsive climate in which respect and nurturance can thrive and ideas can grow.

Dr. Peter Moss (2011), co-author of *Ethics and Politics in Early Childhood Education*, stated as part of his keynote presentation in Toronto that Ethics of Care is

> A practice, not a set of rules … involving particular acts of care and a "general habit of mind" that informs all aspects of moral life and includes attentiveness, responsibility, competence and responsiveness … [and] caring as everything we do to maintain, continue and repair our 'world' so we can live in it as well as possible….
>
> From our (provisional) answers to critical questions, we can then ask more technical questions:
>
> - How should we organize and structure our services (e.g., administration, regulation, access, funding, workforce, type of provision)?
> - How should we practise education? What pedagogy?

- How should we evaluate?
- What pedagogical tools are useful?*

The process of inquiry invites change. Openness to change and the **predisposition** to change are key in creating alternative change in practices. What would questions look like in an observation cycle? Questions offered in Diagram 2.3 illustrate some possibilities.

DIAGRAM 2.3   OBSERVATION CYCLE: QUESTIONS

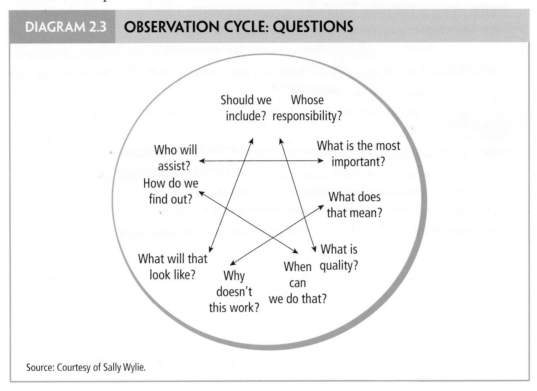

Source: Courtesy of Sally Wylie.

Following the ebb and flow of questions, discussion, and reflection, where might this process lead? Including the children and involved adults allows the shared process to proceed without a scheduled time frame or outcomes driving the process; it is ongoing, vibrant, and transformational. This process involves the children, their work in all forms, and the possibility to revisit the work created as well as the process, as noted in Webster, Belanger, and Conant's (2002) article about Canadian children and documentation in Exhibit 2.8.

PEDAGOGICAL QUESTIONS

Firmly established in the cycle of observation is the fundamental practice of asking questions. These questions can range from basic questions such as educators asking themselves in the morning, "How will I continue to document the children's interest

*Courtesy of Dr. Peter Moss.

EXHIBIT 2.8

THE ROLES AND FORMS OF DOCUMENTATION IN THE INVESTIGATION

"Documentation records a moment in time and contains details that easily fade from memory, thus enabling children, teachers and parents to revisit it and delve deeper into an investigation. For example, it would have been less powerful had we simply told the children about the parents' attempts to 'read' their drawings. As mentioned earlier, we teachers felt that the parents had done rather well, but the children noticed many details that we had missed. Watching the videotape of parents attempting to understand their drawings provoked the children to create new ones. By revisiting the documentation, and following through on the children's ideas, we helped them to generate new ideas and work to further articulate and express them. Reggio educators describe such use of documentation as a cyclical process of inquiry (Gandini & Goldhaber, 2001). Forms of documentation will vary depending on what equipment is available, the nature of the investigation and the information a teacher wants to record. If children are sitting in a circle having a conversation, a tape recorder might suffice to catch the children's ideas. Teachers might make sketches of the construction of a block structure to capture a child's process."

Source: Marilyn Webster, Jessica Belanger, Faith Conant. You Can't Draw on Air: Stretches and Sketches, *Canadian Children*, Vol. 27, No. 2, pp. 4–11. Canadian Association for Young Children (2002).

in the differences of textures?" to divergent questions such as "What are the ways we will display the documentation of the preschooler's ideas about water?" or critical questions such as "What pieces, when compiled together, will best portray the experiences and learning of this child?" These pedagogical questions reflect the thinking of appreciative educators who are transformative in their approach to learning.

Exhibit 2.9 examines other, deeply reflective pedagogical questions inquiring into social responsibility and diversity taken from the British Columbia Early Learning Framework.

QUESTIONS OF SELF-REFLECTION

Questions of self-reflection, such as "Have I seen and documented this child's struggle with self-regulation in an equitable manner?" are critical in this reflective or evaluative function. The process of documenting or reflecting on documentation

EXHIBIT 2.9	PEDAGOGICAL QUESTIONS

My Practice and Social Responsibility and Diversity

Think about

- How are social responsibility and diversity currently reflected in my practice?
- What can I do to bring my practice more in line with the Framework's description of social responsibility and diversity and its learning goals, including the Aboriginal-specific provisions?
- How can I know if social responsibility and diversity and its goals are evident in my program? What can I do to make this area of early learning more explicit in my practice?
- How can I promote a discussion of social responsibility and diversity in my practice, and with families and communities?
- How have I reflected upon the *Questions to Consider* included in the Framework for social responsibility and diversity?
- Have I appropriately accommodated the unique circumstances of Aboriginal children with respect to social responsibility and diversity?

Source: From *Understanding the British Columbia Early Learning Framework: From Theory to Practice*, p. 14, British Columbia Ministry of Education. Copyright Province of British Columbia. All rights reserved. Reprinted with permission of the Province of British Columbia.

invites critical evaluation not only of what has been seen and recorded but also the perceptions of that process by the recorders themselves. Here is where a different phase of responsibility lies—in the reflection and evaluation of those responsible for the presentation or display of the children's work. Adults' self-reflection plays an important role when reflecting on children's capacity for work.

Schools and centres typically support the observation and documentation process as a vital part of their practice. We have all heard of planning time. What about reflection time? Is the reflection process valued? How is the value of it represented within the day? Perhaps that question, if posed at the beginning of the cycle of observation, would have an influence that would be felt throughout our practice. As Hughes (2005) states,

> One of the greatest contributions from the educators of Reggio Emilia is the promotion of discussion, reflection and examination of beliefs and values that are translated into teaching practices (New, 2000). When teachers are serious in their study, they optimize the opportunity to question and to examine the underlying

principles of this approach and apply their understanding to their own unique early childhood education program. (p. 49)

You will find extended conversations and more information on self-reflection and reflective questioning in Chapters 6, 7, and 8.

Before we continue with the reflective, pedagogical questions discussed above in later chapters, let's reflect back to Chapter 1 when the children asked, "What happened to the trees?" With that one question, the children and educators began their journey of investigation, and that's where our questioning will return now— to some of the basic questions which will form the foundation of our self-reflective questioning.

Christopher Futcher/iStockphoto.com

ASKING THE QUESTIONS: WHY, HOW, WHO, WHEN, WHERE, AND WHAT

WHY OBSERVE CHILDREN?

As discussed in Chapter 1, we observe children for a number of important reasons, each of which broadens our abilities to educate and care for young children. Those reasons were

- to observe children's growth and development
- to appreciate the unique thinking processes of every child
- to support early intervention
- to observe daily interactions
- to observe the group as a whole
- to determine how children play with certain materials or equipment
- to discover the variability of skills or temperament within each child
- to involve parents in the process of discovery
- to observe who seems happy and having fun and who seems sad, upset, lonesome, or frustrated
- to observe the environment and make adaptations to it
- to develop pedagogical documentation

This list only begins to reflect the main reasons for observing young children. To continue, let us examine several other reasons for engaging in the observation of young children.

OTHER REASONS FOR OBSERVING YOUNG CHILDREN

Other reasons for observing young children could be

- *To observe the safety and well-being (social, emotional, and physical) of each child in the group.* Taking the time to observe and record physical health or social/emotional behavioural changes enables educators to implement appropriate care practices for each child within the group. Take, for example, children arriving in the morning with their parents. Upon arrival, through observing, the educator may notice that Lauren, one of the preschoolers in the classroom, is tired, has a flushed face, and is clinging to her mother. Observing her behaviour and comparing it to how she typically arrives at her child-care centre—which involves smiling, running toward her peers, and quickly joining various play experiences—prompts a discussion with her parent. As she is examined by both the educator and the parent, they discover together that she has a fever and that her ears hurt. As a result, her parent takes her home. Not only does this decision allow Lauren time to recover, but it also prevents the unwanted spreading of germs among other children in the room. "A healthy start in life has a great impact on the well-being of children and throughout life, providing opportunities for children to develop the attributes and resilience needed to mature into healthy adults in our complex society" (Pimento & Kernested, 2010, p. 20).

  Observing and documenting also provide the information necessary for other optimal health and safety prevention practices concerning a number of different elements of practice, including but not limited to helping children cope with stress, child abuse reporting, protocols for lifting/carrying children, field trip considerations, and the appropriate supervision of children throughout the day. Is your field trip appropriate for your children? With supervision, do the rules within the classroom support the safety of the children? Watching to see if the children sit down before going down the slide or use their walking feet indoors ensures that the children are playing safely. Fortunately, observation of children's behaviours and appropriate follow-up can assist in preventing unwanted consequences. For example, if Matthew persists in sliding headfirst down the slide, he will be redirected elsewhere in the playground. Setting limits and following through means using

Reggio Summer Intensive, Acorn School/ Kristine Fenning

your observation skills to see if the children are listening to directions and playing safely.

- *To expand professional roles and promote reflection.* As educators develop knowledge and skills in the role of educator-observer, they cannot help but be shaped by what they learn and uncover. Through lifelong learning, not only do educators develop a professional body of skills and learning, but their personal attitudes, interests, and beliefs change and evolve as well. Working with children cannot help but change how and what you choose to observe and document but also how you see yourself as an educator within the context of child, family, and community. Go online for more on professional development.

- *To evaluate themselves as a group.* Educators discuss their philosophy and practices not only to reflect together on their observations of children, the environment, and curriculum but also to reflect on their work together. Through reflective conversation, educators practise appreciative inquiry, expand their knowledge through others' perspectives, and develop abilities to think critically about the process of constructing a responsive environment:

> Teams of teachers help each other gain perspective on the class, an individual, a time of the day. Observations can be a means of validating one teacher's point of view. By checking out an opinion or idea through systematic observation, teachers get a sense of direction in their planning. Such an assessment implies self-assessment. A team that looks at what their program is or isn't accomplishing and how their program may be affecting children values the reflective process and professional level of teamwork that goes with it. (Gordon & Browne, 2007, pp. 204–205)

Kristine Fenning; thanks to Reggio-inspired Summer Institute, Acorn School

- *To use a variety of methods, which helps ensure a fair overview of information.* Using a variety of recording methods, such as those in Chapters 4 and 5, helps ensure a fair overview of the child. By using a carefully chosen variety of documentation methods, a more balanced picture of the child will result than that achieved by relying on one type of assessment, type of record, or way of documenting. Obtaining information in a number of ways will assist you in gaining a more thorough understanding of a child. An educator's background in typical growth and development and experience with families from different cultures and countries will contribute to her or his ability to determine the pedagogical documentation relevant and meaningful to use.

- *To observe the environment and make adaptations to it.* Observing how children use and respond to their environment is part of an educator's role. Educators know that a child's behaviour is influenced by the environment or surroundings. By watching the children experience and interact with their environment, educators may see definite **patterns**. Some parts of the playroom may be heavy traffic areas because several popular activities are occurring side by side. The dynamics of the group also determine how materials or toys are used. For example, the room can be arranged to suit a particular group of children by enlarging the space for floor toys. Better use of books and audio can be encouraged by relocating them to a space away from a busy area. Observing how the children interact with the environment gives educators ideas for possible changes or adaptations. Basing curriculum materials and equipment on observations of the children's interests, strengths, and needs avoids a narrow program focus. Further discussion of the environment will be found in later chapters.

- *To maintain occupational standards.* **Occupational standards** in Canada have been developed to define acceptable professional behaviour and the knowledge required for a particular occupation. Knowing what levels of occupational competence to expect from new hires and seasoned educators is integral to the maintenance of quality early learning and care. See Exhibit 2.10 for an example of a task and a subtask core competency. Be sure to go online for a more thorough and comprehensive review of the wide-reaching role that observation assumes in professional practice, remembering that expectations may vary from province to province and country to country.

- *To build capacity and community through networking and the development of community partnerships.* Building community within an early learning program requires its educators to engage in ongoing networking and partnering with team members, families, and outside professionals both within and external to the early learning field.

  Networking within the community contributes to the well-being of children, families, educators, and the overall early childhood program. Educators working effectively as a team contribute significantly to the level of quality provided by the program. No one works in isolation, and early childhood settings are no exception. Staff cannot and should

EXHIBIT 2.10 **SECTION A: CHILD DEVELOPMENT, LEARNING, AND CARE: OCCUPATIONAL STANDARDS FOR EARLY CHILDHOOD**

Example: A.1. Facilitate the Development and Behaviour of Children

Context Statement

Early childhood educators facilitate daily experiences that support and promote each child's physical, language, emotional, cognitive, social, and creative development and behaviour using applicable observational tools while respecting inclusion principles and diversity issues.

Subtask A.1.1. Use A Variety of Observation and Documentation Techniques

Required Skills and Abilities	Required Core Knowledge
ECEs are able to	ECEs know
a. document observations using a wide range of methods (e.g., notes, photos, videos)	1. child development theories
b. seek information from parents' observations of their children	2. effective communication skills to understand and interpret children's behaviours
c. categorize observations into domains	3. theories and approaches about observation and documentation techniques
d. interpret observations	
e. communicate observations with team and families	
f. use non-biased language (e.g., open-ended sentences, non-judgemental terminology)	

Source: Child Care Human Resources Sector Council, *Occupational Standards for Early Childhood Educators*, 2010, page 11

not try to be all things to all people. Staff must establish a network with professionals, agencies, and associations in their community. (Pimento & Kernested, 2010, p. 44)

Observing and reflecting upon the services and supports available within your immediate, national, and international communities will open up a wealth of possibilities and resources that can support a program in numerous ways, such as sharing expertise and knowledge, collaborating on projects, fundraising, and building community capacity, a topic covered in detail in Chapter 8.

HOW TO OBSERVE CHILDREN

How do you go about the act of observing? Practically speaking, there are two basic ways to observe children. These ways or modes may be determined by the observer's role, the program philosophy and practices, or even the environment.

SPECTATOR MODE

Observing children's behaviour from a detached and uninvolved position allows the observer to be a spectator to events in the playroom. Some settings have an **observation room** where an educator or parent can comfortably observe the playroom without affecting the behaviour of the children or being involved in the room. Many clinical, university, and college laboratory schools have the luxury of such a vantage point, and for staff and parents, the advantages of an observation area are numerous. Parents often say that it is a treat to stand back and watch their child just for the pleasure of seeing her play without the child's knowledge.

Taking on the spectator role allows the observer to see the big picture. What does that mean? While observing a specific child, the observer can also watch other children's behaviour, or the educators' behaviour may also warrant attention. With the ability to watch all that goes on, what may be observed is how much time one of the educators spends cleaning up the sink area, going through cupboards, rearranging artwork, and generally spending time on the environment rather than with the children. When stepping back as a spectator, a great deal more can be observed because your role is singular: a detached, uninvolved observer.

Taking the spectator role allows the observer to focus on any event, specific child, or particular dynamic happening within the group. Being a spectator also means the educator has time to reflect upon what is observed as well as to document the observations without interruption.

During a dedicated observation time, the educator-observer should not be counted on to assist in the room. Educators say that this system, when well communicated, ensures a safer and more adequately supervised room because everyone is clear about who is doing what. Educators also say that letting the staff and the children know that they will be occupied with observing is a more honest approach. Instead of divided attention and distractions all around, observation can be done with full attention.

PARTICIPATORY MODE

The participatory mode refers to observing while participating with the children. This means that while you are sitting with a group of children engaging in a matching game, you are also observing one of the children in the group while making notes or perhaps taking a photo or video of the learning and conversations taking place. This type of observation requires multitasking! At first, it will be difficult to observe and document while still being aware of and responding to what the children around you are doing and saying. Yet experienced educators say that the participatory mode most certainly resembles what occurs daily. Being able to function in all these roles, rather than taking only the observer-spectator role, is the most realistic scenario in any early childhood centre. Add to that the occasional visitor, the phone ringing, and other daily occurrences, and you have an educator who does not have the luxury of playing one role at a time. At any time, an educator must respond to a child or event, as in Exhibit 2.11, when Peter and Ahmed are making roaring sounds with their dinosaurs.

Beginning as a new educator in the early childhood field, you may be required to conduct your observations using the spectator mode. This style will allow you to

---

Peter and Ahmed are playing with the dinosaurs in the sand, making roaring sounds. The educator walks over. She says, "I can see a dinosaur lying down."

Ahmed: "He's not! He felled."
Peter: "Mine not!"
The educator asks, "Where are your dinosaurs going?"
Ahmed: "For a walk. They's goin' t' hide in the woods."
Peter does not respond.
The educator asks, "Can they hide in the sand?"
Ahmed begins covering up the dinosaur with sand.

Courtesy of Scotia Plaza Child Care Centre

Source: Courtesy of Kristine Fenning and Sally Wylie.

---

focus on observing without interruptions. However, you may also be asked to adopt a participatory style, which will give you an idea of the skills required by an educator and the challenges and opportunities to problem-solve and develop confidence. Beginning to observe and document those observations represents quite a learning curve. Writing with descriptive language—paying keen attention to specifics and detail while in a busy playroom—takes concentration. Yet once you have had the opportunities to practise and try different types of methods, observing becomes easier, and, increasingly, your observations will become clearer as your ability to communicate what you have discovered about the children evolves along with strategies for documentation.

WHOM WILL YOU OBSERVE?

Your decision to observe a particular child should ideally involve others. Since educators observe all the children in their groups, they are the primary observers. Yet co-educators, volunteers, parents, students, and children are involved in the process as well. Different perspectives, as described throughout this text, should be welcomed and valued as observation of a large group of children is a full-time endeavour. Whom would you observe?

Perhaps a new child has started at the centre, and no one has had much time to observe him. You may want to be part of the team by collecting the initial information, such as with what toys he plays and with whom he plays. Staff may know which parents might be pleased or reluctant to have you observe their child. Make sure to take into consideration the wishes of the parent or caregiver and get permission before beginning the process.

Whom would you choose to observe: the shy, withdrawn child; the rough-and-tumble, active child; or the quiet, independent child? What do your choices reflect about you?

WHEN TO OBSERVE

Timing is one of the most critical elements of observation. When is the best time? Are some times better than others?

As with other decisions, the educators in the room may want input so that you can achieve your intentions as a team. It is a good idea to clarify with your team whom you will be observing and when. As a team, decide how observations might be completed throughout the day. Many possibilities such as outdoor time, indoor free play, small-group experiences, transition or meal times, or walks in the community might lend themselves to capturing more of the learning that is taking place in the environment. What times and aspects of the day have you managed to capture meaningful documentation? The timing of your observations may also depend upon the necessity for particular observations.

Keep in mind that there will never be an ideal time, so do not wait for it. Learn to create opportunities to observe and have your laptop, camera, or notebook handy so that you are prepared. Then, as you are sitting next to or playing with the children as they rummage through the block centre, eat their snack, or pile up brick blocks and laugh as they push them over, you are there, ready to document their play and make their daily experiences and investigations visible.

WHERE TO CONDUCT OBSERVATIONS

Finding a place to observe can be as complex as finding the time! Before you begin, look around the room to find the places (more than one) that will work for you. Try to observe a child in a variety of environments in order to achieve a more rounded or holistic view of the child. Being within hearing distance is important to hear the conversations.

To begin, make yourself as **unobtrusive** as you can. The great advantage of observation is that it does not interrupt children's play or other activities. If the children are accustomed to others conducting observations, the children won't even be aware that someone is watching them. Children's behaviour often changes when they sense that they are being watched. You could appear to be quite busy without signalling that you are observing. The main idea is to be part of the normal rhythm of the room. Again, if you are in an environment where observation is an integral part of the day, then your observation will not be an extraordinary event and will probably go unnoticed by the children.

What if one or more curious children approach you to ask what you are doing? Answer their questions briefly and tell them you will play with them when you are finished. Give them suggestions for things to do until you are ready to join them. Ask for help from your team members: they will be happy to assist! If all else fails—especially if you are working with toddlers—safely put aside your materials and try again later.

WHAT TO OBSERVE

What will you observe? Everything the child is doing? That sounds easy enough, but is it? If you said, "I want to see with whom Kuldip plays," your observations would be straightforward as it is easy to jot down who Kuldip's playmates were during the day.

Suppose, however, that you wanted to document how she played or state your opinion as to why she behaved as she did. Then you would need to determine whether what you observed was actually behaviour or an inference or opinion. For example, you would use clear, descriptive language to record your observations of how Kuldip carefully attached one of the cars to another. Then, as she looked up and smiled, you might add your interpretations about how she felt. Watching and listening to Kuldip talk to her friends while at play allows you to comment on her communication skills and share your reflections.

What you are learning about observation has you already looking at children, and perhaps everyday events, in a different way. These new skills will help you apply what you may be learning in other courses, such as child development and wellness. Integrating your knowledge with emerging observation skills will contribute to your growing sense of confidence and professionalism.

Brasil2/iStockphoto.com

CHALLENGES TO EFFECTIVE OBSERVATION

The following are some of the challenges to effective observation that have been identified by seasoned educators and those just entering the field. Please note the problem-solving suggestions relating to these challenges under the heading "Problem Solving and Teamwork" on page 72.

THE TIME CHALLENGE

In theory, educators will have time to reflect on what they observed and create or enhance their documentation. In reality, the lack of time is the main reason given for not documenting observations. Many educators say that the role of an observer in the classroom competes with other roles, such as facilitator; co-learner; curriculum planner; administrator; liaison person with parents, visitors, and volunteers; room supervisor;

and, most importantly, caregiver to the children. Each of these roles involves time. Reflection, discussion, and documentation of these observations require more time before they are forgotten: the process of observing and recording is a time commitment.

Solving the time challenge means making observation a priority. Before you enter the room, have an idea of what you might observe and how you will do that. Being proactive means you know where the camera is, that the batteries are charged, that there is paper on the documentation shelf. Being prepared also means having ongoing access to documentation materials so as to promote the involvement of others in the process as well as capture the spontaneity of children's inquiries and new wonderings. Have ongoing conversations with team members that include the possibilities for observation.

Observation is not an alternative activity but one that should be ingrained in the daily practice of educators of all age groups. Going back to the cycle of observation, it means taking advantage of every opportunity and possibility to make visible the interests and activity of individual children in the group. Spontaneously taking pictures and/or writing notes will capture the essence of children's investigation and wonderings. Being prepared is essential for that to happen.

But what about the other time, the time needed to fully prepare the documentation for a portfolio or classroom display? That time will need to come from the philosophy and practices of the centre. Is there planning time, reflection time, or time for working on pedagogical documentation in early childhood settings? How the time challenge of documentation can be met is further explored in Chapter 6.

OTHER CHALLENGES

There are further challenges to conducting observations. Some of these challenges reflect a clear lack of focus on observation, and that may be embedded in the philosophy and practices of the setting or program.

- *Lack of teamwork or organization.* In order for reflective observation to take place, educators need to determine the basics: the who, what, why, where, and when of conducting observations. Responsibilities need to be identified, rotated, or shared. If those responsibilities are shared unequally, problems may result within the team. Perhaps some educators fail to see the relevance of observing or do not understand how the observations will be of benefit. If some educators document observations whereas others do not, these inconsistent staff practices may be noticed by parents or others and flagged as a concern. Discussion, organization, and compromise are necessary for the inclusive, reflective practice of observation.
- *Observation not part of the philosophy or practice of the setting.* All child-care settings practise some methods of observation. The observations may be expressed as basic

comments of the day. These comments are made casually, shared informally, and seen more as everyday occurrences than as observations; for example, "He slept for two hours today," or "She didn't seem herself today—she hardly ate any lunch." These comments, although valid information, are feedback about the child's day. They do not represent a systematic, reflective attempt to capture what the child is thinking or feeling, how she played with her peers, or if she understood a complex concept. How can you discover if a setting or school has developed a philosophy or practices regarding the observation of children?

- *Challenges of everyday events.* Educators are busy people! They may plan to observe each day, but because someone left early, or the Humane Society representative came in to show animals to the children, or it was Sammy's birthday or picture day, the observations may not happen or they may not get documented. Special events often preclude systematic observation. Educators say that these events require a dedicated focus, and they are too busy for reflective observation. Yet we would wager that often these events yield the most surprising discoveries about children.

- *Unfamiliarity or lack of training.* Some educators and student-educators say that being unfamiliar with observation methods prevents them from starting or continuing to observe. They feel that they may be doing it incorrectly or are not sure what is expected. If a person feels that writing is not one of his or her strengths, that person may be reluctant to begin the process let alone share his or her observations. How an educator feels about his or her writing skills has a bearing on the willingness to document and share information with families.

- *The misperception of observation.* Observation need not be perceived as a task that must be done "on top of everything else!" If seen in this way, observation would be something done only if there was time. It would be seen as if it were a separate activity educators do only when the schedule permits or the inclination presents itself. But, if observation is perceived as the most essential practice of the day during the entire day, then it becomes everything we see, hear, and do. Our perception of the role of observation is the key. The observational methods described in detail in Chapters 4 and 5 allow educators to integrate observation throughout the day while at the same time meeting ministry requirements and the occupational standards expected of them.

PROBLEM SOLVING AND TEAMWORK

You may encounter other challenges to conducting observations of children. These challenges, however, can be overcome with a willingness to resolve the issues, good communication skills, a sense of humour, flexibility, and a good grasp of what can be realistically accomplished! Working together as a team develops personal and professional growth. Trusting yourself and others to want to work for the common good of the children is the best place to start.

Although this text offers no magic answers or a list of all-inclusive strategies, here are some suggestions to begin the problem-solving process with your team:

- *Include the families.* Parents want to know what their children are doing and appreciate information, cooperation, and sharing. They like to know that they can contribute as well. Find ways to encourage parents to become observers and part of the documentation process. All subsequent chapters refer to families as part of the team, but Chapters 6 and 7 further detail ways to involve families.

- *Include the children.* How children are included in co-discovering and wondering about any daily experience, their thoughts, and their feelings can be reflected in possibilities for documentation. For example, if your pedagogical documentation includes photography, being a scribe (writing down what children say), or any other methods or technology to engage children, then they are able to play a role and contribute. Not including children is a missed opportunity.

Monkey Business Images/Shutterstock.com

- *Work out a plan to observe and a way to involve others in observing.* Supervisors and educators could identify observation time as a priority for the staff-meeting agenda to discuss the strategies involved in developing a plan of observation. Being proactive rather than reactive will create new opportunities and reasons to observe. Although it will also serve to promote "observation time" as an essential part of practice, observation time is not meant to imply that this time would be the only time for observation. Looking at ways to involve children and families in the process of observing is equally as important.

- *Think about, be conscious of, and discuss the tangible benefits of observation.* What are the benefits of pedagogical documentation to the children, families, educators, and the community? List and discuss them and, while doing so, reflect on the incredible power of observation and inquiry to link ideas and create opportunities and a reflective, inclusive environment. How can these benefits be communicated to the parents and families of the children in the centre as well as the community? What is the image of an educator when observation is key to that role?

- *Share your interest.* Communicate your enthusiasm for your role as educator-observer to your colleagues and other professionals. Meet with parents and colleagues to discuss ways in which the observation process can further illustrate the exciting growth and development of the children in your care. In Chapters 4 and 5, you will discover some of the ways to document the imagination, play, and knowledge of children.
- *Communicate!* Discuss your professional goals, philosophy, values, and talents, and also the areas about which you are interested in learning more. By acting professionally, monitoring your own behaviour, and clearly expressing your personal and professional goals, it is possible to create the communication that is necessary for a group of people to work as a team. You could start by saying, "I'd really like to find more time to observe some of the children." Find people who agree with you and are willing to work out possible ways for you to achieve your goal.
- *Make observation a priority and declare it publicly.* This can be done at the supervisory or administrative level in the child-care setting through a mission statement or centre policies and practices. The philosophy of the centre is defined within those documents and will state as goals or specific pedagogy the role observation has in the program. There are several ways in which directors or supervisors can promote and support systematic observations (see Exhibit 2.12).

EXHIBIT 2.12   SETTING THE TONE

Ways in which directors or supervisors can promote and support systematic observations and an appreciative inquiry process are as follows:

- Set aside time for weekly, biweekly, or monthly staff meetings.
- Ensure that each staff member comes to the meetings prepared to discuss individual children, the group, curriculum, environment, and community involvement, and share this information with each other and the supervisor or director.
- Discuss time management and strategies for observation and documentation to ensure that everyone has access to materials for observation as well as opportunities to observe throughout the day. Time is also needed for reflection and discussion of observations so as to develop interpretations. Create an environment of inquiry where questioning is encouraged and supported.
- Brainstorm ways to display the documentation from each room in the centre not only within the centre, but also within the community.

Source: Courtesy of Sally Wylie.

- *Research!* Find effective ways in which others are using observation to create exciting programming or document the progress of individual children. Check out the websites of local centres/programs or national organizations. Ask other educators in your neighbourhood, municipality, or province. What are educators in other countries doing to document the activity of the children in their care? Let your research also include investigating your personal queries or wonderings, as they could lead you to interesting findings of your own. For example, if you wonder which countries have legislated the rights of all children to attend programs for young children, you might find that Finland is one of them. Ask yourself how this information is relevant to child care in Canada (see www.oecd .org/finland/2476019.pdf). This research will generate questions such as "What are the federal child care policies of Canada?"

There is no doubt: observation is **multifaceted** and far from simple. The more we engage in observation, the more we learn, thus leading to more questions and the need for further inquiry and observation. Reflecting upon the systematic and cyclical nature of this process as a team leads us to examine and discuss ways in which we can compile and use this information. Regardless of the philosophical approach, selecting a frame or structure from which to develop and build documentation is necessary. As discussed in Chapter 3, the portfolio is one of these organizational structures with which we can gain insights into the interests, abilities, and uniqueness of children, as well as numerous other aspects of professional practice.

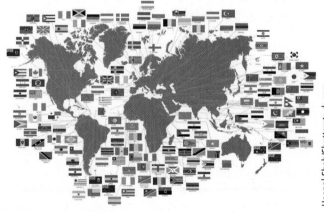

Heenal Shah/Shutterstock.com

THE RIGHTS OF CHILDREN

The United Nations General Assembly adopted the Convention on the Rights of the Child in 1989. The convention lays out principles to protect the rights of all children of the world, set out in 54 rights and optional protocols. Children have the right to be heard, express themselves, and be recognized in their own right. Why does this topic appear in a textbook about observation? One of the main reasons we raise this topic (only briefly) is to bring awareness to the fact that as educators we have a moral and legal obligation to children. They do not vote, and their voices are rarely heard on topics like globalization, economic disparities, and social issues, and yet they are the ones who will inherit the consequences of adult decisions. Children have the right to have their views considered in decisions affecting their lives, while taking into account their age and maturity (see Exhibit 2.13). Yet, many children do not know their rights, may not have their voices heard, and may not be consulted about even their basic needs. As a keen observer of young children, you may be in a position to support the voice of a child who is abused, neglected, or in harm's way.

"The views of the child must be 'given due weight in accordance with the age and maturity of the child.' It is not sufficient to listen to children. It is also necessary to give their views serious consideration when making decisions. Their concerns, perspectives and ideas must inform decisions that affect their lives. However; the weight to be given to children's views needs qualifying. It must take into account of the age and maturity of the child: in other words, the child's level of understanding of the implications of the matter. It is important to note that age by itself does not necessarily provide guidance as to the children's levels of understanding."

Source: Lansdown, G. (2011). *Every child's right to be heard: A resource guide on the UN Committee on the Rights of the Child General Comment no. 12.* London, England: Save the Children UK, p. 23. Retrieved from http://www.unicef.org/french/adolescence/files/Every_Childs_Right_to_be_Heard.pdf

When you walk into many early childhood settings, you will see on the wall a copy of the UN Convention on the Rights of Children. It is posted for all to see, to remind us of our important role in encouraging expression, making sure we listen carefully and deeply, and responding in an inclusive, positive manner to support the child through understanding her or his culture and home life's context and relevance.

Visit the website of the Canadian Child Care Federation/Fédération canadienne des services de garde à l'enfance and the UNICEF Canada website for more on this subject. As you examine these resources, think about how you as an educator might use observation to support the tenets and principles they describe.

CODE OF ETHICS

CODE OF ETHICS AND STANDARDS OF PRACTICE

Educators around the world are responsible for adhering to ethical and occupational standards specific to their role, and in this case when observing children. These standards are represented in different ways and expected at each level of government—municipal, provincial/territorial, and federal—as a number of government and licensing agencies hold those who educate or teach children to specific professional standards. Take a moment to review the information in Exhibit 2.14 and in the paragraphs that follow. Exhibit 2.14 outlines some of the important ethical standards pertaining to educators in Ontario.

EXHIBIT 2.14	ETHICAL STANDARDS PERTAINING TO EARLY CHILDHOOD IN ONTARIO		
Regulatory/ Governing Body	**Document**	**Audience**	**Relevance to Observation and Documentation**
Canadian Child Care Federation (CCCF)	Code of Ethics	Early childhood professionals, at a national level	To promote quality care and "best practice in early childhood education" (CCCF, 2012, para. 1)
College of Early Childhood Educators (CECE)	Code of Ethics and Standards of Practice	Registered early childhood educators in Ontario	"I. Caring and Nurturing Relationships that Support Learning II. Developmentally Appropriate Care and Education III. Safe, Healthy and Supportive Learning Environments IV. Professional Knowledge and Competence V. Professional Boundaries, Dual Relationships and Conflicts of Interest VI. Confidentiality and Consent to the Release of Information Regarding Children and their Families" (CECE, 2011, p. 9)
Ontario College of Teachers	The Standards of Practice for the Teaching Profession and the Ethical Standards for the Teaching Profession	Certified elementary school teachers in Ontario	Frameworks with which to guide all certified teachers in all aspects of their role including the observation, documentation, and assessment of young children (Ontario College of Teachers, 2015).

If you were to replicate this exhibit with ethical standards documents and regulating agencies pertaining to where you practice, what would it look like?

Within Ontario, educators in early childhood settings are expected to register with the College of Early Childhood Educators and follow the Code of Ethics and Standards of Practice in order to practise as a registered early childhood educator. Elementary school teachers also have a regulatory body called the Ontario College of Teachers, which requires teachers to follow its own ethical standards. At a national level, the Code of Ethics pertaining to early childhood educators across Canada is located on the Canadian Child Care Federation website and can be found posted in most schools or early learning centres across Canada. The Code of Ethics begins as follows:

Child care practitioners work with one of society's most vulnerable groups—young children. The quality of the interactions between young children and the adults who care for them has a significant, enduring impact on children's lives. The intimacy of the relationship and the potential to do harm call for a commitment on the part of child care practitioners to the highest standards of ethical practice.

Child care practitioners accept the ethical obligation to understand and work effectively with children in the context of family, culture and community. Child care practitioners care for and educate young children. However, ethical practice extends beyond the child/practitioner relationship. Child care practitioners also support parents as primary caregivers of their children and liaise with other professionals and community resources on behalf of children and families. (Canadian Child Care Federation, 2011, p. 26)

The eight fundamental principles of the Code of Ethics are listed in Exhibit 2.15. Go online for further resources on ethical standards

When a centre posts its Code of Ethics, the staff are telling everyone that they support the values and principles laid out in the Code. More importantly, the staff state their intention to work toward fulfilling these tenets on a daily basis. These principles apply to everyone who is involved at the centre, including you, the educator.

Essentially, the Code of Ethics from the Canadian Child Care Federation is about respect. Demonstrating respect to children means listening to them as human beings with valid feelings and ideas and talking to them about things that interest them. Having a genuine conversation with a child communicates a readiness to learn about the uniqueness of each child rather than being a detached commentator who uses

- Child-care practitioners promote the health and well-being of all children.
- Child-care practitioners enable children to participate to their full potential in environments carefully planned to serve individual needs and to facilitate the child's progress in the social, emotional, physical, and cognitive areas of development.
- Child-care practitioners demonstrate caring for all children in all aspects of their practice.
- Child-care practitioners work in partnership with parents, recognizing that parents have the primary responsibility for the care of their children, valuing their commitment to the children, and supporting them in meeting their responsibilities to their children.
- Child-care practitioners work in partnership with colleagues and other service providers in the community to support the well-being of children and their families.
- Child-care practitioners work in ways that enhance human dignity in trusting, caring, and cooperative relationships that respect the worth and uniqueness of the individual.
- Child-care practitioners pursue, on an ongoing basis, the knowledge, skills, and self-awareness needed to be professionally competent.
- Child-care practitioners demonstrate integrity in all of their professional relationships.

Source: Courtesy of the Canadian Child Care Federation.

such worn phrases as "Good job" or quiz questions such as "What colour is that?" "What shape is this?" "What sound does it make?"

Observing young children and interacting with them provide opportunities for experiences to evolve and for meaningful observation. This reflective process gives educators a chance to uncover the distinctiveness of each child. Does this sound familiar? In what ways do these principles relate to the appreciative inquiry approach discussed in Chapter 1? What about pedagogical documentation and the observation cycle?

ETHICS AND THE OBSERVATION PROCESS

For many years, observations have been the primary responsibility of the educator-observer; children often were not provided the opportunity to know or even be informed of what was being written about them. While observation and documentation is still an important role of the educator, a shift toward pedagogical documentation methodologies is prompting a rethinking of traditional observation paradigms. Resulting from this shift are the inclusion of children's perspectives in all aspects and stages of the observation and documentation process, and a movement toward observation and documentation as a shared responsibility of all—educators, families, and children. This means that children are to be provided the opportunity to participate in the inquiry, observation, documentation, reflection, interpretation, and response stages of the observation cycle, as they have much to offer. By viewing the image of the child in a different way, we see that children have the right and the ability to be co-observers, co-researchers, and co-educators in our early childhood settings.

This transformation in observation methods and practices, particularly in the use of technology as both a medium and a tool with which to transmit our observations to others, has precipitated research and discussion. This discussion has prompted the need not only to be aware of biases in our observations, but also to question how we go about observing in an ethical way and how we communicate what has been learned regardless of the media we are using.

Putting yourself in the position of the child, having your behaviour, actions, feelings, interests, and needs documented continuously without permission, would be an unnerving feeling. How would you feel if everything that you said and did on a daily basis were made visible to others? Would you want to be constantly under this perceived surveillance? It is important to understand that the frequent eye glance or response of a child smiling to a photograph being taken does not imply consent. It begs the question whether what we are capturing is truly informed consent or whether the child has simply resigned him- or herself to not having a voice in the observation and documentation process. The pedagogical documentation approach and our ethical standards demand that we ensure this does not happen. How do we truly know when a child is giving informed consent? Do we understand the impact of documentation through technology and social media on the child, the quality of their play, the environment, and what it is that we see and hear? As we reflect more upon the cycle of observation, it is important to think about our current observing and recording practices to ensure that we are ethical in our practice.

OBSERVATION AND IDENTITY

Children should be involved in decision making throughout the entire observation and documentation process, contributing what they see and hear when reviewing their own observations. Children should always have the right to share their voice and perspective on their developing identity. For years, traditional observation methods did not invite this voice, and as a result it was left to the educator- or parent-observer to interpret and discuss what he or she saw as composing the child's evolving identity. Children should have a voice in how these images are interpreted, and they should have the right to participate and make decisions about what is written about them. Who is to say that the educator or the parent's interpretations are correct? Who is giving power to the child's interpretation of the learning taking place? These questions are worth your consideration.

As you continue to reflect upon ethics in your role, think about putting yourself in the child's place. Would you as a future adult want to have these images shared and viewed by others? Reflecting back upon the rights of children, what are the rights of the child in this case? The UN Convention on the Rights of the Child is bringing into consideration the need to consult with children in the processes of observing, documenting, and interpreting, as they not only have the right to do so but also hold the knowledge to understand and comment on what they know, see, and hear.

Appreciative inquiry is a necessary part of this discussion. For example, in what ways have children been

- asked for their consent regularly?
- asked to have their learning documented?
- involved in deciding what to document and when the observations would take place? For example, have they had the opportunity to participate in deciding which images to use for daily communication, webbing, documentation panels, portfolios, etc.?
- involved in the observation, documentation, and interpretation processes of their own learning?
- invited to review and/or assist in preparing the written narrations of what took place and the meaning-making process (interpretations)?
- informed about how their learning will be interpreted by others or who will be reviewing their documentation to interpret the learning taking place?
- afforded the opportunity to be anonymous and to not have their faces depicted in photos or images?
- asked about which artifacts represent significant learning moments or experiences for placement in their portfolio?
- asked for consent by an adult who comes to the child's level to ensure there is not a height difference, thus equalling the power relationship between adult and child?
- prompted to discuss observations and interpretations with their families to allow them to feel in control of what is shared and communicated?

How would you respond to any of these questions? It is important for responsive, inclusive educators to be aware of this discussion and reflect in ways that are non-intrusive, respecting the integrity and nuances of what is taking placing in children's play with others or on their own.

Observing and documenting does not guarantee ethical practice; it is the choice of the educator to be ethical in the process. Pedagogical documentation introduces other ethical considerations and decision making that must take place when observing young children. One of these new considerations involves not just considering the rights of parents/guardians in decision making, but also considering the rights of children in the process. Based on the UN Convention on the Rights of the Child, "compliance with Article 12 is therefore an ethical, legal and moral imperative (Lundy, 2007) and mandates that all children must be involved in decision-making processes on matters that concern them. This is a non-negotiable and permanent human right afforded to children" (Harcourt & Sergeant, 2011, p. 423). As responsive, inclusive educators, we have a responsibility to uphold this principle by applying it to our observational practices.

ETHICS, PEDAGOGICAL DOCUMENTATION, AND THE OBSERVER

Ethical practices in observation begin with engaging in conversations with other educators, families, and children regarding how well your current observation processes reflect the perspectives and wishes of the children. These conversations also need to be ongoing in order to sustain the level of quality and ethics in your practice. It is through these conversations that processes unfold to engage everyone in the observation process. Providing time and access to observational opportunities as well as the necessary documentation materials is an integral part of promoting pedagogically sound observation practices within an early childhood setting. Other ways to increase access and opportunities for observation could include

- conducting daily discussions regarding how observation could occur in a non-intrusive way throughout the day. This would also help to balance the types of observation being done so as to avoid the overuse and misuse of photos and visual images in the room. Ensuring that there are a variety of observations, methods, and artifacts prepared by different people to put in a child's portfolio is important.
- designating an area of the room where observation materials are available to increase the participation of children and families in the observation process (sticky notes, pens and pencils, lined paper, white boards, digital cameras, iPads, audio recorders, maps of the room, clipboards, etc.)
- ensuring that observations are available at the end of every day to prompt discussion, inquiry, and reflection by both the parent and the child. This could promote a variety of perspectives and interpretations of the observations made.

Regardless of who has made the observation, pedagogical documentation is intended to invite the perspectives of others who are reading or interpreting the visual and written narratives so as to provide their own insights and perspectives on what they see and understand.

CONSENT AND CONFIDENTIALITY

Part of being a qualified educator involves adhering to confidentiality when documenting information about children and when sharing information about children. Ethical standards also require that student-educators sign a **Pledge of Confidentiality** stating that the student will not discuss the events of the centre or the persons involved. Similar confidentiality assurances are required by provincial/territorial law to ensure that the privacy of information on children and their families held in centre files will be respected. Educators must sign such an assurance indicating they understand and agree they will hold all information in confidence. While in an early childhood setting, ensure that you follow the Code of Ethics.

Part of a postsecondary early childhood program is an orientation that involves the discussion of field placement or practicum. Fundamental to that orientation is the discussion of your role and responsibilities while attending an early learning and care setting or school. This orientation, and quite probably the orientation you will receive in the first week of your new placement or practicum, will include the important procedures regarding consent and confidentiality. Compliance with the college's policies of consent and confidentiality and those of the early childhood setting or school you will be attending is mandatory.

As well, each province and territory, through the appropriate government ministry, sets out standards and guidelines regarding consent and confidentiality for qualified educators to follow. Visit your provincial/territorial website for details of the administration of children's records.

Policies and procedures recommend a system for exchanging information between the parents/guardians and the centre. "Records are covered by legislation dealing with privacy and an individual's access to information. A record is defined as almost any form of information, including letters, daily logs, case notes, memos, drawings, videotapes and computer files. Therefore, a record includes all agency records, from the most informal to the most formal" (Valentino, 2004, p. 14). Each agency's, school's, or organization's policies and procedures are guided by legislation such as this and noted in a licensed centre's parents' manual or office documents. In addition, federal legislation, such as the *Freedom of Information Act* and the *Bill of Rights*, must be considered as this legislation guarantees confidentiality and the rights of the individual. Each licensed child-care setting must follow the advisories but may interpret how the consent forms it uses will be phrased.

Centres will have separate consent forms for each child. Some children, if they are enrolled in two different programs, will have specific consent forms. The consent form gives the centre permission to receive and transmit information from one centre to the other.

Whether you are a student-educator or a new educator, you should be made fully aware of the centre's policies and procedures before you begin your new position. Make sure to be advised as to what information you may access and what records and files are strictly confidential. If this information is not forthcoming, it is your responsibility to ask so that you are apprised of the policies and procedures. Parental permission must be obtained prior to any research (observation) being conducted on a child.

Exhibit 2.16 and Exhibit 2.17 provide visual examples of the following consent forms: Authorization for Release of Information and Authorization for Exchange of Information.

| EXHIBIT 2.16 | AUTHORIZATION FOR RELEASE OF INFORMATION |

This form may be used to exchange information when the child is attending more than one program. Please complete and sign this permission form to allow this exchange of information.

I/We give permission to ABC Nursery School and Canadiana Public School to exchange information about my child. This consent form covers the time period from September 7, 2015, to June 20, 2016.

_____   _____
Name of Child   Date of Birth

_____   _____
Signature of Parent/Guardian   Date

_____
Witness

Source: Courtesy of Sally Wylie.

EXHIBIT 2.17 **AUTHORIZATION FOR EXCHANGE OF INFORMATION**

This form authorizes a professional from the child-care centre to obtain information on a child.

I/We hereby authorize ABC Nursery School through its representative

_____

(Supervisor/Director)

from any educational, social, and/or medical authority on

_____   _____

Surname   Given Names

I/We hereby further authorize ABC Nursery School to convey to any educational, social, and/or medical authority information on

_____   _____

Signature of Parent/Guardian   Date

_____

Witness

Source: Courtesy of Sally Wylie.

OFFICE FILES

Every licensed early childhood environment maintains its records according to a set of ministry expectations and policies unique to each setting. All licensed early childhood settings have office files that must be maintained. The office files are kept in the main office or supervisor's office in a secure, locked cabinet. Typically, office files will contain such information as medical records, referral forms, intake information, and financial records. Only licensed educators, administrators, and parents have access to these files. Parents and guardians will have access only to *their* child's file.

GETTING PERMISSION FOR OBSERVATIONS

If you are a student not yet practising in the profession, ensure that parents and guardians are aware of any observations you may complete on their child while you are a student-educator. This is often done through a permission letter of some kind.

It is recommended that an introduction be given stating your name, the name(s) of your instructor(s), and the purpose of the observations. If this introduction is in letter form, it could be shared with the centre supervisor, involved staff, and the parents. You will find examples of permission letters online. If you are a practising educator in an early childhood setting, requirements of your setting for permissions to observe would be outlined in the centre, school, or agency policies. Not all settings will require a letter in their exchange-of-information procedures, but parents do like to know who is in the room with their child and need to know what information on their child is obtained or exchanged.

Whether you are a student-educator or a seasoned educator, be sure to explain to parents/caregivers that observations are part of your studies or role. If the parent wishes to read your observations when you are in a student capacity, it is important to consult with your professor first, as student observations and interpretations are opportunities for practising and learning and are not intended for authentic entry into a child's portfolio. Student observations and interpretations must be vetted and approved by the supervisor or director, as the observations and interpretations may require rewording. While employed educators have permission to use name or centre identifiers within their setting, students do not have the same authority or ability to use real names of children or settings. This is to ensure confidentiality of information gained and used for learning purposes. As a student, it is important to remember not only to transmit written information to parents only with the approval of the educator or supervisor in charge, but also to be aware of and follow the agency's policies and procedures regarding consent and confidentiality.

SUMMARY

This practical chapter has defined observation as a systematic process. We hope we have helped you navigate this process, which included engaging in inquiry, a cycle of observation, and the respectful pedagogical documentation of a child's expression during play. This chapter has begun the pragmatic preparation required for the observation of young children. Making decisions regarding how, why, what, who, when, and where to observe is essential to this process. The discussion of the importance of consent and confidentiality, the rights of children, and the Code of Ethics highlights the considerations necessary before observing young children.

CHAPTER 3

LEARNING TO DOCUMENT THE ACTIVITY OF CHILDREN

René Mansi/iStockphoto.com

Two first-year early childhood education students are loading their books and papers into their backpacks. Their first class of the day is Developing Observation Skills. They have been in class for an hour; for the second hour of class, the instructor has directed them to the lab school observation deck to conduct their first observations of children. "What are we supposed to be doing? I don't get it," says Karyn.

"I don't know for sure, but we're going down to the lab school to watch the children," replies Janelle. "I don't know what we're going to do *exactly*—*she* said we'd be writing down what we see the children doing. Sounds easy to me."

Later, after the class has had the opportunity to try two one-minute observations and one five-minute observation, the students gather together to share their first attempts. The instructor asks, "What did you learn today? What did you experience? What did your observations teach you?" The following are some of the comments:

- "I couldn't believe what a child does in the span of a few minutes!"
- "There was so much going on, I didn't know what to write down."
- "When I looked down to write and then looked up again, my child had moved from his chair to the water table, and I never saw him go!"
- "I saw a child adding a photo and some information to the learning web on the wall and he was talking to some other children about what he had built with the blocks."
- "What are we supposed to do with these observations now?"
- "I can't read mine!"
- "I couldn't think of the right words. I didn't know what to call some of the toys they play with, and I couldn't think of words fast enough to describe what she was doing."

As the discussion continued and students tried to read what they had hurriedly written down, they commented on how much they had actually recorded. If more than one student had watched the same child, they compared observations. They talked about how interesting it was that when three people had observed the same child, although they all recorded some similar things, each person picked up on something that the others had not. Janelle asked, "How do you know what's important to write and what isn't? Karyn noticed that the boy scratched his arm a lot. I never saw that. Compared with Karyn, I hardly have anything written down."

We've been listening. Whether you are a preservice educator, as in the example above, or a seasoned educator in the profession, observation is not as easy as it seems, and we recognize that the process of pedagogical documentation poses yet another challenge. The journey of discovering what interests a child, what a child learns, and what a child loves doesn't stop there. You will be on the same journey, learning about yourself, your biases, and your ability to problem-solve your way through questions and reflection, while coming to appreciate your own unique skills and discoveries. We've anticipated some of your questions and hope in this chapter to provide topics that will enlighten and expand your knowledge.

OVERVIEW

Chapter 3 ends this first section with guidelines and ideas about how to actually write pedagogical documentation. As in the first two chapters, the more we learn about any concept relating to observation, the more there is to know. For example, this text is unique in that writing and the actual writing process are discussed for all students: those new to college/university, mature students returning to school, students with English as a second language, and educators who may wish to refresh their writing skills. In this chapter, you will discover how language usage, combined with observation skills, produces knowledge about children not previously known. That is exciting! But before you begin writing, we'd like you to examine how the careful use of language is crucial when documenting your observations.

Whether your documentation represents a few lines that accompany photographs or comments attached to a chart or a **narrative**, there must be congruence between what was observed and what is documented. As you observe and document, you will begin to understand how writing is also a process of discovering your *own* thoughts about how children learn and your image of a child.

This chapter will also introduce the important step of interpretation and reflection, a process involving making sense of what has been seen and heard. This step is necessary in developing our understanding of children, our environment, and our practice and responding in a meaningful way. With observation and reflection come the values, images, bias, knowledge, and perceptions of the observer. Understanding the various forms of bias that might influence our perceptions cannot be overlooked. In this particular section, evidence of the connections between ethics, confidentiality, and bias will be examined.

This chapter will be most effective when used in conjunction with opportunities to observe. Opportunities for application will help you grow in skills and confidence. It takes time to develop your own observing or recording style, but as you progress, compare your first efforts to other, later observations. Educators say that they can actually see an improvement in their written skills, which gives them another benchmark for measuring their success as a practising early childhood professional. It is through documentation that educators can construct new knowledge starting with a blank page. Let the writing begin!

FOCUS QUESTIONS

1. In what ways does writing observations of children uncover what you believe?
2. Is it possible that objective observations are harder to write than subjective interpretations? Why or why not?
3. How might we prepare our early childhood environment to prompt all participants to engage to share and collaborate in the observation and documentation process?
4. How might we use our understanding of bias in observations to reduce the level of bias in our observations and documentation?

GETTING STARTED

Reflecting back upon Chapters 1 and 2, we now understand that observation is an important responsibility of all educators, regardless of their setting or philosophy. We also know the value of having all members of a learning community participate in the observation cycle and process. Let's take a look at how we might do this.

INCREASING ACCESSIBILITY: SHARING RESPONSIBILITY FOR OBSERVING AND DOCUMENTING

Opportunities to observe young children and to practise recording their activity are fundamental to developing the complex abilities and skills needed in the documentation process. Seizing daily opportunities to observe promotes a natural approach to gathering the information needed to interpret, evaluate, and respond in an inclusive way.

Wiarton Kids' Den/Sally Wylie

Being able to capture and provide open-ended opportunities for observing, wondering, questioning, inquiring, interpreting, and responding requires us not only to plan how these opportunities for observing might happen within the context of our day and other responsibilities, but also to plan for making materials for recording observations available. To create pedagogical documentation, educators need to take the time to create an environment in which all participants have the opportunity to observe, document, and have their perspectives included. What materials could be made accessible to children, parents, families, and educators for documenting and recording? Take a look at Exhibit 3.1 to see how one centre created a culture of inquiry and observation.

When we take the time to make observation part of our everyday pedagogy, it becomes a pleasurable and transformative experience for everyone. Be sure to read Chapter 8 and go online to explore how social media and technology function as a way in which to document, share, and make visible children's learning!

EXHIBIT 3.1   **ENGAGING ALL OBSERVERS**

Tony, a full-day kindergarten early childhood educator, and Liz, his elementary school colleague, had worked together now for just over one year. Their administration had introduced the new changes for the kindergarten curriculum, one of which was a strong emphasis on capturing the play and learning of children in the room. "How are we ever going to be able to document the experiences of every child in the room?" Liz asked Tony as they were preparing for the children to arrive. "I've been thinking about this a lot, and I have an idea," Tony replied. "We should create an observation centre in our classroom." Liz asked, "What do you mean?" As the children started entering the room, Tony explained, "At the end of my shift when the children go home, I'll show you."

The end of the day came and their transformation began. Throughout the day, Tony had gathered a number of materials, bins, and an extra shelf for the classroom. Knowing they had space close to the door of the classroom, Tony and Liz talked about placing a variety of observational materials on the shelf for parents, children, students, and educators to use to self-observe or to observe the experiences and wonderings of others in the room. The materials included

- clipboards
- assorted paper—lined, blank, scraps, sticky notes
- pens, pencils, crayons, and pastels
- mini whiteboards and erasable markers
- mapping sheets of the classroom
- paper with areas for photos and printed lines for narratives/messaging
- paper with basic webs
- two cameras with photo and video functionality
- one iPad in the cupboard above the shelf for signing out and using (the technology had been purchased through their parent advisory board)

Before unveiling the new exploratory area for observers, Tony and Liz organized a night for discussion around the purpose of this new space, opening up dialogue regarding how everyone could participate in the process of making learning visible in the classroom. Before long, children, families, and educators were all contributing transformative documentation of children's learning for children's portfolios, digital photo frames in the classroom, communication boards within the classroom, and documentation panels for the halls.

Source: Kristine Fenning.

LEARNING TO RECORD AND UNDERSTAND WHAT WE ARE OBSERVING

Having a variety of materials available to document is a great start! We will now turn our attention to the writing process. Writing with a purpose in mind can be a complex process. Even writing a simple shopping list requires a series of steps. What are the steps?

1. deciding what you need at the store and why you need it —your purpose
2. making a list—format
3. writing the items down—documentation
4. checking with others—teamwork
5. remembering to use the list! Observations are meaningful only when they are used!

The purpose of this brief, real-life example is to demonstrate that even a shopping list is not simple. There are steps in the process of this familiar task. Writing observations in a clear, descriptive narrative relies on similar steps:

- determining the purpose through appreciative inquiry, while including others in that conversation
- choosing a format or method to suit the purpose or spontaneity of what you are attempting to capture and make visible
- documenting your observations
- consulting with others while sharing your observations and reflections

This basic comparison illustrates the steps required for purposeful writing no matter how simple the task. The purpose of this chapter, therefore, is not only to make visible for the observer the necessary steps to follow within the observational writing process, but also to clarify what an effective observation involves.

THE DOCUMENTING PROCESS

Initially, many students find developing the skills to effectively document and record their observations challenging. Some struggle with appropriate ways to write down what they think or feel: "The way we say things when writing our observations is not how we'd say them in regular conversations, so we find it sort of clumsy to try to write like that." This chapter examines why it might be "clumsy to try to write like that." One of the most direct ways to begin is to find out why writing observations is initially a challenge.

First, observations are factual, based on what actually occurred. Factual writing is about using nouns, verbs, adverbs, and adjectives in a clear, concise way. The following are some of the reasons why learning this skill is challenging:

- using a descriptive vocabulary for detailed writing
- having to observe and record simultaneously
- being unsure about what to actually observe and record
- being unsure of how to compose the observation
- recognizing that discovering how to express your thoughts in writing in a professional manner is a multifaceted skill
- lacking confidence in current writing skills
- being unsure of the nuances of each type of observation and understanding their purpose

Being proficient in documenting clear observations, interpreting children's behaviour, and creating documentation that is inclusive, respectful, and meaningful is expected of all responsive educators. This complex process begins with focusing on starting the documentation process, learning the guidelines for consideration while observing, and laying the groundwork for determining the use and purpose of information we are gathering, such as including it in a portfolio. We hope that as a result of our comprehensive approach, readers will continue to use this text throughout their professional career.

OBSERVER GUIDELINES IN THE COMMUNITY

Once you have had opportunities to observe, either in an early childhood setting or through the use of online clips, you will have begun this amazing process of discovering the world of children. If you are already in an early childhood setting, remember those initial questions discussed in Chapter 2 that followed the basic journalistic approach: who, why, how, when, where, and what. These questions guided your initial decisions. Here are other important guidelines to consider when compiling documentation in a centre or school:

- *Talk with staff.* Inquire about the expectations, policies, and procedures of the setting. Inform staff of what you need to do in terms of observations and find out when that may be convenient. Determine what is best for everyone in terms of schedules and personnel. For example, a good time to conduct observations may be when all staff are present rather than early or late in the schedule when not all the educators are on site.

- *Choose a child.* The careful choice of a child for your observation is important. What is it that you wish to observe? Some student-observers choose the child sitting on a chair at the creative table because she is quiet. This choice may appear easy, but if that child is not active, there may not be a great deal to write about. Choose a child who is active in the group; there will be a lot to write about and more opportunities to learn. As discussed in Chapter 2, ensure that permissions are obtained and ethical processes are followed prior to conducting observations.
- *Be a spectator or participant.* If you adopt the spectator mode, find a place (where) to observe that is unobtrusive. Being off to the side or in the background will ensure you are interrupted less often. If observing while being involved with the children (a participant), plan ahead. How will you record your observations while still interacting and supervising safely with the children? What hard-copy or technology-assisted observational tools will be most helpful to you in this type of situation? Keep your pens in a safe place, particularly with toddlers!
- *Record essential information.* Initially, record the child's name and date of birth. Note that policies of schools or early childhood settings vary regarding how a child's name is recorded. For example, variations may be (1) only the child's first name, (2) initials, (3) a fictitious name or initials, or (4) simply "Child A." Check with the supervisor or director to ensure compliance with policies regarding confidentiality before observations are begun. When you are working or employed in the field as an educator, you will use a child's real names, both first and last, as the information is housed only in the school, centre, or agency.
- *Be consistent with centre policies* as they relate to recording a child's date of birth (D.O.B.). Find out how dates of birth are recorded: as (1) day, month, and year; (2) year, month, and day; or (3) month, day, and year. It may not seem relevant at first, but notice what happens if a child's birthday is December 1, 2014, and the date of birth is represented as 01/12/2014 or 12/01/2014. Consistent use of one format for recording dates also pertains to the use of assessment tools as well as documentation. Ask for clarification; it will help avoid any misunderstandings.
- *Record the essential information as indicated in the example.* These data are fundamental to accurate records.

   Example:
   Observer: Sandy   Date: January 5, 2015
   Child's name: Child A   D.O.B.: December 1, 2012
   Time: 10:15–10:20
- *Assemble your materials.* You will need an electronic device or a pen and paper: one page for a one- or two-minute observation and more pages for a five- or

ten-minute observation. Have more than one pen on hand. If using a laptop or iPad, ensure that the electronic devices are fully charged. It is important to have a variety of writing mediums to accommodate everyone.

- *Invent shortcuts.* Invent shortcuts using abbreviations such as those below or ways to indicate involvement of other children (Child B, Child C).

LH for left hand	A = alone	sh = short
RH for right hand	P = one or more peers	lg = long

- *Use short forms that are meaningful to you.* Jot down key words and abbreviations. Writing or keyboarding in sentence form simply takes too long. When using abbreviations, try to update to a good copy as soon as possible so that when you go back to rewrite, you can understand your notes. A student said, "I found it challenging to first learn to write in rough/short form. I thought I would forget what the short forms meant! But if I didn't use any short forms, then I missed things in my observation! It's not as easy as it seems!"
- *Record dialogue.* When documenting older children who are talking together, you will quickly realize the challenge that recording their conversations poses. It will be impossible to document everything that is said. Two methods to investigate are using an audio recording or **paraphrasing**. Paraphrasing means that you are summarizing or putting into your own words the gist of the child's conversation. For example, suppose that a four-year-old girl is sitting at a table painting a picture. While she paints, she says, "You know what, last night I watched TV until really late, and then my mom said it was time for bed, so I went upstairs and then I had to brush my teeth and get ready for bed, but I wanted my mom to read me a story and so she did, and then I still wasn't tired and I asked if she'd read another one, so she read me another one." Obviously, writing down all she said would be exhaustive, but paraphrasing captures what she said in the following manner: "Nina talked while she painted. She talked in sequence what she did last night, ending with her sharing that her mother read two books to her before she went to sleep." Telling Nina's story in your own words paraphrases or summarizes the conversation. It gives a sense of what she was talking about. When paraphrasing what is said, the use of quotation marks is not necessary. However, when recording a **direct quotation**, use quotation marks, as shown briefly in Exhibit 3.2.
- *Rewrite your observations.* Once you've finished your observations, rewrite them so that not only you can understand what you've written, but others can

EXHIBIT 3.2   **TOMAS AND THE DOLL**

Tomas has propped up the doll on the log. The doll's hair is pulled up and tied atop its head to reveal the stitched hairline of the doll. He pushes the doll's head gently with his left hand, saying, "Ugh, ugh." He waits. Some of the strands of hair now stick out. He tries to press them back into the stitched holes.

Courtesy of University of Toronto, Child Care on Charles Street.

Source: Kristine Fenning, Sally Wylie.

as well. Go back over your notes and rewrite what is needed, or expand on key words and phrases while they are fresh in your mind. The longer the time that passes between the initial observation and the rewriting, the more that will be forgotten.

A student wrote, "I found it helpful for me to put little reminders on my rough notes for things that really stick out. I also tried to write my good copy as fast as I could after the observation so that it was all fresh in my mind."

- *Make words count by using descriptors!* Rewriting your notes is the perfect time for considering descriptors. **Descriptors** act to strengthen the meaning of the action. A descriptor enhances the meaning of the original word used. There is a difference between changing a word from "walked" to "shuffled" and to actually interpreting the gist or essence of your observation. To illustrate this point, note the examples in Exhibit 3.3.

EXHIBIT 3.3	WORDS AND DESCRIPTORS
Original Words	**Descriptive Words (Descriptors)**
Smiled. Watched teacher.	Smiled warily. Regarded teacher carefully.
Tapped fingers on puzzle.	Tapped fingers lightly on puzzle.
Shifted in seat.	Shifted slowly in his seat.
Hummed to self.	Hummed quietly to self.

Source: Courtesy of Sally Wylie.

- Which of the four examples changed the most? Which of the four examples changed the least? These four examples may assist you in understanding the influence words have when trying to convey the clearest meaning possible. Use words that will capture the essence of what you saw or heard. Instead of using "walked," use more descriptive words, such as "waddled" or "shuffled along," to describe the action more accurately. Instead of the verb "said," consider using "yelled" as you remember the child called out loudly about someone grabbing the computer mouse. When recording observations, finding the most appropriate word for the action is not the main focus; recording what is seen and heard is the main objective. For many, recording the actions of a fast-moving child at the time does not allow the luxury of searching for the right word in English or any language.
- Depending on the type of documentation chosen, the words used will reflect whether you are documenting while the observation is occurring or whether you have decided to document after the observation is finished. If an observer discovers that documenting while observing is difficult, then perhaps they might prepare the documentation following the observation. For others, they may document during the observation with short hand or key words but then elaborate following the observation. The key words or descriptors will not only assist in remembering what you saw and heard but also remind

you how he ran or how she smiled. They can be seen as "interpreting" the observation, which, arguably, may be true. But more importantly, descriptors are clues when rewriting to remind the observer: "he ran quickly" or "she slowly smiled."

- Do not add description just to make a lot of words—make the words count and be meaningful. Does exchanging words while rewriting change what was originally written? Adding descriptors to what you write is acceptable providing that the essence of the observation is not changed.

THE ROLE OF THE OBSERVER AND LANGUAGE USAGE

In the role of teacher-observer, you will become reacquainted with language usage—verbs, adverbs, nouns, and adjectives—and how language will become a powerful tool in your oral and written communication.

Remember our definition of observation?

> Observation is a systematic process of watching and listening to children and recording their behaviour in a meaningful way for shared use.

Recording their behaviour in a meaningful way implies that this information will be accessible, useful, and written in an inclusive, responsive manner and is meant to be shared with others. As part of a sensitive, caring team, educator-observers learn to recognize the importance of oral and written communication skills in the early childhood profession.

ADAPTING YOUR COMMUNICATION STYLE IN EARLY CHILDHOOD

Adapting your language with children will represent a shift in your communication style. Finding the words children understand challenges us to look beyond the words we normally use, to rethink concepts, and to reframe them in words children can relate to. This does not mean talking down to children or using baby talk: it means talking to children differently from the way you talk to your peers. For example, if you tell a toddler, "Bring that over here," you might get a blank stare. Why? Children need concrete descriptions. Because toddlers do not understand what "that" refers to or where "here" is, rephrasing the sentence using concrete descriptors will clearly convey what is expected: "Joey, bring me the ball." Another example to illustrate how understanding was achieved through rephrasing took place in a kindergarten setting. When asked if a young girl could draw a picture of a woman, she replied, "No." When the same request was made, but with different words, "Can you draw a picture of your mommy?" the girl responded with a smile and began to draw immediately. Adapting language or rephrasing using concrete words or descriptors makes a big difference in the process of communication with young children.

Instead of the casual conversations you engage in with peers, you have to think through not only what you are going to say to children but also how you will say it. Instead of saying, "Hey, you guys, stop throwing sand on the floor," you will need to use the children's names rather than slang and state your expectations positively: "Aisha and Maribeth, let's keep the sand in the sandbox. We can throw the beanbags and balls instead when we get outside." Adapting your language and monitoring your messages are a critical part of developing your communication skills in early childhood.

Wiarton Kid's Den/Sally Wylie

What does this adaptation of language in the learning environment have to do with observation? Being aware of language usage with young children, we communicate using key words that are descriptive yet concise. One of the reasons we express ourselves clearly as educators is that we are modelling language for young children.

When we conduct observations, we also use key words to focus on what is important. Our adaptation of language influences the way we look for, listen to, and document information that is relevant. We begin to use meaningful words with children, and we write down these words when observing them.

USING DESCRIPTIVE LANGUAGE

Let us begin with the very simple building blocks of language: verbs, adverbs, nouns, and adjectives. Here is where we can begin to build strong images, starting with ordinary words such as "walk" and "talk":

- *alternative verbs for walk:* amble, stroll, saunter, clomp, stomp, march, strut, stride, toddle
- *alternative verbs for talk:* whisper, state, declare, speak, converse, utter, shout, murmur

Each word creates a different mental image—think of the difference between "limping" and "marching." *Verbs* are action words. Sometimes we can get enough action out of a word so that we do not need any other words to get our meaning across. However, if we need to qualify a verb further, *adverbs* are very handy. Many adverbs in the English language end in "ly." Some examples are hastily, happily, and brilliantly. These words add meaning to the action, for example: "walked heavily" or "lightly" or "quickly." Adverbs make the action come alive to help others see what you have seen. For example:

- *adverbs for walk:* slowly, heavily, carefully, briskly
- *adverbs for talk:* slowly, sharply, haltingly, surely

Using imaginative and descriptive language gives us new words and the ability to further our understanding. *Adjectives* are words that qualify nouns. *Nouns* are words that name a person, place, object, or idea. Young children begin learning language word by word, and a baby's first word is usually a noun. Adjectives state the attributes or qualities of a noun—for example, big, yellow, fuzzy. Adjectives perform the same function with nouns that adverbs do with verbs. Adjectives clarify what we are talking about. For example, instead of just a chair, we could have a highchair, a small chair, a lounge chair, a rocking chair, or a folding chair. Instead of a puzzle, we could have a single-inset puzzle, a floor puzzle, or a multiple-inset puzzle.

A clear description of an item (noun and adjective) helps illustrate for the reader what the child sat on or played with. This object could have a direct influence on the child's behaviour. For example, if four-year-old Nadia takes a five-piece, single-inset puzzle off the shelf, sits down, and begins taking it apart, she will probably have no difficulty in putting it back together. But if she takes a thirty-five-piece, multiple-inset puzzle off the shelf, you will likely see a different set of behaviours. Defining the kind of puzzle or contextual information gives us clues and helps us understand Nadia's difficulty—or lack of difficulty—with the puzzle. These words serve to clarify for the reader a child's response to materials in the environment.

Do you see why using descriptive language is important in the process of documentation? The environment also influences the activity of young children. Children who have experience with loose parts and materials, for example, would have the opportunity to practise the appreciative inquiry approach, thinking about possibilities and ways in which they could construct and create based on their imagination and use of these pieces. Puzzles that are missing pieces, torn books, and broken toys also influence children's play and behaviour but in a very different way. In using descriptive words such as "torn" and "broken," clear images are conveyed, helping the reader understand the consequent behaviour of a child—for example, "He picked up the torn book and quickly placed it back on the shelf." Noting that the book was torn and that the child placed it quickly back on the shelf is an important observation. It speaks to the child as much as the environment. As noted in the article "People First Language" by Kathie Snow (2010), "The difference between the right word and the almost right word is the difference between lightning and the lightning bug" (p. 1).

DEVELOPING VOCABULARY

Learning new words is the process of developing a *vocabulary*. Children, as well as adults, have a larger passive vocabulary than an active vocabulary. This simply means that we understand and know more words than we generally use on a daily basis. Documenting children's behaviour means using words in a descriptive way that we may not be accustomed to using. We must make a conscious effort to adapt the way we use language and broaden our active vocabulary in our role as educator. Adapting our communication style means learning the definition of new words and how to use these words appropriately in the early childhood profession.

Learning new early childhood topics includes learning new vocabulary. Key terms are highlighted throughout each chapter. Be sure to also check out the Glossary or meaning of these key terms at the back of this text. Developing and using this new, active vocabulary does not come easily at first, but when you include these new words in your vocabulary, you will also be increasing your ability to express yourself and articulate your views professionally.

SEMANTICS AND PRAGMATICS

Before children attend Grade 1, they have already acquired the grammar, semantics, and pragmatics of their first language. If children have been in child care, nursery school, or private home care, educators have been their first teachers, along with parents/caregivers and other family members. Being in a caring, nurturing environment where children are included in conversations or told stories promotes language development. Children learn that language is giving and receiving—a most social endeavour. Social interactions, particularly those between adult and child, are the most important influence on language development in young children.

Semantics is concerned with the meaning of words. Although words are learned, so too are other forms of communication that often accompany these words: tone of voice, facial expression, and body language. Conversations with people we know tend to be full of body language, sounds, intonations, facial expressions, and code words that have meaning within that social group.

To clarify the meaning of semantics, here is an example: the word "mummy." It is one of the first words a very young child learns and says. Yet look at the powerful meanings in that one word:

- "Mummy!" Translated: "I want the person who feeds me."
- "Mummy?" Translated: "I'm in my room. Where are you?"
- "Mummmyyyy!" Translated: "I miss you and I want to go home!"

That one word is so powerful, but by itself it is just a word. The tone, strength, and meaning of the word are what is important. Family members, like educators of young children, tune in to the semantics or meaning of the child's limited vocabulary. Discovering the meaning behind the word is necessary in order for the observation to convey the appropriate message.

Social interactions give rise to the use of language in a social context—**pragmatics**. In social settings, the child learns how she or he will use language as a means of communicating socially with others. "Hi" and "Bye" are two of the earliest forms of social communication that families and educators model for young children. Waving bye-bye and saying the words convey a strong social message. Greeting people with a "Hi" uses language as a social conveyance. For children to achieve understanding and use of language, there must be a high degree of adult participation and understanding of the language-learning process. One aspect of the language acquisition process of toddlers is taken from the Canadian Language and Literacy Research Network and is provided in Exhibit 3.4.

Maica/iStockphoto.com

EXHIBIT 3.4   LANGUAGE ACQUISITION OF TODDLERS

"By 24 months, most toddlers are able to use over 100 words. In the 25 to 36 month period, their expressive vocabularies increase rapidly. By about 30 months, they may be able to use around 400 words. By 36 months, their expressive vocabularies may have increased to over 1000 words."

Source: Carrie Gotzke and Heather Sample Gosse, University of Alberta, *Introduction to language 25–36 months— understanding and using more words and sentence types.* Canadian Language and Literacy Research Network, 2007. http://www.theroadmap.ualberta.ca/understandings

LEARNING TO DOCUMENT

DOCUMENTING OBSERVATIONS: A UNIQUE STYLE OF WRITING

Writing what was seen and heard requires a unique style. It is not like writing an essay or a term paper, where a topic is chosen, researched, and then composed by the tried-and-true stages of successful essay writing. Many books, courses, and workshops exist for people who are interested in writing a successful essay, a good business report, a technical manual, a romance novel, or a short story. Yet few resources exist that guide educators in developing the appropriate writing skills needed for documentation, **summary reports,** forms, and other reports typical of the child-care field, such as those available online. This text, and particularly this chapter, attempts to address this need.

LECTURE NOTE TAKING VERSUS RECORDING OBSERVATIONS

How is lecture-based note taking similar to writing rough notes during observations? In one way, the process is similar because while taking notes in class (electronic presentation/smartboard/whiteboard notes), you are simultaneously listening, watching, and writing. Taking notes while observing children is similar to writing class notes: you are multitasking—watching, listening, and recording.

Lecture notes represent important academic information. During lectures, students typically receive hints about headings, grouping of information, and examples to illustrate main points—guidance and cues that are helpful when assimilating new information. Lectures provide shortcuts that are used during note taking, such as how to highlight certain terms, bold key words, and organize important points within your notes. You are familiar with this process.

While observing young children, note taking is different; there are no such guides (what to write) or cues (how to write it). There is no one to instruct, give examples, or indicate what is important. Learning how to observe and record and to decide what is relevant to document and what is not is a highly personal process. No one will see the same event in the same way because what we see is filtered through a personal, unique network of senses and perceptions.

Every observation has its own unique perspective. To illustrate this point, refer to the four examples of observations of the same child based on a video clip of a boy (Exhibit 3.5).

EXHIBIT 3.5	COMPARISON OF FOUR OBSERVATIONS: THE BOY AND THE SLIDE

1. Child A is sitting in the sand on the end of the slide. He looks around and then picks up his shoes. He slowly walks to the slide. He leans on the slide while standing and slides down holding his shoes.
2. Child A is sitting at the end of the slide, playing in the sand. He took off both of his shoes and then stood up and walked over to the side of the slide. He puts one leg over and pulls himself onto the slide. He then slides down the slide feet first on his belly.
3. Child A is sitting in the sand of the playground. He starts to take off his shoes by first removing his right shoe and then his left shoe. Child A walks over to the blue slide, but only slides down with the left side of his body on the slide. He then picks up his shoes and slides them down the slide.
4. Child A is sitting on the ground outside in the sand. He doesn't have any socks on his feet. He picks himself off the ground and walks over to the slide. He sits down and takes off his shoes. He stands at the slide and puts his shoes on the slide and lets them slide down.

Source: Courtesy of Sally Wylie.

ROUGH NOTES AND REWRITING: REPRODUCING THOUGHTS

The process of writing rough notes of observations and then rewriting them is more than a skill; it is a process of discovering thoughts. Exhibit 3.6 offers an example of how a student used her rough notes to reproduce her thoughts into observations that are meaningful and easily read.

Sandra's rough notes demonstrate what she recorded during her observation. When she had time to copy her rough notes and reflect on what she had written, she was able to clarify the meaning. Repetition and practice allow us to become better at not only knowing what to write down but also using key words to express our thoughts. The more you practise, the more efficient you will become at conveying clearly what you have observed.

| EXHIBIT 3.6 | **EXAMPLE OF ROUGH NOTES AND THE GOOD COPY** |

Rough Notes – Part 1

> 1:40 Moved to circle area — 1 chair
> Tried to sit on chair w 2 friends one
> fell off + cried stood up and watched
> her cry while teacher helped cryer.
> Picks up toys from floor held toy cat
> undr left arm toy Barbie in left hand
> and watched around room.
> Sat on edge of chair looked all
> around room
> twisted doll leg with right finger tips
> yawned.

Good Copy – Part 2

Running Notes

Child's Name: Jane   D.O.B.: March 2010   Age: 2½ years

Observer: Sandra Weddum   Date: Thursday, October 19, 2012

Time	Observations	Comments
1:40	Jane wanders to circle area. There is only one chair (meant for the teacher). Jane tries to sit on it with two friends. One friend falls off the chair and begins to cry. Jane stands up and looks down at her friend and watches as the teacher comforts her.	Interested in friend
1:45	Jane glances around the room and runs to the cutting table where a toy Barbie and stuffed kitten are on the floor. She picks them up with her right hand and tucks the kitten under her left arm. She holds the Barbie by the hair, in her left hand. Again Jane looks around the room. Jane edges over to a chair and perches on its edge. She continues to look around the room as she twists the Barbie's hair with her right fingertips. Jane grasps the seat of the chair with her left hand.	Appears to have attachment to toys. Seems interested in her surroundings. Perhaps looking for something. Involvement with others?

Source: Courtesy of Sandra Weddum.

An educator wrote, "When I wrote my good notes from my rough notes, I recalled the whole observation and also things that I had not written down originally, such as small things like the expression on the child's face; it all came back to me as I was rewriting."

The first few observations engender uncertainty—uncertainty of what to look for and what to write. With guidance and opportunities to observe, write, and rewrite, students gain skills. As one student wrote, "I found writing from rough notes to good copy very rewarding. Observing made me become aware of looking at what a child does in her play at the centre. Observation is an eye opener!"

WRITING WITH CONFIDENCE

Good writing takes time, reflection, the ability to analyze and critique, the willingness to redo what has already been done, and the courage to self-evaluate. It also requires willingness to make visible your observations to others in order to invite them into the observational experience. For some educators, writing is not a comfortable or desirable exercise. Writing may not engender confidence because of a history of previous struggles.

Students in a continuing education night class suggested that a lack of confidence was a bigger issue than the actual writing process: "I found it to be very difficult. I wasn't sure of myself. I wasn't too certain about what was expected. This was my first assignment in many years, so I agonized whether I was doing it right or not." From a mature student point of view, "Doing it right" or "not sure what is expected" is a typical concern. Students returning to a school environment after some time are concerned that, over the years, they have forgotten how to study or lack confidence in their abilities.

Most colleges and universities have learning centres where students can access free resources, workshops, and tutoring services. Students who have been out of school for some time will find tutors who specialize in the learning issues facing mature students. Students who have learning disabilities that affect the process of writing will also find it advisable to avail themselves of these services early in the academic year.

Some colleges or universities offer courses tailored to the student whose first language is not English. Making use of resources, finding peer tutors, and getting feedback on practice work assist students in developing confidence in their writing skills.

TRANSLATION AND DOCUMENTATION

For students who have recently immigrated to Canada or students who are now returning to school after a period of adjustment in this country, another layer is added to the writing process: translation. Students will often write rough notes of their observations in their own language (or both languages, as in Exhibit 3.7), translate them, and then rewrite them in English.

Students write in their own language while making rough notes of observations because they can think and write faster in their own language. They have said that even finding the right words to capture what they are observing is easier in their own language. Later, when rewriting into English for the good copy, a student has more time to reflect on the right translation, consult an English/other language dictionary, or use a thesaurus. Internet resources are available to assist with translation while they are online.

EXHIBIT 3.7 NAYER'S ROUGH NOTES: URDU AND ENGLISH

Rough Notes

Child's Name: B
Time: 10:30 – 10:40
Date: oct. 16, 2006
Age: 2 1/2
observations:
child is standing to the water bin
because [illegible] stool [illegible] teacher
she cannot reach to the toys
in the water bin She picks the
toy boats. Different colors of boats.
[illegible]
She watches them, looking them
She feels happy. She splash.
She does not talk
[illegible]
[illegible]
[illegible]
[illegible]
[illegible]

Good Copy

Anecdotal Record

Child's Name: B **Age:** 2½

Time: 10:30–10:40 **Date:** October 16

(*Continued*)

Observations

Child B is standing to the water bin. She is standing on the stool to reach the toys in the water bin. She touches all the materials that are floating in the water. At first she picks the green boat then she picks the red boat. One of her friends tries to get the red boat but she does not give it to him. He pushes her but she does not react. She keeps herself busy in playing with the boat. Teacher asks her to share. She listens to the teacher and puts it back in the water. She gets a toy fish. She waves her arms up and down, still holding the toy firmly in her right hand. She looks around at the teacher sitting at the other end of the water bin. She does not say anything but smiles as she leans over the water bin. Her peers are talking to the teacher. She listens to them. She mumbles to herself. She moves her body as the boat floats in the water. She is about to fall. She slopes downward. She wiggles but she controls her body. She keeps balance to stop herself from falling. Then her teacher says, "It's story time." She goes to the reading centre.

Source: Courtesy of Nayer Khan.

It takes extra time and commitment to search for appropriate words from one language to another. Students have said that they think about what they want to say in their own language, mentally translate it into English, and then write it.

Students with language-learning needs may require extra supports to achieve written proficiency and competency. In college or university settings, students can access a language lab, apply for peer tutoring, or take an active role in developing an in-class buddy system. Whatever our own strengths or writing needs, making accommodations for ourselves and seeking support with writing are important steps in achieving confidence and success with this process.

SELF-EVALUATION

When several sessions of observations have been completed, take a look at the documentation you have written. Ask yourself:

- Can I read what I have written?
- Did I use any shortcuts, abbreviations, and key words?
- Did my observations include the people who were involved with "Child A"?
- Did I include contextual information?

You will see a difference between your earlier observations compared to the ones you have currently completed. What has changed? As a lifelong learner, your ability to evaluate your own progress is crucial to your learning. Develop a willingness and ability to evaluate your current skills against your former skills. Only you know where you started with your observation skills and how much you have learned and developed in this area. As can be seen in Exhibit 3.8, self-evaluation and critical reflection provide feedback that focuses on self-constructed skills and knowledge. Those questions play an important role in developing the habit of reflection. Becoming aware of what questions to ask and reflecting and acting upon the answers are part of the pedagogy of observing, listening, and establishing a practice of personal inquiry.

| EXHIBIT 3.8 | REFLECTIVE PRACTICE FROM AUSTRALIA |

"Reflective practice is a form of ongoing learning that involves engaging with questions of philosophy, ethics and practice. Its intention is to gather information and gain insights that support, inform and enrich decision-making about children's learning. As professionals, early childhood educators examine what happens in their settings and reflect on what they might change.

Critical reflection involves closely examining all aspects of events and experiences from different perspectives. Educators often frame their reflective practice within a set of overarching questions, developing more specific questions for particular areas of enquiry.

Overarching questions to guide reflection include:

- What are my understandings of each child?
- What theories, philosophies and understandings shape and assist my work?
- Who is advantaged when I work in this way? Who is disadvantaged?
- What questions do I have about my work? What am I challenged by? What am I curious about? What am I confronted by?
- What aspects of my work are not helped by the theories and guidance that I usually draw on to make sense of what I do?
- Are there other theories or knowledge that could help me to understand better what I have observed or experienced? What are they? How might those theories and that knowledge affect my practice?

A lively culture of professional inquiry is established when early childhood educators and those with whom they work are all involved in an ongoing cycle of review through which current practices are examined, outcomes reviewed and new ideas generated. In such a climate, issues relating to curriculum quality, equity and children's wellbeing can be raised and debated."

Source: *Belonging, Being & Becoming – The Early Years Learning Framework for Australia,* Commonwealth of Australia (2009).

The ongoing learning begun in the process of observing young children and documenting their experiences leads both students and experienced educators to gain insight not only into the pedagogy of documentation, but also into their personal and professional beliefs and values. For examples of self-reflective and personal inquiry checklists, consult with your course instructor and see those available online.

EXAMINING THREE BASIC CONCEPTS IN THE OBSERVATION PROCESS

In an earlier discussion, we explored the personal and professional observations of educators, stating how our personal and professional experiences, culture, and ways of communication all have an influence in our perceptions of what we see and hear. In the context of examining how we observe and, just as important, how we document, we've introduced three basic concepts that all educators consider as they endeavour to portray the children in their care in an equitable fashion. The three concepts to examine are behaviour, internal conditions, and characteristics. You'll note that the definition of observation in Chapter 2 reflects these concepts, yet the definition does not define specific methods or types of pedagogical documentation that educators should follow. For example, learning stories (described in future chapters) are written in a unique style that includes subjective, interpretive words within the body of the text; there is no separation between the observations and the subjective feelings and ideas embedded in that story. Other methods such as anecdotals, however, require a style of writing that separates interpretive words from the body of the observation for objectivity purposes. Chapters 4 and 5 will introduce these and many other methodologies.

SEARCHING FOR A DEFINITION OF BEHAVIOUR

To define *behaviour*, an operational definition is helpful so that everyone understands what behaviour means. A clear definition should be easily read, said, understood, and remembered. *Behaviour* has been defined as "anything that can be *seen, heard, counted, or measured*" (Cartwright & Cartwright, 1984, p. 4). Here we see the influence of the behaviourists, with the words "measured" and "counted"; these words sound very scientific. In this text, our focus is not on promoting this image of educators counting behaviours, although there is a use for precise measurement, as we will see in Chapter 5. We are interested, however, in coming to some kind of understanding of what behaviour is so that as this understanding broadens, we can see how important it is to separate what we actually see or hear from our conjecture. To assist in this understanding, let us begin by imagining the following behaviours:

- stamping feet
- hanging head down
- swinging legs
- sucking thumb
- running in circles
- staring into space

Just a few words like these make it possible to visualize a child doing these things. Can you visualize a toddler running in circles? Is it possible, then, to make a basic inference about how she might be feeling or thinking? What about a kindergarten child swinging his legs under a table? What does that say to you?

Young children express themselves with their bodies. They reflect their learning and feelings not only with their eyes and ears but also their bodies. When toddlers try things out, they practise over and over until they master whatever it is they are trying to do. Young children explore and discover their world using all their senses to understand concepts of over and under, round and soft, sticky and squishy. If we can observe a toddler's behaviour as he climbs in and out of a cardboard box, puffing and grunting, and tugging at a box, we can witness this intense learning that takes place. When the educator says to Jacob, "Can you climb *out* of the box?" and he does, Jacob's behaviour tells us that he has learned what the word "out" means, and he can follow that one-step direction. Five-year-olds love games and pretend play. They, too, learn with their whole being. As adults, we often forget how important the process of discovery truly is for children.

Since young children communicate much of what they think and feel nonverbally, it is even more important to be aware of this "silent talking" to best understand what each child is "saying." You cannot see sadness, but you can hear crying. You cannot see imagination, but you can hear a child in the dramatic centre telling another child to "make some dinner for the baby" or watch children race across the playground pretending to be horses.

On the basis of Cartwright and Cartwright's definition of behaviour (1984), sadness and imagination cannot be behaviours because we cannot see them. Behaviour is something that can be seen. We can see a child crying. We can hear a child proclaim, "My dinosaur is sad today." We conclude from these behaviours that sadness and imagination exist as internal states.

INTERNAL CONDITIONS

Internal conditions are unobservable, internal states of being that are cognitive, emotional, or physiological. Some examples of emotional conditions are disappointment, pleasure, fear, happiness, distrust, apprehension, excitement, and frustration. Some cognitive conditions are thinking, problem solving, remembering, and classifying.

Physiology refers to the body's functioning, taking into consideration physical condition, for example, being tired, energetic, or achy. Physiological conditions refer to internal states that cannot be directly observed, such as a sore throat or a headache.

At this point, we have defined two important concepts: behaviour and internal conditions. Decide which of the following are behaviours and which are internal conditions:

- jumps
- sad
- happy
- stumbles
- frustrated
- hungry
- thinking
- painted

Courtesy of University of Toronto, Child Care on Charles Street

Four of these words are conditions. Consider the word "frustrated": what would you need to see or hear in order to infer that a child is frustrated? If you describe the behaviour using such words as "yelled and threw the puzzle on the floor" or "sighed heavily" or "mumbled, 'I just can't do this puzzle. I'm so upset,'" you may conclude that the child seemed frustrated. Can you see or hear "said," "stumbles," and "painted"? Yes. What about "hungry"? That is a physiological condition because it is an internal state that is not observable. If you were hungry, how would other people know? You would probably tell someone. How does an infant express hunger?

This is why observing young children is so important. Much of what we do as reflective and responsive educators is to capture their learning, interpret what they are "saying," and try to respond to their wants and needs while clarifying their world for them. The early childhood educator also needs to clarify to other adults involved how he or she arrived at these conclusions. Responding to and communicating with an infant who appears upset involve many vital skills, including relaying that information to the parent or caregiver.

CHARACTERISTICS

The behaviours of a child that are typical or usual are often referred to as the characteristics of that child. Characteristics are patterns of behaviour or sets of traits that distinguish an individual from others. Some examples of characteristics could be

- easygoing
- affectionate
- reliable
- considerate

For our purposes, the term "characteristics" will not refer to physical traits or characteristics, such as brown hair or blue eyes, but rather to behaviours. It will refer to characteristics or traits of personality. Characteristics can also refer to a predisposition to behave in certain ways. What is a characteristic of a good friend of yours?

THE THREE CONCEPTS: HOW ARE THEY THE SAME/DIFFERENT?

Behaviours are different from characteristics and internal conditions. Behaviours can be seen or heard and, in some cases, measured or counted.

Characteristics and internal conditions must be *inferred*. An inference is a logical conclusion based on given information or, in this case, on groupings of behaviour. In other words, you would have to observe the behaviour in order to make an inference. Inferences add personal judgment. An inference adds another dimension to the observation so that now your observations have created the possibility to ascribe a characteristic to a person or to surmise that some internal condition is occurring. For example, if a child is crying on the bus, we infer that "the child is upset" as an internal condition. On that same bus, we look around and form immediate impressions about others on the basis of their appearance and behaviour. We observe a man move over to make room for a pregnant woman on the bus and think, "He's a considerate person." We have learned to use our background knowledge and accommodate new information to make inferences. Let us see if we can analyze the three concepts discussed thus far.

Indicate which of the following are behaviours, internal conditions, or characteristics:

- breaks toys
- grins widely
- nervous
- pushes wagon
- easygoing
- patient
- sore throat
- affectionate

"Breaks toys," "grins widely," and "pushes wagon" are behaviours. "Sore throat" is an internal condition. "Nervous" could be a condition (that is, how you are feeling, but no one is aware of it), or it could be a characteristic of someone: "She's a very nervous person." "Easygoing" and "affectionate" could be terms that describe characteristics. "Patient" could be either a condition or a characteristic.

CHARACTERISTICS AND LABELS

What is the difference between a characteristic and a label? Children learn to classify people, things, and events to bring meaning to their world. In the process of ordering and classifying things such as zoo animals, types of cars, or varieties

Wiarton Kids' Den/Sally Wylie

of flowers, children further classify things into categories of "like" and "don't like." As adults, we continue this process. We affix personal values to them. Some people, things, and events are valued or are more important than others. When we value people or things, we ascribe positive value and describe them in positive ways. When we ascribe negative values and describe in negative ways, we are **labelling**. Labelling is often used to describe someone in a demeaning manner. Great care must be taken to define the characteristics of a child in a positive manner and to avoid assigning negative labels. Check out the examples in Exhibit 3.9. Can you think of other examples?

EXHIBIT 3.9	CHARACTERISTICS AND LABELS

There is a fine line between describing people in terms of their characteristics and negatively labelling them. Listed below are some words that have negative connotations. Other words are offered as alternatives. Can you think of others?

Label	Alternatives
skinny	thin, slender
bossy	assertive
noisy	boisterous
selfish	egocentric
babyish	immature
rude	outspoken

Source: Courtesy of Sally Wylie.

When interpreting a young child's behaviour, be as thoughtful as you can when discussing what was seen or heard in order to make reasonable interpretations about that behaviour. For example, imagine that Anthony is gazing out the window at the rain. You observe him tracing the drops of rain with his finger as they trickle down the window pane. What inference could you draw from this one observation? Is he sad, curious, daydreaming, or just waiting for his dad? When you reflect upon what Anthony may be feeling or thinking, you are being a considerate, responsive educator.

This entire process, certainly when engaging in the act of reflection, also causes us to revisit our conversation in Chapter 1 about observation, pedagogical documentation, and the appreciative inquiry process. It also prompts us to examine the importance of viewing children as able and confident learners, as well as how we can phrase our communication about children in a responsive and inclusive way.

Children are children first; they deserve to be treated, and their behaviour discussed and documented, in a dignified and respectful way. Promoting this "person-first" approach can be achieved when we take care in using wording that puts a person first. For example, if we are discussing how to support a child's mobility in the classroom, rather than saying "wheelchair-bound Kevin," we say, "Kevin, who uses a wheelchair for mobility." For further information on the "person-first" approach, see the discussion available online.

Drawing inferences from one situation can often prompt a great deal of reflection. For example, let us assume you just walked into the ABC Early Learning Centre. As you enter the preschool room, you observe Milena screaming at the top of her lungs and hitting Sladjana over the head with a doll, and the educator running toward them. What would you infer from this? Suppose that after things settle down, you find out that Sladjana took Milena's favourite doll from her cubby, the doll she had just received as a birthday present. When you talk to the educator, she remarks that she has never seen Milena act that way before. Now what do you think? Do you still maintain the same impression of what you initially saw?

When examining the behaviour of children, we need to reflect upon many variables before we arrive at conclusions. Remember to establish a systematic practice of observing children on a regular basis to capture their learning, their joys and interests, the things that seem to challenge them, and the ways they problem-solve. Involve children, family, and other educators in the process. Be familiar with a wide range of appropriate observation methods. Ensure your documentation is meaningful, and be creative in making children's learning visible. Judiciously observe and document what you saw and heard in a way that is meaningful to share with others.

VARIABLES AFFECTING BEHAVIOUR: CHANGES IN ENVIRONMENT, SITUATIONS, OR TIME

Let's take a look at three broad categories of variables affecting the experiences and behaviour of young children in group care: environment, situations, and time.

All educators could tell you many stories of how time changes how a child experiences or perceives her or his day. Although young children are not aware of schedules in the strictest sense of time, they do experience what went before or what happens next, and children will tell you after snack, we go outside, or when we come in from outdoors, we eat lunch. Changes to the day will have an impact on the behaviour of some children and how they experience novel or unusual events.

Consider the behaviour of preschoolers starting junior kindergarten in September if it is their first group experience. Will their behaviour or their experiences of their day change by the following April? By then, they will know the routines, understand the expectations, and have made new friends. Those children who cried for mum or dad probably won't be crying anymore. Many children who appeared shy initially will be chatting busily with their friends. Children display subtle and overt differences from one time frame to another. Children can demonstrate variability in their behaviour even hourly or daily! This is all the more reason to keep an open mind about the discoveries that unfold in any setting with young children.

A child's behaviour can also vary from morning to afternoon. Educators will say that variations in an individual's behaviour could stem from family practices at home or the child's disposition. The beginning of the week versus Friday afternoon also makes a difference in the behaviour of some children. Some children are just like adults in that some are "early birds," whereas others are "night owls." Ironically, time is one of the main variables of behaviour, yet it is a concept not totally understood by children. Identifying with children's experiences helps us understand better how time influences their lives.

Although young children do not have a sense of time the way adults do, most of them do have a sense of what adults call "time." Consistent routines at certain times of the day help "set" children's internal clock. An interesting example of the influence of time on young children's behaviour involves the change to daylight savings time in the spring and the change back in the fall. For many children, one hour makes a *big* difference. Even infants will establish a feeding schedule of their own and be quite predictable in terms of their behaviour, beginning to fuss to remind adults it is time to eat!

Changes in the environment or circumstances will elicit changes in the behaviour of young children, in how they act or react. Children may act differently in different situations. For example, educators know that children often behave differently when taken out of a familiar child-care setting on an excursion in the neighbourhood or field trip. Children who are usually shy can become very outgoing and excited, whereas other children who appear quite confident in the classroom seem afraid and cling to their favourite educator.

A change in circumstances at home or school or a dramatic change in the familiar schedule will prompt a variety of perceptions and behaviours in children. Even having a visitor in the classroom will engender excitement, resulting in some, not all, children rushing over to the new person to ask questions and certainly find out, "Why are you here?" Changes at home within the child's family or inner circle of friends and relatives almost always influence how a child responds, acts, feels, and thinks.

Why mention these variables? Change creates change, and it is incumbent upon the responsive educator to be aware of all the children in the group in terms of what excites them, what interests them, and what seems to change behaviour in a child who is accustomed to acting in certain ways and yet suddenly changes. These changes can signal anxiety, illness, excitement—a host of behaviours that flag the educator's attention and create an "aha moment," sparking curiosity in the educator and interest in what those changes may mean.

These three broad categories remind us that behaviour varies at different times and in different settings or situations and will influence the accuracy and depth of your inferences. Recording patterns of behaviour gives us the information we need to understand and reflect upon the children's growth and progress, appropriate curriculum, teaching strategies, and the environment and allows us to talk professionally with the parents and caregivers of the children and other professionals.

Being aware of the subtle or overt changes in the child's life is the responsibility of all educators. In Chapters 4 and 5, many observational methods of documenting will be introduced, some of which, in particular the sociogram, are quite inclusive in looking at the holistic experiences of a child, thus making educators aware of all the variables that influence a child's life.

AREAS OF CHILD DEVELOPMENT/DOMAINS

Early childhood educators agree that some areas of development/domains are more readily observed than others, and those areas are fine motor skills, gross motor skills, or skills involving self-help. Research moves us beyond treating knowledge domains as topics that are no more than lists of facts.

The behaviours that can be grouped in these areas or domains can be observed as discrete units: they tend to have a clear beginning, middle, and end. Exhibit 3.10 provides a list of readily observable behaviours that can be documented with a minimum of probable interpretations. Throwing a ball overhand is a gross motor activity. It can be easily identified and readily interpreted. Without context or descriptors, what other interpretations could be generated? What age group is the most probable for performing this skill: toddlers, preschoolers, or children in senior kindergarten?

Other areas, such as social development or speech and language, are more complex to observe, document, and/or interpret. The same can be said of the emotional and spiritual development of children. We may observe things about children and reflect upon their personality or sociocultural influences, and although the observations may seem clear when documented—for example, he cried when it was

EXHIBIT 3.10	EASILY OBSERVED AREAS OF DEVELOPMENT/DOMAINS

Area of Development	Examples of Behaviour
Gross motor	Hopping on one foot for 1 metre
	Throwing a ball overhand
	Climbing up a playground ladder
Fine motor	Twisting lids on and off
	Using pincer grasp to pick up pom-poms
	Picking up Lego pieces
Self-help	Putting on shoes independently
	Drinking from a cup with one hand
	Choosing creative materials from a shelf

Source: Courtesy of Sally Wylie.

naptime—our interpretation of what that means can be immensely complex. How children take a nap in different cultures plays a role in their response to naptime, a common routine in daycare in Canada.

The cognitive area, which concerns itself with learning, is another area of development that exacts interpretation. **Cognition**, or the capacity for knowledge, is an internal process; we can observe only the behaviours that tell us that learning is taking place. The interpretation of learning based on what we know about a child and his or her family, environmental influences, and many other factors is what makes the observation and interpretation more complex.

A child matching colours is a clear example of a cognitive activity: "This blue bear goes with the blue square." When suggesting examples of thought processes and learning, cognitive skills such as matching, labelling, comparing, ordering, and classifying are immediately associated with the cognitive process. Often overlooked are the examples of social problem solving, which is as much a cognitive activity as matching and sequencing. It is also important to be mindful of individual variations in how children demonstrate problem solving, as well as other skills and knowledge, as it will differ from child to child. Appreciating children's individuality is an essential approach.

On the playground, cognitive function in a social context might be represented by "Who's going first?" or "Let's pretend we're camping!" These behaviours are tangible evidence that the children are learning social problem solving in their environment during play. Yet these play-based examples are usually not the first thing we think about when we examine the cognitive skills of young children. Look at the examples of behaviour in these developmental areas in Exhibit 3.11. Remember from Chapter 2 that a behaviour is something you can see or hear. In Exhibit 3.11, "remembering" is an internal process. What would you need to observe in order to conclude that a child has "remembered"? She or he would have to demonstrate a behaviour, such as telling everyone what she or he played outside yesterday. "Enjoying" is another internal process. Actually, many of the examples are not behaviours at all but examples of internal conditions or processes. These examples invite personal inferences about what is a reasonable attention span or what a child's thoughts are when "talking to no one in particular."

EXHIBIT 3.11	RECORDED, BUT LESS EASILY INTERPRETED, DEVELOPMENTAL AREAS/DOMAINS
Cognitive	Discussing rules to social games
	Remembering where yesterday's play left off before class
	Deciding which toy to select from the shelf
Socioemotional	Demonstrating an ability to wait while turn-taking
	Engaging in pretend play
	Enjoying playing with older children
Speech and language	Imitating sounds of peers
	Pointing to something
	Identifying sounds in the environment

Source: Courtesy of Sally Wylie.

Understanding development and what it is we see children doing takes time, practice, and frequent engagement in appreciative inquiry to make sense of what skills fall within each domain, to plan how we might support children in their next stages of development, and to think about what we might provide within our environment to stimulate development in a particular area. Research, one aspect of our appreciative inquiry process on our journey to understanding children, "helps us understand why some aspects of a domain are easy to understand and other aspects are more complex" (Forman & Hall, 2005, "Review Classic and Contemporary Research," para. 2).

Where might pedagogical documentation fit, then, in our journey to understanding development? Pedagogical documentation, as explained in Chapter 1, is about documenting with the holistic image of the child rather than focusing on specific domains. Yet, understanding developmental areas and how they inform our understanding of a child's growth and development is important, especially when just beginning your career in early childhood. "Pedagogical documentation invites us to be curious and to wonder with others about the meaning of events to children. We become co-learners together; focusing on children's expanding understanding of the world as we interpret that understanding with others" (Wein, 2013, p. 2).

UNDERSTANDING AND INTERPRETING OBSERVATIONS

WHAT ARE INTERPRETATIONS?

Interpretations are our subjective responses to what we have observed. In our daily lives, we are inundated with information. We constantly make observations of people and events around us and spontaneously assign a value to these observations. We have all developed strategies to navigate our way through our busy lives based on our observations. For example, let's say you are sitting on the bus when a scruffy-looking person gets on. You look up. Immediately, you form an impression. Do you want that person to sit next to you? We have become experts at making spontaneous judgments about people, places, or things as we observe them.

Whether we realize it at the time or not, we respond to our environment with a personal judgment: like/dislike, trust/distrust, accept/reject. We may accommodate new information or reorganize it to align with other experiences. This process happens spontaneously and quickly. We have learned to form quick impressions and make hasty interpretations of events or people, partly to compensate for the sheer volume of information in our environment. In our personal lives, we order and classify many experiences, events, and people based on values that are uniquely ours: good or bad, important or trivial. While we filter the daily mass of information, we build our own eclectic views, keeping/discarding information and incorporating new experiences into our existing beliefs. No wonder our initial observations of children will include words or phrases that refer to *our* thoughts or feelings.

Interpretations are reflections upon what was seen and heard. The very nature of reflection implies a pause for thought, whether that reflection happens at the time documentation is being entered on an iPad or later, after the observation has been written. Interpretations, like reflection, suggest that these thoughts are more than a quick, judgmental response, but rather a pause to consider what something means, its relevance, or its relationship to something else.

Interpretations also have their own unique style of expression. Words such as "seems," "perhaps," "as if," and "appears" are used to indicate that interpretations are speculative and subject to personal bias. These and similar words convey the tentative nature of interpretations. They are not the truth—they represent only our best efforts to explain what is meaningful about what was seen and heard within the observation.

As educators of young children, we should pause and reflect, asking the question, "How will my views affect others?" We need to communicate professionally with colleagues and families or caregivers to share our perspectives, not dictate them. This means accommodating the viewpoints of others, including the children: discovering what *they* find relevant, and why. What aspects of the observations were meaningful to families? How did the children interpret and reflect upon their learning? Including the child(ren), other educators, and families is about inclusive communication and developing responsive relationships.

How we portray a child in writing is an immensely important professional responsibility. This applies not only to the child, but also to their families, the context of the observations, and the child-care environment, which includes the staff, policies, and procedures of that setting. Our perception is tightly woven into the practice of pedagogical documentation.

Where perceptions and professional practices converge is in the interpretations or reflections of what is observed, and this is especially true in the documentation. That is why we have included in this chapter conversation about these concepts:

- the differences between behaviour, internal conditions, and characteristics
- the reasons why examining these concepts is important
- areas of development
- methods of uncovering bias
- language usage in documentation

These concepts do influence interpretations. When you read about "interpretations" in Chapters 4 and 5, you will already have an understanding of what interpretations mean, and also what has gone into that understanding, including bias, internal conditions, characteristics, behaviour, language usage, ethics, and professional standards.

Among many other things, we bring to this reflection our values, images, bias, knowledge, and perceptions. Writing interpretations can be even more challenging than writing observations because with interpretations there is also a process to follow. As observers, it is important to

- analyze the observations
- interpret what the child did or said, considering multiple lenses with which to understand what has been seen and heard (including but not limited to socio-cultural theory, child psychology, child development, and the child within the context of his or her environment)

- frame your inferences using inclusive language and a positive, professional approach
- reflect upon what has been documented and what your interpretations are inferring
- share your observations and interpretations with an appreciative inquiry approach, inviting others to wonder and interpret what has been observed, adding the perspectives of children, parents or guardians, and other educators
- remain open-minded to other possible interpretations

Practice in observing and documenting the activities of young children will change not only how we see things but also how we express what we've seen. For example, a novice observer might say, "Sarah was so smart because she placed all five shapes into the shape sorter by herself." A more experienced observer may say instead, "Independently, Sarah spent over 10 minutes placing the square, rectangle, circle, oval, and octagon shapes into the shape sorter. She persisted to rotate and flip each piece using both hands until she found the correct hole for each shape to fit in." Do you see the difference between the two statements?

When observing and recording children's behaviour, you'll need to accommodate new habits of observation that invite change in your professional practice. For example, you will learn to observe first and then interpret. You'll begin to separate those two processes. Separating what we see from how we think or feel about the person or event is exactly the opposite process of what we have spent a lifetime learning to do. For additional practice with interpretations, see the information available online.

VARIATIONS WITHIN INTERPRETATIONS

Interpretations for some methods, such as anecdotals and running records, are meant to be in third person; they are not intended to reflect first person, as in the case of learning stories. Familiarize yourself with the various methods and take time to understand the role of interpretations in each observational approach.

Some texts refer to interpretations as comments, conclusions, inferences, perceptions, judgments, opinions, insights, reflections, or evaluations. This text incorporates reflection as an integral part of the interpretation process as well as throughout all stages and steps of the observation cycle as identified in Chapter 2. Many of these terms and others are often used interchangeably with the word *interpretation*.

FORMS OF BIAS IN OUR OBSERVATIONS

Once you begin observing and interacting with young children, attitudes toward learning, perceptions of equity, and responsiveness develop. Each decision you make, such as whom or what to observe, is a personal choice and is, therefore, subjective. Even if two people observe the same child, very different information will be recorded, as seen in the comparison of four observations in Exhibit 3.5 on p. 104.

ENSURING THE PRESENCE OF ETHICS IN OUR OBSERVATION PRACTICES

Ensuring the presence of ethics in our observations and all aspects of the observation process is difficult but essential. To maintain integrity in our professional practice, it is very important to reflect upon our biases, as well as to think about how we have ensured ethics in our observations. Let's see what we can do to promote this.

BEING AWARE OF BIAS

When educators of young children are asked if they have a favourite in their group, they often say, "Yes." Human nature is such that we just prefer some people to others. Being aware of a bias—positive or negative—is the first step in treating all children fairly and professionally:

> A way to find out about individuals or families is to be more observant. To be a good observer you have to suspend judgments. Only then can you begin to understand someone who is different from yourself and who operates out of another system. The idea is to learn the deeper meaning of what you are seeing. Observation combined with communication helps you seek out other perspectives. (Gonzalez-Mena, 2008, p. 4)

In your role as an educator, you should be perceived by children as someone who is just and reasonable; their trust in you as a nurturing, caring adult depends on it. Being or becoming a just and reasonable educator is primarily about relationships, ideals, and values—not something you would think would be part of observation and documentation. Yet there are many practices that enhance that notion in any child-care setting:

- Document your observations in a manner that is respectful, inclusive, and professional.
- Use descriptive language that clearly captures the essence of your observations.
- Share and compare your observations and documentation and discuss your reflections with colleagues at your school or centre.
- Get to know those with whom you work. Talk about their perceptions and expectations, ask questions, and be open to sharing ideas. Discuss the children, issues, feelings, and ideas concerning learning and teaching. Discuss the curriculum and the environment. Some educators tend to favour certain aspects of the curriculum, such as creative projects that require extensive sitting. These activities suit the interests, materials, and ideas of the educator but perhaps not the mix of children in the group. Be aware of your curriculum biases so that you set up a balanced curriculum for the children, not one that reflects just what you feel comfortable doing.
- Bring in outside resources. When working with a group of children for some time, it is easy to become biased after a while. Requesting other professionals to observe, question, give ideas, and share suggestions about your room, curriculum, methods of observation, and routines introduces a new perspective and offers opportunities to reflect and learn.
- Maintain motivation and accountability. One of the attitudes when observing children is the belief that nothing is ever done with the information anyway, so why bother? If staff members feel an ever-dwindling interest on the part of administrators to conduct observations, the staff's motivation to do so may also lessen. Accountability involves standards and a desire to achieve what is best. Having the support of administrators—valuing the process of observation and supporting this effort—is critical. Remember, however, that it is ultimately your responsibility to be accountable for the children in your care. Saying, "Oh, we don't do observation in this centre" means that you have agreed not to do it either. It is a slippery slope from enthusiasm and commitment to doing the bare minimum.
- Be aware of your biases. Take the time to observe and document through the eyes of the children and families in your classroom. Including the perspectives, values, beliefs, and norms of the children and their families in your observations and documentation approaches not only aims to reduce bias in your own observations but also supports a holistic, equitable, and shared approach to

teaching and learning for the teachers, the parents, and the children. As Hyland (2010) states, learning becomes a reciprocal experience when you "take opportunities to learn from and educate families, because they can offer you new ways of interpreting children's behavior as well as present you with opportunities to persuade them to reconsider their own assumptions (Derman-Sparks & ABC Task Force 1989; Derman-Sparks & Ramsey 2006; Derman-Sparks & Edwards 2010)" (p. 89).

We all bring to our teaching practices our unique personality, attitudes, culture, philosophy, and background or life experiences, as noted in Exhibit 3.12. Every one of these components will influence your perceptions of children and the evaluation of their behaviour and skills, their families, your team, and numerous other elements of professional practice.

What are your values, perspectives, and beliefs concerning each of those areas of bias? Although we are trained to be caring, professional, and objective in our

| EXHIBIT 3.12 | AREAS OF BIAS |

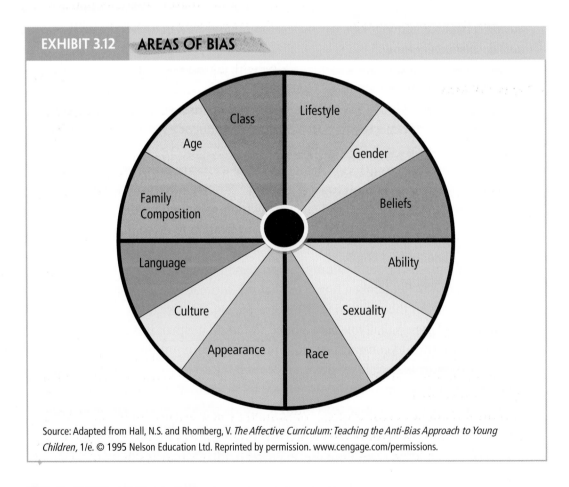

Source: Adapted from Hall, N.S. and Rhomberg, V. *The Affective Curriculum: Teaching the Anti-Bias Approach to Young Children*, 1/e. © 1995 Nelson Education Ltd. Reprinted by permission. www.cengage.com/permissions.

early childhood role, we cannot remove all elements of bias, but we certainly can look at strategies to deepen our self-awareness and how our backgrounds and experiences influence how we teach or educate. "Because beliefs and biases influence what we choose to ignore or act on, it is important for teachers to reflect on their family values, how they were raised, and what behaviours they view as acceptable or not acceptable" (Chen, Nimmo, & Fraser, 2009, p. 3; see also Marshall, 2001). For example, if educators believe that children should have free choice to do whatever they like, then their appraisal of certain behaviours will be quite different from that of an educator with plenty of rules for everything. When we begin to understand our values and beliefs, we enhance our ability to remove as much subjectivity and/or judgment as possible in order to be responsive and inclusive in all areas of our practice. Furthermore, this awareness can assist in avoiding the superficiality of a "tourist curriculum" as well as support in-depth understanding and increased sustainability of learning about respect for diversity for children and adults alike (Derman-Sparks & Edwards, 2010). Being aware of our biases or judgmental errors in our observational practices or approaches is the first step in addressing them. Further resources on this topic are available online.

FORMS OF BIAS

Leniency is the most common form of judgmental error or bias; it means being overly generous in rating children's behaviour. One type of leniency error we have all experienced is that of the "teacher's pet." Most educators can remember their own school experience of being the teacher's pet or knowing classmates who were favoured. They can also remember the feelings associated with this bias. Perhaps as a result of these memories, educators working with young children express the intent to work very hard not to have favourites and to treat each child with respect and dignity.

For every educator who has a favourite, there is one who has a least liked child. Perhaps the child's appearance, habits, or mannerisms bother the teacher, leading to a negative bias toward that child. Often a child who is disruptive or displays unacceptable behaviour (such as constant fighting) is labelled a "troublemaker" or "problem child." Sometimes there is no obvious or conscious reason to dislike a child, but the bias against her or him exists, and the child's behaviour is consequently rated with a severity bias.

A central tendency error is often committed by new teachers in the field of early childhood. This type of error occurs when all children are evaluated the same way, regardless of the children's individuality. Central tendency may result from a lack of confidence in expressing opinions, being new to the field, or simply a lack of experience in drawing conclusions about age-appropriate behaviours.

Expectancy or logical error refers to assumptions made about two seemingly related behaviours. This type of error is made when the observer makes assumptions or has certain expectations that are not based on direct observation. For example, if Miguel is the first one to put on his coat for outside play, waits first in line at the door, and dashes outside the second the door is opened, we conclude quite logically that he loves to be outside. Knowing how active Miguel is and watching him run around or ride a bike, we might assume he has excellent gross motor skills. However, if we were to observe his gross motor skills closely, what we might find is that Miguel runs and rides a bike but has yet to throw or catch a ball or to walk a balance beam. As a result of systematic observation, we may conclude there are other gross motor skills he can improve upon that are demonstrated by children of his age. The logical error is made when we relate Miguel's active nature outside to his enthusiasm for outdoor play and from this derive a faulty conclusion. We were expecting that because he did that, he was good at it. Without systematically observing and recording the behaviour of young children, even experienced teachers can make expectancy errors.

Observational drift is another common error when observing young children. This error occurs during the observation process or defining what to observe. For example, when teachers are asked to observe and record "children sharing," each may begin observing with a firm idea of the target behaviour. Teacher A may record examples of children sharing only materials, whereas teacher B may record examples of children sharing space or ideas. When the teachers compare their observations, they find that they have "drifted" with their own interpretations of what constitutes sharing.

ZoneCreative/iStockphoto.com

Does it matter if children are rated on different criteria? Yes, it does: **interrater reliability** means the extent to which two or more people rating the same behaviour will yield the same results. Teachers need to agree on what exactly to observe, the type of record to be used, and how to obtain the data. This systematic approach does not guarantee objectivity, but it does tend to eliminate much subjectivity and increase the reliability of the information.

BIAS AND PERCEPTIONS

Bias or preconceived ideas can lead to erroneous assumptions about a child. Bias can lead to a focus on the child being the problem rather than a focus on discovery, which includes the teachers, environment, or other factors. If the child has already been identified as "a problem," then the likelihood of that perception remaining is quite high. One of the perceptual errors of human nature is to see what we believe rather than believe what we see. Being proactive, rather than reactive, in observing children and their environment expands the early childhood educator's attention to all behaviours, not just those that are problematic. Keep this in mind.

Another form of bias is called **cultural bias**. It occurs when people of one culture make assumptions about another culture. These assumptions could pertain to beliefs, values, and practices. People who demonstrate this type of bias interpret and judge events and circumstances in terms particular to their own culture. People with a cultural bias see through the narrow lens of only their culture. In early childhood settings, becoming acquainted with children and families from many different cultures helps us all better understand one another, so the lens is widened to embrace more clearly the visions of many. An example of efforts to combat cultural bias and cultivate a **culturally responsive** classroom is found in the article "Culturally Responsive Classrooms: Affirming Culturally Different Gifted Students" (Ford, 2010). This article is based on experience in the United States, but it raises questions such as "Are teachers eager and enthusiastic about working with students who are different from them culturally?" and discusses culturally responsive teaching and how to create a culturally responsive learning environment.

In her book *Diversity in Early Care and Education: Honoring Differences*, Janet Gonzalez-Mena (2008) states:

> You can't remove from your cultural framework the ways you relate to children and guide their behavior, plan a curriculum, set up the environment, handle caregiving routines, and carry out parent education. Your behaviors are determined by what you consider normal, which can be influenced by your race, ability, social status, income, sexual orientation, religion, age, and/or the messages you've been given about yourself in regard to these aspects of your background and identity. (p. 14)

Becoming aware of personal bias and judgmental errors is an important step in identifying and dealing with attitudes that influence the children and other adults with whom you work. This process is essential if we are to become early childhood educators who demonstrate sensitivity and inclusivity, engage in appreciative inquiry, and show a fair and professional approach in all aspects of our relationships with children, their families, and the community.

PORTFOLIOS

Educators might ask, "So what now? What do I do with this new knowledge? What do I do with these observations and interpretations?" Portfolios are one way in which educators, children, and families can collect and present information about a child. Let's begin a basic examination of portfolio development here.

WHAT IS A PORTFOLIO?

Although the definition varies, there seems to be general consensus that the portfolio is a purposeful collection of work that conveys relevant information about a child. A portfolio profiles in a chronological collection the growth and development of a child and how that child changes over time—earlier documentation as well as current information. The concept of portfolio development involves a philosophy, teamwork including families, and practices that support this ongoing process.

WHAT IS THE PURPOSE OF DEVELOPING A PORTFOLIO?

A portfolio should be a work in progress—a dynamic process that reflects the individuality of the child. At the heart of any portfolio lies its purpose, which should reveal what is important to the children, educators, and families. However begun, a portfolio offers opportunities for interpreting growth and development and revisiting and reflecting upon the child, group, family, culture, and community. Depending on a number of factors, such as philosophy and observational approaches, a portfolio can be assembled in a number of ways and therefore could

- reflect the many languages of children—a child's communication, projects, artwork
- be open-ended so that the collection process represents a child's interests, skills, participation, health, growth, and development
- if relevant, compare a child's learning and current level of functioning to previous entries
- demonstrate a child's involvement and interactions with a group of children
- reflect the child's culture and family and may include input from involved professionals

WHAT IS IN A PORTFOLIO?

A child's portfolio will reflect the centre's philosophy, practices, and culture; the child's family culture; and other considerations. Portfolios may include the following:

- artwork samples (paintings, project work, masks, rain sticks, collage, constructions)
- photographs (individual children, a group of children, and/or the process of a project)
- observations: examples from open methods, such as anecdotal records, as well as records that target specific behaviours, such as checklists and rating scales
- combination methods such as ecomaps and anecdotal comments or sociograms with accompanying audio recordings

These basic descriptions regarding portfolios are only a brief introduction to this topic. We'll provide more in-depth, detailed treatment of this topic in Chapter 6 and online.

SUMMARY

Chapter 3 is about getting started with the actual process of observing, documenting, interpreting, and reflecting upon the learning experiences of young children. This chapter examined how language usage, combined with observation skills, produces knowledge about young children. We also learned about the importance of understanding how bias influences how and what we document and the important considerations we need to make when engaging in the observational process. From this knowledge, we hope you will begin to reflect on your thoughts and beliefs about children. Through careful observation and documentation, we form our beliefs about how children learn, how we respond to their learning, and how we develop our attitudes, skills, and knowledge, which help form our philosophy. As we interpret what we see and hear, we begin to understand our role in creating a culturally responsive environment and how our role is interwoven with those of the children and their families. We then begin as educators to appreciate the role of the family and its cultural influence on a child's development.

In this chapter, we hope you have begun to understand the writing process: learning what to write and finding the appropriate ways to say it. It takes time to develop your own observing or recording style. Practising educators say they are excited when they actually see their own progress when comparing their earlier observations with their current work. They can see how much they have progressed, and that encourages reflection, the ability to self-correct, and the practice of appreciative inquiry.

HOW IS OBSERVATION DOCUMENTED?

Part 2 is clearly the "how-to" section in this text, as well as the most pragmatic. Found here are numerous ways in which to document the learning experiences of young children, the interactions of adults and children, and the environment. The methods found in these two chapters are inclusive; they can be used with all children. Each method discussed has application to the appreciative inquiry process and the cycle of observation introduced in Chapters 1 and 2, giving breadth to pedagogical documentation. Any documentation, with the intent to be meaningful, requires ongoing reflection on, inquiry into, and responses to what we are seeing and hearing. Dialogue with educators, parents, and children is part of this process.

Some exhibit examples in Chapters 4 and 5 include the work of educators that exemplifies the notion that through observation, educators can construct their own knowledge starting with a new page. Other examples will demonstrate the transformative nature of pedagogical documentation whereby children, like educators, can participate and assist in co-constructing and co-educating to create shared knowledge and understanding. Through their choice of documentation method, whether it be hard copy, electronic documentation on an iPad, a photo narrative, a learning story, or some other form, observers will be presented with opportunities to listen and observe so as to see, capture, and interpret the thoughts, natural curiosity, and actions of children. It is through pedagogical documentation that educators are able to be responsive and transformative in their practice, in how they communicate their image of children, in understanding how learning takes place, and in their approaches to observation.

THE MAIN CATEGORIES

The pedagogical documentation represented in Chapters 4 and 5 explores and illustrates the current, practical ways in which the observations of young children are documented. The examples in these chapters represent a continuum of observational methods from simple checklists to descriptive storytelling narratives. Some of the examples will not be useful or of interest to some educators, as they may not reflect their philosophy, whereas others may find the various types of records useful.

The purpose of Part 2 is to provide a variety of observational tools from which to choose, considering which one would be most appropriate for a philosophy, a set of practices, a population, or an intent. The types of documentation can be grouped into two main categories:

1. Documentation used for recording unanticipated behaviours and events—to discover something new or to uncover something unknown. This particular grouping includes methods of pedagogical narration to capture the inquiry process and to narrate a story or moment in time. These methods could also reflect more visual or auditory ways of documenting, such as photographs, videos, audio recordings, or combinations of text, visual, and audio.
2. Those records used to target a specific learning experience or event—documentation to be used to capture specific skills or knowledge for a particular reason, objective, or outcome.

Chapter 4 features those methods best suited to capture or discover daily experiences, behaviours, or happenings as they unfold or immediately after they have occurred. Chapter 5 examines the observational tools that are purposefully preselected by the observer to target specific skills, knowledge, experiences, or events.

All methods in each chapter require us, the observers, to pause, reflect, and question the purpose of our observation. When we ask ourselves a number of questions such as why do we want to observe, what do we want to observe, as well as when and where do we want to observe, we are more likely to be led down a path of meaningful observation and documentation.

In Part 3 of the text, discussion of the application and compilation of documentation will include topics such as portfolio development, development of curriculum through documentation, and pedagogical documentation through social media. This section will assume knowledge of the types of methods presented in Chapters 4 and 5.

OBSERVING AND RECORDING UNANTICIPATED BEHAVIOURS

Rob Hainer/Shutterstock.com

Paired observations were not uncommon for the educators of six-year-old boys and cousins Sebastian and Rocco, since they were inseparable. Their parents had provided permission for their names to be used in each other's portfolio. This was the case for one Monday afternoon. Sebastian and Rocco had raced to the block centre at their before- and after-school program as soon as they walked in the door, running fast past the teacher who had just welcomed them in. Sebastian had just gone with his family to see Old Fort Henry on the weekend and was talking quickly the minute he arrived to the classroom. As he ran past the teacher who was calling his name for attendance, he raised his voice and shouted, "I want to build a cannon just like the one I saw to keep all the bad guys away. I can't talk right now, I gotta get the blocks fast! Rocco, you comin'?" Rocco nodded his head and quietly ran after Sebastian. As Sebastian ran, he jumped in mid-air with both feet and landed with his whole body lying on his side on the floor, both feet stretched out touching the block shelf. "Phew, I'm safe," he said in a quiet tone to Rocco, who came to sit beside him. Rocco sat with his bottom on his heels and bent his back and head forward as he crouched down behind Sebastian. "That's how I do it in baseball so they don't put me out," Sebastian whispered to Rocco. Rocco remained silent, just looking at Sebastian. Rocco reached up to the highest shelf to pull out the bin of Tinkertoy blocks. He picked up a tube and a circular block, one in each hand, and put them together, repeating the same action until he had a metre-stick length of tubes and blocks all put together. "There, mine's ready," said Rocco to Sebastian, who was lying beside Rocco and facing him. Rocco pointed to his creation, which he had placed on the floor between them. "That's not gonna work," replied Sebastian, who had created a triangle of the same blocks. "Here, it's gotta be put on this thing so that it can go over the wall to reach the battle ships." Sebastian picked up Rocco's creation, pulled off several block lengths, and then attached it to his triangle of blocks. "There, now you watch for the enemy while I get some blocks to build our fort," whispered Sebastian to Rocco as they both peered into the first block, pointing their creation out toward the rest of the room. Rocco nodded his head up and down and watched Sebastian as he rolled over to the shelf to begin construction of their fort.

OVERVIEW

Observational methods that capture unexpected, spontaneous imaginative play such as that of Sebastian and Rocco are like fishnets cast out to sea—you never know what you may catch. This **open method** of documenting spontaneous behaviour is flexible and unstructured. It suits the catch of the day: unanticipated behaviours.

Unanticipated behaviour means unexpected, unpredictable, or unknown behaviour. Part of the excitement of unanticipated events or behaviour is the element of discovery and inquiry, and part of the excitement of discovery and inquiry is doing something new, uncovering something unknown, or having to respond unexpectedly. It also means being open to learning possibilities and listening to children. Developing new relationships and perspectives with how we know, view, and document children opens the door to creating meaning from what we observe. Being open to the possibilities of what you may see and hear, being ready with the appropriate methods in which to record those times of discovery, and engaging in shared reflection with families, children, and other educators are key strategies to becoming a responsive observer.

Educators will tell you that unanticipated behaviour in the playroom is a daily occurrence. Children, by their very nature, are spontaneous, and their behaviours and responses are unpredictable. The uniqueness of each child will be reflected in the observations and, ultimately, the documentation created and the decisions made. As Turner and Wilson (2010) describe,

> Documentation is not just a technical tool, but an attitude towards teaching and learning. Gianni Rodari (1996) urges us to consider that everyday things hide secrets for those who know how to see and hear them. In this sense, documentation is an essential tool for listening, observing, and evaluating the nature of our experience. We need to be clear about this mental habit, this cultural attitude, rather than simply focus on the technical or professional practice of documentation. (p. 6)

Assuming this attitude and making the choice to be a reflective and responsive observer requires understanding of all observational methods and pedagogical documentation. This chapter is the first of two chapters that will describe various observational methods that are used to document the experiences and learning of young children. In this chapter, the featured types of records are

- anecdotal records
- running records
- ABC analysis
- photographs and text
- audio/digital voice and sound recordings
- video recordings
- learning stories

The first three methods—anecdotal records, running records, and ABC analysis—are methods historically used by educators to observe young children. These records still have significant value to the early childhood role and profession, and as such will be discussed at great length in this chapter. The next five methodologies—photographs and text, audio recordings, video recordings, and learning stories—challenge observational practices to look at new variations, technological and social media applications, and other ways in which we can observe young children. While most records within this chapter demonstrate the practice of separating objective information from subjective interpretations of that information, the purpose and intention of pedagogical documentation may transform this traditional paradigm of thinking, wondering about, observing, and documenting in new and different ways.

ANECDOTAL RECORDS

One of the most well-known recording methods in early childhood education is the **anecdotal record**. Anecdotal records capture spontaneous behaviour as it occurs. When the educator documents a child's learning experience, she or he is telling a story—an anecdote. The story, however, is not fiction—it is real. Anecdotal records of children's behaviours should be as objective and accurate as possible. They record important information. The roots of anecdotal records extend back to the 1800s when Jean-Marc Gaspard Itard, a French physician, wrote of the extreme behaviours of "the Wild Boy of Aveyron." Piaget's observations are another example of anecdotal roots as his observations led him to conclude that children develop different constructs of learning at different ages and stages. Anecdotal records have been a valuable tool in establishing the difference between popular thinking and legitimate investigation. As noted in Chapter 1, observation can be used in formal settings, such as testing or research, or informal settings, such as early childhood settings, private home child care, or any informal early learning and care program.

PURPOSE AND UNIQUE FEATURE

Anecdotal records have been described as a word picture, a description so clearly written that when read, the image of the child and the learning moment or learning experience immediately comes to mind. An anecdotal record could consist of a few lines, a paragraph, or a page or more, depending on what spontaneous situation is being observed. Anecdotal observations can originate in many ways; they could be written by the educator, self-reported or documented by a child to highlight his or her learning, or created by parents as co-observers.

Anecdotals follow the appreciative inquiry process and are part of the cycle of observation as they narrate a story, prompt further inquiry, inform planning and curriculum development, prompt extensions of play or play experiences, or become the basis for many other decisions made by the team (including parents). An anecdotal record is written in narrative form; it is a description of what the observer saw and heard (see Exhibit 4.1). This methodology has the capability of making learning visible in some way.

EXHIBIT 4.1	ANECDOTAL RECORDS

Anecdotal records
- document unanticipated behaviours
- are open-ended, enabling the documentation of contextual information
- consist of objective observations and subjective interpretations
- are used in informal settings to document behaviour that is natural and spontaneous
- are setting-independent (can be used in any early childhood setting) and can be written by any observer (child, parent, educator, outside professional, etc.)
- are intended to capture how learning happens

= Flexibility

The **key feature** of anecdotal records is their flexibility; they can be used to record the behaviour of children in any setting, within any philosophy or set of practices, and under any conditions. All you need is paper or a sticky note, and a pen/pencil, laptop, iPad, or any electronic device to begin your observation.

FORMAT OF ANECDOTAL RECORDS

Anecdotal observations can be presented in different formats, as this method is considered both flexible and open-ended. Simply noting the date, the age of the child, and the essential information is all that is needed to begin the observation process. Anecdotal observations within the early childhood environment are natural observations, that is, events that happen spontaneously in familiar surroundings. Using anecdotal observations in informal settings captures behaviours that are unanticipated.

In the example of Robert's quiet play in Exhibit 4.2, the observer wrote what actually occurred. Even with such brief episodes, we can learn a lot about Robert. The familiar setting, combined with the open-ended style of the anecdotal observation, means that the observer could take advantage of free playtime to record their behaviours.

EXHIBIT 4.2   TODDLER ONLOOKER

Anecdotal Observation

Name of Child: <u>Robert</u>   Age: 22 <u>months</u>   Date of Birth: <u>July 5, 2013</u>

Date of Observation: Location: <u>Toddler Playroom</u>   Time: <u>9:35–9:38 a.m.</u>

<u>May 8, 2015</u>

Observation

Robert is standing in front of a rectangular table, with his stomach gently leaning against the side and his feet planted on the floor. He looks for a brief few seconds silently over at his peers in the book and block centre but then looks back down on the items in front of him on the table. On the table are two containers of glue with sticks, along with paper, trays, and items for gluing. As he looks at the table, his right fist is inserted slightly into his mouth, with his other arm slightly extended in front of his stomach. He takes his fist out of his mouth and reaches into the small bowl and selects a sticker with the number two printed on it with his right thumb and pointer finger, places it on its edge on the table, and begins sliding it forward and backward on the tablecloth. He puts it back into the bowl and then looks down again to select another item in the bowl, which he places back in the bowl immediately. As he does this he is moving his lips up and down, saying something inaudible. Two times he grasps the lip on the side of the bowl on his right but doesn't pick it up. The second time he pushes the bowl closer to the other bowl with his right hand. He continues to remain silent, occasionally moving his lips but not vocalizing loud enough to hear. Despite several louder voices of educators and other children in the room at various learning experiences, he remains focused on the materials in front of him. He looks to his left and squats down to pick up a small piece of paper with his left thumb and pointer finger while extending his right hand flat on the table. Robert then examines the paper item in both hands. He stops and pauses for a few seconds, mouth open in a circle, and begins looking out the window across the room in front of him. He stands, again silently, as his educator comes to wipe his nose, and remains looking forward until she is done, at which time he looks back down again. He twists his upper body and moves his feet slightly to look at the educator, who is now in the washroom washing her hands. He then begins glancing around at different areas of the room, including areas where children are, as well as looking at items hanging from the ceiling. Robert does this for one minute twenty seconds, at which time his educator calls another child to go outside. He glances at the teacher, his mouth slightly open, and walks slowly toward her, not saying anything.

The educator says, "Let's go outside and see so many snails. You can bring the books with you if you like." Robert looks over at the book centre, pauses as other children come over to see the educator, and then begins to slowly follow the educator as she sings, "Follow, follow, follow Asima."

Interpretations

It seems that Robert is able to engage in both solitary and onlooker play as he stands at the table interacting with the materials on his own and occasionally glancing at his peers to see what they are doing. He appears to demonstrate some interest in the materials, as he selects different ones, looking at them and placing them back down. He also seems to demonstrate interest in what is going on around him, as he pauses for over a minute to look at what others are doing around him. He appears to demonstrate reaching and a pincer grasp as he holds on to paper and sticker items consistently using his right hand. He seems able to squat and stand independently, and is able to follow a one-step direction when the educator in the room says that it is time to go outside.

Source: Courtesy of Kristine Fenning.

These notes should be transcribed at the earliest available time and used to support further learning. After Robert's educators wrote their initial rough notes, they transcribed them soon afterward, noting key words such as verbs, adverbs, and adjectives. As we learned previously, the systematic recording of children's behaviour involves investigating strategies for efficient ways to document observations.

Although the focus of documentation is primarily on the children, their environment or setting is of particular importance. The open-ended style of an anecdotal observation recorded in a familiar environment includes contextual information:

- What was some of the contextual information in Exhibit 4.2 with Robert?
- What happened in the environment that influenced Robert's behaviour?

When you record your observations of children, make sure to include appropriate references to other children, adults, and the environment. Remember the considerations of confidentiality when including other children and adults in your observations.

The observation of Robert in Exhibit 4.2 represents the first part of the anecdotal observation: the factual account of a child's learning experience. The actual observation could stand alone; it could serve to provide others with a written account of this event. Typically, however, an observation is accompanied by an interpretation. Take a look at the format of the interpretation. What do you notice that is different from the observation section?

ANECDOTAL INTERPRETATIONS

Interpretation plays a role in all open-ended types of records that capture unanticipated behaviour. As discussed in Chapter 3, for many methods of observation in this book (anecdotals, running records, participation charts, mapping, etc.), interpretations are professional reflections upon what we see (the factual descriptions of events and behaviours) and what we hear. They are intended to reflect upon what was learned about a particular observation and are not intended to be definitive in their singular form. When we observe a child over time, we are able to see patterns and repeated demonstration of knowledge and skills and as such are able to draw more meaning and conclusions when we integrate this information with the perspectives of parents and other children on the same information. *Remember that your interpretations and reflections rest on your observations, and your observations achieve significance with your interpretations and reflections.*

As we review the interpretation section in Exhibit 4.2 and recall what we learned about interpretations in Chapter 3, we see the importance of

- considering the context of the learning experience, development, and interests of the child. This includes language examples where possible.
- phrasing interpretation as "it seems or appears" to indicate the information is being discussed based on only one observation and, as such, would not be representative of **patterning** or multiple observations to indicate mastery of a skill or domain of development
- avoiding the use of first person and keeping the information in third person
- providing opportunities to children, parents, and educators to interpret and talk about what is seen and heard, supporting increased awareness and understanding of how a child learns and what might be appropriate supports or curriculum to assist each child in furthering her or his development and unique identity

While reading over the brief anecdotal observation in Exhibit 4.3, ask yourself the following questions:

- What have we learned from this brief observation?
- In what ways can we gather insight into Payton's personality using this information?
- What can we learn about Payton's interests and development?

EXHIBIT 4.3 **THREE-YEAR-OLD PAYTON IN THE DRAMATIC CENTRE**

Anecdotal Observation

Name: <u>Payton</u>   DOB: <u>Aug. 5, 2012</u>   Date of Observation:

Time: <u>9:00–9:03 a.m.</u>   Location: <u>Preschool Indoor Playroom</u>   <u>Aug. 19, 2015</u>

Observer: <u>Xinyu</u>

Payton runs quickly over to the dramatic centre, where she confronts Child A standing at the play sink pretending to wash dishes. "That's mine," says Payton to Child A. She grabs two of the red dishes and rushes over to the table, where she picks up the pretend iPhone. She says, "Hi, Nana, I come over now," while she taps the screen randomly and puts the phone to her ear. "Goo-by, goo-by," she then says and drops the phone on the table, twirls around, and looks around the room.

Exhibit 4.4a represents a poor example of what an anecdotal observation might look like. To test what we have learned so far, let's critique the anecdotal observation in Exhibit 4.4a. What is wrong?

EXHIBIT 4.4A **POOR EXAMPLE OF AN ANECDOTAL OBSERVATION**

Child's Name: <u>Lacey Borders</u>   DOB: <u>January 5</u>   Date of Observation: <u>March 10</u>

Learning experience: <u>Playdoo table</u>

Observation	**Interpretation**
Lacey was playing with the pink playdoo. She and Crystal played together. She communicated to her that she wanted the wooden roller. The educator walked by. She was bored, so she got up and left the table. She went to the drama centre and started to play. She was there for quite a while.	Lacey loves to do all the creative activities in the room. She gets bored easy. She didn't really want to play with Crystal because she went to the drama centre. Lacey is so easygoing. She likes to play in the drama centre because she's always in there.

First, in the essential information section at the beginning of the observation, the last name of the child was included. Proper names of children should be used only by the registered educator in the room. For observers not yet registered or qualified, the real name of the child should be kept confidential. The name of another child also has been included in the observation about Lacey. Next, the word "play dough" was spelled incorrectly. Correct spelling is important because incorrect spelling of a word may change the entire meaning.

What about the observation itself? Did you find any interpretations within the observation? The term "bored" is both an unprofessional and highly subjective word that should not be used in an observation or interpretation. The word "went" was used, which is neither detailed nor descriptive. Saying the child "was playing" gives very little information and could be expanded. How did the child "communicate"? To whom does "she" refer to in that sentence? How long was "quite a while"? Was the educator walking by worth adding to the observation? It appears from this observation that the educator had no interaction or any real effect on the children's behaviour; therefore, there is no reason to include the educator in the observation.

Now take a look at the comparison example in Exhibit 4.4b. Did this observation give you a more accurate picture of what happened? Did the examples of dialogue help?

EXHIBIT 4.4B   COMPARISON EXAMPLE

Child's Name: <u>Lacey</u>   DOB: <u>January 5, 2011</u>   Date of Observation: <u>March 10, 2015</u>
Learning experience: <u>Playdough table</u>

Observation	Interpretation
Lacey rolled the pink play dough around the wooden rolling pin. She laughed when Child A said, "Let's make a roll pie." Lacey asked, "Want to make a pie?" Child A told Lacey she wanted the wooden roller. After a few minutes, Lacey looked around the room. She watched Child A roll the play dough. Then, she pushed her chair back and ran over to the drama centre. She picked up a dress from the floor and began putting it on. Next, she looked for a pair of shoes in the cupboard, found a hat and put it on, and then found a doll and carried it to the table.	Lacy appeared to have a sense of humour when she considered the "roll pie." It seemed she felt comfortable with her own company as well as that of her peers. As she selected a dress, shoes, and hat, she appeared to make her own decisions, was able to problem-solve, and independently helped herself.

What about the concrete description of Lacey's actions? Detail and description are key elements to writing a true anecdotal observation but also to understanding one that has been written.

What about the interpretation? For anecdotal observations, interpretations must reflect the observation and the context of what took place. The observer should be querying what has been learned from the observation. In Exhibit 4.4a, should the observer comment that Lacey "loves to do all the activities in the room" when there was no evidence of that in the observation? Did Lacey walk to the dramatic centre because she did not want to play with Crystal? How can an interpretation like that be made when there is no evidence to support it? What are the implications of such assumptions? They may lead to inaccurate information and, more importantly, create an unfair image of Lacey. Saying Lacey was "always" in the dramatic centre is erroneous; the observer should comment only on the actual content of the observation and not on what she may generally know about the child. There are other errors in the observation and interpretation that could be highlighted for discussion. Can you find them? The interpretation in the comparison example speaks only to the actual observation and not what the observer saw earlier that day or on a different day. It also picks up on Lacey's laughter over the "roll pie." The social development of a child is always worth commenting on, and in Lacey's observation, it showed she could play with a peer and also by herself. It doesn't make assumptions about what Lacey didn't want to do or wanted to do. What else could have been included in the comparison interpretation? Yes, some comment could be written about what she enjoyed doing in the classroom. How could this information now be used to inform planning? What **provocations** might you suggest for this child now?

INTERPRETING EXPANDED OBSERVATIONS

When observations describe the *quality* of the behaviour, reasonable inferences can be made from them. This is true even with **expanded observations**, which include multiple observations of one child from different settings, during different times, from other observers or educators and, as a result, will include multiple examples of behaviour. With a variety of anecdotal observations of a child, you would be able to net some meaningful samples of behaviour that would offer more opportunities for reflection and interpretations. Although quantity is no substitute for quality, expanded anecdotal observations will allow you to see more behaviours that are similar or related and to see patterns that you could say are characteristic of that child. When educators observe with intent, they begin to see into the surface behaviour of a child to ask questions about what it means, as stated in Exhibit 4.5. This process reframes our role, influences our practice, and changes how we observe. For example, we may ask, What was Arya's purpose when she took all the red blocks from the shelves and arranged them in a row on the windowsill?

EXHIBIT 4.5	RETHINKING THE ROLE OF OBSERVATION IN EARLY CHILDHOOD DEVELOPMENT

"Through careful and intentional observation and critical reflection educators can begin to see children differently, as capable learners who are continually constructing knowledge and theories. Rather than deciding what children 'need' to know, we can begin to see what children already know. If we begin to view children as competent and capable, as continually researching the world and how it works, then new ways of being with children emerge, new ways of thinking and doing in our practice. If we reframe how we see children, we then need to reframe our role; instead of transmitters of knowledge, we become co-constructors of knowledge. If we observe children carefully and intentionally, we can begin to ask different kinds of questions about what we see." (p. 4)

Source: Atkinson, K. (Fall 2012). "Pedagogical Narration: What's It All About?" *The Early Childhood Educator*, pp. 3–7.

INTERPRETATIONS AS AN EVALUATIVE FUNCTION

Observations compiled over several days or weeks demand a more complex set of skills and increased depth of interpretations. As discussed earlier, interpretations compiled from multiple observations involve making comparisons, analyzing, and reflecting. What makes this kind of interpretation different from interpretations previously mentioned? Interpretations based on expanded or multiple sets of observations usually take on an evaluative function. This evaluative function could be part of an overall assessment process, as described in Chapter 7.

ADAPTING ANECDOTAL RECORDS

As previously discussed, due to the flexibility and open-endedness of this methodology, various adaptations to the format can be made, such as those found online. The observer can check off whether or not the observation was remembered or live, as well as whether it was a natural or a contrived observation. **Contrived observations** refer to those that are staged by the educator, teacher, researcher, or **play therapist**. The majority of references to observations made in this text are about **natural observations**, that is, events that happen spontaneously in familiar surroundings. Can you think of an example of when an educator would want to stage a contrived observation? Some anecdotal records have the observations and related interpretations in column form, side by side, displaying the objective information and the subjective information in left-to-right sequence. This format has the advantage of making connections between the two columns relatively easy. Others would suggest that the anecdotal record format in Exhibit 4.6 is easier to write, as the observations are generally written first and the interpretations are added afterward in a before–after sequence. Fortunately, the location of the interpretation comes down to observer preference. Which do you prefer?

EXHIBIT 4.6   **ANECDOTAL FORMAT**

Child's Name: _____ DOB: _____ Age: _____

Observer(s): _____ Date(s): _____

Observations

- objective and factual
- a word picture; a narrative of context and actions; a moment in time
- a style of writing different from the interpretation

Interpretations

- subjective (uses terms like "seems," "appears")
- speculative
- requires the observer to query what has been learned from the observation
- discusses the development and the interests of the child
- reflection based on personal views and professional values

Source: Sally Wylie.

Regardless of which format is used, the focus is the recording of unanticipated behaviour. Not having a preconceived idea of what to look for keeps the windows of **perception** open to numerous discoveries. Just the process of wondering opens our eyes to a new lens of opportunity. As noted in Chapter 1, appreciative inquiry is exactly that: wondering, considering, and questioning our pedagogical practice. With an open-ended method like anecdotal observation, we might wonder what to document in the classroom on any given day. We most likely wonder what significance our observations have on developing curriculum, what to share with parents, or how to make public in the community what we have discovered about how children think and process their world. For example, an educator might wonder why a child was jumping up and down and running around in the playground, only to discover the child was chasing her shadow. They wondered together about shadows. They engaged other children in the preschool room about the subject of shadows, and before long, the educator and the children were wondering how they could take pictures of their shadows, and while all that wondering was going on, the educator documented the entire adventure until she hung it on the wall for all to see.

Jorg Hackemann/Shutterstock.com

If we want to observe Joey because it has been a long time since we have done so, then we will probably be open to whatever it is Joey says or does. Recording information only to learn more about the child reduces bias on the part of the observer, and that is an advantage for everyone. Paradoxically, the anecdotal observation may be one of the most biased types of records because of the strong role given to personal interpretation. Could this be both an advantage and a disadvantage? Check the advantages/disadvantages chart in MindTap to see if it answers this question.

COMBINATIONS AND ADAPTATIONS

Anecdotal observations can be combined with many other pedagogical documentation methods, such as learning stories and participation charts. A participation chart (see Chapter 5) targets particular behaviours and does not include a narrative or anecdotal record. Yet educators often like to include a comments section for contextual information or for information about the child that does not "fit" in the chart but is still highly relevant. Combining or adapting certain methods to include the narrative of the anecdotal record is a common practice. The methods in Chapters 4 and 5 can be easily adapted to include an anecdotal section.

These methods may be adapted to include anecdotal observations or a comments section for other reasons. The adaptations may reflect a specific request for information from parents or professionals working with a child. Suppose educators kept an ongoing checklist from September to November on the developing language skills of the toddler group, and in this group, there is a child with a diagnosed special language need. The resource educator and the child's family may want specific language samples used by the child with peers and adults. The early childhood educators may be requested to record contextual comments, such as those in Exhibit 4.7.

| EXHIBIT 4.7 | **CHECKLIST WITH ANECDOTAL SECTION** |

Child's Name: _____   DOB: _____   Age: _____

Observer(s): _____   Date(s): _____

Time: _____   Learning experience: _____

| **Behaviour** | **Yes** | **No** |

- Repeats key words such as "me, no, mine, go"
- Imitates sounds of others during play
- Engages in play, making sounds and using gestures to communicate with peers
- Imitates actions of others during play

Child A imitated the children outside in the sandbox when they made formed shapes out of the wet sand. Child A imitated the boys using boats and sponges in the water play. Last Monday he imitated the sounds of the children making car sounds in the block area. Child A approached several children during the week, touching their body or trying to take their hands.

Source: Courtesy of Sally Wylie.

Similar adaptations can be made when the educators provide topics and special projects for the children and the resource educator or consultant has specific objectives for a child with special needs. Observing the group and the individual child supports team teaching and a planning process that benefits all the children.

PERCEPTIONS AND CULTURAL INFERENCES

Before we go any further, let us re-examine the notion of subjective influences in anecdotal observations. Although we try to be as equitable as possible, some subjectivity is bound to influence our observations. Writing a "sly smile" is different from writing a "winning smile." An "awkward-looking walk" is laden with perception, isn't it? A few words placed here and there can make a difference between a child being perceived as assertive and confident and being perceived as aggressive and bossy. Reading too much into an observation that may be based on inexperience or misunderstanding can bias our observation and potentially portray that child as someone quite different from who he or she really is. Reading too little into our observations can also mean that although we have clear, factual observations, we will not be able to use them to their full advantage by providing insight and perception into the child's behaviour, experiences, or learning, thereby losing the potential for better understanding.

As noted throughout this text, Canada is a diverse, multilingual society, which is reflected in group settings where not only children and their families but also educators and staff represent a microcosm of this society. How could differing cultures affect how a child's behaviour is perceived? In what ways could we involve our entire observation team in collecting more information that truly reflects the uniqueness of each child?

An understanding of diverse backgrounds, cultures, and lifestyles helps educators be in tune with their children and families and be open to differences even in a common routine such as naptime, as illustrated in Exhibit 4.8.

EXHIBIT 4.8   BASIC ROUTINES AND CULTURAL SENSITIVITY

When observation and cultural sensitivities are discussed, most often the focus is on environment, curriculum, or documentation of children's free play or activities at learning centres. Yet we know that throughout many basic daily routines, observation continues to be part of an educator's mindset and practice. Naptime is one of those routines for infants, toddlers, or preschoolers.

During enrolment, family practices regarding naps and naptime are part of the supervisor's interview. Communication about this routine is important so that staff can discover rather than assume the values and practices of families, particularly newcomer populations in Canada.

Consider this story of a family-centred program where, one afternoon when the children were napping, a child woke screaming. This scream could not be comforted by the educator, and another staff member ran down the hall to get his mother. Mother and child sat on the cot together, not saying a word. The child was immediately comforted. He stayed in his mother's arms until he fell asleep again. Later it was discovered that this child had experienced separation and war in his country of origin. He did not like the darkened room.

What do we learn from this? We cannot assume that basic routines are common to everyone, nor can we assume that every family practises naptime in the same way. Seeing how the child acted and reacted, and learning from the mother–child relationship and discussing what happened, the centre made adaptations. Soft lighting was introduced in an area of the room. An educator sat with the child until he fell asleep. If there were days he could not sleep, he was encouraged to participate in quiet activities with the other non-napping children. An awareness of family experiences and documentation of what is learned enhances professional sensitivity, responsiveness, and knowledge.

Being aware of a child's home culture, the dynamics of the children within the group, and your own bias helps you understand how to interpret a child's behaviour in ways that are reflective, meaningful, responsive, and inclusive. As discussed in Chapter 3, being aware of your own biases is a good starting point when writing in a fair manner about your observations. As you observe young children, how will you maintain a professional approach, ensuring that your values, reactions, and biases aren't projected onto others?

To learn more about the advantages and disadvantages of using anecdotal records, refer to the chart in MindTap. Studying the breakdown of advantages and disadvantages for the methods found in this chapter will help you determine which best suits your purpose for observing.

RUNNING RECORDS

PURPOSE AND UNIQUE FEATURE

The **narrative** or **running record** documents a child's learning experiences in the narrative and, as such, is similar to the anecdotal observation. The main purpose for using a running record is to focus on a child and record the child's learning experience over time. There are many reasons why an observer would wish to conduct a running record, such as documenting the social interactions of a child with peers, logging the verbal exchanges of one child with adults and other children, or noting the physical efforts of a child with special needs to maintain safe mobility within a busy room.

The unique feature of the running record is that it is chronological in nature, a series of observations in a sequence: minutes, hours, days, or weeks. This open-ended approach to collecting information on a child over time requires dedicated observation time and considerable commitment. A running record generally focuses on a child throughout the day, recording samples of behaviour from morning until the child leaves the centre, perhaps every day for weeks or even months. Ideally, the observer should be a nonparticipant in the playroom. As educators rarely have the opportunity to devote hours of time solely to observing one child, outside resources could be enlisted to conduct this function. Centres that have access to a resource educator or consultant are fortunate that they can call upon this professional for assistance in this process.

FORMAT OF RUNNING RECORDS

This method records behaviour as it occurs. The narrative may be recorded in detail or captured as a sketch of events to be filled in with more description after the events. The reason for the documentation will, in effect, determine the number of entries and their detail.

What should be the length of a running record? No set number of days or number of entries per day is recommended, as it depends on the purpose of keeping the record and many other variables.

What else could be included in the running record? When formatting the running record, an observer could include the learning experiences frequented or a description of the setting or the adults and children involved. The actual formatting of the running record would include the variables that are relevant to the purpose. John, in Exhibit 4.9, was referred from a behaviour clinic to a community program.

EXHIBIT 4.9 **EXAMPLE OF RUNNING RECORD**

Child's Name: John   DOB: February 3   Age: 3

Observer(s): Aline   Date(s): March 15

The setting: Free playtime indoors in the morning (5:40–11:45)

Time	Observations	Comments
8:40	Runs around corner into room. Yells "Hi, guys!" Stops, looks, runs over to water play, dashes both hands in water (still has winter coat on), splashes until educator removes him.	Loves program. Mom seems unable or unwilling to direct him to cubby upon entry to room. Second week in program.
9:10	Runs to easel and stops, grabs brush, smacks brush on paper, laughs, runs to dramatic centre.	Appears eager to try things.
9:30	Pulls truck out of B.'s hands, J. yells, B. laughs, J. pulls harder at truck, glances at educator, drops truck.	Perhaps still enthusiastic about everything new—sharing.
9:55	J. is screaming. Educator is holding on to his hand. Children lining up at the door.	Work on transitions?
10:10	Volunteer walks with J. in the hall. J. is doing the talking.	Seems to calm him. Appears happy.
10:30	Cloakroom. Chatting to K. about TV program. Animated. Listening to K.	Responds to K.
11:45	Runs to other end of playground when parent arrives, refuses to leave, cries and screams, throws self on ground. Educator intervenes. Parent watches.	Second time for this occurrence. Yesterday less intense reaction.

Source: Courtesy of Sally Wylie.

The example in Exhibit 4.9 illustrates briefly the sequence of time, the behaviour that was documented, and the comments. The comments show that the observer makes brief notes that are open-ended and speculative. The pages and pages of similarly recorded observations that must be presumed to continue would yield a wealth of information. Perhaps then, after days or weeks, patterns could be identified, strategies developed, and resources identified for John during this transition to the community program.

To report on his progress during this transition from one program to another, a running record was required. The running record appears to be appropriate in the short term. Running records can also be created to record the dynamics of a group of children, such as in Exhibit 4.10 with Tabitha, Hanna, Meghan, and Cassidy. In Exhibits 4.9 and 4.10, the educators had reasons for their observations that were compelling enough to take the time to learn. Most early childhood settings, however, simply do not have the capacity to conduct these intensive kinds of observations regularly; therefore, running records are the exception rather than the rule.

| EXHIBIT 4.10 | **RUNNING RECORD FOR A KINDERGARTEN GROUP OF CHILDREN** |

Date: <u>July 15</u>

Centre: <u>ABC</u>

Time: <u>Afternoon Outdoor Play (2:00–3:00)</u>

Observer: <u>Karen</u>

Children/Ages: <u>Tabitha (6), Hanna (7), Meghan (6), and Cassidy (6)</u>

Kristine Fenning

Observation

- Tabitha, Hanna, Meghan, and Cassidy spent over 20 minutes today shouting out to the open air around them "we are monkeys, we are monkeys" as they hung and climbed up on the monkey bars in the playground.
- Tabitha and Hanna identified themselves as the mom and dad and could be overheard trying to feed "bananas" to the baby monkeys known as Cassidy and Meghan.
- "Let's pretend we are in the zoo and a whole bunch of people are coming to pay money to see us," exclaimed Cassidy.
- "Yeah, we could put on a show!" exclaimed Tabitha.

(continued)

- The girls set to work, each moving their arms and legs, one after the other, climbing up on the ladder up to the top bar, and then hanging and moving on the bars in ways they wanted to move for the show that they were going to put on.
- The girls shared their ideas back and forth, and they also paired up to hold hands and do movements together for a paired performance.
- "Ladieeeeeeeeees and Gennnnnntelman, welcome to the silly monkey show!" said Meghan.
- "Wait, we haven't collected the money yet," said Hanna.
- "I'll do it," said Cassidy, and dropped down from the monkey bars to the areas in front, whereby she reached forward with her hand several times in front of her toward open space, putting her hand in her pocket each time. "There, I collected one hundred dollars. That should be enough to feed all the monkeys in the show," she said.
- "Okay, now let's start. WELCOME TO THE SHOW," shouted Meghan.
- "Oooo, ooo, ahhh, ahh," the girls began shouting out loud. Each girl began moving, making a variety of faces, repeating the sounds they each made. Meghan and Cassidy were holding hands and letting their bodies hang from the bars for 30 seconds, and Hanna began flipping her body backwards while the bars were behind her knees, allowing her to hang upside down. Tabitha kept hanging by one arm, with her other arm scratching her armpit.
- "That was awesome!" piped up Tabitha. "Yeah, let's do it again tomorrow," shouted Meghan.

Reflection/Interpretation

How might this be interpreted?

Source: Kristine Fenning.

What did you learn from the observation in Exhibit 4.10? What interpretations could be made of the observation? Interpretations for this particular methodology follow the same format as anecdotals; take a moment to reflect upon the group observation in Exhibit 4.10.

Educators have learned that observation plays a key role in understanding each child as well as discerning the dynamics of the group. It is through observation that educators are more equipped to understand and appreciate the diversity within our learning environments, enabling the co-creation of responsive and inclusive environments.

DIARIES: A TYPE OF RECORD SIMILAR TO RUNNING RECORDS

Diaries are similar to running records. Historically, diaries are one of the oldest methods of recording children's development (remember Piaget's diaries of his children's cognitive development?). The diary typically documents a child's development over an extended period of time and includes logged specimens of that child's behaviour. In that traditional sense, diaries are rarely carried out in early childhood settings. What many people refer to as diaries today in early childhood settings are daily **at-a-glance records**, feedback books, logs, or **specimen records**. What is important and universal to them all is that they collect daily information that is meaningful and useful.

To learn more about the advantages and disadvantages of using running records and diaries, refer to the chart in MindTap.

ABC ANALYSIS

PURPOSE AND UNIQUE FEATURE

ABC analysis is an open-ended way to record a child's behaviour, interactions with other adults or children, and interactions with materials, equipment, and/or setting. If educators are unclear about what is causing certain behaviours or how the behaviours affect others in the room, the ABC analysis type of record is a good choice for this purpose. ABC analysis can also be used to examine educator–child interactions or to assess how children are interacting with one another or coping with various transitions of the day.

ABC analysis is recorded as a three-part sequence of related events:

1. What happened prior to a particular behaviour occurring is called the stimulus or **antecedent**.
2. The **behaviour** is what the child did.
3. The **consequences** are what happened as a result of that behaviour.

Because ABC analysis is a cause-and-effect method of observation, the observer is looking for reasons for certain behaviours. What could be *causing* (antecedent) Kristie to act in such an aggressive manner (behaviour)? Keeping an open mind concerning causality is vital when using ABC analysis. Often a number of factors combined are the catalyst. Teasing out those reasons, uncovering why Kristie behaved as she did, is the strength and power of this method. Here the observer is the detective looking for clues that will help solve the perceived problem or issue.

But that is only the "AB." What about the "C," the consequences? What follows, or consequences, can be just as important as the antecedent in understanding a specific behaviour. If Kristie was acting aggressively (behaviour) and getting what she wanted (consequences), what kind of detective work would be needed to uncover how the consequence was supporting or rewarding the behaviour? The method of ABC analysis is ideal for examining complex behaviours.

ABC ANALYSIS AND THE BEHAVIOURISTS

ABC analysis bears a resemblance to the studies of behaviourists such as Pavlov, Skinner, and Watson. These theorists centred on animal learning as an **analogue**, or model, for human learning and focused on external stimuli in the learning environment rather than on internal states or conditions of the learner to explain learning behaviours. The application of their theories is still seen in education settings today. B.F. Skinner's concepts of **operant conditioning** and **reinforcement** are commonplace in modern social learning theories, and educators are familiar with the statement that often typifies his theory: "Behaviour that is rewarded is likely to be repeated." The use of rewards, such as stickers for completed work or candy for sitting during educator-directed small-group time, can find its roots in behaviourist theories. Behaviourists tend to maximize the importance of external reinforcers, such as rewards (consequences), and minimize the importance of the internal cognitive states.

Theories that examine *antecedents* or *consequences* are looking for explanations for certain actions or behaviours. The behaviourists applied their theories to learning situations that either centred on enhancing the learning process or reduced or redirected unacceptable behaviour or inefficient learning. Using ABC analysis to uncover reasons for certain behaviours or to unravel complicated behaviours reflects a reliance on the scientific principles of these theories of learning. See the further examples of ABC analysis available online.

Often parents ask educators for advice on what to do at home about certain behaviours, such as acting out at mealtime, sibling rivalry, or temper tantrums. Most home-based problematic behaviours are highly complex, personal, and certainly not solvable by a quick conversation. It is wise to listen carefully and to engage in appreciative inquiry before giving suggestions. The child's behaviours are usually only one part of the equation. The ABC analysis model can be effective in uncovering the concerns or expectations of the parents. Assisting the parent to see what caused the behaviour and/or identify how the consequences may be adding to the problem is a positive outcome. How the parent feels is also important. Talking through this process may assist the parent in unravelling and, therefore, understanding the complex nature of the situation. A team approach, that is, discussions of information gathered with the parents or educators, is key to changing the response or consequences following the behaviour.

FORMAT OF ABC ANALYSIS

The antecedent is the catalyst that triggers a certain behaviour. What the child says and does is obviously the child's behaviour. But we also want to find out what happens because of or as a result of that child's behaviour. What happens to the consequences if the antecedent or the behaviour changes? How do the consequences become the antecedent for future behaviours? Knowing the consequences helps, in turn, to understand how future behaviours may be influenced.

To see how ABC analysis is part of our everyday life in various ways, let us take a look at Exhibit 4.11. Can you think of other examples?

EXHIBIT 4.11	EXAMPLE OF ABC ANALYSIS	
Antecedent	**Behaviour**	**Consequence**
Alarm clock rings	Wake up; shut it off	Get up
Let us change the antecedent in the example:		
Forgot to set the alarm clock	Sleep in	Miss exam
Let us change the behaviour in the example:		
Forgot to set the alarm clock	Dad wakes you up	GET UP!!!
Source: Sally Wylie.		

By using ABC analysis, the observer is able to analyze what seemed to cause the behaviour as well as to examine the consequences of that behaviour (see Exhibit 4.12). The primary reason for using this type of record is to document behaviours that may be unacceptable, unusual, or atypical. These behaviours could be aggressive behaviours such as hitting, pushing, biting, or swearing; bullying behaviours; destructive group dynamics; or episodes of mild or severe seizures. Observers use ABC analysis to record, unravel, analyze, or explore the relationships between the observed behaviours of a child or group of children and the environment, social dynamics of peers, or influences of educator behaviours.

Embedded in the purpose of using ABC analysis are expectations: expectations of age-appropriate, acceptable behaviour; cultural and familial expectations; or, given our knowledge of a particular child, expectations of what is typical behaviour for this child. These expectations can be the underlying reason for the perceived issue or problem.

| EXHIBIT 4.12 | ABC ANALYSIS: GILLIAN |

Child's Name: <u>Gillian</u>   DOB: _____   Age: _____

Observer(s): _____   Date(s): _____

Time	Antecedent	Behaviour	Consequence
8:45	After sitting with Gillian for 10 min., Mom gets up to leave for work.	Gillian, who had been lying on the floor next to Mom, starts crying.	Educator intervenes, picks up Gillian, waves bye to Mom.
9:30	Gillian sits quietly on educator's lap. Tidy-up song is sung, and everyone goes to cloakroom.	Gillian clings to educator and begins to cry.	Educator takes Gillian, still crying, with him to the cloakroom.
10:00	Gillian sits on edge of sandbox alone and cries (peers and educators have left area).	Educators encourage Gillian to play with peers.	Gillian continues to cry, not moving from sandbox.

Source: Courtesy of Sally Wylie.

ADAPTING ABC ANALYSIS

ABC analysis can be used with a group of children to monitor specific group relationships or to evaluate the environment. This methodology will vary depending on what is being observed. For example, perhaps educators have noticed that the transition time between free play and outdoors seems to result in children pushing, shoving, or crying and the educators having to remind, remove, and reproach. Usually, no one has the luxury of objectively observing this transition because everyone is caught up in it! Yet if educators took time out to observe, they might find the following:

> The transition time from indoor free play to outdoor learning experience begins at 9:30. The educators give warning of the transition by singing songs, reminding children, assisting the children in getting started by tidying up with them, and establishing a presence in the cloakroom. As in most centres, some children run immediately to get dressed to go outside, others dawdle, and still others move their chairs even closer to the tables, sending a clear message that they intend to stay inside.

Anyone who has been in a playroom at a time such as this can predict quite accurately what types of behaviours will occur. Transitions can be difficult for young children; having to stop playing is like asking a theatre full of moviegoers to stop watching the movie, tidy up the area around them, and leave the theatre! Scheduled time is relevant only to older children and adults. Educators are well aware of this fact, but the point of the observation would be to examine the behaviours in the context of the morning transition. The children are telling us something—we need to listen. Children exhibit behaviour to communicate that their needs are not being met in some way. It is our role as investigators to determine what that might be. Once the observations are completed over a number of days, analyzing and interpreting the data and looking for patterns may indicate what acts as an antecedent to the behaviours at morning transition time. Perhaps the behaviours of some children are inconsistent, and the only pattern is that there is none. That, too, is always a possibility. However, other interpretations may indicate how the noisy routine evolves or who may be the major players in the complex set of events. Observing and recording behaviour in a meaningful way can and does make a difference. Perhaps moving the schedule around to allow more playtime or putting playtime earlier or later in the schedule may be the answer. If, after making these observations, the educators conclude that only a few children seem to be having a difficult time during this transition, then they can try to find the best solution for each child. Perhaps the obvious answer is simply to change the amount of time needed in the cloakroom, but to avoid not seeing the forest for the trees, a step back to observe is necessary.

As inferred above, interpretations for this type of methodology will look different from the types of interpretations made for perhaps an anecdotal or learning story. The purpose of this method leads us to look at what might be precipitating a response in a child or group of children, and as such, our interpretations may lead us to conclusions that focus on the role and influence of the educator, the response of the adult or child to what is taking place, and the impact of the curriculum, environment, or materials/equipment in the room, as a few examples. What is often discovered is that many of the behaviours and actions communicated by children are a result of the adult who has either set the stage or responded in a particular way. Take a moment to reflect on this. Why might this be likely? Would you agree and why? When we take the time to reflect upon what is taking place, we are better equipped to increase desired behaviours or decrease undesirable behaviours taking place in the classroom. It is our responsibility to figure this out, as children communicate through their actions how best to meet their needs. Take a moment to reflect upon the ABC analysis examples available online. How might that information be patterned and interpreted? What can be learned?

ABC ANALYSIS AND CURRICULUM DEVELOPMENT

ABC analysis can also be effective when used in curriculum development. For example, in Exhibit 4.13, the junior kindergarten room is exploring the concept of making a town, using for its base a plastic toddler wading pool filled with sand. Into

EXHIBIT 4.13	ABC ANALYSIS OF CURRICULUM	

Antecedents	Behaviours	Consequences
Monday Introduced sand learning experience. Added cars, trucks, small blocks. Limit of four children.	Four children (boys) dove into box. Some disagreements, much verbal and physical pushing for space.	Reminders about noise level and sharing materials. Eventual sharing of space around sand pool.
Tuesday Reintroduced materials. Added pieces of cardboard. Role-modelled making a city with streets.	Three girls and one boy sifted through the box, watched, and participated in getting more cardboard, space, and materials.	Quiet shuffling of cardboard in the box. Children took up spots around the sand pool. Children played together, sharing.
Wednesday Reintroduced materials. Added pinecones, popsicle sticks, odd bits of wood, trucks, toy people.	Two girls and two boys rustled through variety of materials.	Quickly set up city and named what things are and what they are used for. Added people. Children played cooperatively, sharing ideas.
Thursday Reintroduced materials. Added cars, train tracks, animals. Provided large mural paper on wall next to sand pool and markers to draw.	Four boys piled materials in arms. Two girls took markers and watched and drew cities.	Major discussion of who does what. Three boys and a girl began to set up a city. One boy and one girl drew set-up of the city on mural paper.

Source: Courtesy of Sally Wylie.

the sand, educators added open-ended materials, and observation of the children began. The focus of the observation was how each child responded to the materials and the new experience. Each day new materials were added. Using the open-ended materials described in Exhibit 4.13, you can see, through ABC analysis, how materials influenced behaviour and how, when the children used the materials, there were differing outcomes and consequences. What were the implications for further planning or changes from Monday to Friday?

From the example in Exhibit 4.13, it is easy to see how varied materials affected the behaviour of the children, such as the choice to participate. Close examination of each day and the antecedents, behaviours, and consequences of the daily experiences shows how play exploration became on one day the antecedent, and on another day, the consequence. It confirms the assumption that curriculum affects behaviour, and behaviour affects choices in curriculum development. What has been the role of the ABC analysis in developing an inclusive and responsive curriculum?

Setting out these materials in plastic toddler wading pool with sand provided easily accessible experiences for children. Set-up of the environment in this fashion illustrates how the environment can become an antecedent of behaviour. The novel, on-the-floor set-up approach was enticing and interesting, acting as a lure in itself, inviting exploration and discovery.

To learn more about the advantages and disadvantages of using ABC analysis, see the chart in MindTap.

PHOTOGRAPHS

Photography as a form of visual literacy and communication can be traced back to at least 150 years ago, when the photographic process evolved enough to allow for public use. For years, photos have been used to document history and historic moments, societal changes and trends, innovations, milestones, human behaviour, and posed situations of icons, leaders, children, and families. Every moment of every day people use visuals (photos or real experience) for a variety of reasons, such as to understand what they see as well as get to where they need to go. Technology is changing at an ever-rapid pace, and we find ourselves having access to a multitude of technological tools transforming the way in which photos can be taken, adapted, used, communicated, and shared. Staying abreast of technology changes and its presence in observation and documentation is a subject explored in Chapter 8.

Photos in early childhood have most often been associated with the **Reggio Emilia** philosophy, an approach known for its authentic commitment to documenting the learning journey of children, and for capturing the image of the child through a variety of documentation methods, one of which is photos. Photos are powerful. They have the ability to

- transcend all early childhood philosophies
- break down perceived language barriers in order to bridge cross-cultural communication

- promote visual literacy no matter where we are in the world
- serve as communication for individuals with special needs, support responsiveness, and promote inclusiveness
- enable everyone to have access to early learning environments so as to view the learning taking place

Observation through photo documentation prompts pedagogical inquiry, further observation, interpretation, and the co-construction of new knowledge for all learners: children, educators, and families. As a result of this common practice, photos are now a part of observation and pedagogical documentation in most types of philosophies around the globe.

Gladskikh Tatiana/Shutterstock.com

PURPOSE AND UNIQUE FEATURE

Familiar to many educators are the photos of family members, pets, special toys, and objects from home visually posted around the rooms in early childhood settings. These photos often find their way to traditional bulletin boards, a child's cubby, or a portfolio, or are mounted low enough on the wall for the kisses and smiles of infants and toddlers. Photos of family members help ease children's stress at being away from family for the first time. Together, educators and parents make up photo albums of pictures from home for the child to have at the centre. These purposes still hold validity; as educators, we recognize how important it is for children to see themselves within their learning environment as they engage in their journey of constructing their identity. To do this, many educators will keep their camera ready upon parent request to record their special moments. Taking a picture of a young child standing on his or her own for the first time is a celebration for educators and parents alike and provides a worthy photo of a milestone in the child's development for the child's portfolio. As Linda Good (2005–2006) states in her article "Snap It Up: Using Digital Photography in Early Childhood Education," photographs of children are used in a variety of ways:

> Educators of young children can use digital photography to build a sense of community and belonging, promote feelings of security, build children's self-esteem, aid in classroom management, communicate with parents, document children's growth, promote language

and literacy, provide choices for children with special needs and enhance other areas of the curriculum. (p. 79)

Many early childhood settings maintain their own photo albums, which are kept in a special place in the playroom. The children can sit and look at pictures of themselves, school trips, special holidays, birthdays, family members, and their friends. These albums are a rich source of learning—of developing memory for past events and sequence of time and of becoming aware of a shared past with people other than family members. Photos appeal to children and parents alike, providing opportunities for paired or small-group discussion.

The camera can also be used for other specific purposes. As Luckenbill (2012) points out, "The camera can document children's interests and patterns of behavior, assisting caregivers in following the children's lead. The camera/video camera can pinpoint environmental stimuli and caregiver behavior patterns that may be triggering problematic behaviors" (p. 31).

Providing opportunities for this inquiry, reflection, and responding to children's interests and actions promotes a responsive and inclusive approach. Understanding the impact that educators have upon children, interactions, and the environment is worth examining so that we might continue to improve all aspects of our practice. Using a camera to understand our impact upon children's behaviour and interactions with others is a great tool for team discussion and reflection so as to improve our building of relationships and resiliency in all learners. Using documentation as a means to further reflect upon professional practice is an important concept explored in later chapters. Engaging multiple perspectives to reflect upon visual documentation communicates to children, families, and educators that all learners are valued, all learners contribute knowledge, and all learners are capable and competent in their ability to learn. Photographs open the door to inquiry and the sharing of perspectives. How might photographs be formatted to communicate all that we have discussed and much more?

FORMAT OF PHOTOGRAPHS

Photos make children's learning and other forms of documentation visible. Like a chameleon, photos can absorb the power, richness, and vitality of what is going on around them, and they have the ability to stand alone or be adapted or paired with other forms of documentation to aid a specific observational purpose. Formats will vary for a variety of reasons, including photo combinations with other methodologies, early childhood setting preferences for documentation methods, and purpose of observing, to name a few. Let's examine the role of photos with other forms of documentation and text to further assist our inquiry.

PICTORIAL COMBINATIONS: PHOTOGRAPHS AND TEXT

As explored in the learning stories section of this chapter, the photograph and text do more than answer the question; they may illustrate visually and narrate in print the event, the inquiry, or the thinking that occurred. They provide opportunities for parents, children, and educators to make further inquiries and to respond. In short, photos and text encourage and support inquiry. Adding a page on which anyone can respond is an inclusive practice. That documentation promotes co-learning involving, in this case, the key participants: educators, children, and parents. Photographs have become learning/teaching tools that capture in unique ways the activity of young children as they play and learn. As Margot Boardman (2007) notes in the article "I Know How Much This Child Has Learned. I Have Proof," "Educators indicated that using digital cameras facilitated children's reflective thinking processes: It was good to show other children [the digital photos as a follow-up to the initial learning experience], as they can explain and talk about what was happening and what they were doing in the photos and so you got a lot more information out of this" (p. 61).

Digital technology has given us the ability to economically use photographs with greater flexibility than before. Several good pictures out of many can be chosen for their strong visual images that capture a particular behaviour or event. These photographs can then be further enriched with brief narratives, such as those found in Exhibit 4.14.

EXHIBIT 4.14	EMMA MAKING BREAD

Emma is able to pour the flour with stable hands without the teacher's help. She looks focused on what she is doing.

Emma is enjoying playing with the flour and maybe that's because it's soft. She pretends to make dough by mixing the flour. She looks like she is imitating her mother because in her culture, the mom used to make the dough all the time to make bread. Her facial expression reflects her hard work to mix the dough.

Source: Text and photos courtesy of Bushra Qasim and Hassan Fayad.

What do these photographs and narratives tell us about Emma? Bushra Assad, who provided the material in Exhibit 4.14, wrote that "she can create many things when given the materials. She seemed very patient, and focused on her work. She likes to be independent." Visual imagery can be complemented by educators and/ or parents adding significant written commentary, as in the example of Emma in Exhibit 4.14. Note in this example how the text enables the story portrayed in the photographs. Text accompanying photos can be varied in length and can be written in the narrative by the parent, the child, or educator.

VISUAL COMMUNICATION AND CHILDREN WITH EXTRA SUPPORT NEEDS

Visual communication with pictures and text embraces the concept of **total communication**. Photos are used to assist all children to understand what is taking place in their day. This helps children to self-regulate and reduce anxiety about new experiences and aspects of their day. Photos have been particularly effective with children who require supports to communicate. Photos can be pointed to, looked at, named, and used as a visual means of communication. Children with special needs might use pictures of learning materials or toys in a personal photo album to show what they would like to play with. Their photos can also represent meal choices, functional items they need, or experiences in which they wish to engage. The pictures are supplied and organized by family members, teachers, and professionals. To provide this kind of pictorial aid, these people must be aware of the child's interests, likes and dislikes, needs, and skills. Carefully observing any child who might benefit from visuals will give the teacher clues about what pictorial aids would be most useful and appropriate. Ongoing monitoring will also be necessary to make sure the choices are significant, relevant, and helpful to the child. Go online and visit Pinterest or other apps and websites for examples of communication boards used with children.

PHOTOGRAPHS AND OTHER DOCUMENTATION METHODS

Photographs can also be formatted with other documentation approaches, including mapping and webbing. Using photos on a mapping diagram either in hard copy or on a tablet/iPad can assist the documenter in visualizing the areas frequented by the child or children being observed. Positioning photos within a web on a wall in the classroom enables children, families, and educators to respond and contribute to the interests, inquiry, and learning taking place through additional discussion, the addition of new materials, or written comments to extend the thinking or perhaps stimulate new questions and inquiry for exploration.

Photos are also a great addition to digital or hard-copy portfolios to document a child's learning journey, questions, and interests, and how the child's learning might be happening. The Learning Stories section on page 179 and the section online provide apps and programs for using photo documentation. Photos can also be used in discussion of curriculum planning for both individuals and groups, and they can accompany other methods of documentation discussed in this text.

PHOTOGRAPHS AND DOCUMENTATION PANELS

Photos intended or formatted for the purposes of **documentation panels** enable the learning and thinking of children to be visible in unique ways, as they allow the viewer to understand and appreciate how learning and inquiry occur for a community of learners. Selected, prepared, and created by one or more observers (including children, families, educators, and community), documentation panels may be composed of a variety of methodologies, such as a combination of artwork or illustrations, photos of creations or sculptures, narratives, conversations or captions, hypotheses, a group or individual experience or moment in time, a telling of a story or timeline, a depiction of interconnecting relationships, or narrations of an individual/group journey of discoveries. Intended for viewing and visibility, conversation, questioning, or additional contributions of other perspectives, these panels are often placed on a variety of surfaces, including walls, display boards, electronic devices such as digital photo frames, or movable room dividers. Documentation panels often serve as provocations for meaningful conversations at arrival and departure times or during planned community nights within an early childhood setting. Having these panels available regularly for children to discuss, review, and evaluate their learning and inquiries with families and others supports the creation of a responsive, inclusive curriculum and environment that is reflective of its learners. See the examples of documentation panels available online.

PHOTOGRAPHS AND PEDAGOGICAL DOCUMENTATION: REFLECTIONS AND CONSIDERATIONS

In pedagogical documentation, the photograph taken is expected to hold meaning. Framing what we see in a context we want to communicate requires some thoughtful reflection about things such as

- ensuring that a separate consent form has been signed for sharing and communication of photos in a digital, web-based, and/or hard-copy format. Ensuring that families understand how photos will be used is necessary for informed consent. Examples of consent forms are available online.

- ensuring access to documentation for all learners (educators, children, and families) to take photos of what they feel captures meaningful learning or moments in time. For ideas on how to promote access to observation and documentation, visit Chapter 3.
- watching and listening to children's conversations and taking photos of them in action (rather than posed photos). It is recommended that if narrating or adding text to the photo, the observer document the context and language of the situation at the time of the photo for authenticity and realism of the moment captured in time.
- selecting posed photos only if children wish to document something they have made, perhaps photos of friends or family they want to share, proud moments, and so on. Ensuring a balance of photo and photo/text combinations assists in ensuring a more comprehensive approach to authentic representation of the image of a child and her or his interests and abilities.
- including both single and groupings of photos. Single photos are great for capturing singular inquiry instances or moments in time, while grouped and sequential photos of a process or learning experience can demonstrate how learning evolved and how the inquiry, discussions, and reflections led to the outcome of the experience. Children would then be able to narrate or replicate the experience if they so choose to do so.
- seeking observation opportunities that promote the strengths and interests of children
- seeking opportunities to visually document relationships, interactions with the environment, manipulation of materials, new inquiries and questions, and social interactions, among many other things
- determining how photos will be stored and organized right after they have been taken. Photos lose their meaning if simply left on the camera or downloaded with no organization.
- exploring different online photo documentation apps or programs that will enable remote access to children's learning for families, if this is appropriate and reflective of your learning community.
- exploring how opportunities might be provided to elicit perspectives and interpretations of the photo documentation captured.

What other possibilities should we be thinking about? As we reflect upon this question, it brings us to the important conversation of ethics and the photographic process. As discussed in previous chapters, we must take care to be ethical and respectful in the decisions we make and in our observation and documentation processes.

ETHICS AND PHOTO DOCUMENTATION: ETHICAL DILEMMA OR NOT?

Chapter 3 introduced us to the ethical conversations we need to have with fellow educators, families, children, and communities regarding the observation and documentation process. Often it is perceived that the camera or the photos we take are nonintrusive; however, this is not the case. If we take a moment to first think critically about ourselves as human beings and educators, it is easy to recognize that as adults we might not be comfortable in having our own photos taken and then used on Facebook, Instagram, and Pinterest. What if someone took or posted a photo of you without permission? Have you consulted with the children regarding having their photos taken? Have you taken a moment to reflect upon the privacy laws guiding the practice of taking photos with your cellphone or iPad? What if the photos were misused? Sent to the wrong email address? Lost or stolen? What about photos being downloaded onto apps or websites for viewing? To answer these questions, be sure to review the ethics conversations in previous chapters. Later in this chapter, we will examine ways in which to promote confidentiality with the storage of visual media. Articles, legislation, and ethical resources for educators in early childhood settings are available online. Exhibit 4.15 poses some other important questions for consideration.

EXHIBIT 4.15	PHOTOS AND ETHICAL REFLECTIONS FOR EDUCATORS

1. Separate from the conversation with parents regarding consent forms, in what ways have you determined that every child has agreed to be videotaped and photographed daily?
2. In what ways have children decided what is of value to them to be photographed, videotaped, and documented?
3. In what ways have you considered how children's voices, perspectives, and insights have been included in the observation, documentation, and demonstration of them through visual methods?
4. How have children been invited to select the photos or videos displayed within the environment for others?
5. In what ways have children been invited to create and communicate their own documentation?
6. How are the child's needs being met when taking photographs, videos, or documenting? Might it be our needs and responsibilities that we are fulfilling and not the child's?

7. What if a photo was taken that makes visible a child's concerning behaviours in a "negative" light? What might you do?
8. What would happen if a child refused to be documented? Do children have this right?
9. What does the UN Convention on the Rights of the Child say about the rights of children in relation to visual documentation?
10. In what ways are you ensuring that the photos are protected from use by others?

Pedagogical documentation is about appreciating what we see, and this requires attention to ethics. As Lindgren (2012) insists, "Further discussions need to occur about ethics and what it means for children and adults to produce pedagogical documentation, and particularly when using visual technology" (p. 338). This is particularly true when photos are used to communicate learning through social media. When using the social media platform, how are you ensuring confidentiality, integrity, and appropriate use of the images shared? In what ways have families been consulted? Be sure to visit Chapter 8 to reflect upon social media as a different digital platform to share children's learning visually.

To learn more about the advantages and disadvantages of using photographs, consult the chart in MindTap.

AUDIO/DIGITAL VOICE AND SOUND RECORDINGS

Hard-copy **audio recordings** or voice recordings have been part of the early childhood educator's repertoire of educational tools for decades. Educators have always known that sounds are important to young children in sorting out the **aural** world. Children love to listen to themselves and others sing and talk on recordings. Do you remember the first time you heard your voice recorded? Most people's reaction is one of stunned amazement, followed by, "That's not me. That's not what I sound like!" We know the reasons why we sound different on a recording, but children generally do not. This is a great opportunity to ask questions, generate discussion and inquiry, and explore with them how our ears function and what sound is, and to expand the subject to include animals' ears, animal sounds, and so on. Children also love to identify themselves and their friends on recordings and take pride in participating in recorded singsongs, whether just for fun or for a special musical event.

This text's definition of "observation" includes *watching and listening*. Sounds can tell us much. In familiar surroundings, the sounds you hear will be enough; you do not have to look around to confirm what you heard. Children who live in rural Saskatchewan or northern Manitoba will learn different auditory cues than children who live in downtown Vancouver or Halifax. Sounds are part of a specific environment. Think of the sounds in the playroom that are alarms for teachers: sudden crashing sounds, cries, and screams. Educators can tell you quite easily, "The group is louder today than usual" or "They're very quiet; it must be Monday morning." Experienced educators will observe with their ears as well as their eyes to gauge the mood or feeling of the group.

PURPOSE AND UNIQUE FEATURE

This methodology engages a number of pedagogical documentation principles, as it enables the authentic audio gathering of real moments, conversations, and communication, attuning the listener only to the auditory components of the experience. For example, when on their own or paired with another methodology, recordings have the capacity to capture many unique experiences happening within a learning environment, including role playing and conversations between children in the dramatic centre, children narrating a story as they look at pictures in a storybook, a bonding moment between an adult and child, and much more. Children, families, and educators are able to use these recordings for revisiting, reflecting, and discussing what took place, why something was said, and what thinking might have been occurring, and experience new inquiries as a result.

Emin Kuliyev/Shutterstock.com

There are a multitude of purposes for audio/voice recording. Audio recordings can be used effectively to capture samples of children's communication or speech and language. A parent, a speech pathologist, or an audiologist might be interested in a profile of sounds that may further clarify the patterns of a child's speech and language development.

Audio recordings can also serve as a temporary substitute for writing. An educator could conduct a one-on-one interview with a child for a variety of reasons. When writing is not feasible at the time or is not fast enough to keep pace with what is occurring, audio recordings are a viable option.

FORMAT OF AUDIO/DIGITAL RECORDINGS

Audio/voice can be recorded in a variety of ways using digital technology devices. For many years, the simple hand-held voice recorders commonly used for interviews had been an option for many educators. This approach required the observer to audio record and write simultaneously, or later transcribe the recordings on paper. While any observer has the ability to transform audio to handwritten or word processing formats, many no longer choose this option as a result of the technology available. Recent digital technology has enabled audio recordings to be transformed even further with the variety of apps and programs available online to users around the world. New digital programs not only enable the production of hard-copy audio notes into digital form, but they also provide access to digital resources that enable the observer to voice record and then digitize the notes simultaneously. This saves the observer a significant amount of time in transcribing the information.

With the introduction of smartphones and tablets, as well as new digital hand-held devices, recording audio has become quite easy. Depending on the type of device, particularly if it has a removable secure digital (SD) card, programs may use individual SD cards with different children so that the documentation can stay in audio form for future listening and reflecting upon with children and their families. Certainly a strength to keeping the documentation in digital form is that this reduces the amount of paperwork, but keeping it digital isn't always the best use of information if it's not organized properly for storage and communication with others. The tricky part for most educators is the time needed for the transcription of data.

Depending on the type of recording device used, educators may need to transcribe the audio recordings immediately following the observation so as to remember the context of the situation being recorded. Take a moment to think about the relevance of understanding the context of an audio or voice observation. Why might it be important? New apps, assistive and online programs as discussed in the section on photo documentation, and learning stories sections would be of significant assistance in recording and documenting audio or voice. With a **Livescribe pen**, observers are able to write and record at the same time using special lined paper and the pen to take notes. The pen itself records the audio/voice while the observer makes notes. Observers are then able to connect the pen to a PC or an iPad and transform the notes into digital form. Many apps and programs, such as Dragon NaturallySpeaking, allow you to record the language or audio straight to a word or working document for easy formatting into a document ready for printing, sharing, or including in a child's portfolio.

Digital audio/voice recordings aided by a voice-to-text program can also assist any observer who finds it challenging to simultaneously listen to and document audio of a child or group of children. Programs and technological aids like those identified above also create opportunities for English-language learners to document in their first language and then use the audio recordings to enhance in English what they may not have been able to translate.

AUDIO/DIGITAL VOICE RECORDINGS AND CHILDREN'S PORTFOLIOS

Having the capacity to replay audio for clarity, reflection, and understanding assists in ensuring accuracy of information gained on a child or group of children to contribute to their online or hard-copy portfolio. As with video recording, audio and voice recordings in digital form allow children to listen to and reflect upon what they were saying or perhaps how they resolved a situation and the language they used. Eliciting a child's perspective on his or her own audio recording gives further insight into the questions we might ask to prompt further inquiry, as well as into the other knowledge and skills the child possesses. This inquiry may prompt further questioning and reflection by the child and inform curriculum planning by the child or educator based on what was discussed.

Take a look at the online audio exhibits, which include portfolio entries and transcriptions as narratives for a wall exhibit demonstrating the questions children had on a particular day in their classroom. Examples to practise writing in quotations the conversations happening between children are also available online. How might you translate some of these into portfolio entries? In what ways could this information inform a profile for a child? How might this audio be used further with a child and curriculum planning?

To learn more about the advantages and disadvantages of using audio/digital recordings, refer to the chart in MindTap.

VIDEO RECORDING

It is well known by those who coach sports teams that using visual methodologies such as video playback assists the team and individual players to reflect upon past plays, new strategies, and their role in the team to enhance their future success. The use of video playback is no different for early childhood education. As a pedagogical documentation methodology, **video recording** provides a unique opportunity to watch children, listen to them, understand their thinking, as well as appreciate how learning and knowledge might be demonstrated in different ways.

PURPOSE AND UNIQUE FEATURE

Video recording in the classroom, in its use and application by children, parents, and educators, poses numerous opportunities for revisiting, reflecting upon, interpreting, and discussing observations made on video. In Exhibit 4.16, we see that Enoch changes his image and perspective of Child A as a result of introducing and using a video camera in his kindergarten classroom. In this example, Enoch learns the importance of providing opportunities for children to build and scaffold their

EXHIBIT 4.16   **VIDEO RECORDING AS RELATIONSHIP BUILDING**

Enoch, a kindergarten educator, recently attended a session on pedagogical documentation with his peers. In this session, they had discussed the idea of using video as a way to prompt inquiry. Intrigued by this session, Enoch and his team member Rebecca decided they would place some pretend video cameras in the classroom for the children as a provocation. They were pleasantly surprised with what they saw and heard. On one occasion, Enoch was able to capture a narrative of two children discussing how delicate the camera was, where to place their eyes, how to ensure the strap was around their neck, and how it "was so expensive."

The time soon came for the real video cameras to arrive. The children were squealing with delight as Rebecca opened the boxes. Concerned about the expense of the cameras, Rebecca raised her eyebrows, put her finger to her mouth, and stated, "Hmmm, I'm really confused on how to use this camera and how to take care of it so that we have it for a very long time in the room. Can any of you help me to understand how I am going to be able to remember?" One child piped up, "READ THE INSTRUCTIONS, SILLY!" Rebecca chuckled in response. "Oh yes, that is a good idea. But I'm not sure I am going to remember all this information." The same child replied, "Let's make a poster of the rules of the camera and how to take videos. That will make sure everybody will remember." "I think that will really help everyone, Child A. Would you like to prepare this, Child A?" asked Rebecca. "Yeah," responded Child A. Over the next three days, Child A recruited his father to video record him talking about how to hold the camera in different positions and where to store the camera. He also asked another boy in the classroom to help him to print photos of his video to put on a poster board. Rebecca and Enoch ensured that Child A had the materials he needed when required.

Child A soon completed the project and selected where to place the poster, as well as where and how to store the camera. Quickly, Child A became the "expert" in camera care and video recording as other children consulted with him about the new video they had on their classroom computer. As each child played his video, Child A would stop it at different points to ensure that his peer was imitating exactly what he was showing on the video. As Enoch sat down with Child A and his father to reflect upon Child A's experience, he learned just how significant this opportunity was. Child A's father discussed how touched he was that the educators in the room trusted his son to put this together, something he was not used to experiencing. Child A's eyes widened and he smiled. Enoch said, "Child A, we were very fortunate to have your help. In what ways have you been the teacher in helping our

(continued)

class?" As the conversation continued, Child A elaborated for 15 minutes on all the ways it would help others and how he would continue to be of assistance in the room. It was at that moment that the image of this child and the relationship he had with this child changed for Enoch. Given the opportunity, Child A had become the educator, the researcher, the documenter, and the inspiration for new ways of knowing and learning.

Source: Kristine Fenning.

own knowledge by using video recording as a process to capture what they know and understand. He also learns how video can be used as a way to communicate children's learning to others, as well to reflect upon and assess what they don't know and want to learn more about. These new insights serve to support his understanding of how children learn. The multi-purpose application and format of video recording is further reflected in Bullard's (2010) ideas and his reference to the video recording of George Forman:

> George Forman has labelled video recording "a tool of the mind" (1999), an aid for reflection for both teachers and children. It is easier for children to consider their thinking when they are not also engaged in the action. As children watch themselves participating in different interactions and then reflect upon them, they might also see the incident from another child's point of view. Once used only to record special events in the classroom, video cameras are now small enough and affordable enough to be used to document everyday events. Video cameras with foldout screens allow children to watch their activities immediately after they happen and to discuss them with a teacher. (p. 296)

Video capture, of course, is not limited to video cameras. Many centres are now using tablets, iPads, or smartphones to capture video footage as a result of their portability and multi-purpose usage. Video recordings, then, have two very distinct and important elements: they combine the visual aspects of photos with audio recordings. In early childhood settings, video recordings can enrich learning and awareness for all involved—from parents to educators to children.

Video recording can serve a number of functions, including but not limited to the following:

- *Educator self-awareness.* Educators constantly analyze their interactions, relationships, and all aspects of their practice. Video is viewed as a powerful tool to support educator learning because of its unique capability to capture the elusive classroom practice for later study (Borko et al., 2008, cited in Zhang, Lundeberg, & Eberhardt, 2010). Video recordings allow educator-researchers to replay classroom events and notice aspects of classroom situations that they are too busy to notice during the act of teaching; as a teacher-participant said, "You see things that you don't realize in the heat of teaching" (Zhang et al., 2010, p. 3).

- *Curriculum planning and implementation.* Video captures a large volume of information regarding children's interests, where they prefer to play and with whom, their engagement in each aspect of the learning environment, and the interactions that took place, among many other elements. This information could be used to inform future planning; to prompt discussion between educators, children, and families regarding planning; and to enhance educators' abilities to meet the needs of the children.

- *Environmental design.* Video recording enables the examination of different elements of the physical environment and the possible influences on children's behaviour and actions. This would include everything from the availability and accessibility of equipment and furniture to items on the wall, levels of natural light, and developmentally or culturally relevant materials.

- *Modifications and adaptations.* Monitoring of modifications and adaptations helps ensure that they are effective and appropriate. This video-recorded information could help outside professionals who are supporting a particular child or group of children or the educator and family who are looking at ways to scaffold children's learning, therefore recognizing each child's individuality.

- *Children's self-assessment and connectedness to the world.* As in Enoch's experiences with his group of children, videotaping can be used by children to inquire, reflect upon, or demonstrate their learning.

> Video will more likely capture how the child deals with and solves problems in real time; the decisions, false starts, corrections, and clever strategies that exemplify the child's intelligence in action, as opposed to a simple check list for what the child can or cannot do. Such an orientation to the child will improve the teacher's ability to enter the child's mental world, support the child's thinking, provide constructive provocations, and raise the child's consciousness of his or her current assumptions about how the social and physical world works. (Forman, 2010, p. 32)

It is an authentic approach for children and students to embrace, share, and connect their knowledge, feelings, and emotions not only to their own learning experiences but also to the learning experiences of others within their own classroom or anywhere in the world. Using video technology as a platform to express one's connections to learning can be a very affirming and positive experience.

- *Educator–parent interviews and developmental monitoring.* Videos can be used to record special events or brief clips of children at play to share with parents. During parent meetings or parent get-togethers, videos can provide an amazing provocation for dialogue about the importance of play, child-initiated thinking and exploration, mastery, attachment, language, and independence, for example. By watching the video, parents are able to appreciate and become a part of their child's day, which may have been invisible to them before for various reasons. Setting aside time for parents, educators, and children to view video clips together encourages communication and can be an interesting starting point for dialogue. The immediacy of a video recording available on an iPad, digital photo frame, or computer helps those watching to see firsthand and respond spontaneously. Parents who may not feel comfortable sitting with an educator at a desk with written communication might find viewing a clip of their child at play with an educator a more comfortable experience. In some centres, Internet video streaming with remote access by password is also a viable option for families wishing to see their child in action within their classroom without having to be physically present with their child.

- *Digital portfolio documentation.* To further enhance the discussion between parents and educators, videos have the capacity to document electronically a child's developmental journey and variations in development. Videos might also demonstrate important achievements or experiences worth capturing, skills yet to be obtained, children demonstrating their own learning and understanding, or children expressing their creativity in some way (see Learning Stories on p. 179 for examples of digital portfolio documentation programs and apps).

FORMAT OF VIDEO DOCUMENTATION

At first, it might seem unnecessary to discuss the format of video documentation when traditionally, the format of videos has simply entailed watching a "movie" of a memorable event or experience in video form, captured on DVD. While this may be one way of viewing video, it is limited in its scope when applied to early childhood education and pedagogical practice. The multi-purpose, unique features of video have resulted in a transformation of formats, viewing capabilities, and pedagogical applications of this methodology.

Depending on the video app, site, or program used to format video footage, video can be transferred to MP3 or MP4 formats on USBs, SD cards, or chips for portability and viewing on laptops, tablets, and iPads. They can be formatted and zipped for easy uploading or downloading onto password-protected websites for virtual viewing.

Understanding that this methodology has the capability to be mass distributed or shared with more people than just the child and family, it is important to revisit and reflect upon the confidentiality and ethical implications associated with visible documentation outlined in earlier chapters. Prior to using this video methodology, it is imperative that educators think about "ethics and what it means for children and adults to produce pedagogical documentation, particularly visual technology" (Lindgren, 2012, p. 338). Video recording or any electronic transmission of documentation through formats such as social media (Twitter, Pinterest, Instagram, or Facebook, for example) requires a separate and distinct permission form, stating exactly where and how the videos will be used and accessed, to be signed by a child's parents or guardians. Examples of ethical considerations and questions, as well as a special permissions letter for video recording, are available online.

As with the other methodologies in this chapter, it is important for the observer to interpret and reflect on video documentation. Interpretations can be prepared in the same format as interpretations for anecdotal observations, or they may be as simple as capturing word for word the verbal interpretations being made of the video by the child and/or the parent and educator. Interpretations can be captured via hard copy in a child's portfolio or file, or they can be filed electronically in a child's digital portfolio. The knowledge gained from this interpretation process can then be used for further inquiry, curriculum planning, or a multitude of other purposes.

VIDEO RECORDING WITH A SPECIFIC PURPOSE: SOCIOEMOTIONAL DEVELOPMENT

The area of socioemotional development in young children has been highlighted in current literature, along with other topics, such as redefining diversity, special needs, resiliency training, health and development, and brain research. This is not to say that the social and emotional development of children is a new topic but, rather, that it is new in light of the changes in families, the reordering of social structures, advances in technology, changes in social communication strategies, stresses upon children and families, and socioeconomic factors. These effects and many other variables require educators to challenge themselves to re-evaluate their perspectives, strategies, and curricula in order to support all children effectively. A primary example of the use of video with socioemotional context can be found in the article "Show Me Again What I Can Do: Documentation and Self-Determination for Students with Social Challenges" (Cox-Suárez, 2010). This article speaks to the use of video documentation by educators who are assisting children in Grade 7 who were diagnosed with pervasive developmental disorder to self-assess themselves in social interactions. Their purpose and intent was to assist the children to use their reflections and conversations regarding the video footage to further grasp the strengths of social strategies they were using, as well as to think of other ways in which they might invite a friend to play or respond appropriately to social conversations, among other things. One child, named Johnny, "grew to depend on these visual images as a visual reminder of his abilities particularly when he felt too frustrated to continue on any given day" (Cox-Suárez, 2010, p. 26).

This video was also transformed into video **social stories** that Johnny could revisit frequently to independently self-regulate and build his self-confidence. Video in this particular circumstance also enabled the educator to do some self-inquiry and reflection, resulting in better strategies that she and other educators and support staff could use to assist Johnny and other children within their classroom.

As researchers, psychologists, and educators research and discuss socioemotional development, it is no wonder that they have used video in early childhood to learn more about the importance of social relationships and to understand the role of play in the child's social development. There is no doubt that using this methodology can assist us in learning about the complexities of social expectations and circumstances for any child or individual.

IS VIDEO RECORDING AN EFFECTIVE METHOD?

When video recording, there is a planning process: decisions have to be made in terms of ethics and use, purpose of use, time, cost, resources, responsibility, and management. The technical aspects of obtaining and setting up apps or video-editing programs, as well as the actual editing, maintenance, repair, and storage of any mechanical or electronic media, can be an involved process if this is a new experience. Once understood and mastered, however, video capture and downloading can be quite quick, efficient, and easily accessible for viewing, interpreting, and application.

As with every method of observation, evaluating whether or not this is the most effective method for the purpose or event is a major consideration. The information from this type of documentation must still be interpreted, reflected upon, and compiled with other information. (Using media-assisted documentation does not mean that the educator escapes his or her responsibility for interpreting and communicating that information.) When video is used meaningfully, the outcome can be quite positive, profound, and transformative for all involved.

To learn more about the advantages and disadvantages of using video documentation, consult the chart in MindTap.

LEARNING STORIES

Learning Stories, originally created by Dr. Margaret Carr and colleagues in New Zealand, continue to gain momentum and recognition in Europe and North America as a pedagogical narrative approach that documents how children learn, as well as the individuality of children as competent and curious learners. Dr. Carr initiated her research in 1998 with a group of early years teachers to determine the effectiveness of an "assessment story approach" as part of the New Zealand curriculum. These teachers "storied" their observations on paper, as digital technology was not yet available and computers were not readily accessible to most teachers. It was this research and the addition of many new articles and books on the topic of learning stories that led Dr. Carr's research to become popularized around the world. Her leadership in this area has led to the examination of this method as a way to engage and reflect upon the perspectives, voices, cultures, and languages of children, their families, and educators within their communities.

Learning stories are the most malleable of all of the methods discussed in Chapters 4 and 5, as their narrative feature can accompany many different types of observational methodologies to make children's learning visible. Rooted in sociocultural theory, this particular methodology challenges the traditional developmental approach to documenting only developmental achievement or non-achievement.

> A situated/socio-cultural viewpoint looks at knowledge and learning not primarily in terms of representation in the head, although there is no need to deny that such representations exist and play an important role. Rather, it looks at knowledge and learning in terms of a relationship between an individual with both a mind and a body and an environment in which the individual thinks, feels and interacts. (Carr & Lee, 2012, p. 5)

As stated in Exhibit 4.17, this theory proposes that children are to be viewed as beings connected to culture (self and societal), to family, and to their diverse communities (child care, family, friends, where they live and play, etc.). Some of the many forms this methodology may take within a child's portfolio might include narratives that accompany artwork, photos, work samples, interview notes, videos, and documented conversations. Like other methods, this methodology is not setting-dependent, as it lends itself to many types of philosophies and curriculum

"Many educators, policy makers, and program consultants working in Indigenous communities suggest that many mainstream assessment tools are culturally inappropriate, meaning that elements in the testing, including both the instruments and the processes, do not make sense to the person being tested because, for example, the language or pictures used are not familiar or have meanings inconsistent with local knowledge (Rowan, 2010b). In Nunavik, where 90% of children speak Inuttitut (Duhaime, 2008), an assessment tool in English or French is unsuitable because these languages are not the language of the children and families in the community. In Nunavik images of farm animals and city buses are out of place—they are unfamiliar and therefore not recommended for use with young Inuit children for assessment purposes (Rowan 2010b)....

... Pedagogical documentation, or learning stories, supports practices of communication, reflection, and action, thus it holds great potential to contribute to the development of stronger, fairer, more just relationships among families and communities in Nunavik."

Source: Rowan, C. Thesis document, University of Victoria. pp. 19–23 retrieved from https://dspace.library.uvic.ca/bitstream/handle/1828/3483/Rowan_Marycaroline_2011-1.pdf?sequence=1)

frameworks, including Reggio Emilia, Emergent, Maori, *Te Whariki*, the Ontario Early Learning Framework, and approaches based upon appreciative inquiry, responsiveness, and inclusiveness.

How might the learning story in Exhibit 4.18 inform curriculum for Ethan? How might this be used as a portfolio entry? What has been learned from this information? How might his family be further involved in this experience and new learning?

PURPOSE AND UNIQUE FEATURE

Although written, interpreted, and formatted somewhat differently around the world, learning stories are a unique story narrative approach that combines a number of traditional elements, including observation, interpretation/reflection, analysis, and a responsive plan or next steps. Some may argue that learning stories have prompted a paradigm shift from the traditional anecdotal style of observation to a forward-thinking, pedagogically sound way of documenting, capturing a moment in time, and making learning visible. There are a number of elements

EXHIBIT 4.18 **ETHAN'S NEW PURPOSE FOR OUR DUMP TRUCKS**

Exploring a New Purpose with Our Dump Trucks

Yesterday Ethan had been talking about the dump trucks that kept passing by our playground to dump sand into our new nature playground being built. When he came into the classroom, he immediately went to the bin of toy trucks and was pushing them along on the shelves in the room going "vroom, vroom."

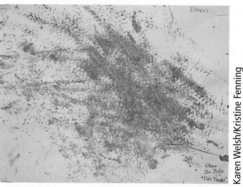

Painting at the easel soon caught his eye, and he sauntered over to the easel with a truck in each hand and began to put the wheels of the truck into the paint, and then in broad side-to-side and diagonal strokes he made these patterns on his paper. His eyes widened, he displayed a huge smile, and he inspired his peers to come over after him to try this new experience!

<u>**Ethan's Interpretation**</u>: "I went up and all around with the truck. I 'maded' these tracks and put the colours like that. Daddy's four-wheeler makes tracks in the mud just like that."

<u>**Parent Reflection**</u>: "Ethan loves mud exploding all over his back when we go through the mud puddles. I can tell he was trying to recreate our recent trip to Algonquin Park here in his picture. We will have to put this picture alongside the photo of us covered in mud!"

Source: Kristine Fenning.

that differentiate traditional documentation from learning stories. Exhibit 4.18 is a primary example of how

> Learning Stories offer a thoughtful and reflective window into a child or children's learning as this learning happens and how these stories attempt to describe unique experiences or moments that cause teachers to pause, wonder or consider a particular event. At their best, Learning Stories inform future curriculum paths and directions, serve as assessment in children's portfolios, develop into invitational and engaging democratic documentation, are gathered into classroom journals and can be quickly reformatted to email to families as a newsletter. (Kashin & Jupp, 2013, "So What Is a Learning Story?" para. 1)

Exhibit 4.18 and other examples online also showcase the structure of a common learning story. The learning story models in a very visible way the appreciative inquiry process and strengths-based approach, as well as its ability to capture the context of the experience. "Children's voices … are included … in the creation of their own narrative accounts, using visual elements and a variety of textual forms, and communicating within a framework of active listening, inviting children to be skillful communicators, rights holders, and meaning makers (Clark et al., 2011, p. 6)" (Burke, 2012, p. 6). A learning story presents a framework in which the child, parent, educator, and community function as co-educators and co-learners, each playing a role in questioning, prompting, dialoguing, wondering, and scaffolding new learning for the other. Through a sociocultural lens, learning stories enable children to revisit real events, memories, theories they have tried, problems they have solved or are facing, social relationships, contexts, and situations. In doing this, children are more apt to experience feelings of mastery, achievement, pride, and confidence; generate new cultural and community identities and knowledge; and build upon their language and relationships.

FORMAT OF THE LEARNING STORY NARRATIVE

How we document a learning story is influenced not only by our philosophy of teaching and learning, but also by the views we have of a child or children. When we take the time to reflect upon our image of each child as a unique individual with her or his own strengths, talents, abilities, interests, and rights, we are more apt to practise the appreciative inquiry approach and wonder how we might capture that individuality and that child's "story" in a thoughtful, positive, responsive, and inclusive way. Learning stories can be visually portrayed in a variety of ways, such as in traditional hard-copy printed photos and accompanying narratives; through documentation panels on walls; in storybooks prepared by children narrating their own learning journeys; in blogs, tweets, or video vines (footage of 15 seconds or less); and on **webbing** boards/visual mapping boards outlining photos and narratives scripted by educators, children, and families. The flexibility and open-ended nature of this "storied" approach also allows for multiple interpretations of the same story and, in fact, invites other perspectives to interpret what took place.

Common elements to consider when writing a learning story include the considerations that follow.

SECTION ONE: CAPTURING AND DEVELOPING THE STORY

- The story is written in the child's home language or language of choice, recognizing that the main audience of the story is the child.
- Characters of the story are identified, including who is being storied, as well as the context of the situation or event.

- What took place in the story is narrated, including the thoughts, feelings, and conversations/language heard. Unlike anecdotal records, where additional details allow the reader to re-enact the actions of the observed, learning stories do not capture every single detail.
- Stories may take place in one moment or over several days or months. This includes the option of one or more photos to communicate the story that unfolded as well as subsequent stories that follow as a result of the initial learning story.
- First-person narration is permitted to reflect the perspective of the person telling the story.
- Stories are also told by the child—allowing for the child's voice.

SECTION TWO: REFLECTING UPON AND INTERPRETING THE LEARNING THAT TOOK PLACE

- This section follows the learning story. This portion not only interprets the learning that took place, but also links the learning to curriculum frameworks or learning outcomes used or practised by the setting/observer.
- This section should include an area that invites interpretations and perspectives of others, including the child, parent, and educator.

SECTION THREE: DISCUSSING NEXT STEPS, FUTURE OPPORTUNITIES, AND EXTENSIONS OF LEARNING

- This section discusses how the learning might be extended or scaffolded to lead to other opportunities for learning.
- This section should also have an area to invite the interpretations and perspectives of others, including the child, parent, and educator.

For more information or examples that explore and present templates for learning stories, please visit websites such as the Aussie Childcare Network, Pinterest, and Technology Rich Inquiry Based Research.

As identified above in the structure of a learning story, the style and expectations of learning story narrative writing and forming interpretations/reflections are quite different from those of other observational methods. Less structured and more "storied" in approach, in learning stories the interpretations and reflections of the observer are included in the narrative simultaneously at the time of recording, contrary to the discussion in Chapter 3 of how interpretations are formed and written. In methods such as anecdotal observations, running records, ABC analysis, and others, interpretations are separated from the observation to heighten objectivity, they are written following the observation, and they use language that poses what skills, knowledge, and behaviour might be visible in a particular observation. Learning stories, however, invite outside perspectives of the child, family, or educator to comment on the learning story in an interpretive way. Exhibit 4.18 also illustrates these qualities. It is in that exhibit that the child interprets his own experience in the photo of the artwork and presents it to his parent, who has a complementary yet entirely different perspective on what was being communicated through the artwork. What are the implications for documenting children's learning if the perspective of the observer is included in the observation? Take a moment to reflect upon the pros and cons of the methods of observation. Is one approach more ethical than another? For whom is each more ethical—child, educator, or parent?

Certainly a goal of being an effective educator is to ensure objectivity and ethics in our observations and documentation. These can exist within the learning story approach, as observers can employ a number of the strategies discussed in Chapter 3 to keep observations and interpretations objective. Remember, there is no method that is fully objective—all methods require interpretation at some level and as such are subjective in their approach. It is again important to think about how the child or children have been involved in documenting their experience or event and whether they have been consulted to provide approval for documentation of their learning. Involving the children helps them to develop an awareness of how they learn.

For ideas and strategies concerning how to ensure as much objectivity as possible in your learning story narratives, be sure to revisit the discussions in previous chapters as well as to employ the strategies outlined in Exhibit 4.19.

EXHIBIT 4.19	PROMOTING OBJECTIVITY IN LEARNING STORIES

- Continue to use "it seems" and "it appears" to communicate to the reader of the narrative that this is one perspective on what is seen (in the photo, video, art sample, etc.) and is not necessarily the perspective of all who view the documentation.
- Use evidence from the observation to support the narration: "It seemed you were really proud of the cupcake you made today as you were clapping your hands, smiling, and showing your cupcake to all your friends."
- Co-author the learning story with the child, parent, or other educator who saw the experience or event take place.
- Try to avoid using words such as "good," "great," and "wonderful" to qualify level of achievement or demonstration of skill, as they run the risk of implying that a child has

mastered a skill or a set of skills based on only one demonstration or little evidence. Avoiding these terms does not imply that a child is not these qualities; it merely implies that mastery is evident with repeated demonstration of a skill and that discussion with all co-educators and co-learners (child, family, and educator) about all the knowledge and skills evident or demonstrated over time within a domain is important for accuracy in drawing conclusions.

- Pull the knowledge and skills demonstrated within the learning story and place them into a **profile** within a child's portfolio to build evidence of a child's learning over time for discussion within the team.

What other strategies can you think of?

Take some time to review the online examples that compare and illustrate objectivity, ethics, and different styles and formats of the learning story approach. Some styles more than others may reflect your philosophy or setting.

TECHNOLOGY-ENABLED LEARNING STORY FORMATS

Technology devices and availability of these devices within the early childhood setting have enabled opportunities for learning stories to be created digitally. According to Carr and Lee (2012),

> Digital story-telling by young adults has provided eloquent reflections of the views of self that the teller wishes to tell, and for the very young, the ease of digital photography has provided new ways of contributing to their own assessments; taking their own photographs, being able to "read" assessments, and setting up visual cues for remembering after the event. The new information communication technologies enable Learning Stories to document both vividly and quickly the range of multimodal pathways and affordance networks that have always characterised the early childhood educational environments. Photographs and DVDs capture drawing, painting, three-dimensional constructions, gesture, drama, movement, digital imagery, often in progress. A number of Learning Stories are developed from DVDs, and a number of stories are DVDs. (p. 36)

For these reasons and others, many centres are choosing to digitize their learning stories for remote and in-centre access to learning stories. Parents, educators, and children would all have access and the convenience of uploading new stories or commenting on older ones when at home or at the centre. The interactive and responsive nature of this approach would promote real-time discussions of children's learning as it occurs, and could lead to co-development of responsive curriculum and planning to further support the interests and development of children. Observers who are considering any type of electronic documentation must remember that observation permissions need to be obtained separately from hard-copy permissions because of its accessibility.

Observers who are keen to document learning stories directly on their computer can access various e-portfolio sites (discussed in Chapter 6) or other learning story programs such as Storypark, Educa, and Kinderloop, all of which are protected and accessible by families to add documentation as well. Note that password protection is very important for digital and technology devices when saving photo and digital media. In addition to the passwords on the app sites, think about password protection for opening the devices being used for documentation as an extra protective feature. Storypark lends itself to a more open-ended learning story approach that is not defined by a particular framework or curriculum. It also allows the creator to add learning tags reflecting the Ontario Early Learning Framework to uploaded stories. Educa is more specific to the New Zealand curriculum framework yet is adaptable to fit other approaches as well. Kinderloop also allows educators to post digital observations for parent access to updates of their child's day and experiences. What other apps or websites can you find? For further examination of apps and their use in practice with young children and the role of the early childhood educator, be sure to visit Chapter 6.

To learn more about the advantages and disadvantages of using learning stories, consult the chart in MindTap.

SUMMARY

This chapter introduced a number of pedagogically sound observational methodologies with different purposes and structures, all of which could be used by any educator in any classroom or location around the world. Evident in the purpose and unique features for each method was the importance of observers understanding the intent of each method prior to engaging in the process.

The open-ended and flexible nature of many methodologies in this chapter enables the recording of unanticipated and spontaneous actions and behaviours of young children as they investigate, wonder, and test their theories about their world. To maintain quality in our observations, in each methodology the observer is expected to practise an appreciative inquiry approach, seeing the image of the child as capable and knowledgeable. Exhibits within this chapter demonstrated this approach, and emphasized the important role that educators play in preparing quality pedagogical documentation. For each method, the observer engages in all stages of the observation cycle as she or he observes, documents, interprets, and reflects upon what was seen and heard so as to give meaning to the information gained. Providing opportunities for discussion and other interpretations of observations is a necessary step in this process to aid our understanding of how to be responsive and inclusive in our observations of children and in our application of the new knowledge gained. We will explore this idea further in later chapters as each methodology holds value and significance to our understanding of each and every child.

CHAPTER 5

OBSERVING AND RECORDING TARGETED BEHAVIOURS

MNStudio/Shutterstock.com

Three-year-old Sonja comes to school neatly dressed. She complies with her educator's requests. She displays manners by saying please, thank you, and excuse me if she wants to interrupt her peers or educators. As shown in the photo above, it seems she usually engages in solitary play, but when the educators in her classroom think about Sonja at the end of the day, it is hard for them to recall what she did the entire day!

Children like Sonja are not always noticed because they are independent and self-reliant. They can go through the day without drawing attention to themselves. Children who are shy, reserved, or content with their own company can be overlooked in a lively classroom of young children.

Systematic, purposeful observation helps ensure that no child is overlooked. If an educator had completed a **participation chart** on all the children in her group, she would have included Sonja and learned more about this quiet child. Educators may have learned where Sonja spent her time each day by using a participation chart such as the one displayed below.

EXHIBIT 5.1	PARTICIPATION CHART

Name: Sonja   **DOB:** July 3, 2012   **Age:** 3

Observer: Afton   **Date:** _____

Learning Centres	Monday	Tuesday	Wednesday	Thursday	Friday
Dramatic centre	✓✓✓	✓✓✓✓	✓✓	✓✓✓	✓✓
Listening centre	✓✓✓	✓✓✓✓	✓	✓✓	✓
Creative area	✓	✓	✓✓✓✓✓	✓✓✓	✓✓✓
Projects area	✓	✓✓	✓✓	✓	✓✓
Construction centre		✓	✓		
Interest centre	✓✓	✓✓✓	✓✓	✓✓✓	✓✓

This chart provides an at-a-glance visual of the learning centres Sonja frequented. Looking at the learning centres and check marks from Monday to Friday, what were the centres most frequented? What does that tell us about Sonja? How would this information be helpful in discussing with her family what she seems to enjoy in the playroom? Questions like these arise when we observe and reflect. How does this inquiry-based practice based on information from the participation chart inform curriculum planning for Sonja? What provocations or invitations might the observer prepare for her?

OVERVIEW

Chapter 4 used the analogy of the fishnet cast out to sea "catching" information and experiences through documentation. Those narrative methods are "open-weave" and represent an open-ended method of recording observations of unanticipated behaviours. Not surprisingly, closed methods are used to document preselected behaviours, contextual factors, use of the environment, or social dynamics, to name a few. This chapter groups together a second broad category of observational tools preselected by the observer that may be used to record a variety of "targeted" aspects within an early learning environment, as well as targeted behaviours exhibited by a child or group of children.

The featured types of records discussed in this chapter are

- checklists
- rating scales
- behavioural tallying and charting
- participation charts
- profiles
- pictorial representations
- sociograms and ecomaps
- mapping

These types of records do not have the storytelling characteristics of the narrative but, rather, are precise, brief descriptions that are easily recorded as single words, diagrams, marks, codes, or point-form notes. These closed methods are specially designed to encompass the "I wonder why or how …" inquiry approach, thus enabling the observer to catch and reflect upon specific information.

The kinds of observation and documentation tools used in Chapter 5 are different from those presented in Chapter 4 in yet another way. The narratives in Chapter 4 captured the moment with no specific form or diagram to organize, design, and implement. The methods of observation in this chapter require considerable reflection and preparation before the observation begins. Using the methods of documentation in Chapter 5 requires organizing and conceptualizing the format, essentially designing it to reflect the reasons for the observations.

As we reflect back to the cycle of observation introduced in Chapter 2, it is easy to see the connection these closed methods have to the cycle and the appreciative

FOCUS QUESTIONS

1. In what ways might each observational tool be adapted or used to inquire about children or aspects of your practice?
2. Describe how the purpose and design of these methods differ from those of the methods discussed in Chapter 4.
3. How could all the methods described in this chapter be used to create or fit into a cycle of observation?
4. What are some basic questions educators might ask when selecting a particular type of record described in this chapter?

inquiry approach. Using appreciative inquiry in the application, implementation, and reflection components of these methodologies assists educators to participate as co-inquirers, to query and understand the behaviours/skills/events seen, and then respond to their findings in a supportive and inclusive way. As you reflect upon each methodology, think about their relationship to pedagogical documentation. How might we involve everyone in the process?

MAKING DECISIONS

Once the purpose for the observation has been established, there are many other decisions to be made to ensure you are gathering the information you need. The questions below highlight some of the possible queries and decisions to consider:

- How might we determine the behaviours to observe?
- In what ways can we define those behaviours clearly and in such a way that anyone using the form will have the same understanding of what those behaviours are?
- How might we decide, if applicable, which symbols to use: numbers, check marks, or specific descriptors?
- How would the observer consider the diversity of the group: age ranges, children who require supports, personalities, and social dynamics?
- In what ways could we consider environmental factors that influence how children act, including space, equipment, and materials?
- In what ways could we design our methods to gather contextual information to assist in understanding the behaviours and skills seen?
- How might we involve our team (including the family) in the inquiry, design, and implementation aspects of the observational process?

WHAT COULD BE OTHER CONSIDERATIONS?

Making choices about which descriptors to use or how to ascribe certain symbols to represent some kind of evaluation is a complex task. Even defining the behaviour to be targeted and monitored is a challenge. For example, if "sharing" is the targeted behaviour, educators may interpret sharing in a variety of ways. Some educators may refer to sharing in relation to toys, whereas others consider the sharing of space, ideas, or friends to be more relevant. If the educators have different ideas about what kinds of sharing are important to observe and record, then the information they collect will not be consistent. Furthermore, determining how the observation will take place and how each member of the team will contribute observations to form a holistic response to the information learned is a necessary conversation to have prior to observing. Reflecting upon what we learn from a variety of perspectives promotes validity and accuracy of our interpretations and reflections of what is seen and heard and therefore results in a more appropriate response.

FREQUENCY VERSUS DURATION

Before examining the types of records in this chapter, there needs to be a discussion about the concepts of "frequency" and "duration." These concepts are totally relevant to understanding what is meant by choosing behaviours for charts, checklists, maps, or rating scales that are easily identifiable, requiring the least amount of interpretation.

Recording frequency, or the number of times something happens, relies on behaviour or factors that are stated in well-defined terms. The preselected behaviour must be a discrete unit and sharply defined to minimize subjective interpretations. Some examples of behaviours that are easily observed are "kicks ball," "folds paper," "draws a circle," and "removes shoes." Each of these samples is a distinct behaviour, and its frequency of occurrence can be recorded with ease. See Exhibit 5.2 for examples.

Duration refers to how long the behaviour occurred. Duration refers to how long it took a child to put away his toys, complete a project, or eat lunch. The purpose of observing and recording duration may be quite different from the purpose of observing frequency. See Exhibit 5.2 for examples.

EXHIBIT 5.2	EXAMPLES: FREQUENCY AND DURATION
Examples of Frequency Behaviours	**Examples of Duration Behaviours**
throwing ball	wandering
printing name	crying
hitting	gazing
zipping up jacket	painting
Source: Courtesy of Sally Wylie.	

Recording duration is effective for the types of behaviours that do not appear to have definite boundaries. These behaviours occur over a varying amount of time and are complex, encompassing other behaviours. For example, while Joseph is painting, he is watching other children, scratching his nose, and wriggling; during small-group time, even though Muriel is sitting, she is talking, tickling her neighbour, and leaning from side to side.

Frequency behaviours are those discrete, self-contained behaviours with a beginning, a middle, and an end. When they are observed, they can be checked off. Duration behaviours are complex, occur over a period of time from minutes to hours, and include subsets of behaviours. The following are examples of an observed behaviour with subsets:

- "wanders around the room at the end of playroom time"
- "plays cooperatively with peers"
- "communicates with her peers"

For ease of observing and recording, these examples could be separated into more distinct subsets of targeted behaviours such as those in Exhibit 5.3.

EXHIBIT 5.3	EXAMPLES OF SUBSETS OF BEHAVIOURS
Wanders around the room at the end of playroom time	Takes books off shelf and puts them back, pulls toys out of container and walks away, asks what time it is
Plays cooperatively with peers	Gets blocks for peers, tells friend the plans for the fort, listens to peers
Communicates with peers	Asks questions, listens, smiles, yells, cries, hits, hugs, laughs

Examining the concepts of frequency and duration help educators in understanding what behaviours they actually want to observe and record. Do you want to document how many times Mattie and Christy argue during the day or how long the behaviour lasts? What is the significance of this behaviour? Reflecting on the focus of your questions or the purpose of your observations is at the heart of appreciative inquiry.

By taking time to reflect and observe, we can be proactive, responsive educators who understand and support each child. Investigating new methodologies supports our inquiry-based practice and helps to ensure we are using the most effective methods in our observations. Observation, inquiry, and reflection form the cycle of observation.

DESIGNING AN OBSERVATIONAL TOOL

Considering the complexity of designing types of records, it is not hard to understand why commercially produced observational tools, such as checklists or rating scales, are popular. Developing an observational tool is a lengthy process involving

- a defined purpose and vision of outcomes
- effective communication among team members
- research

- an educated application of child development knowledge
- previous knowledge or experience concerning what constitutes quality in early learning environments
- strategies for monitoring the process
- careful reflection of both the process and the outcomes.

This thoughtful process is supported by the cycle of observation depicted in Exhibit 2.5 on page 52. Active reflection occurs throughout the cycle as it systematically engages educators, families, and children in inquiry-based thinking. Observation is supported through reflection and inquiry-based practice, and further observation emerges from those discussions regarding why, who, and how, thus creating the cycle.

Through ongoing dialogue and reflection using an appreciative inquiry approach, educators are able to choose the observational tool most suited to their purpose and most appropriate for their children and families. Each of the records in this chapter will provide opportunities for educators to discover valuable information and respond meaningfully.

CHECKLISTS

PURPOSE AND UNIQUE FEATURE

The checklist is the most fundamental of the recording methods discussed in this chapter and a good place to start. In its most basic form, the checklist is used to record the presence (yes) or absence (no) of what is observed. Checklists are a useful tool in recording distinct, preselected, targeted behaviours or elements of the environment or relationships that influence people. The unique feature of the checklist is that it is formatted to allow for easy recording of achieved outcomes.

Checklists are used so routinely to gather information in our everyday lives that they are already very familiar to us. We are often asked to respond to a questionnaire, as anyone who has strolled through a mall or been interrupted by a telephone survey will attest. Does this sound familiar? "Hi, I'm calling on behalf of the XYZ Association. Would you mind taking a few minutes of your time to answer yes or no to the following questions?" Organizations that use checklists are aware that people are busy, and they use this method in order to gather as much information as possible in the least amount of time. In addition to the checklists examined within this chapter, other predefined standardized checklists may be found in Chapter 7.

FORMAT OF CHECKLISTS

The format of a checklist begins with basic but relevant information such as child's name, date of birth, and age; the name of the observer; and the date of observation. A checklist should also contain the same essential information if specific to a child or group of children. Checklists are not specific to the behaviour of children; they can be used for assessing the environment or as indicators of relationships connecting educators and families. Gathering input from all team members in the design of the checklist can assist in ensuring that the content within is both culturally relevant and respectful of the population being observed, and allows for the capturing of variations in development.

In a checklist, columns of data are listed in a grid: one column lists the behaviours that are to be observed, followed by separate columns for "yes" and "no." The speech and language checklist in Exhibit 5.4 is an example of a simple checklist format to be used with children. In this exhibit, the team of preschool educators began a checklist to ascertain the speech and language skills of a new child starting in their room. What other skills might you add to this checklist to reflect the preschool age range? An infant age range? How might you ensure the expectations or skills you are looking for are appropriate? How might your checklist be adapted so that it might be used with a group of children?

EXHIBIT 5.4	SPEECH AND LANGUAGE CHECKLIST

Child's Name: _____ DOB: _____ Age: _____

Observer(s): _____ Date(s): _____

Item	Yes	No
1. Defines simple words		
2. Follows a two-step direction		
3. Describes similarities and differences in objects		
4. Uses contractions (can't/don't)		
5. Uses plurals other than by adding "s"		

Comments and Examples

_____

_____

Source: Courtesy of Sally Wylie.

Columns using a check mark indicating the presence or absence of a behaviour can also be organized by using an alternative coding scheme. Educators have used coloured stickers instead of check marks to indicate skills; for example, yellow means "yes," green is "emerging," and red is "not evident." Instead of yes or no, educators may wish to accommodate degrees of skill acquisition by using abbreviations such as in the following examples:

NE	Not Evident
Em	Emerging
WO	Working On
Es	Established
NO	No Opportunity
NA	Not Applicable

Why the variations? Some behaviours do not always lend themselves to a yes/no answer. Depending on the circumstances of the day, the environment, or feelings of the child, the documentation of observed behaviours may not be accurately described as yes/no but rather, for example, "Amber is working on …" or "We notice that Veejay sometimes demonstrates self-feeding, but other times waits for an adult to feed him." Recording variations allows parents to see that their child shows the same pattern of inconsistent behaviour at the early childhood setting as at home. Discussing with parents the outcomes of the checklist documentation that shows varying degrees of skill acquisition provides yet another opportunity to share information.

Using other abbreviations when discussing outcomes also gives educators a chance to explain what they are and why they are used. NO means "No Opportunity," which could mean a variety of things: the child was home for those days or for those days educators did not have the opportunity to observe. NA means "Not Applicable," which means that the item or section is not applicable for a particular child. For example, if a child with cerebral palsy had yet to "walk backward for 2 metres," adding an "NA" would mean that it was not applicable or appropriate to consider this item for that child. What if the child in this circumstance was beginning to walk backward? What abbreviation would be used then?

Further examples that might relate to environmental checklists may use qualifiers such as "Does Not Meet Expectations" to indicate no evidence of inclusive planning that reflects children's interests and development or perhaps poor quality of planning. "Meets or Exceeds Expectations" suggests that there is either evidence of planning that satisfactorily reflects the interests and development of individual children within the group or that creativity and care were taken to develop experiences for the children that reflect a responsive and inclusive approach to planning. These types of abbreviations, plus comments and examples, help educators not only to communicate a child's current level of functioning or the ability of an environment to stimulate learning for children, but also to explain how the documentation is gathered and factors that affect the outcomes.

When constructing a checklist, decide what the focus will be, what should be included in it, and what the time frame would be, for example, completed during part of the day or every day, and for how long, such as one week or two weeks. The purpose of the checklist should be clearly reflected in its composition.

Review the checklist examples available online. How is the design of each of those checklists related to their purpose? How might you respond considering the information learned in each?

DEVELOPMENTAL SEQUENCE OF SKILLS

A sound knowledge of child development continuums and variations in development is essential when creating specific types of checklists. Choosing the developmental area(s) or behaviours to be included is of critical importance. If gross motor skills are the focus, then the skills reflective of the age group(s) should be listed in sequence. For what age group would a checklist with the following fine motor skills be considered?

- transfer a toy from one hand to another
- use pincer grasp
- play pat-a-cake
- put objects into a container

For the educator in any setting, using a well-constructed checklist provides an understanding of **prerequisite skills**, which are a precondition or foundation upon which other skills are built. Appreciation for the subsets of skills that form a learned behaviour contributes to an overall awareness of how children grow and develop. For example, an educator of a group of three-year-olds in the cloakroom may not find the term "can dress self" as accurate as a breakdown of that skill:

- assists in dressing
- puts on front-opening sleeved garment with assistance
- pulls on boots (may be on wrong feet)
- zips front zipper if catch is done up

Prerequisite skills can also indicate which skills in a subset have yet to be accomplished, assisting educators with identifying the kinds of planned experiences needed to develop them. For example, if children in a group were able to identify most facial body parts but unable to point to their chin or teeth, then the educator could easily incorporate provocations into any aspect of the day for children to learn new body parts. Educators should consult with standardized checklists to assist in identifying appropriate prerequisite skills, as well as skills and behaviours requiring observation.

KNOWLEDGE OF CHILDREN WITHIN THE GROUP

Experienced educators know that a wide range of skills and abilities exist within any group of young children. Among other things, these variances can be attributed to but not limited to culture, opportunities, family experiences, linguistic differences, or the unique needs of a child with special needs. Knowing the children and their families is as critical to developing a checklist as knowledge of child development. Each child demonstrates emerging skills at different times and different ways. This knowledge can be reflected in the composition of the checklist. How can the understanding of a group of children with unique differences be accommodated without changing the checklist for each child? How might we include and consider the context of the environment in the design of the checklist? If you refer back to Exhibit 5.4, you will note

- a section entitled "Comments and Examples"
- in the list of behaviour items, a number of items that identify receptive language as well as expressive language

Do these two additions to this checklist allow educators to document the variety of skills and behaviours they observe within the group of children? Yes, they do. How? In the section entitled "Comments and Examples," the educator could include comments that illustrate how the child accomplished this skill or cite examples of any variation to a particular item, such as "follows a two-step direction," by stating, "Petra can follow two-step directions when gestures accompany the verbal instruction."

Children tend to understand more than they can communicate, so having items that address a child's receptive as well as expressive language skills gives a more comprehensive look at a child's ability. It also reveals patterns that may not be expressed with a yes/no response.

The comments section gives the observer an opportunity to record important information, such as "Celine has been away for two days and just returned today." That one piece of information speaks volumes. When an educator combines that sentence with knowledge of the individual child and his or her family, it will give insight into the results of the checklist for the day or week. With the documentation of comments comes further understanding of the child's progress in acquiring a new language if English or French is not the home language. If the child is responding in his or her own language to questions in English, the comments section is the place to note that; it is an important piece of information.

KNOWLEDGE OF CHILDREN WITHIN THE CONTEXT OF THEIR ENVIRONMENT

Understanding the relationship between the children in a group setting and their environment will be covered in Chapter 8 in more detail, yet here is a good place to remind ourselves that when using methods such as a checklist, we need to keep in mind the group itself and the environment. If toddlers are climbing on the dramatic play furniture or cupboards, educators will take steps to make changes. If these behaviours occur deep within the winter months, do educators need to bring in the gross motor equipment for more tumble-and-roll experiences? Who is initiating the climbing? Are the other toddlers following the child's lead? What questions could be asked? What would result from those questions or inquiry? Questions help to jog people out of their usual thinking or ways of doing things. Those questions create reflection concerning the relationship between children, the children and the environment, and curriculum questions. This process is another example of inquiry and the cycle of observation.

MAKING CHECKLISTS USER-FRIENDLY

When constructing any checklist, make the form user-friendly. Keeping the format as consistent as possible with the essential information listed first goes a long way in identifying what information is needed for each child. Maintaining the same list of behavioural data for each child is systematic and therefore contributes to fairness; each child is observed for the same skill sets even though there will be differences between children.

When designing a checklist, some of the following criteria for behavioural data should be considered:

- Is the behaviour readily observable?
- Does it occur frequently?
- Can it be observed unobtrusively during routines of the day?
- Is it easily elicited from the child if not observed, such as the clapping of hands?
- Is it consistent in construction (same word order and verb tense)?
- Is it stated positively?

Given these criteria for an item-appropriate checklist, look back at the speech and language checklist in Exhibit 5.4. Do the items meet the aforementioned criteria? What about other types of checklists found online?

Targeting behaviours that are likely to be repeated and seen during the day gives the educator and others many opportunities to observe and document. The educator can adopt a spectator role or a participant role, create openings for communication with parents, or document a group-friendly experience. Take, for example, the arrival-time ritual that children engage in as they enter their early childhood setting. Adopting a spectator role to observe and document how all children transition into your environment would be a great opportunity to review the role of the educator in these types of circumstances. Why is it that Mamta has tears throughout the day and particularly upon arrival?

Elaine Campana/Kristine Fenning

Devising a checklist or using a commercially prepared checklist that explores self-regulation for children, or one that outlines important roles for the educator or parent to check off as yes/no, might assist in your exploration. Perhaps the checklist could accompany another observational method that provides more context of the situation. Using this information would then aid further inquiry and inform planning for this children, while respecting their interests and abilities.

PREPARED/COMMERCIAL CHECKLIST EXAMPLES

Prepared checklists can be found on the Internet or in published textbooks or trade publications. The key to finding a checklist that is appropriate for a child or group of children is knowing what you are looking for and how to find it. Some commonly used commercial checklists used across

Sally Wylie

Canada are the Nipissing District Developmental Screen (NDDS) (see Chapter 7) and the Ages and Stages Questionnaire.

Each of these commercial checklists is chosen by educators or resource professionals for a variety of reasons. For example, if you look at the NDDS in Chapter 7 (p. 320), you will see that the checklist is quite easy to follow. It asks the question, "By 18 months of age, does your child …" to give an age guideline. Parents and educators could check off the yes/no items together or independently. On the following page of the NDDS is a list of activities that "will help you play your part in your child's development"; it is geared toward parents.

Checklist items from the Hawaii Early Learning Profile in Exhibit 5.5 illustrate sign-language skills and wheelchair skills; these are items that are not commonly found in checklists for young children and therefore would be appropriate for those settings where children need assistance with their mobility. If sign language is used as a primary means of communication, then the Hawaii Early Learning Profile would be a good choice to evaluate the child's progress in this area.

EXHIBIT 5.5	CHECKLIST ITEMS FROM HELP®

3–9 Wheelchair Skills

Date	Credit	ID#	Age (y.m)	Skill	Comments
	3.208		Stops wheelchair in any manner		
	3.209		Moves wheelchair forward using 1 push forward and release		
	3.210		Moves wheelchair backward using 1 pull back and release		
	3.211		Turns wheelchair in a circle to the right		
	3.212		Turns wheelchair in a circle to the left		

2–8 Sign Language Skills

Date	Credit	ID#	Age (y.m)	Skill	Comments
	2.184		Watches face and body of speaker to get clues as to meaning signed communication		
	2.186		Responds to single signs pertaining to own wants or needs when signed by another		
	2.187		Imitates single signs expressing own wants or needs when signed by another		

Source: Reprinted by permission of the VORT® Corporation from HELP®: 3–6. © 2010. All rights reserved.

Reflecting on the use of checklists prompts us to consider several notions. First, we should keep an open mind about the different ways skills can be demonstrated. Take running, for example. Some children run quickly and with agility, dodging and weaving among their playmates with ease, while others run stiff-legged or stumble often. But all the checklist asks is "Can the child run? yes/no." Is being satisfied with a check mark good enough? Variations in how children run are important to note. Record that in the comments section.

Pausing to reflect on the information found in a checklist and how it correlates to norms for child development is also important. Use the items in a checklist as reference. Instead of trying to match the items with what are deemed age-appropriate guidelines, use them to help guide your knowledge and practice. Recording a "no" on a checklist should not prompt the educator or observer to jump to a conclusion that "this is something a child should do at this age." Instead, begin with an appreciative inquiry. Ask yourself and team members questions like "What other kinds of gross motor skills does this child have?" "What have we seen this child do on the play-ground?" "I wonder why …," or "I wonder if.…" Wondering is another way of being reflective and being an inquiry-based educator. Finding other means to investigate and gain knowledge of the child in a variety of environments is what's important.

ADAPTING CHECKLISTS

The simple format of a checklist allows educators to adapt or create a "homemade" version, one that will reflect the group's ages, abilities, cultures, languages, gender, or unique setting. For example, checklists can be adapted to include linguistic examples from languages spoken by the children and families for a more responsive and inclusive approach, such as by including the corresponding words or sign language for "hi," "bye," "help," or "hungry."

Checklists have a place in the evaluation of early childhood environments and what constitutes inclusive quality and design. Although there are many commercial checklists that capture these components, many educators and organizations have designed their own checklists to include what they perceive as the important pieces that compose the "ideal" environment for their children, families, and staff. Checklists in individual infant charts provide opportunities for dialogue with parents about their child's needs for nourishment, care, safety, interaction and relationships, communication, and emerging play interests—to name a few! Checklists also play a role in evaluating the performance of student-educators and are part of educator performance evaluations.

Use of checklist adaptations is a good opportunity to reflect the social and cultural uniqueness of the centre's population. Adding items to include or illustrate linguistic and social skills or providing comments is a way to identify or monitor the progress of each child in languages such as Cree, Urdu, Chinese, and Spanish.

INTERPRETING AND REFLECTING UPON INFORMATION FROM CHECKLISTS

Reflection upon information from a basic yes/no checklist would appear to be fundamental. Yet even from a column of "yes/can do," there will be patterns to examine.

These patterns may be an individual child's portfolio or points of educators' discussions with a child's parent. For any observational tool we use, we are in a position as educators to make numerous professional judgments to generate meaning from what we see and hear, thus informing our decision making and responses. When educators take time to interpret and evaluate the outcomes and then reflect upon the information gained, it tends to inspire inclusive responses and a pedagogical process that supports transformation. This process supports change in many areas of practice, such as examining philosophical approaches, child guidance techniques, and family-centred discussions, or re-examining teaching strategies. Educators could also reflect on whether or not the checklist was, in fact, the most appropriate methodology for their purpose. Did they discover what they had expected, or were the outcomes inconclusive or simplistic for their purpose? Did they find a disproportionate number of "NO"s or empty spaces where check marks should have been? In addition to patterning the documentation, further reflections and appreciative inquiry might include the following:

- What have I seen and heard? What have the children or families seen or heard?
- What interpretations or views do other team members, including the family, have of the information gained?
- If pertaining to a child or a group of children, what insights or interpretations were gained regarding development (both their strengths and skills to be developed), their unique abilities, and approaches as a group or as individual children, taking care to preserve the diversity of each child?
- Considering the environmental context, what environmental influences may have had an impact on the information gained?
- What more needs to be known? Why?
- What are the next steps? How will this information be used to inform and change current teaching or educating practices regarding children? The environment? Interactions with families?

Investigate checklist examples online. How would a checklist be used in a child's portfolio? Which ones consider the reflective processes and are used to inform responsive inclusive practice?

To learn more about the advantages and disadvantages of using checklists, please consult the chart in MindTap. Studying the breakdown of advantages and disadvantages for the methods found in this chapter will help you determine which one best suits your purpose for observing.

RATING SCALES

PURPOSE AND UNIQUE FEATURE

Rating scales are similar to checklists: they record behaviours or other elements of professional practice or learning environments that have been targeted in advance. Instead of the yes/no recording of a checklist, the rating scale provides a broader range of possibilities for documenting. The rating scale's unique feature is a scale against which the behavioural items or those factors relating to an early learning setting are rated. The rating scale is used to judge the degree to which the behaviour occurs along a chosen continuum. The rating scale is, therefore, a kind of checklist that includes judgments about the behaviour or components being observed; it can tell us the degree to which the targeted behaviour or aspects of professional practice being rated are present.

FORMAT OF RATING SCALES

The process of choosing the items for the rating scale is similar to that of choosing items for a checklist: the items or behaviours are preselected prior to the observations. Essential information is gathered (name of child, date of birth, age, dates of observation, the observer's name) and recorded before observations begin, just as in all the types of records previously reviewed. Rating scales designed with environmental quality indicators would have a different set of essential information, which may include only the date, the name of the observer, and the school room number. What essential information would be needed for an educator performance rating scale?

Rating scales, like checklists, are set up as a grid with the items or behaviour listed, such as the basic rating scale in Exhibit 5.6. This rating scale describes how the children use the books in the book centre. In this example, the educators wanted to get an idea of not only whether the children were using the books but also, more importantly, how they were using the books.

The skills judged along a continuum provide educators or any observers with information such as who in the group was most successful in achieving an outcome and who needs to achieve that skill. The continuum of a rating scale provides educators with a scaffolding approach: who might need the most support in their learning and who might require less.

EXHIBIT 5.6	RATING SCALE FOR BOOK CENTRE

Child's Name: _____ DOB: _____ Age: _____

Observer(s): _____ Date(s): _____

	Not Descriptive or True		Moderately Descriptive or True			Very Descriptive or True	
1. Turns book right side up	1	2	3	4	5	6	7
2. Hands book to adult to read	1	2	3	4	5	6	7
3. Points to and names pictures	1	2	3	4	5	6	7
4. Turns pages one at a time	1	2	3	4	5	6	7

Source: Courtesy of Sally Wylie.

Rating scales can include numerical ratings (1–10) or statements along a continuum ranging from terms such as "strongly agree" to "strongly disagree," or they can be a combination of both. The range of judgment is determined by the descriptors or qualifiers, as in Exhibit 5.6, and they are *not descriptive or true, moderately descriptive or true,* and *very descriptive or true.* These descriptors are then given a value on a numerical continuum. Along this continuum, there are three different descriptors with a total of seven possible numbers from which to choose. There are two sets of numbers for each descriptor. These numbers allow some flexibility in interpreting the behaviour, for example, "turns pages one at a time."

If a researcher or consultant evaluates these behaviours along the continuum by adding up these and other numbers, he or she would derive a **summative evaluation.** A summative evaluation is one that takes place at the end of an observation cycle and yields data that can then be analyzed and critically evaluated (see Chapter 7, p. 331).

COMMERCIAL EXAMPLES OF RATING SCALES

Prepared rating scales can be found in early childhood textbooks, in trade publications, or on the Internet. (See the resources and examples of rating scales available online.) Once the purpose for the rating scale has been established, educators, consultants, or others can begin the task of researching this observational tool to determine which one(s) would be most appropriate. Rating scales in early childhood may be used for such things but are not limited to uncovering information about children or evaluating staff relationships, curriculum, and the environment.

RATING SCALES IN EARLY CHILDHOOD

Valid rating scales are complex to construct. Their design requires a good deal of research, not only in terms of the components or behaviours to be rated but also in terms of the rating system itself.

The possibilities for judgmental error can exist at several levels:

- the components of what is to be observed
- the order in which these components are listed along the continuum
- how the observer is allowed to rate the behaviour along the continuum
- the possibility of multiple inferences from each descriptor
- the type of scale used
- the appropriateness of the scale in relation to the descriptors being rated
- the weighting of each descriptor
- the appropriateness of the wording of the rating scale

Long as this list is, it represents a limited view of the entire process. The purpose of identifying these variables here is to explain them rather than to dissuade you from developing your own. Rating scales are a major form of evaluation; their value has been proven.

By understanding some of the complexities involved, we can appreciate the efforts of those who have already devised rating scales, such as Thelma Harms, Richard M. Clifford, and Debby Cryer.

ADAPTING RATING SCALES

Early childhood educators rarely design and develop rating scales to evaluate children; rather, they rely on rating scales already on the market and available from educational institutions and publishers. Professionals contributing years of empirical research have developed commercial rating scales for children, and many good examples exist for different populations. These assessment tools can usually be ordered as a package containing a manual, scoring sheets, and other materials. The Childhood Autism Rating Scale (CARS2) is suitable for use by a variety of professionals with children over two years of age and uses observation as well as parent reports and other information to rate each child. The child is rated along a seven-point continuum, indicating the degree to which the child's behaviour deviates from that of another child of the same age.

See the examples of adapted rating scales available online.

RATING SCALE DESIGN CONSIDERATIONS

Adaptations of existing rating scales can be accomplished while still maintaining the reliability and validity of the rating scale by using only sections rather than the scale in its entirety. However, if different rating scales were combined through a "cut-and-paste" approach, then the validity of the information gathered would be in question, as well as the inferences drawn from such data. The norms from the various tests may not be congruent, which again influences the reliability and validity of the information.

Examples of prepared rating scales can easily be found. The key to selecting a particular rating scale is to inquire about the following:

- Is it appropriate for the purpose?
- Does the language and content reflect the values, beliefs, and philosophies of the children, family, environment, centre, and community appropriately? Are ability, gender, and other areas of diversity considered?
- What kinds of outcomes are the users hoping to achieve by using a rating scale, for example, to measure literacy?
- Can this information be gathered in ways that are more closely aligned with the practices inherent in the centre philosophy?
- Is the scale consistent with expectations of the licensing and regulatory bodies to ensure its usefulness to inform practice?

Creating your own rating scale modelled on existing rating scales for a particular age group, linguistic needs, or distinct mobility or communication needs leads us back to the issues: are we measuring what we intended to measure, and are the results of our rating scales reliable? Rating scales are complex to construct. The process requires a good deal of time and commitment if the rating scale, and therefore the information gathered, is valid and reliable.

INTERPRETATION OF INFORMATION FROM RATING SCALES

Reflection upon and interpretation of information from rating scales requires the same kind of reflective practices outlined in Chapter 4 and in other sections of this chapter. What was discovered? What does it mean for the child or children, the curriculum, the program, the environment, and future decisions? How will this information be communicated to the parent(s)? How will this newly learned information now inform your practice?

When interpreting data from the rating scales, begin by ensuring that you have all the completed pages. Reflect upon the purpose of the observations. Did you obtain the intended information? Are there patterns? What did you uncover that you did not intend to find? If other observers collected the same data, were the findings consistent? Was there inter-rater reliability? Critically analyzing the information, the methods used to gather the information, and other data will lay the foundation for productive discussions with those who observed. What reasons would prompt you to include a rating scale in a child's portfolio? Go online for possibilities.

It is once again very important to ensure our observations are conducted in a responsive and inclusive way. As we observe, gather information, and progress through the observation cycle, it is imperative to include the family and the broader team in the discussion of what we know and have learned about the children, the environment, or aspects of our practice. This then aids ongoing inquiry and decision making to continue to promote quality in everything that we do.

To learn more about the advantages and disadvantages of using rating scales, please see the chart in MindTap.

BEHAVIOUR TALLYING AND CHARTING

PURPOSE AND UNIQUE FEATURE

Behaviour tallying counts the frequency of behaviours: how many times does it happen? Behaviour tallying works in tandem with other observations as it generates substantial data rather quickly, demonstrating that a behaviour has occurred and how many times. When using this tallying and charting method, the behaviour must be clearly defined so all observers know what to observe and record. Defining what to do helps us do it.

A behaviour tallying chart has typically recorded concerning behaviour such as hitting, biting, or swearing and rarely, if ever, prosocial behaviour such as hugging or smiling. Why is that? we wonder. Perhaps we believe that prosocial behaviours do not need to be monitored or recorded. Instead, we focus on those inappropriate behaviours that cause others discomfort or even pain. Biting can be an issue within a group of young children. We want to know "how many times does Joey bite the other children?" We want to know the frequency with which the behaviour occurs so we can begin to understand how to respond in a supportive manner for all children. A toddler biting another child once is quite different from a toddler who is using biting to communicate or show frustration.

If we again use our appreciative inquiry approach, documenting and understanding when, how frequently, and what types of prosocial behaviours are evident will assist us in building on what is working well. This type of proactive approach is often forgotten, yet it is an integral component to being responsive to our learners and environment. This natural inquiry also forces us to ask other questions like the following:

1. How might we promote the usage of words among our toddlers?
2. How might we alter our role to prevent some of these behaviours from reoccurring?
3. What is it that we are not doing to decrease these behaviours, and how do we play a role in this?

What questions can you think of?

BEHAVIOUR TALLYING

Behaviour tallying usually takes on a connecting position in the observation process. Some types of observational tools lay the groundwork for behaviour tallying, which is then followed by further observation. Let's use the behavioural example of hitting to illustrate this process. First, the hitting behaviour may be uncovered by an observational tool, such as an anecdotal record. The behaviour to be tallied or counted is then identified: hitting. When the question is answered (How many times?) by using behaviour tallying to record the frequency, then based on the data, further decisions can be made. Certain behaviour is significant enough to warrant a closer look. Further observations, such as ABC analysis, could be selected to determine if the educator intervention strategies have been successful in decreasing the number of times the child hits others. To observe and modify behaviour, initial observations are taken, decisions are made, and then a different measurement is used to see the significance of any change.

FORMAT OF BEHAVIOUR TALLYING

The first format is a simple tally of the number of times a child demonstrated a particular behaviour. The numbers can be added on a premade chart or grid or recorded on a calendar.

The behaviours to be observed are defined, the times they occurred are checked off, and then conclusions are drawn on the basis of the completed data. Alternatively, a list of chosen behaviours can be checked off in terms of frequency and then displayed in chart or graph form. The chart or graph will give you a visual picture of a certain set of behaviours over time. From the display, conclusions can be drawn; for example, from Monday to Friday, the number of unacceptable hitting behaviours decreased from ten instances on Monday to five on Friday. What happened? What patterns were seen? Why the decrease in hitting from Monday to Friday? What conclusions can be drawn? From these questions, collaborative discussions can take place and strategies can be generated for teaching and learning. Many different kinds of charts are used within an early childhood environment, and the toileting chart in Exhibit 5.7 is one

EXHIBIT 5.7	TOILETING CHART

Child's Name: _____ DOB: _____ Age: _____

Observer(s): _____ Date(s): _____

	Monday	Tuesday	Wednesday	Thursday	Friday
8:00–8:30					
8:30–9:00					
9:00–9:30					
9:30–10:00					
10:00–10:30					
10:30–11:00					
11:00–11:30					
11:30–12:00					
12:00–12:30					
12:30–1:00					
1:00–1:30					
1:30–2:00					
2:00–2:30					
2:30–3:00					
3:00–3:30					
3:30–4:00					
4:00–4:30					

Legend	D = Dry pants W = Wet pants B = Bowel movement–pants
	X = On potty–nothing P = On potty–urination
	BP = On potty–bowel movement

Comments	

Source: Courtesy of Sally Wylie.

commonly used in the toddler or junior preschool room. In this toilet education chart, we can see how life skills might be tallied or counted to assist educators or any observers in finding patterns of events.

A coding system displayed as a legend provides a quick visual reference. The toilet education chart includes a legend with a relevant coding system. The educator can quickly see that "W" = wet pants and use that rather than write out the words. The use of symbols or letters to represent a particular concept makes recording behaviour quick and easy. How might this chart be adapted to support a child who is catheterized for toileting? What about a child building independence in dressing?

Behaviour tallying and charting can also be used to determine a wide range of entry skills in a junior or senior kindergarten class, such as cutting skills. In-class activities often assume that children have mastered the skill of cutting with scissors. Charting the skills of the children within each class will allow you to determine which children have limited experience with scissors and those who can use them with ease. A practical approach to using task analysis is provided online. In this example, children started off cutting simple strips of paper and ended up cutting out specific small objects from magazines without difficulty. The skills were graphed for each child in class. Check out the tallied results of the class after they had been provided many opportunities to use scissors in class.

USING A CONVENTIONAL GRAPH

Constructing a conventional graph (see Exhibit 5.8) to display data is easy to do. The standard graph has a vertical axis on which you plot ordinates, or vertical coordinates (the levels of behaviour). The horizontal axis, where you plot the abscissas, or horizontal coordinates, is where you indicate the dimension of time (hours, days, weeks), quality, or another indicator.

Perhaps you are engaged in research on the outdoor play preferences of children within your centre or organization and wish to present your data in visually interesting ways. Entering your raw data into a spreadsheet format will allow for conversion of the information into graph form. As you can see in Exhibit 5.8, a graph can display complex data in a less print-dependent way. The curriculum area of sand was most popular in which week? What would be some questions to ask given the data in the graph? In what types of situations might we want to present our information in this way?

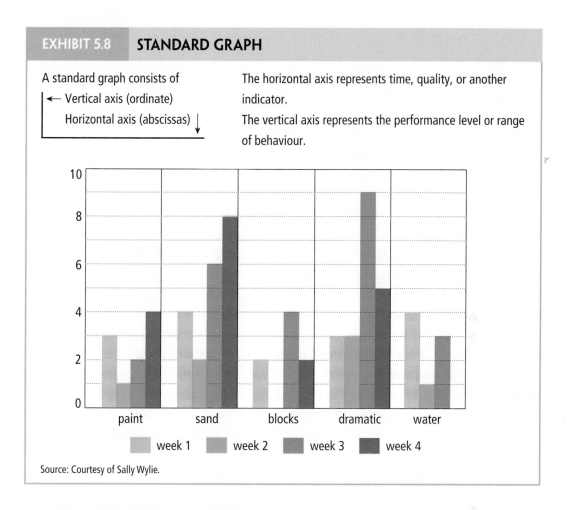

EXHIBIT 5.8   STANDARD GRAPH

A standard graph consists of
← Vertical axis (ordinate)
Horizontal axis (abscissas) ↓

The horizontal axis represents time, quality, or another indicator.

The vertical axis represents the performance level or range of behaviour.

week 1   week 2   week 3   week 4

Source: Courtesy of Sally Wylie.

TEXTBOOK/INTERNET EXAMPLES

Examples of graphs can be found throughout the Internet and early childhood texts on topics such as child development, use of curriculum, or almost any related topic in early childhood. "How-to" examples also exist for creating a graph, organizing a chart, or highlighting how to begin constructing a chart and can be found in texts or on the Internet.

INTERPRETING OBSERVATIONS, CHARTS, AND GRAPHS

Counting how many times a particular behaviour occurs yields a very different kind of interpretation than those from narrative observations. If your purpose is just to observe how many times a particular behaviour occurs or how many children can accomplish a particular skill, then the interpretation should be straightforward.

However, if you want to look for reasons behind the behaviour or reflect on why the frequency of a certain behaviour increased during certain days of the week, then your interpretation will be more reflective. It will include knowledge of other factors. It may include what you know about family circumstances and so on. If 10 out of 15 children in a Grade 1 classroom can label the secondary colours, do you need to continue reinforcing this concept? Who in the group has yet to accomplish this task? You would also likely evaluate each child's performance through a number of lenses, including development and culture, to determine if your expectations are appropriate.

A two-week time span for behaviour tallying is most commonly used in early childhood settings, as that time frame is often adequate for patterns to emerge. On the basis of those patterns, the team can make interpretations and form conclusions. However, after two weeks, a pattern may not seem apparent. The question often asked is, What do we do if there is no pattern? Depending on the child, the context, and the purpose for using this observational tool, a variety of possibilities exist. The observation may be continued for another one or two weeks. There may have been extenuating circumstances that prevented a real pattern from emerging. Another option is to stop recording and analyze the information that has already been collected. Perhaps it is time to re-evaluate the purpose and the type of form being used. There are no easy answers, no magic wands, and no one right way. The important key is communication: sharing of information, ideas, and strategies.

EXAMPLES OF BEHAVIOUR TALLYING ADAPTATIONS

Using an example of two educators on the playground on Friday afternoon talking and watching the children, let's examine how behaviour tallying can be adapted. Educator A mentions that it seems Daniel has been regressing in his toilet training lately; he has soiled his clothes during the week. Educator A asks Educator B if she thinks this is an area of concern. In consultation with his parents, Educator B suggests that they observe Daniel. They decide to record how many times Daniel soils his pants in the coming week.

Educators A and B discuss their observations and ideas with Daniel's parents. Since their new baby's arrival, the parents have also noticed that Daniel seems to be regressing. The educators and the parents agree that the educators will monitor Daniel at the daycare to see if, indeed, accidents are increasing. Use the online exhibit to evaluate and reflect upon the outcome of their documentation.

To learn more about the advantages and disadvantages of using behaviour tallying, please see the chart in MindTap.

PARTICIPATION CHARTS

PURPOSE AND UNIQUE FEATURE

The participation chart, such as Exhibit 5.9, targets a child's participation at various learning centres. Participation charts can be organized to record the participation of each child in the group experiencing a particular curriculum area. Participation charts can also be organized to include all children in the group participating in all areas available in the playroom. The unique feature of the participation chart is that it can record the participation of one child, a small group, or the entire group of children. This versatility allows the observer more possibilities to collect information than some of the other methods. The observer may also vary the depth of information sought. For example, he or she may collect basic information on all the children (their participation during outdoor play) but may also choose to focus on one child during this learning experience and include some quality indicators (what types of play the child is engaged in). If desired, a number of variables can be presented on the chart:

- a column for frequency: how many times the child visited the learning experience
- a column for duration: how long the child stayed at each learning experience
- a comments section: an area to comment on the child's playmates, their interactions, types of play, or specific information relevant to the educators

EXHIBIT 5.9	PARTICIPATION CHART FOR ONE CHILD				
Child's Name: _____ DOB: _____ Age: _____					
Observer(s): _____ Date(s): _____					
Learning Centres	**Monday**	**Tuesday**	**Wednesday**	**Thursday**	**Friday**
Sand play					
Science table					
Listening centre					
Book corner					
Constructing centre					
Dramatic centre					
Creative area					
Computer area					
Floor toys					
Project area					

Source: Courtesy of Sally Wylie.

FORMAT OF PARTICIPATION CHARTS

Organization of the participation chart begins the same way as the checklist and rating scale: the listing of essential information. Just below the information is the grid listing the items based on a child-centred curriculum. The set-up of the participation chart will depend on whom you want to include: all the children, some of the children, or only one child. If the chart is set up for one child, then the initial organization will be similar to that in Exhibit 5.9.

However, if the participation chart is to be organized to include a group or all the children, your set-up will be quite different. For example, if you wanted to observe the group during morning free playtime, you could set up your chart as in Exhibit 5.10. The information provided by this chart is significant. With just a brief look, you can immediately see who played where that morning. Are there any particular learning centres or centres based on children's interests that were seldom used or not used at all? Judging from the number of children who used particular areas, which were the most popular areas? Why? Does this information give you any ideas about the curriculum? Does the chart confirm your hunches about who usually plays with whom? How can this information further facilitate your planning of new and additional responsive and inclusive learning experiences that continue to reflect the interests and developmental abilities of the children? How might you reflect their interests and extend their learning? In what ways could children and families participate in this documentation? How might they co-plan responsive and inclusive curriculum with the educator?

EXHIBIT 5.10	PARTICIPATION CHART FOR MORE THAN ONE CHILD

Observer: <u>Heather</u>   Date(s): <u>Week of October 10 (Mon.–Fri.)</u>

Setting: <u>Indoor learning experiences</u>   Time: <u>9:45–10:30 am</u>

Name	Creatives	Dramatic	Blocks	Bookshelf	Sand Play
Lakesha	✓✓✓✓	✓✓		✓	✓
Devon	✓		✓✓✓	✓	✓✓✓
Tiffany	✓✓✓✓	✓✓			
Ahmed	✓✓	✓✓			✓✓

Source: Courtesy of Sally Wylie.

Let us assume that the participation chart in Exhibit 5.10 was implemented on Friday after four straight days of thunder and rain and no outdoor play. Based on what you would have previously observed of the children, if you arranged the same or similar experiences on Monday after a weekend of beautiful weather and implemented another participation chart, would you find the same clustering of children at the same areas? What changes might you expect? How have the children's interests changed? Were all children engaged? Why or why not?

Using a participation chart with a group of children several times over a three-month period presents a rudimentary pattern of group activity. From that information, a variety of educational decisions can be made. You may want to pay particular attention to the group dynamics. Perhaps these charts have indicated a child whose time spent in solitary play at various learning experiences is of concern to you. The simplicity or complexity of participation charts provides educators with many possible educational and managerial decisions.

ADAPTING PARTICIPATION CHARTS

If you wanted to focus on social skills or specifically comment on the social skills of the child as he played, you could set up a participation chart such as the one in Exhibit 5.11 used by a centre practising an eclectic approach to planning experiences for children.

EXHIBIT 5.11	PARTICIPATION CHART FOR SOCIAL SKILLS		

Child's Name: _____ DOB: _____ Age: _____

Observer(s): _____ Date(s): _____

Learning Activities	Frequency	Duration	Comments on Social Skills
Block area			
Literacy centre			
Sand/water play			
Projects			
Woodworking centre			
Dramatic centre			

Source: Courtesy of Sally Wylie.

Adding an open-ended comments section targeting social skills is one way to further adapt a participation chart. Another way to adapt the chart could be by adding other columns or dimensions. Instead of the open-ended comments, you could include the types of play, such as the example in Exhibit 5.12, and arrange them so that each item need only be checked off.

EXHIBIT 5.12	PARTICIPATION CHART WITH TYPES OF PLAY					

Child's Name: _____ DOB: _____ Age: _____

Observe: _____ Date(s): _____

Learning Centre	Unoccupied	Onlooker	Solitary	Parallel	Associative	Cooperative
Block area						
Bookshelf						
Sand/water play						
Projects						
Creative interests						
Constructive play						
Dramatic centre						

Source: Courtesy of Sally Wylie.

If you observed and recorded over a two-week period, you would collect 10 days of interesting behaviour! What types of play would you expect to find in the dramatic centre? What types of play would be most documented in the projects area?

If you choose to have a comments section, it is a good place to jot down any observations you deem interesting or relevant. Recording behaviours that reflect the socio-emotional area might be your focus. What evidence could you find for the following?

- accepts/rejects direction
- is a leader/follower
- is independent/dependent
- is active/passive
- initiates/responds

When you are looking for patterns over time, using indicators such as these will help focus your search and classify similar behaviours that are representative of the socioemotional area.

The participation chart for an outdoor plan found online is similar to the chart in Exhibit 5.12. An educator could modify the chart by adding outdoor learning opportunities instead of indoor learning centres. What would be the kinds of things you could add to an outdoor participation chart? Do you think the outdoor play would reveal different kinds of play than indoors? Would the children play with the same peers as they did inside? Reflect on these questions: why or why not?

INTERPRETING AND REFLECTING UPON PARTICIPATION CHART INFORMATION

Before you begin writing your interpretations and reflecting upon what was learned, organize the information you collected from your participation charts in rough draft form.

- Use headings that might include but are not limited to frequency, duration, development, environmental considerations, and relationships.
- Lay your charts out and systematically go through them, compiling the behaviour you observed under each appropriate heading. Note any contextual information or other information that might give insight into what was observed.
- Present the chart in a way that children and families might participate in the documentation and interpretation/analysis of the results. Children have a lot to offer to the conversation with their thoughts, hypotheses, and opinions regarding how things happen.
- If you made interpretations in your comments section, make sure to record them using "seems," "appears," "as if," and "perhaps" to indicate your opinions.
- Now reflect and respond. Begin to analyze the information, summarizing it in a meaningful way as the basis for discussions with your team, which includes the parents and children. Some of these aspects could include the curriculum, the environment, the program approach, individual children, or the group as a whole. This information can also be included in the children's portfolios.

The number of times a child engages in an experience over a period of two weeks should indicate a number of possible conclusions: the child likes this experience, he or she demonstrates a number of strengths with a particular learning experience, he or she likes the other children who frequent the learning experience as well, he or she demonstrates an attention span reflective of his or her age, or he or she is attracted to the physical environment of that space. These suggestions are not an exhaustive list but rather provide examples of the information that can be generated by one segment of the participation chart. As you engage in your reflection, check your interpretations of the child's behaviour with those of the child, family, and other educators. Did they come to the same conclusions you did?

Similarly, how would you interpret the information in the duration column? What reasons did the child(ren) state for staying/visiting that experience? For a long time? When reflecting upon how long or how little a child's time is spent with another child or in a particular area, consider not only likes and dislikes but also the culture of the child. Is it important that some cultures value silence more than others or that time in other cultures is not meant to be "filled" as it is in North America? A child's upbringing will influence how the child plays and spends her or his day. Other questions to be asked include the following:

- In what way is the child's behaviour reflective of the age group? Of her or his own individuality and variations in development?
- What can be said about the interest in the learning areas?
- What can be learned about the child's interests, learning style, or peer relationships?

These are some of the questions that may arise during an appreciative inquiry discussion among educators, children, and families interpreting information from the participation charts. Take time to reflect and gain meaning from what has been seen and heard. In what ways could a participation chart be used in a portfolio?

George Brown/Kristine Fenning

To learn more about the advantages and disadvantages of using participation charts, please see the chart in MindTap.

PROFILES

PURPOSE AND UNIQUE FEATURE

Profiles focus on specific areas of child development, such as fine motor or communication skills, rather than specific behaviours. Targeting a developmental area or domain appears rather broad, yet it does help focus the observer on one area of development at a time. This narrowing of focus typifies the closed methods of conducting and documenting observations.

The unique feature of the profile is the discoveries that are found when using this type of documentation. Its focus allows the observer to gather specific behaviours within that developmental area that might be demonstrated independently or with support. The observer now has the flexibility of gathering positively worded examples of behaviours and skills, as well as the interests of a child that are meaningful in terms of his or her environment, family, and cultural influences. This contextual or ecological approach offers a broader perspective of a child than the narrow confines of preselected skills.

Profiles can be used for a variety of reasons. The purpose for developing a profile will influence what information is gathered and in what ways. For example, if parents ask for feedback about their child's ability to take care of his or her personal needs, an educator will collect information concerning toileting, dressing and undressing in the cloakroom, and mealtime behaviours. The educator would make point-form notes throughout the day for several days or until a number of representative behaviours were collected. When combined with information from the child and family members on what they see at home, the completed profile would provide the parents with examples of how their child manages his or her personal needs. An additional benefit perhaps could be the sense of confidence it would give the parents not only in the child's abilities but also in their parenting skills. The behavioural examples would confirm for them that what is being taught at home is being transferred to the early childhood setting. This information may be quite significant for families who have been working on these skills at home or for newcomers who have recently immigrated and wish to gain insight into different methods of learning basic life skills. Exhibit 5.13 provides feedback from student-educators that suggests some advantages of using profiles.

EXHIBIT 5.13   STUDENT-EDUCATOR FEEDBACK ON PROFILES

- I found out information my teacher did not know about Meika (she speaks English).
- I like to do profiles on infants because it helps me understand what they can do.
- I thought this one child was dependent on the others, but I found out he's not!
- I like the point form because I'm not a very good writer.

Source: Courtesy of Sally Wylie.

FORMAT OF PROFILES

The format for recording profiles can be structured easily by starting with the essential information and then listing the developmental area and allowing space between each area for examples of behaviour and interests displayed by a child to be recorded. In Exhibit 5.14, Haseena has organized examples of Nadia's behaviour under Cognitive Development. There are some typical examples of cognitive development, such as "matching primary and secondary colours," but there is also an example that obviously takes place in the child-care setting (contextual information).

EXHIBIT 5.14	**PROFILE OF COGNITIVE DEVELOPMENT**

Child's Name: <u>Nadia</u>   DOB: <u>December 1</u>   Age: <u>3 years</u>

Observer(s): <u>Haseena</u>   Date(s): <u>October 17–22</u>

Developmental Area: <u>Cognitive</u>

Examples of Recorded Behaviour
- Matches all primary and secondary colours
- Can sort and classify farm animals from zoo or forest animals
- Tells her playmates how to take paintings off easel and put them on the drying rack without getting paint on anything

Source: Courtesy of Sally Wylie.

ADAPTING PROFILES

Profiles are used in the elementary school system, inclusive early childhood settings, and specialized settings that may be supporting children with special interests or needs. Imagine the wonderfully unique behaviours that you would observe in the following environments:

- an infant room
- a drop-in centre in a diverse or multilinguistic community
- an inclusive centre with children with a variety of extra-support needs
- a family grouping in private home child care
- a full-day kindergarten room
- a parent cooperative preschool

Grouping behaviours under a developmental area or domain creates parameters that say, "You can observe and document any behaviours that you would consider to be under this particular domain." For example, if you were asked to document examples of gross motor skills within a preschool grouping of young children, do you think you would see jumping, hopping, walking, climbing, rolling? What if there was a child with a walker in the group? Would you record examples of balance, or how the child could let go of his walker to get onto the ground or how he manoeuvred his walker from one place to another? This holistic approach targets the domain of gross motors skills and includes all the well-known ways of locomotion, but also leaves observations open to all kinds of everyday examples.

Glenda M. Powers/Shutterstock.com

In early childhood settings, profiles are developed and used in a variety of ways. In an infant-care setting, parents will want to know how much food their baby ate, how many bowel movements she or he had, and how long she or he slept. A brief list of point-form notes could be given to the parents on "what Christopher did today." Dramatic changes in development occur during infancy weekly, if not daily. One of the authors of this book remembers a student-educator who had her field placement in an infant room. She was struggling at first with this new age group, and we decided that in the back of her binder she would keep a profile on one child. The purpose of the profile was for the student-educator to become acquainted with what infants can do (see Exhibit 5.15). When the student-educator told the baby's mother about the observations, the mother was pleased to see the documentation.

EXHIBIT 5.15	INFANT PROFILE

Child's Name: <u>Christopher</u>   Age: <u>18 mos.</u>

Profile of Areas of Development (Observations from April 27–May 15)

Gross Motor	Climbs onto low mat/in and out of low chair
	Crawls easily from one area to another
	Balances upper torso while sitting and playing with toy
	Squats to pick up objects on the floor
	Walks sideways and forward
Fine Motor	Uses palmar grasp to hold toys and release
	Has eye–hand coordination as he moves objects such as … from one hand to another
	Exhibits pincer grasp as he picks up small objects with his thumb and pointer finger

(continued)

Self-Help	Uses spoon to pick up food and place in mouth
	Pulls off own shoes independently
	Holds cup with both hands when drinking
	Seeks out adult for comfort
Communication (Nonverbal)	Listens and responds to greetings and basic directions such as "go get your coat"
	Smiles
	Pushes other child when child is too close
	Approaches new learning experience readily
	Waves "bye-bye"
	Gives kisses upon request
Communication (Verbal)	Cries when upset
	Babbles and "la-la"s to himself (sings)
	Says a dozen words besides "mama" and "dada," such as "doggie, cat, eat"
	Laughs aloud
	Uses key words to express needs and wants, such as "up," "more"
Socioemotional	Plays by himself (solitary play)
	Offers hugs to caregivers and peers
	Is cooperative throughout routines, that is, sleep time/mealtime/change time
	Is interested in exploring and manipulating his environment through mouthing of objects, touching, and looking
	Separates easily from parents
Cognitive	Can find object if only a part of the object is in view
	Displays understanding of cause and effect, that is, presses pop-up top
	Points to simple objects upon request, such as spoon, coat, and shoes
	Imitates adults and peers, such as patty-cake, and plays social games as in peek-a-boo

Source: Courtesy of Sally Wylie.

Documentation such as this example demonstrates a dedication to understanding the infant development of Christopher. Examine the profiles in each area of development. Based on those examples, an educator could develop an emergent curriculum. Setting up an infant obstacle course might be part of those further learning opportunities. Imagine how the parent would enjoy seeing pictures or a video of Christopher crawling and climbing. Those examples could prompt dialogue between educator and parent and give the parent some ideas of what she or he could do at home. When profiles of a child's progress are included in the child's portfolio, they represent the child's growth and development at a particular stage at a certain time. Particularly for this age group, profile examples are invaluable to all of the child's educators.

To illustrate the flexibility of this type of record, let us consider Child A, who at age two demonstrated a unique set of gross motor skills in Exhibit 5.16.

EXHIBIT 5.16   **PROFILE OF CHILD IN HOSPITAL**

Child's Name: <u>Child A</u>   DOB: <u>March 23</u>   Age: <u>2</u>

Observer(s): <u>David</u>   Date(s): <u>September 12 and 13</u>

Relevant Medical Information: <u>Acute myelocytic leukemia</u>

Gross Motor Skills

- Sits in rocking chair on her own
- Uses both hands to lift objects that are heavy (e.g., tape recorder)
- Demonstrates good upper torso flexibility (stretches to reach for objects)
- Walks in very small steps (due to IV unit)
- Good sense of balance (bends over, picks up objects from the floor)

Source: Courtesy of David Fenech.

Here we must qualify that this example is not typical. Returning to our knowledge of consent and confidentiality, we remember that in providing the "relevant medical information as Acute myelocytic leukemia" means that prior permission must have been requested and granted. This example helps us to understand that in the case of Child A in a hospital setting, commercial or more traditional checklists would not have been appropriate. No preformatted list of anticipated behaviours could ever take into consideration the unique circumstances and settings that occur in a hospital. The skills of kicking a ball or walking a balance beam would not be relevant. In the example in Exhibit 5.16, what was relevant was Child A's small steps while pulling her intravenous (IV) pole down the hall. Devising a profile list of relevant behaviours in point form allows the observer more flexibility in delivering such information.

The details that this brief hospital profile reveals are more than abilities. Lifting heavy things is not only a demonstration of gross motor skills but also an indication of confidence. Confidence and self-esteem are important to a child when hospitalized. Hospitals can be intimidating settings for anyone, so when a child demonstrates behaviour that communicates confidence, we know it contributes to the child's well-being. The information gathered on this child will form the basis for communication with parents and others.

For each of these settings and many other examples, educators need an observational tool with some flexibility to allow for the variety of possible ways to record a child's habits, needs, abilities, interests, and characteristics. The profile records behaviours sensitive to the subtle influences of the home culture, the playroom environment, and even media influences. Profiles can include all developmental areas or only one or two, and the format of the profile may vary. The observer may record periodically throughout a two-week cycle. How do you know what is worth writing down? When you first observe a child, almost any data are relevant. Later, after the child has been observed for several weeks, patterns may begin to form, along with new discoveries about that child. Some of your notes may reveal significant milestones in the child's life. Others will be more subtle but represent, for example, a shift from one area of interest to another or a deeper understanding of a concept. Go online for more information and examples.

REFLECTING UPON PROFILES

Similar to the many observational tools previously discussed, profiles offer opportunities for communication between educators, children, and families. What we learn from our observations gives rise to questions: an appreciative inquiry. For example, in a toddler room key questions to ask are, How do toddlers communicate? Are they beginning to understand that words are power? What nonverbal ways of communication could be documented? How could pictures and text be combined to show parents and others the toddler's use of communication?

To begin to answer those questions, let's take a look at the following example. One afternoon it snowed heavily and the toddlers were delighted to look out the window and see it snow. We set the dolls along the low window ledge so the dolls could "see" the snow. The toddlers were busy pressing the dolls' faces against the window while repeating the word "snow" and making all kinds of excited sounds. What a rich opportunity to document that experience and then continue to reflect how this brief experience could inform practice. Documentation should hold the stories of the children—not only their skills and development but also their experiences of the world around them. Recognizing their behaviours and interests and discovering ways to meet variations in the needs of all children support an inclusive, responsive approach.

To learn more about the advantages and disadvantages of using profiles, please see the chart in MindTap.

PICTORIAL REPRESENTATIONS

Pictorial representations are, as the term suggests, pictures, images, or graphic drawings that represent persons or objects. Sketches, pictures, or other graphic representations can be useful to illustrate an idea. These images give visual appeal to text-laden publications. But how can they be used to assist in documenting children's behaviour?

Using prepared pictures with key words, phrases, or sentences is another way educators can communicate what they have seen. These prepared pictures can represent a key developmental milestone, such as walking or sitting independently. The pictures could represent a type of grasp, such as palmar grasp or pincer grasp. For example, in Exhibit 5.17, the age group is infants.

The pictorial examples, such as the images in Exhibit 5.17, are accompanied by phrases or sentences depicting the action that is portrayed. The person who observed the child demonstrating these skills can merely circle the picture or copy the description into the child's record book.

Educators with seasoned skills in working with children who have not yet achieved a high degree of writing skill may find pictorial representation a welcome alternative to print-dependent documentation. Not being able to communicate effectively in writing does not mean that an educator is not a good observer. How unfortunate it would be not to use the skills of a good observer! What are some ways to put those skills to use? Less print-dependent, more visual or graphic ways of recording information provide the means for educators to use their observation skills to full advantage.

Media-assisted observation or graphic representation are methods that can be used with people who are culturally unaccustomed to developing documentation on children yet possess an observant, reflective manner with children. Accommodating their skills within a team approach is a positive and innovative way to use the many ways of documenting children's behaviour.

EXHIBIT 5.17   DEVELOPMENTAL PROFILES

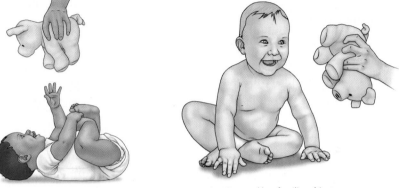

Focuses and reaches for objects.

Recognizes inverted but familiar objects.

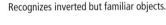

Responds to own name.

Still friendly with strangers.

Source: ALLEN/MAROTZ. Developmental Profiles, 4e. © 2003 South-Western, a part of Cengage Learning, Inc. Reproduced by permission. www.cengage.com/permissions

Many early childhood settings use the Boardmaker system to create a daily communication and observation system for a child. These visuals would be in pictorial form and would be arranged on a communication sheet for children to circle and self-assess their daily learning experiences for the day. This information would then function as a great document for inquiry for the parent/guardian to prompt the child to communicate, or it may empower a child who otherwise might not yet be able to communicate effectively either verbally or nonverbally to show and point to what she or he did while at child care or school. Applying this to the observation cycle, this natural conversation could also prompt provocations to occur at home or at child care as the child debriefs and visually communicates her or his interests and experiences during the day.

PICTORIAL REPRESENTATION WITH A GLOBAL FOCUS

During a community workshop in Singapore attended by early childhood supervisory personnel, considerable time was spent finding ways to document children's activity with which everyone felt comfortable. In Singapore, as in Canada and other countries, educators who work in the early childhood profession have emigrated from other countries with differing child-care practices. During the workshops, we brainstormed ways to include *all* staff in the documentation process. Not all staff members were writers. Finding ways to include their observations was critical in establishing a positive climate of acceptance and collaboration. Pictorial representation was one of the methods determined to be successful in achieving this purpose. Including all staff in the process of documentation is important, acknowledging that any group of educators will demonstrate a wide variety of skills in documentation while still being good observers.

Examples of these visual observation and communication systems are available online.

SOCIOGRAMS

A sociogram is one of the types of social maps used to examine the social context of a child. Social maps can be graphic or pictorial representations of how a person interacts within a group.

A common form of a social map is the family tree. Compiling a family tree is popular practice for children in elementary school—drawing a tree and then adding pictures of themselves and their families to the branches. Family trees are a graphic representation of family history and can be represented in several formats, such as the oldest generations at the bottom and the newer generations at the top. Extensive examples of family tree structures and themes can be found on the Internet.

The type of social map that is most useful in documenting social structures of young children is the sociogram. Sociograms are used in the field of early childhood to document and track social acceptance and relationships. For example, in September, children in a group may be relatively new to one another, and an educator may want to monitor who plays with whom, how often, and for how long. Instead of using pages of written observations, the educator can construct a sociogram. Using this format, shown in Exhibit 5.18, she can indicate by a picture or simple graphic representation children's social connections, using arrows going from and to individual children. A few months later, the educator can, using the same graphic representation, see what new relationships have been formed or see if the same social patterns from September still hold. Sociograms are also known by the new term sociometry.

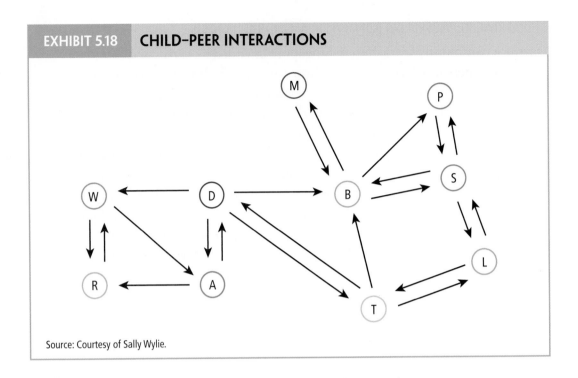

EXHIBIT 5.18   CHILD–PEER INTERACTIONS

Source: Courtesy of Sally Wylie.

Sociograms have also been used extensively as a research technique. Sociograms are useful in obtaining information on a particular child, a child within a group, or group dynamics. A sociogram can be created with input from the children; this variation would be used with older children. For the construction of a sociogram of which child in the group is most likely to help others learn, a child would need the understanding and maturity to define the parameters of the educator's questions.

SOCIOGRAM VARIATIONS: ECOMAPS

Sociograms can also be created to visually communicate the social influence of others in the life of a child. How many groups of children does a child socialize with on a regular basis? How can the groupings of family, friends, child care, and other extracurricular events be represented? Examine the social differences between Sarah and Joel in Exhibit 5.19. What is similar? What is different? How would this knowledge of Sarah and Joel assist the educator in developing an awareness and sensitivity to the child's social home culture and the influences in his or her life?

As discussed in other chapters, the family is not the only social influence in a child's life. Discovering the social influences in a child's life is enlightening. Consult with the exhibit online titled Sociogram Variations: Moyra's Examples. In this example, Moyra constructed a type of sociogram or ecomap to get a sense of the

EXHIBIT 5.19 **ECOMAPS OF SARAH AND JOEL**

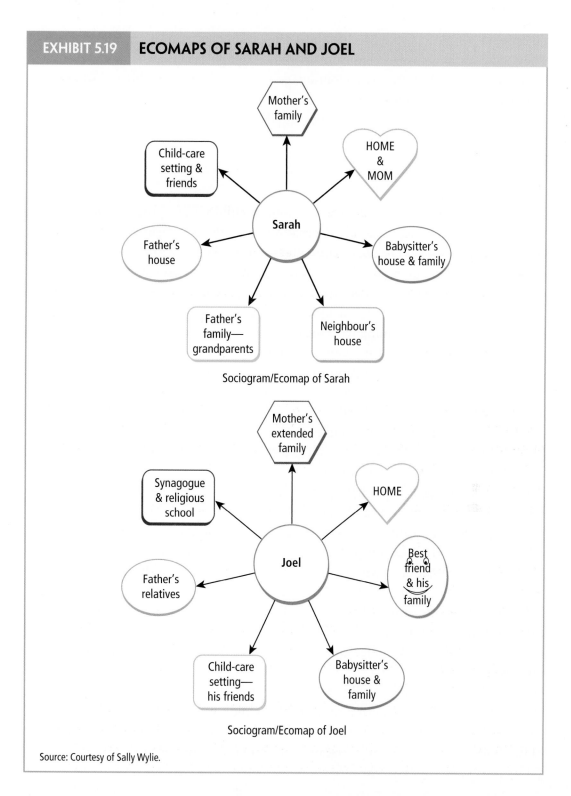

Sociogram/Ecomap of Sarah

Sociogram/Ecomap of Joel

Source: Courtesy of Sally Wylie.

diversity of people in Child M's life and a sense of her socioemotional development. The sociogram was constructed from an audio taping during several interview sessions with Child M. In this sociogram, you can get a sense of who and what is important in Child M's life.

To learn more about the advantages and disadvantages of using sociograms, please see the chart in MindTap.

MAPPING

Mapping is a visually interesting way to monitor children in a group setting. Mapping includes the contextual information of the environment and, therefore, adds another dimension to the documentation. Like the earlier observation methods examined in this chapter, mapping requires the observer to organize and set up the observation record before the observations begin. A map of the environment must first be drawn before the actual mapping of a child's activities can be done. Using mapping requires preplanning with the creation of a diagram of the room with all essential areas and items appropriately indicated, such as the curriculum area, equipment, furniture, supplies, and space. The diagram would have to be relatively accurate, portraying effectively, for example, the distance between areas in the room and spaces between pieces of furniture.

A basic mapping chart of a toddler room is shown in Exhibit 5.20. Mapping is an ideal method to record behaviour such as a child's wandering within the classroom or how toddlers use the environment.

When designing a mapping diagram, leave a space for comments where time spent or other information can be entered. Whatever information is judged by the educator to be significant can also be targeted for her or his attention. From the mapping and brief notes, it is possible to gather inferences and ascribe meaning.

Mapping preschoolers who tend to travel significantly in a short time would pose a challenge! Using a different-coloured pen or marker could be one way of tracking the various routes of each child. If coloured markers are used, a legend can be created. Mapping the behaviours of children represents another option for those educators who prefer an alternative, less print-dependent means of documentation.

Mapping adds a different dimension to documentation. This type of record allows the observer to monitor and record the child's movement throughout the room. Point-form notes can accompany the mapping to detail the significance of the child's activity. This information can be used in conjunction with other

EXHIBIT 5.20 | MAPPING CHART

Child's Name: <u>Ayla</u>　　　DOB: <u>October 16</u>　　　Age: <u>27 months</u>

Date: <u>June 20</u>　　　Time: <u>8:55–9:30</u>

1　Sits on edge of mat watching the children
2　Crawls into and out of the tunnel 2 times
3　Throws balls to educator and other children
4　Stands in the middle of the play equipment and watches
5　Crawls around on the low beams, lies down and bangs feet on the beam
6　Lines up at the door with peers when her name is called

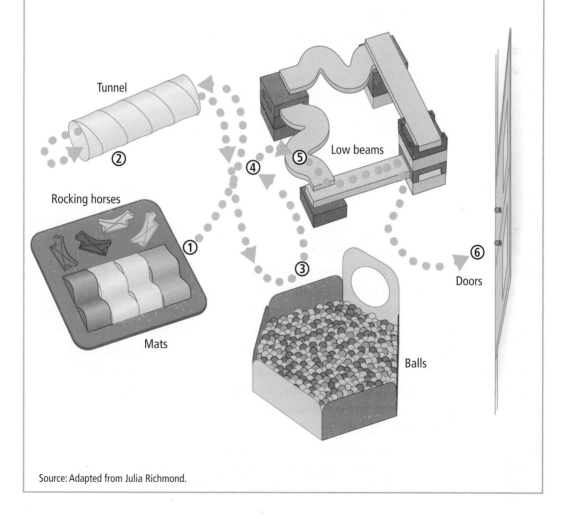

Source: Adapted from Julia Richmond.

documentation in a child's portfolio. Presented with other documentation, mapping provides a new way of presenting information to others. Mapping is an interesting visual tool to engage children in self-reflection and documentation and reflect upon where they played, whom they played with, where they spent the most time, and so on. As we revisit pedagogical documentation, it is important to think about how each methodology, in this case mapping, can be used with children, families, educators, and the community. How might you explain mapping to parents and involve them in documentation? What message might you want to convey when offering the mapping as a revealing piece of documentation?

Mapping can also be used to monitor the mobility of a child with special needs within the playroom. A child with spina bifida who uses a wheelchair for walking may gravitate only to specific areas of the room. Upon examination of the map, in collaboration with the parent or child, the observer recognizes how the set-up of the room is preventing the child from accessing certain learning experiences. As a result of the inquiry, changes can be made to the learning environment allowing the child to move between spaces in the classroom. Monitoring this change over a period of time using mapping can not only show areas of preference over time but also provide a measure for self-confidence.

To learn more about the advantages and disadvantages of using mapping, please see the chart in MindTap.

SUMMARY

In this chapter, many types of records have been featured that represent practical, commonly used observational tools for recording targeted behaviours in early learning settings. These types of records are used when the behaviours or the movements to be observed have been targeted in advance. Each of these closed methods has its own unique features and uses, which allows educators to choose the most appropriate one. These observational tools can be self-designed or commercially made. They can stand alone or be adapted to reflect the children, families, staff, philosophy, or setting. Combining the specific preselected items of a closed method with open-ended documentation reflecting the uniqueness of each learning community provides a contrasting cross-section of knowledge: a concentration of exact, targeted outcomes and relevant, contextual information to include in a child's portfolio. Making decisions based on research and the data that have been compiled encourages and empowers educators and parents, builds self-confidence, and develops trust in their ability to construct their own work together.

THROUGH THE LENS OF REFLECTIVE, TRANSFORMATIVE PRACTICES

Part 1 of this text started us on our journey with the mantra of a good observer: no matter how much you learn about children, there is always more to learn. Part 1 began by examining the observation process and discussing why observing and recording the activity of young children is such a complex and valuable process in the field of early childhood. In Chapter 1, we stated that observation is a practice that is setting-independent, requires the voices of all participants, and is the substance of all pedagogical documentation. Chapters 2 and 3 investigated the writing process and introduced the observer to what constitutes observation and interpretations, while emphasizing the importance of ethics and confidentiality in our practices. These chapters also explored the knowledge and skills needed to prepare different documentation methods, appreciate and understand the importance of inquiry and asking questions, and understand how these actions guide us through the cycle of observation. Part 2 included two comprehensive chapters detailing the many possible methods of pedagogical documentation, from the most basic checklist to complex social narratives and technology-enabled documentation approaches. Fortunately, we are not done—we know that simply engaging in one type of observation will not suffice or give us the information we need to make appropriately informed decisions regarding all areas of our professional practice.

Part 3 is about living in a society that is ever changing, with research and practices that constantly evolve and reframe our thinking. For example, since the time of writing the fourth edition in 2012, our profession has transformed so dramatically that some of the chapters in that edition have been completely deleted, with only a few pictures left standing.

This vibrant process of investigating, learning, and reflecting brings us to the philosophies that are currently evolving and influencing our practice. As Dahlberg, Moss, and Pence (2007) stated, "the greater our awareness of our

pedagogical practices, the greater our possibility to change through constructing a new space" (p. 153). That is the purpose of this text. Through appreciative inquiry and the cycle of observation, we invite you to create a new space in your mind where you will see new possibilities that could transform your practice and what you believe.

In Part 3, we continue to explore how our beliefs and practices around observation are reflected in day-to-day interactions, family, community, and the global village. With the immediacy of the social media and the Internet, we are affected by global events, and it is no wonder that we look not only to our own neighbourhoods but also outward to others for their philosophy and practices regarding children and families. Guided by responsive, inclusive practices, we look to models and principles, goals, and core values to reaffirm, discover, and reflect. Exploring alternative methods that assist us in creating the most useful, meaningful ways of sharing the learning and development of children is part of appreciative inquiry and an attitude of reflection, and is fundamental to developing learning communities.

Acknowledgment and encouragement of parent involvement are equally important if we are to create caring communities. Through dialogue, educators are able to learn about their families, what is important to them, and how they see themselves within the community. Urie Bronfenbrenner's ecological model of human development describes how a child is influenced first by the family and those with whom the child has direct contact, later moving outward from the family to the neighbourhood, to eventually being part of the patterning of environmental events and transitions over the course of life. In this text, we began with the discussion of the observation of children, but through the chapters, we have expanded our discussion to highlight the importance of including not only the voice of the child, but also the voices of the family, educators, and the community in our observation and documentation practices.

Chapters 6, 7, and 8 assist the educator-observer to understand how observation, inquiry, and documentation change one's professional practice. We examine the environment, how portfolios and e-portfolios are created for children and educators, the steps and processes involved with assessment and early intervention, and the role of the community in our observation and documentation practices. Chapter 8 introduces the transformative role of the educator-observer as leader, researcher, mentor, lifelong learner, and community-capacity builder. Observation and sound pedagogical documentation practices rely on team members who are committed to teamwork and participation in the cycle of observation.

CHAPTER 6

INFORMING PEDAGOGICAL PRACTICE THROUGH THE LENS OF REFLECTION

Ke Yu/iStockphoto.com

Tammy Bryngelson/iStockphoto.com

OVERVIEW

How do we determine a framework in which to organize our pedagogical documentation, and how do we share that information? The answer lies in this chapter. Here is where the application of much that has been covered in previous chapters is explored. Chapters 1 through 5 provided for the early childhood educator a number of tools and approaches to support the use of observation in various aspects of practice, specifically with young children. How do we go about informing and creating curriculum from observation? Not until this chapter has this question been answered, and yet it seems to be one of the most asked questions in early childhood. The application of philosophy, developing new child-centred practices out of concepts of responsive, inclusive, emergent, or play-based curriculum, can be puzzling and sometimes intimidating. Will the documentation meet ministry expectations and satisfy parents? How will we know if we're "on the right track" with our play-based curriculum? In response to these questions, the topics in this chapter explore methods of determining strategies and approaches to find or integrate documentation time with our professional practice, fostering collaboration and co-inquiry, and finding a pedagogical framework within a community of learners. We have created examples to illustrate these concepts, and nowhere else in this text will the online site be more important, as it hosts many more examples for each topic.

A major focus in this chapter is the topic of portfolios in all its complexity. It is important to understand that portfolios are part of the cycle of observation and appreciative inquiry. A portfolio is developed while engaging in and observing children's inquiries, collecting their work, and, of course, collaborating with and dialoguing with parents. As educators, we do not see the portfolio as an end product but rather as an ongoing process; thus, we would encourage you to think of the portfolio as a visual continuum of a child's interests and "wonders" and a reflection of the child's growth and development. Many types of portfolios are outlined in this chapter, from hard-copy file folders to electronic variations. Please see the various examples available online.

FOCUS QUESTIONS

1. Describe the importance of reflection and the preparation of questions within the cycle of observation. How do they support our practice?
2. In what ways does the cycle of observation support community building?
3. Define strategies for creating time for documentation and reflection.
4. What are the stages and content in portfolio preparation? How might we connect portfolios to pedagogical documentation?
5. What strategies and approaches enable educators to document daily the experiences and growth of young children?

Finally, we cannot forget the role of our own personal philosophy, beliefs, values, and attitudes. Subconsciously or consciously, they directly influence everything we do. Through the reflective process, we can continue to gain perspective into each area of practice, so let us begin!

APPRECIATIVE INQUIRY REVISITED

We premise this chapter with a return to appreciative inquiry. As stated in Chapter 1 and reinforced in Chapter 2, appreciative inquiry is a strengths-based approach focusing on people's positive energy and passions; it brings openness to seeing new potentials and possibilities from a collective knowledge. In this approach, children and educators teach and learn together, co-discovering new concepts, finding ways to problem-solve, or wondering "what if" together.

The process of appreciative inquiry encourages early childhood professionals to be collaborative and equitable within the workplace. By listening, educators learn what is relevant, important, and meaningful to others. Sharing ideas, being supportive, and being respectful of one another demonstrate an appreciation and understanding of others' perspectives and reality. For example, imagine Lisa, a kindergarten educator, asking what it would be like to document the experiences of the infants rather than her kindergarten class. She thinks she would struggle to appropriately capture the daily activity of infants with pedagogical documentation. Both educators talk about the challenges and joys of pedagogical documentation with different age groups in their respective rooms.

What questions would Lisa ask in regard to documenting the behaviour of infants? How would the educators compare the documentation of socialization between the two age groups? The process of learning and understanding allows for the sharing of knowledge and inquiry, but more importantly an appreciation of each other's strategies, observational methods, and inventive ways of documenting the lives of the children in their care.

Engaging in a systematic and appreciative inquiry approach when observing and recording considers the child's learning and development. Equally important is the documentation that captures contextual factors that have an impact on children's learning, such as relationships, culture, environment, family or diversity, language, gender, philosophy, and values. Consider the winter of 2014—one of the coldest in recent records. How do cold and snow (culture and environment) affect opportunities for expression, documentation, and routines of the day?

How do these experiences prompt questions? How could the answers inform and create curriculum?

In their own way, each of these factors will affect what is observed, how we interpret and reflect upon what we see and hear, and, finally, how we respond. For how family experiences can influence relationships at school and curriculum, see Exhibit 6.1.

FINDING A PEDAGOGICAL FRAMEWORK

As we reflect back to the earlier chapters, it is important to think about how we might apply the concepts presented. Thinking about questions like "How can we do this?" and other related questions targets the most complex part of the observation: finding a pedagogical framework that reflects the school or centre's philosophy, mission statement, policies and procedures, responsibilities to the provincial/ territorial ministries, community, and families. Educators would agree that pedagogical documentation should illustrate their philosophy and practices, their views of learning and educating, and, most importantly, their image of a child and their values of childhood. Creating this documentation involves dialogue, respect, reflection, and a willingness to explore and discover ideas.

EXHIBIT 6.1   CHAIRS AND DOLLS ON A PLANE

Jacob sauntered into the dramatic centre. He picked up a child-sized rattan chair and looked around. He leaned over the shelf and said to Gilly, "My mom and I rode on a plane, you know. We went to Florida." He plunked the chair down and shoved a doll onto the chair. "Do you want to ride on an airplane with us?" The question invited participation, and soon the two children had all the dolls sitting expectantly in the chairs, the chairs lined up in a row.

Bruce Peninsula Family Centre/Sally Wylie

The educator who observed the activity and listened to their conversation asked them about their trip. "What did you see in Florida?" She then asked, "What did you pack in your suitcase?" One of the girls ran to the dramatic area for dress-up clothes. The teacher found a box for the suitcase. From that day and for the next two weeks, air travel became the intense subject in the drama centre. Soon the drama centre stretched into the block centre, and eventually into the book area with shelves of books and comfy chairs and a sofa. The educators brought in posters and they collaboratively made a cardboard box cockpit, used a console as the control panel, set up a table and chairs to take reservations. Props were added: hats, a grass skirt, leis, seashells, bags for luggage, and so on. The travel industry flourished in many forms, all documented by artwork, constructions, photos, text, and stories until the children's interest waned. What educators discovered with the children was a wealth of new vocabulary, understanding of air travel, role playing and relationships, and a glimpse into the experiences of the children in their families.

Finding a systematic process or a pedagogical framework can be especially challenging when no established philosophy or set of practices is adopted. From Vancouver to St. John's, professional educators have developed documentation to best represent their practices and reflect their values, cultures, and philosophy. A wide spectrum of pedagogical frameworks illustrates the point that there is no one right way to observe and document the daily experiences of young children. The environment and methodology also have a significant influence on pedagogical framework, making them crucial to the process.

REFLECTIVE AND TRANSFORMATIVE: REVISITING THE CYCLE OF OBSERVATION

The cycle of observation is not a structured, **didactic**, prescriptive formula for teachers to direct and demonstrate their observation, planning, and reporting process. Rather, the cycle of observation is first an interactive and responsive process involving a team of others: parents, community professionals, educators, and children. Employing a pedagogical framework representative of those involved in this observational cycle allows for the gathering of multiple perspectives from all participants.

How a cycle of observation is represented, however, varies depending on philosophy and practices, the focus on the program and age groupings, parent involvement, community demographics, and other factors. Traditionally, the cycle of observation focused on the teacher and how observations were used to develop curriculum. This involved planning curriculum based on themes supported by documentation and planning curriculum based solely on observations of the children's interests. Some teachers continue to use themes and subject planning as their primary means of developing curriculum; however, with the introduction of research in Ontario and around the world supporting the need for reflection, inquiry, and sound observational and documentation pedagogy, this thinking has changed. Pedagogical documentation prompts new perspectives and processes of observing and documenting, and the cycle of observation supports this movement.

VARIATIONS OF THE CYCLE OF OBSERVATION

We first introduced the cycle of observation in Chapter 1, conceptually presented it in Chapter 2, and have continued to apply our learning to this cycle throughout the text. What we do know is that every setting will have their own philosophy and their own approach. Depending on a number of variables within your setting, variations might occur with the cycle of observation. For example, a variation of the cycle of observation could look like the one in Exhibit 6.2. With specific reference to the child, this particular cycle shows relevance and pertinence of observation and documentation to a centre that is perhaps just beginning their journey of observation and documentation, and directing their process to the creation and development of documentation for a child's portfolio.

How is this similar to or different from the cycle of observation presented in Exhibit 2.5 on page 52? Revisiting the cycle of observation in this chapter with

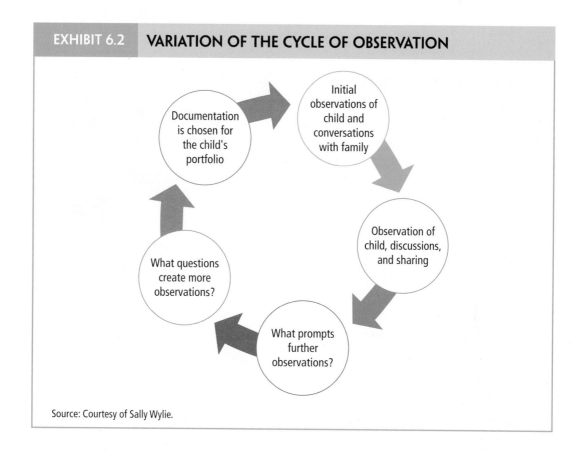

EXHIBIT 6.2 VARIATION OF THE CYCLE OF OBSERVATION

Documentation is chosen for the child's portfolio

Initial observations of child and conversations with family

Observation of child, discussions, and sharing

What prompts further observations?

What questions create more observations?

Source: Courtesy of Sally Wylie.

the application of examples will illustrate some concrete strategies of pedagogical documentation. Exhibit 6.3 is an example showing how the questions of children supported by a responsive educator can create an emerging curriculum ("What prompts further observations?"). Observation plays that key role. It brings the educator to a reflective place where she or he learns and uncovers with the children by paying attention to the artistic desire of a preschooler, the talents of a parent, or the interests of a co-educator in the room.

When interest waned, the educators assembled all the artwork, magazine pictures, photographs, children's narratives, and activities, such as the boats made out of popsicle sticks. They laid it all out and took photographs of it. Now they had electronic copies of their boat investigation for centre records and individual portfolios ("Documentation is chosen for the child's portfolio" in Exhibit 6.2), as well as hard copies to post on their documentation wall. Beginning with one question, the children's interest took their voices into the marina community, caught the interest of the parents, and created the foundation

| EXHIBIT 6.3 | DOES YOUR GRANDPA HAVE A BOAT? |

Discussions resulting from children's questions can generate a collaborative interest that can start with a simple question during lunchtime such as, "My grandpa has a boat. Does your grandpa have a boat?" The educator waits and listens for the responses of the children. "My Bompi has a boat." "My grandpa has a really, really big boat!" Just

gvictoria/Shutterstock.com

such a conversation was started in Wiarton Kids Den. The discussion of boats had begun during lunchtime, but when the first opportunity arose, many of the children dashed to paper and markers to draw a boat and continue their interest. Fortunately, they had an educator who fostered that interest, and for the entire week boats became the major interest. The educator arranged for a community visit on Friday to walk down to the marina and see the boats.

When the preschoolers came back, one of the educators interviewed the children individually while the beds were being set up for naptime. After naptime, interviews continued, and the children shouted out, "Chris is asking me what I saw!" "She's writing down what I'm saying!" They were delighted that their individual stories were being recorded. They were happy to be listened to. Then one child asked another child if he could sleep on a boat. Their investigations of boats led to another topic: camping on boats ("What questions create more observations?").

for further exploration. The cycle of observation included their artwork, their stories, pictures, paintings, and new information. It was relevant and meaningful, and it reflected the community in which the children lived. The days of discovery demonstrated a true interest, where educators and children learned together, and extended their conversation into the community while discovering what was meaningful to them.

Another example to show the continuum of the cycle of observation through documentation is the story of Colin and how he found a new identify and purpose at the Family Day events. See Exhibit 6.4 for Colin's story.

These examples demonstrate how appreciative inquiry creates possibilities out of dialogue and how joint collaboration between adults and children creates focus

EXHIBIT 6.4　**THE FAMILY DAY EVENT**

Debbie enrolled Colin, aged four, at the Cambridge Springs Child Care Centre in the spring of 2014. When she met with Lorie, the supervisor, she confided that she had just filed for a divorce and needed a secure place of comfort for Colin while she was at work. During the initial interview she said that Colin was quite the soccer player. He was

excited that the World Cup would be played in Brazil in the summer ("Initial observations of child and conversations with family" in Exhibit 6.2).

Lorie kept in close touch with Debbie and Colin's educators, sharing how he had been settling in, the friends he had, the things he liked to do, and, most importantly, how he was feeling ("Observations of child, discussions, and sharing").

At the end of the day, Lorie asked Debbie if she thought it would be a good idea to put Colin in a leadership role in the upcoming Family Day events. Lorie and others had observed Colin's talents with a soccer ball and wanted him to teach the other children. The child-care centre asked parents to bring in flags, shirts, and other soccer items for the event. Colin was excited and seemed to thrive in his new role ("What prompts further observation?").

In the days leading up to Family Day, the educators took pictures, transcribed the stories of the children, and generally documented the daily process of what it takes to stage a big event. Documentation came from educators, the children, and the families ("Documentation is chosen for the child's portfolio").

and develops curricula. This process applies to all age groups, not just the children who can articulate their interests, draw elaborate pictures, or challenge accepted meaning. This process includes the age groups of toddlers and infants as well. What may be different are the strategies employed by the educator to draw out the subjects of interest or the

complexities of a problem known only to a child in the infant or toddler room. Several examples applying the cycle of observation to professional practice are available online.

More attention to the behaviour of the children is necessary, as the younger children do not have the ability to verbally express their understanding in words of what is before them; however, they are able to articulate through sounds and actions their intentions and understanding. It is through behaviour, then, that we can observe, reflect, and learn from them, as perhaps is the case with an older infant outside in the sand who is trying to fit the sand from a large container into a smaller container. Besides puzzlement and problem solving, what is evident is one child's enjoyment of being in the same place with another infant shuffling sand around.

THE CYCLE OF OBSERVATION AS COMMUNITY BUILDING

In Chapter 1, we talked about the initial exchanges between educators and families and how through daily practices a bond is formed while scaffolding values and expectations. If we could see those educators and families now when discussing the ideas of their shared documentation, we would see how the cycle of observation we have discussed throughout this text becomes a tool of collaboration that extends into the community.

As each adult involved gains insight into the children's learning and development and contributes to that process at various stages, a group of learners is formed. Let's apply this to a specific context. It may begin, for example, with the children in a fishing village whose classroom work contained literacy and numeracy examples reflecting life in the village. With interest generated by the children's work, parents may be inclined to comment on the work or perhaps contribute artifacts such as fishing nets to further interest. Parents or grandparents may want to talk about fishing life in class. Would their children contribute new ideas about the stories or add to that of their parents or grandparents? How would a rural community wish to talk about, document, and reflect upon the miles of fence made of rocks pulled from the fields by their grandparents? What would children from rural areas tell us about the old photos of their ancestors, and how would they and the class reflect upon those stories? What would their grandchildren tell us in their learning stories at school?

Stories of the old days mingled with the observations of the young can create a rich documentation of heritage, pride, and sense of belonging. This intergenerational, neighbour-to-neighbour oral history is a valuable social construct

Sally Wylie

Sally Wylie

for schools and communities. That history creates community memories of events and places such as county fairs, gatherings, and festivals, which are often reflected in school activities for all to see. In some communities it could be the local heritage events, the pumpkin toss, the maple syrup week, or the Royal Winter Fair.

In the Arctic, Igloolik celebrates the re-emergence of the sun after weeks of total darkness. Many Inuit consider this celebration more important than New Year's Day. Traditionally, they celebrated the return of the light when they had enough food to last until spring. Today, this festival is a five-day extravaganza filled with igloo building, dog sledding, and talent and fashion shows. Those community ties and events bind families and create a local culture that is echoed across Canada. When children in an early childhood setting are involved, it presents a wonderful opportunity to document that experience, whether the child is 12 years or 12 months. Documentation tied to the community says "we belong" (see Exhibit 6.5).

EXHIBIT 6.5   OUR COMMITMENT TO ALL CHILDREN

"We view children as competent, capable of complex thinking, curious and rich in potential. They grow up in families with diverse social, cultural and linguistic perspectives. Every child should feel that he or she belongs, is a valuable contributor to his or her surroundings, and deserves the opportunity to succeed. When we recognize children as capable and curious, we are more likely to deliver programs and services that value and build on their strengths and abilities."

Source: Ontario Ministry of Education. (2013). *Think, Feel, Act: Lessons from Research about Young Children*, p. 7. Retrieved from http://www.edu.gov.on.ca/childcare/document.html

JOINING THE CYCLE: A COMMUNITY RESPONSE

Inviting organizations within the community can also be part of the cycle of observation. As we reflect back to Exhibit 2.5 on page 52, we can see opportunities for the voices of community members in our observation and documentation processes. No one works alone anymore. Collaboration is the key with the goal in mind that everyone benefits. For example, let's say the playground of a school yard has not been updated in years, and the supervisor, while outside at recess, has discovered that the concrete is full of holes, raised chunks, and uneven surfaces. The walls near the playground are continually marred by graffiti, and playground equipment has been removed entirely because of vandalism. Some money is available for the playground refurbishment, but not enough. What can be done? Wisely, the supervisor decides that she and the educators will document with photos and text all areas of the playground. Then they take the documentation, including the photos of the graffiti, to the next community consultation meeting. At the meeting, they give a PowerPoint presentation that illustrates what they have recorded. They discuss the issues. This was an effective way of taking clear documentation to an organization to ask for a solution to the problem.

Sharing documentation is a beginning: a way to get others involved. With the appropriate permissions, observations regarding how children play within such an outdoor area could also be included in the documentation. As part of the cycle of observation, some provocative questions could be asked, such as, "What do the children learn to play here? Is this an ideal place for our children to play?" The observation cycle can be used effectively to **advocate** for the environment. The next stage might be to get professionals from the community to join a discussion and bring their views, ideas, and suggestions as part of a community process. Discussions may point those arrows of the observation cycle in Diagram 2.3 on page 58 back to what can be done, who can do it, and other issues, such as examining avenues of funding or raising awareness of the fundamental tenets

of outdoor play for children. When gathering the perspectives of others, the load is shared as well as the responsibility. The inclusion of others promotes a holistic approach for the community. This process builds community capacity, which we will explore further in this and subsequent chapters.

Courtesy of University of Toronto, Child Care on Charles Street

THE CYCLE OF OBSERVATION: A TRANSFORMATIONAL PROCESS

During the cycle of observation, there should be freedom to stop, reflect, question or inquire, revisit, change direction, and/or include others. When including the viewpoints of others, this process can be transformational as people begin to see things in new ways, participate where they had not before, and change practices to reflect those involved. Different perceptions of others are uncovered through close involvement. Discussion based on observation, appreciative inquiry, and documentation is more than something done in a classroom. This community-inclusive process creates a space for dialogue and involvement, as stated in Exhibit 6.6.

EXHIBIT 6.6	A FOCUS OF DIALOGUE AND INTERACTION

"Perhaps the most significant element … about documentation, whether the Reggio approach or one's own, is that it not only makes learning visible—but it also encourages participation, in the holistic support of children's learning that takes full account of the emotional dimension. It is a focus of dialogue and interaction—it is not simply a means of 'reporting.' Thus, incorporating space in documentation for comments from parents, practitioners, children and others is a vital part of the process of undertaking it. Katz and Chard (1997) suggest that documentation adopted in this way contributes to the quality of early childhood practice in that it signals how seriously children's ideas and work are taken, and fosters awareness of practitioners in continuous planning and evaluation."

Source: Paige-Smith, Alice and Craft, Anna eds. (2008). *Developing Reflective Practice in the Early Years*. Berkshire, UK: Open University Press, p. 19.

For all concerned, this cyclical process invites multiple perspectives so as to provide insight into what is seen and heard. As discussed in Chapter 2, there is no single entry point to this cycle. The educator may begin at any point of the process because observation occurs at any time in any philosophy. Active reflection occurs throughout the cycle as it systematically engages educators, families, and children in inquiry-based thinking. A further benefit of engagement within this cycle is that it leads to discoveries that foster self-awareness, the improvement of professional practice, and experiences that promote learning for all. Another outcome that may be a result of the observation cycle is the pursuit of further assessment concerning a child or the environment.

COLLABORATION AND CO-INQUIRY

The process of appreciative inquiry and the practice of beginning the cycle of observation with a team—parents, educators, related professionals, and the children—represent a collaborative process that for 21st-century learning makes sense. But is it so new?

> The co-inquiry process was originally introduced by John Dewey (1933, 1938) [who] believed that teachers construct knowledge through inquiry with the assistance of colleagues and faculty, who help them refine and clarify their ideas about their learning and teaching experiences in the classroom. [Research into the co-inquiry process shows] a positive correlation between professional development experiences, teacher collaboration, and program quality/child outcomes (Honig & Hirallal 1998; Edsource, 2005). (Abramson, 2008, p. 4)

The benefits of the co-inquiry process as part of the cycle of observation are that it encourages dialogue and offers opportunities for meaningful parent participation other than being on committees, participating in the bake sale, or taking on telephone duties. Being a co-inquirer includes parents not only in the observing and documenting processes, but also in the process of reflecting and evaluating to inform and explore curriculum, as well as investigating new ideas and simply being a part of the conversation each day. Instead of "this is what she ate, did, how many hours slept, etc.," parents can be part of " what did we today." Co-inquiry prompts conversation and involvement beyond the maintenance issues of food, sleep, or diapers.

The writings of Dewey, Vygotsky, Malaguzzi, Piaget, and Skinner refer to co-constructing knowledge through inquiry and are summed up well in the article entitled "Skinner Meets Piaget on the Reggio Playground: Practical Synthesis of Applied Behaviour Analysis and Developmentally Appropriate Practice Orientations" by Warash, Curtis, Hursh, and Tucci (2008). Co-inquiry, they say, is an invitation to rethink relationships and communication not only between educators and related professionals but also with parents and families.

In communities across Canada, parent and family literacy teams work cooperatively with families to encourage oral language and parent participation in children's play. Documentation of adult–child play provides families and parents with opportunities to begin to understand how children learn and grow. Providing opportunities such as a simple adult–child group activity of messy goop or finger painting reminds parents how much fun play still is, as well as giving them a realistic idea of how play feels rather than being a spectator of play. This playtime also offers an opportune time to document the interactions and dialogue, giving another lens from which children and families view themselves.

MUTUAL EDUCATION

When getting to know parents and families right from the very moment we begin the cycle of observation, educators may become informed of a variety of issues that may arise as children grow and develop. Families may communicate about concerns such as discipline at home, child relationships with adults, eating and food preferences, communication styles, napping, and independence versus dependence. When beginning new relationships with families, then, plenty of opportunities to dialogue must be built into practice to allow for mutual understanding and education to take place. The uniqueness of each child and family needs to be encouraged, included, and appreciated so that the educator can be responsive within the early childhood setting. In the text *Diversity in Early Care and Education: Honoring Differences*, Janet Gonzalez-Mena (2008) provides revealing examples of cultural misunderstandings and uses those examples to explore how potential differences of opinion can be resolved when families and educators come together in a common place with different perspectives. Among many strong suggestions to creatively problem-solve, she offers the concept of "mutual education," as noted in Exhibit 6.7.

EXHIBIT 6.7   MUTUAL EDUCATION

"Sometimes conflicts can be solved through creative problem solving. When teachers can move from dualistic thinking to holistic thinking and put their heads together with parents, they may come up with solutions that neither party would have thought of on their own .... When we stop thinking in terms of opposites such as right or wrong, good or bad, appropriate or inappropriate, black or white, we can come up with ideas we never even dreamed of. What I am calling holistic thinking, the [developmentally appropriate practice] book calls both/and thinking. That is, when viewed in a larger context, the two views may fit together and create a whole new view that encompasses both and takes them out of an oppositional stance. Isaura Barrera, a professor of special education at the University of New Mexico, uses the term 'third space' to describe a way of reconciling diverse perspectives. She isn't talking about 'meeting half way.' Third space isn't a compromise but a whole new territory."

Source: Gonzalez-Mena, Janet (2008). *Diversity in Early Care and Education: Honoring Differences*, 5th ed. New York: McGraw-Hill, p. 56.

The idea of mutual education is fundamental in creating trust and building relationships founded on respect and caring. The "third space" Gonzalez-Mena refers to is a concept that means putting away judgments and assumptions. It suggests views are expressed by one person while the other listens attentively, and then the roles are reversed. From that dialogue and understanding will emerge key ideas or parts of the conversation that they could both agree upon. Perhaps the two people create a totally new perspective dramatically different from either of their previous points of view. This process also illustrates how appreciative inquiry (asking questions in a respectful and kind way) and reflection (considering other's point of view) converge to create an atmosphere of openness to possibilities, creating the third space to which Gonzalez-Mena alluded.

The concept and practice of mutual education should be extended to children of all ages, not just adults. How many times have you heard educators say that they probably learn more from their children than the children learn from them? That is quite a statement. What does it reveal? It may refer to an educator's modesty or humbleness or to the educator's regard and value for her children's articulation of what, why, and how they have learned. There are many possibilities, and one of them is mutual education. In his article "Reading the Intentionality of Young Children," George Forman (2010) confirms that "just because infants or 1-year-old children cannot tell us what they are trying to do does not mean that they are without plans or expectations. Young children have many intentions that we can read by careful attention to their subtle movements and glances"(p. 1). In this article and six accompanying video clips, he clearly demonstrates not only the social intentions of very young children but also, importantly, the value of careful observation, with the message to us all who work with children to "slow down." When we take the time to observe, not only do we begin to understand and appreciate, but also we are rewarded with uncovering the world of children in ways we never thought of before.

Taking that same idea of learning from the children, Hallam, Fouts, Bargreen, and Caudle (2009) examined the issue of quality care in the field of early care and education in the United States. Their article, entitled "Quality from a Toddler's Perspective: A Bottom-Up Examination of Classroom Experiences," follows up on Lilian Katz's framework of child-care quality study by exploring the relationship between factors that attempt to identify quality care from a toddler's perspective. The complexity in determining a measurable indicator of quality is well reflected in this article, but their findings "are consistent with previous empirical studies of child care environments and underscore the need for more attention to be paid to teacher-child interaction in toddler group care settings" (p. 8).

THE REFLECTIVE EDUCATOR: RESPONDING TO AND SUSTAINING THE OBSERVATION CYCLE

We've taken a comprehensive look at many integral steps and processes within the observational cycle in this chapter; it is a complex yet dynamic process that requires educators to be mindful of and reflective upon all aspects of practice. To be able to do this effectively, it is important to now think about how we might begin to prepare pedagogical documentation.

A FOCUS ON REFLECTION

Seasoned educators have used the term "planning time" so long that even when they are part of an emergent curriculum that no longer focuses on "teacher planning time," the term is still used. Realizing the importance of reflection within the observation cycle, perhaps what we need is a term like "reflection time." Rather than planning a weekly curriculum in advance, educators might replace this time with the sharing of observations and reflections, perhaps collaborating with children and other educators to document inquiry and learning taking place. Resulting from this collaboration and mutual education might be a variety of documentation artifacts, and in the case of the example below, educators experimented with a few documentation methods in their new journey.

> Centre A and its educators were new to the documentation process, and in particular the capturing of inquiry demonstrated by the children. Not knowing exactly where to begin, they decided to start this new process with a question: "What is something we can all agree on that we observe in the infant, toddler, and preschool rooms?" Educators listened and watched, and what they agreed on was observing the senses of sight and hearing, as this was an interest consistently demonstrated by the children. What evolved from each room

was a curious and interesting mix of questions and responses, which were documented and later posted for all to see. In the toddler room, their documentation was prompted by the interest of one of the toddlers in eye colour. Documentation began with some basic questions posed by the educators, and as time progressed, their documentation methods became increasingly connected to children's actions, words, interests, and inquiry. In this new documentation experience, the educators also related the inquiry to the Ontario Early Learning Framework (OELF), as indicated by one of their entries below.

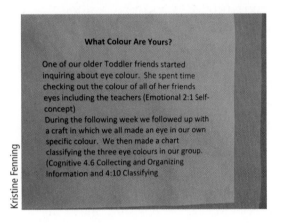

What Colour Are Yours?

One of our older Toddler friends started inquiring about eye colour. She spent time checking out the colour of all of her friends eyes including the teachers (Emotional 2:1 Self-concept)

During the following week we followed up with a craft in which we all made an eye in our own specific colour. We then made a chart classifying the three eye colours in our group. (Cognitive 4.6 Collecting and Organizing Information and 4:10 Classifying

Kristine Fenning

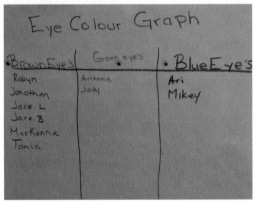

Kristine Fenning

This is a primary example of simply beginning with a question, reflecting upon what it means to look and listen, and taking a leap to try to experiment with new and emerging documentation methods. As knowledge and skills in observation and documentation grow, so too will the complexity and types of documentation produced. With time, practice, and new learning, educators can also look for opportunities for co-participation from children and their families in the process.

CREATING TIME FOR DOCUMENTATION AND REFLECTION

When creating time for documentation and reflection, the first consideration is to respect the educator. What does that mean? It means that when educators of young children are asked to document during the day, that request needs to consider the age of the children, the number of children in the educator's care, and other factors such as the physical environment, professional responsibilities throughout the day, the need to meet licensing and ministry expectations, scheduling constraints, and other expectations. In our genuine desire and excitement to document the wonderful discoveries of young children, care must be taken to ensure that educators are not pressured by unrealistic expectations of what should be accomplished.

This caveat reminds us of our conversation concerning pedagogical documentation in Chapter 2. No matter our profession, we have to be able to work within the time we have. Being proactive is a good attitude toward meeting that challenge. Instead of waiting until you get in the door of the centre or school, reflect upon yesterday and today before you get on the bus or behind the wheel. Think about what you've been documenting with the children, where you might want to lead a discussion today, or what kinds of materials would prompt a further investigation of a topic or exploration already visited. Create your own headspace before you walk into the classroom, and take the time to engage in the moment with the children. Know in advance where the materials are for your documentation, and ensure access to materials for others so that they can engage in the process. Think before you walk in the door not only what to document but also how you'll do that. Ask yourself some of these questions: How will I include some of the reflections from yesterday? How might we document today? How have we contributed to the portfolios of children? How will we refocus today? Self-reflection, dialogue, and inquiry will begin the process of inventing possibilities with your colleagues, the children (regardless of their age), the supervisor, and families.

The following questions often arise from pedagogical documentation: Of all the interests in the classroom, whose ideas or inquiries do we follow/document? What if some children are not interested? How do I keep the concept going, how do I expand it, whose ideas of the children do I follow, and when do I stop with the children and take a different topic? Educators also wonder, are there multiple ways to present documentation, and if so, can each room in the school do things differently or does it all have to be the same? How can we document in the moment? When do we call what we're doing "curriculum"? Will that be acceptable to the ministry or regulatory bodies? These are all provocative questions: begin the conversation with your team!

REFLECTION, APPRECIATION, AND INQUIRY

Other topics within the cycle of observation requiring our reflection include bias and ethics. It is important to question, think about, and plan for how we might consider and respect the rights of children, families, and educators, as well as how we might promote and sustain ethics in the workplace. We also need to be aware of our own biases in order to be positive, responsive, inclusive educators who are open to change, possibilities, and reflection. Appreciation of self and others prompts us to

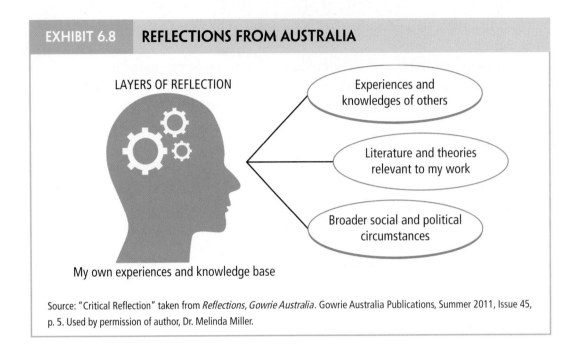

EXHIBIT 6.8   REFLECTIONS FROM AUSTRALIA

LAYERS OF REFLECTION

Experiences and knowledges of others

Literature and theories relevant to my work

Broader social and political circumstances

My own experiences and knowledge base

Source: "Critical Reflection" taken from *Reflections, Gowrie Australia.* Gowrie Australia Publications, Summer 2011, Issue 45, p. 5. Used by permission of author, Dr. Melinda Miller.

consider all points of view and discourages a superficial, surface-level understanding. As noted in Exhibit 6.8, a commitment to embrace the knowledge and practices of others in early childhood is relevant to an educator's professional practice.

Whether you are a seasoned educator in the profession or a beginning student of early childhood, perhaps some of your reflections include what prompted you to become an educator of young children. Maybe you reflected on people in your past who influenced you to become an educator. As you progress through your studies and career, you will be called upon for your thoughts and feelings about various theories, subjects such as discipline, or issues like the need for a federal child-care system. As your experience grows, your views will be influenced, changed, or challenged. This is important as it helps you formulate your own philosophy about education and learning.

Early Learning for Every Child Today: A Framework for Ontario Early Childhood Settings (Ontario Ministry of Children and Youth Services, Best Start Expert Panel on Early Learning, 2007), more recently known as the Ontario Early Learning Framework, includes indicators of "taking another person's point of view," listed under the social domain, for the preschool–kindergarten age group (2.5 to 6 years). See Exhibit 6.9 for the domains and skills, indicators of the skill, and interactions for that page.

A brief glance at the interactions in Exhibit 6.9 shows the kinds of questions or comments an educator might make to encourage or reinforce these concepts. Referring back to the example in Exhibit 6.3, what kinds of questions could be

EXHIBIT 6.9	PRESCHOOL–KINDERGARTEN (2.5 TO 6 YEARS)	
Domain and Skills	**Indicators of the Skill**	**Interactions**
Taking Another Person's Point of View	describing their ideas and emotions recognizing that other people have ideas and emotions understanding the ideas and emotions of others beginning to accept that the ideas and emotions of others may be different from their own adapting behaviour to take other people's points of view into consideration beginning to respond appropriately to the feelings of others beginning to take another's point of view engaging in the exchange of ideas and points of view with others	Create discussion of an experience that was shared by all. "When we were at the fire hall yesterday, I took these photographs? Look at this one, Jed. What do you remember? Becky, Jed remembers…. Do you remember that? What do you think?" This gives practice in describing ideas and hearing the ideas of others who had the same experience. In this way, children can recognize the ideas of others and see that they may be different from their own, e.g., theory of mind.

Source: Ontario Ministry of Education. *Early Learning for Every Child Today (ELECT): A Framework for Ontario Early Childhood Settings*, p. 46. © Queen's Printer for Ontario, 2007. Reproduced with permission of the Government of Ontario.

generated to re-engage the children in reflecting upon the subject of boats? How would those questions and interest encourage this age group to take another person's point of view? What new reflections might be added to the conversation? How would those remembrances contribute to sharing feelings and ideas with others?

There are many theories concerning how, when, and to what degree we reflect upon our professional practice and personal lives. When you observe, interpret, and document what you have seen and heard, you will be reflecting upon many aspects of one event. You may reflect almost immediately as you consider a decision or perhaps pause and think later in the day about the same incident, but in a different way.

Using a ministry document does not preclude educators from using other pedagogical documentation or engaging in appreciative inquiry. They are not exclusive of each other, but rather inclusive practices demonstrate a willingness to create a wide variety of documentation using anecdotal observations, charts, photos, and text—whatever makes visible the daily activity and thinking of children.

As we will see later in this chapter, when co-creating a portfolio with colleagues, families, or children, you will express your views, share your reflections on your observations, and invite others to do the same. Making those connections helps you realize your beliefs and values as well as acknowledge those of others. When you develop a portfolio, many questions along the cycle of observation will be asked, such as, "How will I show the talents and gifts of this child to others?", "How has this child's voice been captured?", or "Have I fairly represented the growth and development of this child over the past six months?" These questions are not only a reflection of what you wonder about but are also about you, the educator. These questions are reflections of your professional philosophy. Discussed further in Chapter 8, they illustrate what you have learned about the complex nature of being an educator of young children.

WEBBING: A MULTIPURPOSE TOOL

Webbing is central to and most identified historically with the concept of developmentally appropriate practice (DAP). It is a versatile and visual tool for inclusion in portfolios to explore and reflect upon key ideas or events with children while building on their ideas, learning, and interests. For example, a child-care setting in northern Ontario had moved from a theme-based curriculum approach to an emergent curriculum. One of the strategies they experimented with was webbing. From the photograph of the summer web, we can see the brainstorming that took place with children and educators. From that exercise, a new direction for resources, energies, and focus began. Since then, the educators have used webs to help give direction, purpose, and even a sense of how to gather evidence of children's learning. Webbing is a visual method to assist in inquiry, decision making, and planning, as seen in Exhibit 6.10. Ensuring that a variety of documentation is obtained addresses the need for diverse observational

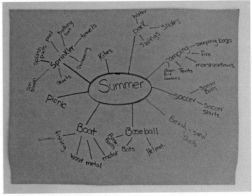

Courtesy of Wiarton Kids Den

lenses—seeing the child from many perspectives and acknowledging that what educators may wish to know can be quite different from what families, the children, or indeed the community in which the child lives wishes to know.

"The first web of types of documentation was developed for the staff of the Valeska Hinton Early Childhood Education Center. The purpose was to assist teachers in expanding their concepts of how they might collect evidence of children's learning and to support their developing skills in documentation. As seen in the Web showing types of documentation, groups the variety of ways of gathering evidence about children's learning around the central topic of types of documentation. Radiating out from the web are five clusters: individual portfolios, narratives, observations of progress and performance, child self-reflections, and products (individual or group). Each of these types of documentation can provide a way to view children's work."

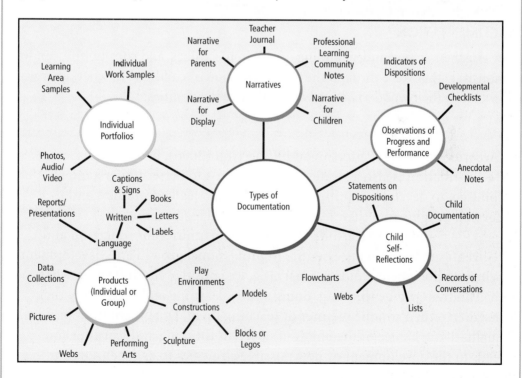

Reflecting back upon our discussion of various observational methods in Chapters 4 and 5, what other methodologies could we include in this web?

WEBBING AND EMERGENT DOCUMENTATION

Using a web to portray inquiries, questions, various hypotheses, the creation of ideas or concepts, or a framework is a discovery process. The process should include the children as much as possible so that the team is representative of many people in the room. At Wiarton Kids Den educators brainstormed many ideas and concepts, such as developmental domains, body parts, shadows, water, eye colours, and wind. The topic of fishing licences evolved from a child in the preschool room who was pretending to fish with a plastic pole trying to hook on to a plastic fish. Before long, every child in the room had asked for one, except one girl who received a babysitting licence. This fishing licence web looked something like the one in Exhibit 6.11.

"THINKING AND WONDERING" IN PEDAGOGICAL DOCUMENTATION

How else then, in our understanding of children, families, and community, can we demonstrate that voice through the documentation of children? In what other ways can we show their wonderings and our collective possibilities?

"According to Fleet, Patterson and Robertson (2006), pedagogical documentation is also a strategy that allows us to better understand children, to develop meaningful curriculum, to lead an inquiry, and to develop insights into their learning. Using pedagogical documentation of individual and group learning provides opportunities for reflection and reinvention, components essential to professional growth and development. When we document children's learning, we consider and reflect on what the children may be thinking, doing and/or learning and then apply their insights to their unique manner of teaching them. Documentation provides qualitative evidence of the children's current thinking and learning and leads to the development of new possible strategies to assist children in reaching the next learning steps."

Source: Bowne, Cutler, DeBates et al., "Pedogogical documentation and collaborative dialogue as tools of inquiry." *Journal of the Scholarship of Teaching and Learning,* 10(2) p. 49.

EXHIBIT 6.11   A FISHING LICENCE

I was at a child-care setting in northern Ontario, and a four-year-old was trying to catch a plastic fish with his toy fishing pole. We talked for a few minutes, and then I asked him if he had a fishing licence. He looked at me, blinking, and said, "No." I asked him if he would like one. "Yes," he said. I scribbled a reasonable facsimile of a small rectangular fishing licence and gave it to him. He beamed. The children around us, of course, felt they needed one as well, until almost all had a fishing licence. The supervisor of the centre happened to come into the room, and when she discovered what the conversation was about, she left and returned quickly with her official fishing licence. The children had to inspect it. Then along came Mabel, who said she doesn't fish, but she had finished folding washcloths with one of the educators. She asked for a folding licence. I made one for her and then asked her what were some other things she could fold with that licence. Below are the two brief curriculum webs we created when we pursued the new ideas.

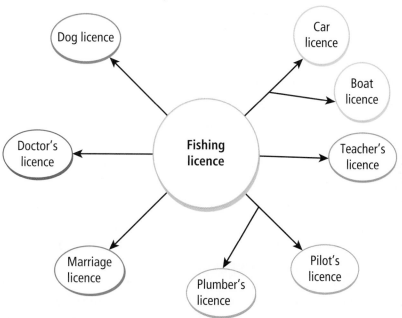

Emerging Inquiry: Why do some people need a licence to do something? Why does a dog need a licence? What is a licence? How long does it take to get one? Why does a pilot need a licence? How does he or she get one? How much does a licence cost? How long can you have a licence?

Source: Wiarton Kids Den/Sally Wylie

(Continued)

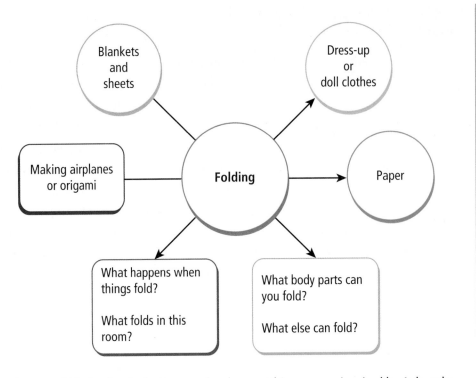

We made several kinds of webs in the preschool room. This one was inspired by Ayla, who apparently loves to fold. Pictures and text would support the investigation of this concept. Take pictures of children folding. Ask them what they are learning and write it down. Include the paper kinds of things they folded. Create a representation of their learning, which is what emergent curriculum is all about.

Source: Wiarton Kids Den/Sally Wylie

PORTFOLIOS AND E-PORTFOLIOS: AN IMPORTANT PART OF THE CYCLE OF OBSERVATION

Earlier sections of this chapter have introduced us to the importance of understanding the steps and processes within the cycle of observation. Let's turn our attention now to portfolios, an important part of the cycle and a necessary part of being a responsive educator.

Trends and changes in observation and documentation methods and expectations within the early childhood profession have prompted change in both the format and usage of portfolios for children. While the value of the traditional paper portfolio has not changed, the infusion of technology, apps, and digital media has opened a flood of new possibilities for portfolio use, conversation and reflection, sharing, and accessibility.

WHAT CONSTITUTES AN ARTIFACT?

Deciding what to put into a portfolio isn't easy, as it requires reflection and understanding of the intent of the artifact. Once you know what type of portfolio is being created, the artifacts can then be

selected. In previous chapters, we introduced some of the types of documentation that could be submitted into a child's hard-copy or digital portfolio. Some of these included photos, anecdotals, sociograms, and audio files. Other meaningful evidence or artifacts might include but are not limited to the following:

- photo narratives
- art samples
- math samples
- certificates of achievement
- language or writing samples
- audio files reflecting language use or social conversations between children
- videos of inquiries, conversations, experiences
- self-assessment scripts or pieces of writing
- group projects or inquiries (names of other children must be withheld if inserting into a child's portfolio)
- running records
- ABC analysis
- learning stories
- documentation panels
- charts or profiles of information whereby artifacts are combined to inform more holistic and comprehensive interpretations
- sticky notes or information collected at a glance
- events or moments in time/learning experiences that hold meaning for the child, family, or educator
- goals and objectives

What other examples can you think of? What have you placed into a portfolio? What has a child or family placed into a portfolio? For your convenience, examples of portfolios and portfolio entries are available online.

PORTFOLIO PREPARATION, STAGES, AND CONTENT

Reflection is at the heart of the portfolio process, as artifacts gain their meaning through this process. To engage in reflection, we again begin by formulating questions to prompt inquiry. As McCoy-Wozniak (2012) puts it,

> Inquiry is a continuous cycle of learning that involves questioning, investigating, analyzing, communicating, and reflecting on the knowledge gained. Reflecting on the evidence and conclusion produces more questions and the cycle of learning and discovery continues. Reflection connects the components of the inquiry cycle and serves as the catalyst to move to the next level of learning and discovery. (pp. 220–221)

Let's reflect, then, on the various types of questions we need to consider when embarking upon this process. Taking the time to reflect upon how the questions below might be answered supports appreciative inquiry and responsive practice. Questions that an early childhood team, including the educators, families, and children, might reflect upon include the following:

- What type of portfolio is best for the setting? For children and families? Who is your audience?
- How will the identity of the child be respected and preserved? If in electronic or e-form, it is important to think about password protection. Families have the right to choose how their child's information is conveyed, portrayed, viewed, and accessed. If hard-copy portfolios are preferred, it is important to consider the same question. Only families and authorized users should be able to access the child's file. Educators also need to consult with their licensing or ministry expectations regarding storage and confidentiality requirements for information on children; with the ethical standards for their profession and organization regarding observation and documentation; and with families and other educators concerning setting preferences.
- Where and how will the portfolio be stored?
- How will the information be organized? How will each child's story be told? How will each child be introduced? What will the headings be? Will they be sorted by connections to development or curriculum standards, by profile entries or dates throughout the year, by interests and strengths, or in some other way? Organization of a portfolio will depend on a number of variables and should reflect the voices and preferences of children, families, and educators collectively. Exhibit 6.12 presents two ways in which two different settings organized and linked their portfolio artifacts to frameworks or standards that guide professional practice.

EXHIBIT 6.12 **PORTFOLIO ORGANIZATION: TWO SETTINGS COMPARED**

Kristine Fenning

Jada and her baby
September 1, 2015 – Written by Asima

<u>Observation:</u> Jada was observed spending approximately 30 minutes today at the dolly centre. From the very moment Jada entered this area, her curiosity was evident and her actions were purposeful. Attempting to grab a baby from a peer, Jada stated "mine" and held the baby tight to her chest. When Asima introduced a different baby to Jada, she quickly accepted the baby and gave the other baby back to her friend. Holding the baby by its arms, Jada walked over to the easel and selected a piece of chalk. She began to draw straight lines on the belly of the baby while whispering "dere, dere you go baby." "Oh oh, your baby is all dirty." Asima began to wash a different baby and then asked Jada to wash her baby too. Jada immediately said "no." Asima then said "the baby needs a bath." Jada replied "yah, baby all dirty" and with a cloth she began washing off the chalk from the baby's belly.

<u>Reflections and Interpretations</u>
Educator: Jada seemed to be very interested in cause and effect as she would colour the baby and then wash the baby several times. Jada appeared to be able to participate in parallel play with her peers as she engaged in her own imaginary play scenario.

Parent: Jada is always very curious, wanting to do different things with materials she uses. At home she is fascinated with her easel chalk board as she is able to wipe her markings clean.

Jada: "That's my baby. I bathed baby."

<u>New Inquiry Possibilities/Extension of Learning:</u> Jada and her teacher will put out some baby bathtubs with washing materials to build on Jada's interests in cleaning her baby and to further her participation in pretend play (2.1.)

OELF Toddlers :Social/ Emotional	OELF: Indicators
1.1 Social Interest	☐ observing and imitating peers ☐ beginning to play "follow the peer games" ☑ observing and playing briefly with peers – may turn into struggle for possession ☐ offering toys ☐ engaging in short group activities
1.2 Perspective Taking	☑ In simple situations beginning to take the point of view of others
1.3 Parallel Play	☑ playing in proximity of peers with similar playthings without an exchange of ideas or things
2.1 Expression of Feelings	☐ expressing aggressive feelings and behaviour ☐ beginning to show self-conscious emotions (shame, embarrassment, guilt, pride) ☑ expressing feelings in language and pretend play

(Continued)

Observer: Cassandra Date: May 12, 2015		OELF Domain /Skill/Indicators	Centre Principle
	Observation: As Oliver sat and watched the bubbles come out from the bubble machine, he imitated a peer who had previously said "pop" and repeatedly said "pop, pop, pop" as he broke the bubbles on the floor. Oliver was also heard saying "bub" as the educators in the room said "look at the bubbles!". He watched and listened to his educator quietly.	Provocation was based on the following domain(s): 3.3 Expressive Language 5.3 Visual Exploration and Discrimination	This experience and suggested extensions of play reflect: #1Healthy development is built on relationships #3 Experiences should reflect the voice, interest, and development of each child within the group.
Bubble Bubble Pop!	Interpretation: Oliver seemed to use two new words today "pop," and "bub" for bubble. He was also able to use his pointer finger to pop the bubbles as he smiled. Parent reflection: "Oliver is attempting to repeat a lot of words lately. Tonight we will add bubbles to his bath to build on the words he was using today."	Indicators demonstrated in experience: 3.3 – using one word to communicate 4.4 Spatial Exploration – tracking moving objects with eyes 4.7 (Imitation) of adult actions and words	
	Extension of Oliver's Play: In addition to home suggestions, we can build on Oliver's curiosity with bubbles by providing a sensory bin with water, bubbles, and floating animals for him to stand to pop the bubbles in the bin, express and label materials in the bin, engage in cause and effect, and interact with peers and educators.	Linked to: 4.7 Symbolic Thought, Representation and Root Skills of Literacy 4.3 Cause and Effect Exploration	

In the first example, the observer has linked the overall learning to the Ontario Early Learning Framework by checking off what has been demonstrated. In the second learning story example, we see a centre linking the experience, what has been learned from the experience, and extensions to the play experience to the Ontario Early Learning Framework. This centre also links this learning to the centre's mission principles.

Source: Domains and indicators retrieved from Ontario Ministry of Children and Youth Services, Best Start Expert Panel on Early Learning (2007, January). *Early Learning for Every Child Today: A Framework for Early Childhood Settings*. Retrieved from http://www.cfcollaborative.ca/wp-content/uploads/2010/10/ELECT.pdf

Other questions we might reflect upon include the following:

- Who will determine what is submitted? Where and how can children, families, or educators write, document, and reflect?
- How will it be ensured that a variety of artifacts are submitted?
- How will the voices of the child, family, and educator be reflected?
- How often will artifacts be submitted?
- How will we know what is permitted to be placed in the portfolio?
- When and how might the portfolio be used to support and extend children's learning/inform practice?

- How might educators increase accessibility and use of the portfolio by children and families to encourage shared and collaborative observation, documentation, interpretation, reflection, and application of knowledge gained?

By considering these and other important questions, educators follow the observation cycle while supporting the integrity of the information being collected, selected, and reflected upon. This process also helps users to steer clear of using portfolios as a scrapbook. While scrapbooks are a great tool for capturing special memories and life events, the intent of portfolios is different in that they are meant to prompt reflection, discussion, demonstration of learning and the voices of children, evaluation, responsive planning, and new inquiries. Understanding the difference between the two is important. What other questions might you consider?

First introduced in Chapter 3, portfolios are a multipurpose, systematic form of **authentic assessment** and a forum in which to present a child's progress over time. Portfolios are not scrapbooks of information. Portfolios are strengths based and inquiry driven, and they reflect each child's interests, abilities, individuality, and diversity within his or her natural learning environment. Rather than a series of checklists or prescribed **standardized assessments**, portfolios are meant to contain a variety of informal observational methods and information. Portfolios are malleable, for they constantly change as each child grows and develops. Portfolios are a holistic way for educators, families, and children to document each child's learning journey, developmental and meaningful life experiences, and their thoughts and feelings, all within the context of the child's family and world.

Portfolios for many years have traditionally been based on a developmental perspective, with artifact submissions often tied to developmental milestones or skills demonstrated. This is still important, as understanding where children are developmentally, what skills they have yet to achieve, and what skills they are working on do enable educators to respond in ways to extend children's learning. However, if we challenge this single-lens paradigm and invite a sociocultural lens to the portfolio process, a more holistic lens of understanding about a child is attained, as the portfolio then contains information, interpretations, and evidence from a variety of sources and people. Portfolios are a rich resource of information to inform inclusive responses to children's interests, hypotheses, and queries and the co-creation of new curriculum and learning opportunities that reflect the voices and perspectives of each child within the learning environment. They are an important part of the observation cycle, as they create opportunities for appreciative inquiry and reflection. It is through team discussion of this information learned that relationships are built and quality environments are created. Further examples of portfolio entries and artifacts are available online.

ROLES OF THE EDUCATOR, CHILD, AND FAMILY

Educators continue to assume the primary role of ensuring that each child within their program has a portfolio, and they usually are responsible for ensuring that specific types of documentation are present. This role is often largely due to a centre's or setting's philosophy, or it may be due to licensing or legislative requirements. During this process of preparing portfolios for each child, the educator may experience a variety of roles including but not limited to the creator/co-creator, gatherer of information, editor, communicator, questioner, inquirer, provocateur, monitor, and decision maker. By sharing these other roles with children and families, the potential for a more holistic view of a child is gained. Everyone should have a voice and a role in developing, evolving, and discussing which artifacts represent most meaningfully a child's experiences, special or aha moments, learning, proud moments, a milestone or achievement, or something of interest. Sound pedagogical practice emphasizes the importance of portfolio creation as a collaborative process. The educator continues to collect and organize the material with the cooperation of children, parents, and colleagues right from the time in which they begin in a setting. Collaboration in the beginning stages and throughout prompts collective reflection upon and interpretation of artifacts for submission and their meaning. It might also prompt reflection upon opportunities experienced and how learning took place, areas for further growth, strengths and interests, environmental variables that support growth and development, and ways that a child's learning might be extended.

Ultimately, eliciting all perspectives assists in reducing bias and misperceptions, therefore leading to a more accurate and comprehensive understanding of a child. Take a look at Exhibit 6.13, for example. Without the accompanying descriptive story of Chelsea sharing her experience with her stepdad, one might think the photo is simply of a child having fun, making a silly face into the camera. This was not the case. Chelsea's review of the narrative in Exhibit 6.13 spawned a whole reflection by Chelsea of her experience in the situation and how she might prepare for future teeth to fall out.

Take a moment to review these reflections online. There you will find various portfolio examples in addition to Chelsea's reflection and subsequent interpretations by her educators, dad, and stepdad prompted the creation of "lost tooth" stories for the bookshelves in the room.

What does Exhibit 6.13 tell us? It portrays the unique and important perspective of the child, and the excitement children have to share their learning and experiences. Having the opportunity to share this learning is what makes these moments special. Take the time to sit and reflect with children on an event in their lives; you'll be surprised by what you hear and learn when you truly listen. Meeting regularly

EXHIBIT 6.13 **LOST TOOTH PORTFOLIO ARTIFACT**

Conversation and Situation at Pick-Up Time:

"Dad, DAD, DAAAAAADDD! Come and see what I did today! I have to show you something." Chelsea brings her stepfather to the digital photo frame mounted on their classroom wall, where the classroom teachers have inserted the SD card of the day. On the card are photos of the experiences that children had earlier in the day. Chelsea exclaims, "Dad, when you see my picture, you have to guess what is different, okay?" "All right," her stepfather replies. "Come closer, Dad, so you can see." Chelsea walks her stepdad up closer to the frame and prompts him when her photo

Anastasia Tveretinovae/Shutterstock.com

appears. "Quick, look! Do you see anything different?" "No, I see you making a goofy face at the camera." "DAAADDDD, I want you to look again, but now you need to wait until my photo comes back." They wait and watch about 20 photos go by before Chelsea's photo comes up again. "Dad, now look better, okay?" "Okay, Chelsea. I don't see anything different," her stepdad says with a smirk on his face. "Ugh, I lost my first tooth!" "I was just joking, Chelsea. How exciting! We are going to have to celebrate. Do you have your tooth?" "Yeah! I can't wait to show Daddy at home. I was so scared when it was dangling at lunch, but my friend said it wouldn't hurt if I pulled it. Then I bit into a soft sandwich and it came out. Did you know that soft things are good for sore teeth? Can we have ice cream to celebrate?" "Wow, I'm glad you figured it out, Chelsea. Way to go! Sure. You, your dad, and I will have a special dinner tonight," her stepdad replies.

Days later, Chelsea and her educators place the photo in the digital Dropbox they had set up for Chelsea and her family, something they had done for every family in the room to document experiences and learning that was happening in the room. Chelsea prepares her reflection on the experience.

with families and children to review and discuss a portfolio, whether it is daily, spontaneously, or at designated times throughout the year, is a necessary step in the pedagogical documentation process and is an important role of the responsive educator. According to Caspe, Seltzer, Lorenzo Kennedy, Cappio, and DeLorenzo (2013),

> Involving families in this process enables them to share their expertise about their children and creates an exchange of information between families and teachers that supports children as their strengths and needs change.... Moreover, children thrive when they are part of a community in which families and teachers understand children's strengths and areas of need and then individualize teaching to match the children's capabilities (Copple & Bredekamp 2009). (p. 9)

Being a responsive educator means using this information in way that supports the preparation of co-created and inclusive curriculum for both individual and groups of children in the same setting.

ROLES OF THE SUPERVISOR, DIRECTOR, OR PRINCIPAL

All early childhood settings have an administration department or office, for it is the role of the administrator to ensure that the staff and educators are fulfilling their responsibilities as per their licensing, ministry, legislative, or board of directors requirements. An important role of the administrator is supporting the educator to create opportunities for portfolio creation and entries for each child. This support could come in the form of

- assisting educators to introduce the portfolio process to families and children when they first start the program
- supporting educators, families, and children to attain materials and the room necessary for ongoing access to documentation to promote joint ownership of observing and documenting how learning happens for children
- scheduling time for educators to meet with children and families to select representative artifacts for insertion. This would include time for preparing documentation that would invite reflections and interpretations from children, families, and educators. This time would also include discussion of where the team sees a child's strengths and opportunities for growth, as well as providing time for a child to reflect upon and discuss meaningful moments in her or his learning. These discussions are great opportunities for revisiting how children learn through play as educators and families listen to children recalling events that took place. Often we are consumed by whether or not a child knows his numbers, shapes, or colours, and we lose track of how a child might be building friendships; resolving conflicts or handling changes in his or her life or day;

forming hypotheses and taking risks; or exploring various aspects (or not) of the learning environment. These are just some of the inquiries we might have in building our understanding of a child. What else might be important to a parent? A child? An educator?

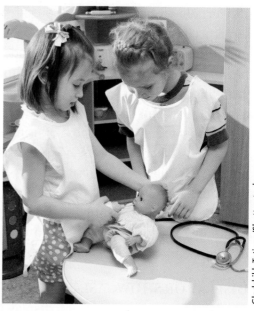

- scheduling time for writing, rewriting, and editing documentation, or for preparing documents in hard copy for a portfolio or in digital form for an e-portfolio. This process includes making connections between the documentation collected and what can be learned or gained by reflecting upon what has been gathered. This step might include building a profile of a child's abilities or co-preparing curriculum that scaffolds upon the child's learning and interests.
- providing time for planning for individual supports if identified through discussion that a child is struggling with an aspect of her or his development, an Individual Educational Plan is necessary, or referrals for outside support are needed. For more information on Individual Education Plans and early intervention, please go to Chapter 7.

Understanding how to build a sustainable portfolio system for every child in a room requires a commitment from all participants in a setting. When everyone understands what the process is and what is required, the value of portfolios as a means to inform practice is increased.

PORTFOLIO AND AUTHENTIC ASSESSMENT: TYPES AND FORMS

The authentic context of the portfolio allows it to be associated with a variety of curriculum approaches, philosophies, and settings. With the evolvement of pedagogical documentation and observational/assessment methods that reflect the individuality of children within familiar environments, it is important to understand that there are various types of portfolios and many forms they can take as a means for documenting progress of a child. Portfolios as a means for documenting the professional learning continuum of educators is a topic that will be further explored in Chapter 8.

Portfolios for children can be prepared in either paper or digital format; it is a philosophical choice of a setting. When in traditional paper form, portfolios may be prepared in a file folder format with tabs, in a binder with sleeve protectors, or in an accordion file, for example. A number of variables might influence the format of the portfolio, including philosophy, storage capacity, stage of portfolio development, skills and knowledge of those contributing to the portfolio, number and type of artifacts submitted.

Understanding the purpose of using a portfolio and who the audience might be can assist in determining the type of portfolio most appropriate for a child, family, or setting. While the organization of a portfolio will vary with the setting, hard-copy portfolios are traditionally presented in three different ways depending on the purpose and intention of the documentation being collected. The three most common and traditional categories of portfolios are display or showcase portfolios, working or developmental portfolios, and assessment portfolios. Let's examine each below.

DISPLAY OR SHOWCASE PORTFOLIOS

The intention and purpose of a **display or showcase portfolio** is exactly as it sounds. Ranges of artifact submissions from informal to formal are appropriate for insertion in this approach. Selected artifacts demonstrating a child's "best" work are presented for review and reflection. The educator with this type of portfolio is often charged with the task of selecting a child's best work or traits so as to show connections to curriculum frameworks, professional standards, or skills and knowledge as outlined in standardized assessments. Children and families might also have the opportunity to perform this task; however, they tend not to provide authentic artifact evidence that shows other elements of a child's experiences and interests, or moments in time that are of significance to the child.

Take, for example, Exhibit 6.14. Ms. Smith, the educator, had been selecting writing samples she felt represented Rachel's growth and development and her "best work." Take a look in this exhibit at Ms. Smith's rationale for not only including the artifact she had collected but also placing Rachel's choice and her rationale beside hers. What do you notice about these two artifacts? Why might it be important to keep both?

This portfolio may house formal and standardized assessment information; however, it is imperative that the educator check with his or her licensing body to determine if this information should be in a more separate and secure location.

WORKING/DEVELOPMENTAL PORTFOLIOS

A **working/developmental portfolio** is sometimes seen as a temporary home for information because it evolves and changes as the individual grows and changes. Others will argue that it is not temporary but rather a portfolio system that is

EXHIBIT 6.14   A COMPARISON OF "BEST WORK"

Artifact Submitted By Rachel, Age 10.1

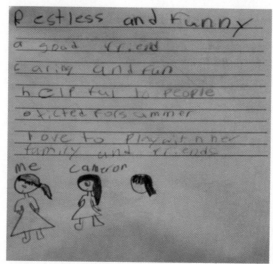

Kristine Fenning

Grade Four Portfolio Artifact

Name of Child: Rachel **CA:** 10.1 yrs **Date:** September 8, 2012
Submitted by: Rachel

Type of Artifact	Rationale for Entry	Reflections on Artifact
Poem	"I think this is a good poem because I wrote it with my friend Cam and she is my best friend. This poem has words in it that we both like, and it is my favourite. We used some really good adjectives that show how I feel about Cam, like restless and funny and helpful."	**Ms. Smith:** Rachel, you have really put your thoughts into some great words that describe your friend. She is lucky to have you as a friend. **Curriculum strand:** *Writing* -Reflects understanding and organization of ideas to reflect an intended audience

Notes: Share at parent–teacher conference

Source: Kristine Fenning

(Continued)

Draft Journal Reflection Artifact Submitted by the Teacher

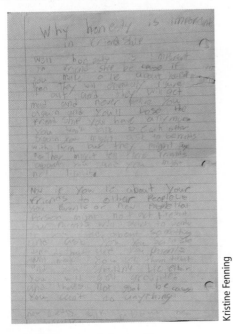

Kristine Fenning

Kristine Fenning

Grade Four Portfolio Artifact

Name of Child: Rachel **CA:** 10.1 yrs **Date:** September 8, 2012

Submitted by: Ms. Smith, Grade 4 teacher

Type of Artifact	Rationale for Entry	Reflections on Artifact
Draft writing sample	This draft was prepared as a reflection on a guest speaker who came in to speak about bullying and the importance of friendships with everyone. It demonstrates Rachel's connection to the concepts presented by the speaker. Rachel was to then proofread it and word process it for display in the classroom.	**Parent comment(s):** We didn't realize she was thinking at this level about the ways in which she needs to act to maintain friendships. This is great to see. **Curriculum strand:** Demonstrates processing skills, forming opinions, forming some connections to concepts

Note: Was reviewed by Rachel and her parents in the parent–teacher conference and compared to her final revised version on display—final grade was level 3+

Source: Kristine Fenning

continually building and changing so as to reflect the learning journey of a child. "It includes selected but typical Work Samples along with teacher documentation to show the child's progress as well as the teacher's observations. It is on these Portfolios that curriculum is based and future actions planned for the child, with input from the child, the family, and other professionals if needed" (Nilsen, 2014, p. 9). This particular type of portfolio resonates with appreciative inquiry and pedagogical documentation principles, as artifacts are more often culturally, developmentally, and authentically relevant, capturing the diversity of the child within the learning environment. Any artifact that holds meaning for the child, family, or educator can be included in this portfolio. Standardized checklists and information should be stored separately from this type of portfolio in a secure location.

ASSESSMENT PORTFOLIOS

The **assessment portfolio** is most commonly associated with the demonstration of knowledge and skills related to curriculum outcomes. This does not necessarily mean that only a child's best work is entered to reflect mastery or attainment of an outcome; instead, artifacts are submitted that provide opportunity for assessment of the level of achievement for a particular standard or grade. The child or the educator may create artifact submissions, which are open for discussion in a parent–educator meeting. Confidential storage of assessment information is particularly important as you will see in Chapter 7.

Robert Kneschke/Shutterstock.com

E-PORTFOLIOS/DIGITAL PORTFOLIOS

It is an increasing expectation that children will use technology as an information source for new learning and exploration. In education today, children are expected to be self-driven with technology and to access the knowledge needed for just-in-time learning. **E-portfolios** provide opportunities for children to practise these skills, while furthering self awareness of their strengths, their aha moments, and areas for growth and development. Common e-portfolio sites such as Weebly, Mahara,

Notability, Desire2Learn, Three Ring, Kidblog, Easy Portfolio, ePortfolio Mashup, Google Docs, and Dreamweaver are set up to allow different types of users to populate the e-portfolios with artifacts and text in various ways. It is strongly suggested that educators research these and other e-portfolio sites to find the best fit for them.

E-portfolios are conducive to capturing the individuality of children's learning and thinking, thus promoting, recognizing, and valuing learning that happens in different ways for different children. This is important for all children. E-portfolios are not restricted to specific types of artifacts, and they provide ongoing opportunity for reflection, interpretation, conversation, and connection to new learning.

In many circumstances, families also benefit from e-portfolio use. According to Bates (2014),

> Digital portfolios can give families a glimpse into their child's day because one of the advantages is the capability to share a child's work. To ensure privacy, teachers control who has access to the portfolio. When sharing it, different levels of permission are available, including the *view* and *modify* options. The view option lets families see the contents of the portfolio, and the modify option lets them contribute by uploading images and recordings from home. This approach supports family engagement and provides a more complete picture of children's development. (p. 56)*

Let's take a look at the excerpt of a parent who added to an artifact in her child's portfolio in Exhibit 6.15.

EXHIBIT 6.15	A PARENT'S ARTIFACT ENTRY TO A DIGITAL PORTFOLIO

Ammentorp Photography/Shutterstock.com

*Bates, C.C. *Digital Portfolios: Using Technology to Involve Families,* National Association for the Education of Young Children, (NAEYC), Sept. 2014, p. 56.

Name of Child: Alexander **Date:** March 19, 2015 **CA:** 3.2 years
Name of Observer: Mary (Alexander's mother)

Digital Artifact Rationale

I took this photo of Alexander at the table doing some artwork as it demonstrates Alexander's imagination and love for superheroes and explosions. When I asked him about this artwork, he said, "The bad guy's car went boom like that when he crashed." I feel this demonstrates his ability to make lots of different movements with his crayons, including large circles, squiggles, and swirly lines.

Reflections

Alexander (written by his mom, Mary): "Yeah, the bad guy's gone now. The fire in his car is out 'cause of the water."

Educator A: Alexander seems to have demonstrated fascination with superheroes and science here because of his interest in explosions. It seems he has demonstrated several fine motor movements with his left hand tripod grasp, as indicated by his parent above.

Development Interpretations and References (Prepared by Educator A)

*Alexander seems to have demonstrated such fine motor movements as drawing a diagonal and zigzag line independently, forming a closed circle, and making purposeful markings. These are evident by the various markings he made on his paper. His tripod grasp seems to be evident in the photo as he holds the crayon in his left hand. It appears that Alexander can speak in 6- to 11-word sentences, as indicated by the language examples above. Alexander is also able to demonstrate recall skills as he elaborates on the story he is imagining that represents his artwork.

*OELF

3.5: Using Descriptive Language to Explain, Explore and Extend
3.9 Retelling stories
4.8 Communicating Findings

New Inquiries and Extensions of Play

We will have Alexander help us to prepare some science experiments with vinegar and baking soda to expand his expressive language and to engage him in forming hypotheses, as well as add some superhero capes to the dramatic and block centres to expand his imaginary play.

More information on the e-portfolio suggestions above and examples of e-portfolios are available online.

PORTFOLIOS AND ACCESSIBILITY

The hard-copy portfolio typically remains at the early childhood setting for viewing until the child leaves a setting or the portfolio has reached its capacity and a new one is created. The e-portfolio has the capacity to be accessed at any time by any authorized user with computer and Internet access no matter where they are. With the introduction of web-based and app-based portfolios, hard-copy portfolios can be transformed into digital formats by simply scanning, taking a photo, and then loading the information onto a computer. As the child changes, the portfolio can be personalized with the simple click of a button to add, remove, or alter information.

Electronic portfolios have a number of capabilities that hard-copy portfolios do not. Audio and visual capabilities of the e-portfolio enable the revisiting of a moment in time so as to allow those viewing the information to experience the situation as it occurs. For example, video vignettes or audio files provide opportunity to dialogue and reflect upon a learning moment together. This gives authentic insights into what took place, thus increasing the accuracy of knowing what has been seen, heard, and understood.

Portability of the electronic portfolio is often an asset. However, the early childhood setting needs to consider whether those who wish to contribute to the electronic portfolio have the necessary electronic skills and abilities to prepare, modify, view, post, or even access technology. Time is a valuable asset for early childhood settings, and thus it is important that educators not be bogged down with trying to figure out systems rather than spending time with the children. Technology also may or may not increase a family's access to their child's information, as some families may not have a computer at home or access to the Internet. This is something to consider when planning for accessibility.

Digital portfolios also allow a large volume of historical information to be retained over long periods of time, whether it is password protected in a web or e-based portfolio site, on a USB or DVD, or on a computer mainframe. Finding opportunities to allow a child to compare his or her learning to previous learning is a great opportunity for a child to engage in self-assessment. This poses a number of benefits for the child, including recognition of his or her individual learning and developmental journey, increased self-awareness, and a supportive dialogue regarding a child's progress and the setting of new goals and personal objectives of interest or relevance to the child.

E-PORTFOLIOS AND VOICE-TO-TEXT PROGRAMS

Voice-to-text programs open up a whole new world for e-portfolios and use by children. With popular voice-to-text programs like Dragon Dictation, Evernote, Voice

Texting Pro, Voice Assistant for social media users, and other apps specific to different educational subjects, users can translate their speech into text that then can be used for an e-portfolio or printed for hard-copy viewing. These programs enable children to be less dependent on adults in navigating and populating their portfolios, thus enhancing literacy and increasing opportunities for the child's voice to be a part of the reflection and dialogue process in parent–educator–child meetings. These programs are also a viable option for educators and families who are constrained for time to write reflections or interpretations during or following an observation or who may struggle with the writing process. These types of apps do change frequently, as technology changes happen daily and new apps come out while others become obsolete. Every app also has its own strengths and limitations, such as specific devices required, price, and usability.

Individual Education Plans (IEPs) or standardized assessments may be a part of a child's files but are often stored separately from a child's portfolio for confidentiality reasons. Again, it is important to check with your licensing or governmental regulations to determine how confidential information is to be stored and viewed. More information on standardized assessments can be found in Chapter 7.

Exhibit 6.16 demonstrates the uniqueness of entries in children's portfolios. Based on the entry below, what types of entries might we see in an infant portfolio? The portfolio of a child in full-day kindergarten? Be sure to see the examples available online.

EXHIBIT 6.16	**SHORT LANGUAGE SAMPLE**

This language sample has been voice-to-text transcribed from the Voice Memo App on Santos's digital portfolio dated January 4, 2015.

Name of Child: Santos   **DOB:** February 14, 2013   **CA:** 25 months
Date: April 24, 2015
Documenter: Erik
(student-educator)

Location: Book centre—Santos is sitting with his legs crossed on the floor beside a student-educator with a social story book created for Santos called "My New Baby Sister."
Student-Educator: "Santos, what are you reading?"
Santos: "Dis, my book."
Student-Educator: "Who is in your book, Santos?"
Santos: "Bith. Bith cying. Stinky dipa."

(Continued)

Student-Educator: "Oh dear, a stinky diaper. What do we do with a stinky diaper?"

Santos: "Wipe bum. Put garbage dere." (he points to the garbage can in the bathroom for diapers)

Student-Educator: "What do you like to do with Elizabeth?"

Santos: "I hoded Bith."

Student-Educator: "I bet you held her very carefully, Santos. Did you feed her a bottle?"

Santos: "No, Mum feed er."

Interpretations

It seems that Santos is able to use approximated and intelligible full words in two- to three-word sentences to communicate, and he appears to be able to answer the questions of his educator with information in context, such as identifying who is in his book and what he does with his sister. It seems he uses past and present tense (hoded, cying).

Reflections/New Inquiries

Educators to offer baby supplies, blankets, dolls, and beds in the dramatic centre to build on Santos's interest in his new baby sister. Building on this book with things he does with his sister might be an option to explore to further build on his expressive language.

Parent Reflection

It is great to see Santos so interested in his new baby sister. We were worried about how he would adjust to this new situation. We would like to prepare a book for him on why he is such a great big brother, as we think this will help him to be more gentle with his sister.

As we explore assessment tools in Chapter 7, it would be interesting to apply our learning from portfolio entries like that in Exhibit 6.16 to a screening tool to determine how we might continue to support a child in his language development. If we were to apply this portfolio example to the Ontario Early Learning Framework and the Ontario Ministry of Education *How Does Learning Happen?* document, what else might we learn? What new questions or inquiries might we have?

PORTFOLIOS: SUPPORTING CHILDREN'S METACOGNITION

As can be seen, portfolios provide a lens to capture the voice of the child. Reflecting, thinking about, interpreting, and communicating about one's learning and progress is a complex and important skill to practise and master. Portfolios provide the platform necessary for this self-reflection to take place. Velez Laski (2013) describes metacognition as

> "thinking about thinking" such as knowing what we know or do not know, monitoring the outcomes of our work, setting goals, and planning ahead.… Essentially, children with good metacognitive skills are self-directed learners who are able to self-evaluate and select new strategies when appropriate rather than rely on someone else to guide them (Bransford, Brown, & Cocking 2000). (p. 38)

When children are provided the materials necessary to self-document and reflect, and ongoing opportunities for conversation and reflection are available, they develop awareness of their strengths and skills requiring development. During these opportunities, children are able to recall proud, exciting, or challenging moments in their learning; revisit old and develop new hypotheses; and develop a passion for literacy as they authentically review their developmental progress and perhaps set goals of their own for future learning. Children of all abilities are able to view their portfolios and communicate through imagery, pictures, and artifacts selected to share with others what they know and understand.

Elementary school teachers with older school-age children at a school in the United States were asked to think about why they wanted system-wide e-portfolios for children in their classes. Reflecting upon the reasons provided in Exhibit 6.17,

---

EXHIBIT 6.17   SCHOOL-WIDE E-PORTFOLIOS

The following "are several important reasons driving us toward school-wide e-portfolios. Central among these reasons:

- students learn to think beyond the grade;
- students increase their self-awareness;
- students develop the essential dispositions for lifelong learning—self-motivation, self-discipline, self-scheduling, responsibility, and organization;
- students understand, set, and discuss their learning goals and strategies for getting there;
- teachers individualize the student learning experience;
- and teachers, students, and parents become partners in the student's learning experience"

Source: Taken from "E-Portfolio: A 21st-Century Tool for 21st-Century Learning" in *Independent Schools*, Winter 2014 issue, p. 72. Used by permission of the author, Chris Shriver.

---

we can see that their reasons centred on children's learning and the development of metacognition.

PORTFOLIOS AND PROFESSIONAL STANDARDS, FRAMEWORKS, AND DOCUMENTS

In the process of preparing and creating portfolios for children, making connections between selected artifacts to defined professional standards, curriculum frameworks, environmental design, ministry documents, or developmental continuums is a common role and expectation for educators around the world. When meaningful artifacts are collected, selected, and reflected upon, the process of applying and connecting the new knowledge gained to developmental continuums, to professional standards of practice, or to standards held by a particular setting becomes more defined. Exhibit 6.18 connects a documentation artifact to the *How Does Learning Happen? Ontario's Pedagogy for the Early Years* document prepared by the Ontario Ministry of Education (2014). What do you notice about this documentation? How might you structure your documentation to link to frameworks or guidelines that inform your practice? Remember that all the documentation methods we have discussed can be formatted in digital or hardcopy form and can be configured in ways that align with your centre, agency, or school requirements.

| EXHIBIT 6.18 | MAKING THE CONNECTION |

Kristine Fenning

Lauren, Age 4.2 years. Date of artwork: July 22, 2015.

"The Pumpkin Patch"

Lauren made lots of pictures using orange today. This one she proudly shared with everyone in the room. Lauren said "this pumpkin is growing so big, even bigger than the other plants in the field cause of the sun and the rain. We brought this pumpkin home and we are going to make lots of pies."

Parent Post-it:

We weighed it and it was 15 pounds! Lauren has been scooping out the seeds and so far she has counted 50! She wants to show her friends.

Educator Post-it:

Lauren's family are bringing in the pumpkin for the group to explore. We are going to compare our pumpkins from the centre garden to this one to provoke new inquiries.

If we link this artifact, experience, and accompanying reflections to the *How Does Learning Happen?* document (Ontario Ministry of Education, 2014), we can see its pertinence to the goal of engagement as the educators and Lauren connect her family experience to the inquiries of the children in the room who are already interested in the growing pumpkins in their centre garden. Inviting the participation of the family is responsive to Lauren's interests, it prompts inquiry through play and exploration of the natural world, and it presents a number of provocations and new questions for the children as they explore this large pumpkin. In what other ways can you connect this experience and Lauren's learning to the Ontario Early Learning Framework?

Source: Kristine Fenning

What questions might the children have when the pumpkin is brought in? How might these connections and this information now inform curriculum? How might families, children, and educators use this information collaboratively to extend learning? How might it inform additions or changes to the environment? What would you suggest as a response to the question in Exhibit 6.18?

Other provincial documents also remind us to be mindful of the needs and desires of newcomer children and families and, when documenting the activity of children from other cultures who speak languages other than English or French, to do so with awareness and respect.

In Ontario, documents such as *Many Roots/Many Voices: Supporting English Language Learners in Every Classroom* (Ontario Ministry of Education, 2005) are inclusive and supportive of newcomers to Canada:

> Newcomers from all backgrounds have a wide variety of interests and skills and often can contribute a great deal to a school's co-curricular activities. Some may have highly developed skills in a sport that does not have a long history at the school. Others may want to form a language club. Many newcomers will have talents and stories to contribute.… All of these activities provide opportunities for English language learners to participate in school life. (p. 41)

Alberta's document *Working with Young Children Who Are Learning English as a New Language* (2009), advises,

> Research shows that when young children are developing two languages at the same time, the two developing languages build on each other rather than take away from each other. The stronger the first (or home) language proficiency is, the stronger the second language proficiency will be, particularly with academic literacy. Maintaining the home language is key to a child's success in school.…
>
> Family, community members and the children themselves are great resources as you seek to establish a learning environment where cultural and linguistic diversity is valued. As you get to know families, you will want to be responsive to what you see, hear and observe. (pp. 5, 7)

Both of these provincial documents speak to responsive, inclusive practice respecting the cultures of families of Canada.

SUMMARY

Ever since the observations of Piaget and those before him who kept records of children's learning, observation has been the means to discover what we know about children today. In the informal, familiar playroom, teachers learn about the effects of socialization and culture on children's personalities or about how the environment shapes their behaviour and attitudes. In addition to learning about each child, our observations have become more complex, requiring us to interpret a child's behaviour through lenses of the bigger world outside the centre: families, communities, and society in general. Formulating an observation cycle connects the child-care setting with the influences of the child's family, home life, culture, and general community. Creating early learning environments for young children provides early childhood educators with ideas to enhance the space that children occupy. Educators think intentionally about how to organize the space and involve the children to provide accessible materials that engage children and enhance their play experiences. Creating healthy and inviting environments encourages all participants to explore the many possibilities for learning and living in a caring community.

This chapter took a broad look at the process of documentation, considering the environment, the stakeholders, and how philosophy and practice merge to produce unique pedagogical documentation. Through the lens of the reflective cycle of observation, appreciative inquiry, and mutual education, we hope that new spaces in your mind will creatively transform your philosophy and practices.

CHAPTER 7

INFORMING PRACTICE THROUGH THE LENS OF EARLY IDENTIFICATION

Courtesy of Scotia Plaza Child Care Centre

OVERVIEW

In Chapter 6, we discussed the reflective cycle of observation, creating curriculum, community awareness, portfolios, and other aspects of transforming possibilities to practice. This process inevitably requires us to step outside the box to look back in. As educators, we look outward to inform our practices; that process can provide the lens to see how we would like things to be. We also need to look from the outside in to assess ourselves as a community of learners, to partner with families, and to ensure optimal development for all children in the community.

Some of the main topics in this chapter include assessment, family-centred practice, early identification, and early intervention in the early childhood profession. A core focus will certainly be on practical insights into working with children with special needs and families. Included will be the importance of comprehensive data collection during the **early intervention/early identification** process to ensure that the child's actual needs are being addressed.

As new definitions of play-based learning, curriculum, and environment emerge and new practices within community consultation are evolving, it is important to look with the lens to what is needed by and provided to the children who have special needs or require special supports and/or services. As has been often said, it takes a village to raise a child; therefore, our focus in this chapter is not only on the child and family but also on services, resources, and relationships in the community.

FOCUS QUESTIONS

1. What is the role of observation in the early identification of children with special needs?
2. Whom might educators collaborate with in the early intervention process?
3. What are the components of family-centred services or practices?
4. What considerations might a professional make in designing an early identification plan based on appreciative inquiry principles and the cycle of observation?

THE CYCLE OF OBSERVATION AND EARLY INTERVENTION

Reflecting on content from other chapters, we are reminded that appreciative inquiry is a strengths-based approach to change, focusing on an openness to see new possibilities from a collective knowledge. Also, remember that the cycle of observation is a reflective process that is transforming, allowing participants the flexibility of thought and action to observe, discuss, reflect, monitor, and plan. This team-directed, multiperspective approach is most represented in this particular chapter as we learn about the process of early intervention, the role of assessment and children with extra support and/or special needs, family-centred practice, and the importance of working with our team and community partners. Although the cycle of observation in Chapter 6 includes the same process and terminology, another aspect of that cycle represents the unique process of early intervention: initial observations, assessment, an individual plan, strategies with adaptations and supports, implementation, monitoring, and evaluation. This process, as you can see from Exhibit 7.1, is part of the cycle yet uniquely on its own.

EXHIBIT 7.1

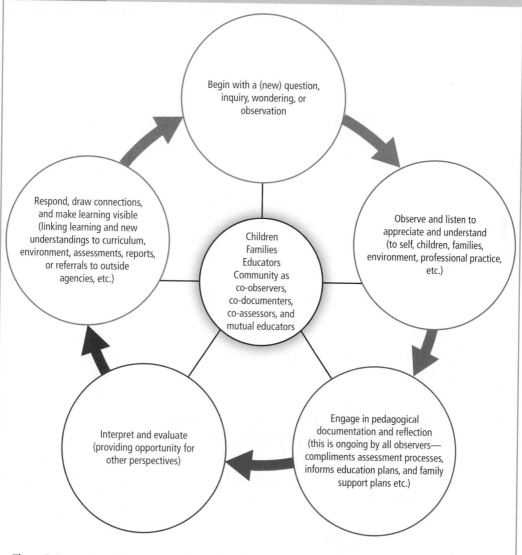

There is interaction throughout the cycle. Through application of appreciative inquiry, observers can begin at any point and can move fluidly through the process. Examples demonstrating the application of this cycle to early identification and intervention are available online.

Source: Kristine Fenning

To illustrate the process of appreciative inquiry and the cycle of observation in the classroom, let us consider Michael. This is a true story about the role of careful observation, inquiry, and the importance of relationships. Imagine a half-day community program that has a professional support network and therefore is able to have within its enrolment a number of children who have been referred from the community for additional support. The child in the following scenario is described by an educator.

Michael is a young boy of three who was referred from the community hub to our program for behavioural issues identified by his family. Initially, Michael lived up to his referral with outbursts of temper, refusal to cooperate, and, more importantly, almost constantly pushing and shoving other children around him. Michael wore glasses, which I discovered he had been wearing only for the past 6 months. I observed him over a number of days, and one observation in particular was highly interesting. Michael was sitting at a table trying to construct a 12-piece single-inset puzzle. This was the first time I had seen him attempt a puzzle. As I watched, he fumbled with the pieces, bringing each one up to his face and leaning over the puzzle before he wiggled each one into position. When his mother arrived to take him home, I asked her about his vision. "Oh, he can see fine," she said, "now that he has his glasses." Several days passed. As I completed more observations, I began to suspect that he might not actually be seeing all that clearly; perhaps his glasses were not helping him see as well as they could. After much discussion with Michael's mother, my supervisor, and colleagues, we decided it might be worth investigating further into his vision and glasses. Michael's mother finally was able to get an appointment with an ophthalmologist to have his eyes tested again. This time, he was diagnosed with strabismus in one eye and was immediately scheduled for an operation to correct his field of vision. When he returned from his operation with his new glasses, it was not long before we saw a changed child; he seemed happier and more confident and was less aggressive with his peers. His mother noticed a change at home as well.

Michael's referral to us from a different program as a perceived "unruly" child was based on his behaviour. Staff had labelled him without uncovering the cause of his behaviour. Michael pushed and shoved because he could not see. Perhaps he pushed and shoved because he felt anxious and vulnerable, and that frustration poured out into almost all aspects of his social encounters. He could not see, but because he had glasses, the assumption was that he could see. Michael did not really understand that his vision was challenged; he just tried to cope with life around him.

In what ways does this story provoke our thinking? How does it challenge us to see beyond what we consider to be obvious?

These kinds of stories and questions are reminders that there is no substitute for appreciative inquiry, reflection, and informed observation. The sustainability of learning, rather than a "Band-Aid" approach to learning that is short lived and often superficial, is key to understanding behaviour. Observation gets to the core to uncover the cause. The For Goodness Sake Program (https://ascy.ca/goodness-sake/) offered through the Affiliated Services for Children and Youth (n.d.) in Hamilton, Ontario, is one example of an "applied approach to behavioural intervention for young children [and] is a resource for early childhood educators, community health nurses and teachers …" (para. 1). This program integrates the knowledge and the processes necessary to develop action plans for addressing challenging behaviour and promoting **prosocial behaviour** in children. Children communicate through behaviour that something is "not right" or that a need is not being met. It is our role as responsive educators to listen, learn, observe, document, and collect the information necessary to understand and respond.

It takes a community to build collective knowledge and a paradigm of possibilities for children, their families, and the community itself. This is especially true for children with special needs, children who are vulnerable, and children who need extra supports or services. How well we construct a plan for observing and documenting, develop a model for early intervention, implement our required ministry policies, or prepare and follow policies and procedures in our early childhood settings hinges on our discussion of our collective beliefs and commitment, our services and resources, and our vision of what can be. How creatively do we problem-solve perceived barriers or challenges? How do we scaffold new knowledge by rethinking our perspectives to see things in different ways? Asking questions like these helps us create quality inclusive and responsive practices and environments. If we can engage in appreciative inquiry and mutual education, we will make a significant difference in our approach to the welfare of our children and families.

BEGINNING WITH OBSERVATION

In this chapter, we again pick up our primary thread of the observation process to illustrate a multistep complex process of early identification, observation, assessment, evaluation, and community building. Educators are important contributors to all aspects of this complex process and interactive cycle.

CREATING AN OBSERVATIONAL PLAN

Establishing observation as an everyday practice and dialogue requires every participant within an early childhood setting to participate in establishing an observational plan. All members of the team—child, family, teacher, and supervisor—are integral to the creation of a sustainable and realistic observational system.

> "Early Childhood Educators observe, assess, evaluate, document and report on children's progress along all domains of child development. As they work with children, families and other adults, Early Childhood Educators set goals, make decisions, resolve challenges, decide on developmentally responsive activities and experiences, provide behaviour guidance and work collaboratively in the best interest of the children under their professional supervision." (p. 19)
>
> Source: *Code of Ethics and Standards of Practice*. College of Early Childhood Educators, 2011, p. 19, www.college-ece.ca.

As we dialogue about what a plan might look like, we realize that each member in our team places value and priority on different aspects of learning, teaching, and observation. As new members join the program (families, children, and staff), the team needs to revisit their observational plan to ensure shared understanding of their varying values, centre philosophy, and priorities in order to support effectively the success of their entire learning community. These varying perspectives, if discussed professionally and proactively, can stimulate some new and exciting observation and documentation approaches. Implementing a system that works for everyone requires a collaboration of ideas from all members, as well as a commitment to following through with the plan.

It is through observation, documentation, reflection, and evaluation that decisions can be made by the team. These decisions might include or inform curriculum changes for individuals or groups of children based on their strengths, opportunities for growth, and interests. They might also inform changes to teaching approaches, environmental design, the need for more observation, or perhaps the introduction of assessment and early intervention for children requiring extra support. How does your early childhood setting implement observation as part of everyday practice? Within your setting, do you have an early identification plan based upon a strong observational foundation? How might your plan be connected to an appreciative inquiry approach? How are families and children involved in that plan? The inquiry process will generate these and other important questions, which will focus and guide the cycle of observation and observational plan. More information on the Ontario Ministry of Education observation and documentation expectations, as well as examples of how observation and documentation inform aspects of our practice, including early intervention, is available online.

Iakov Filimonov/Shutterstock.com

Let us look at some of the factors that would contribute to the development of an early intervention plan that works for our children, our families, and our settings and reflect upon our role in the whole process. Remember, it takes a community to create a community—we *all* need to be part of the observation journey.

WHAT ARE EARLY INTERVENTION AND EARLY IDENTIFICATION?

Early intervention and identification no longer have the connotations of being both a system and a group of services exclusively designed to support only children with diagnosed special needs and their families. A significant change in the field has been an attitudinal one, looking at special needs as something experienced by all people. As societal attitudes and the needs of children and families change, so, too, do the terms of reference, legislation, and policies that guide the delivery and availability of services and early learning spaces for children. While services may change regularly, what we do know is that *all children* are entitled to have access to quality early childhood settings, opportunities, and early intervention and identification services.

The terms *early intervention* and *early identification*, while complex in terms of systems and processes, are actually simple in their intentions. At the heart of early intervention and identification is the process of supporting and nurturing the individual variations in growth and development demonstrated by every child, and providing the necessary supports, materials, resources, and services to enable them to flourish and thrive to be the best they can be.

EARLY INTERVENTION AND IDENTIFICATION: WHERE DOES THE PROCESS BEGIN?

The early intervention and identification process starts the moment any child and family begin a program. It begins with a conversation about the relevance and importance of observation, as well as how an observational plan will lead to understanding how to support a child's inquiry, learning, and development.

When time is taken to explain what early identification and early intervention mean to the child's overall success and the responsibilities of educators to support children's learning to be the best they can be, then a shared value and understanding of why it is necessary to observe, inquire, dialogue, reflect, and respond is established. This open-ended communication-based strategy essentially creates a proactive rather than a reactive approach to this process, which then enables the building of reciprocal trust between the educator, parent(s), and child and, ultimately, the promotion of teamwork and collaboration.

Collaboration means many different things to different people and professionals within the early childhood profession. At its core, it is a relationship between a group of people, agencies, or organizations who share a common vision while fulfilling related or different roles to achieve an agreed-upon outcome. It is a process, an action, a value, a skill, and an attitude, and it can exist at any level (program, municipally, provincially, nationally, or internationally). While it is not without complexity, it is an important aspect of practice not to be underestimated. It is recommended that family priorities and needs direct the collaboration and the process and direction of the intervention. Building into this process open communication and appreciative inquiry helps to keep the flexibility needed for an inclusive response.

Some outcomes of this ongoing process of learning about each child within the group might involve further assessment and use of **screening** or **functional assessments** or further pursuit of **diagnostic assessment**, either done simultaneously or in conjunction with ongoing observation. In any context or situation relating to observation, assessment, or early intervention and identification, parents and their child(ren) are seen as key contributors and decision makers. Their involvement is accorded deep respect for their expertise and perspectives. In addition to authentic observational methods (such as those discussed in Chapters 4 and 5) capturing the inquiry, interests, and abilities of each child, many early childhood settings may choose to conduct screenings on each child with permission and participation from their family (and the child). This process further considers such things as prerequisite skills evident or requiring further development, how to better break down a task for a child, what materials and resources might support a child the best, and so on. In many circumstances involving assessment, outside **paraprofessionals** will be involved.

Note that in Exhibit 7.2, every family's experience with early intervention and identification is unique and therefore prompts constant movement and exchange within the entire early intervention system and process, as indicated by the arrows.

EXHIBIT 7.2   AN EARLY INTERVENTION/IDENTIFICATION PROCESS EXAMPLE

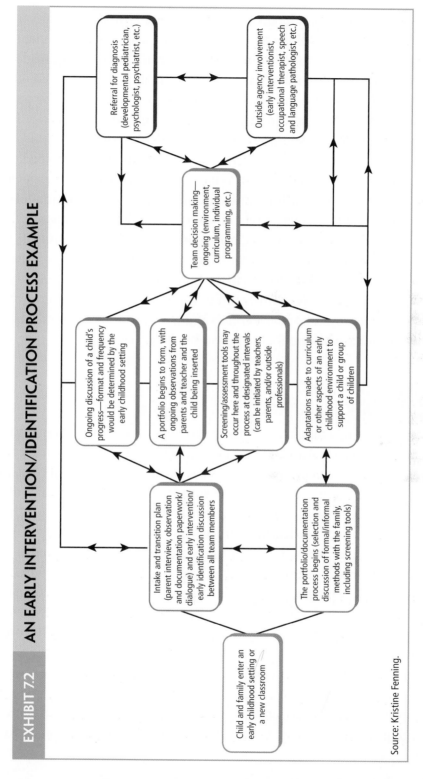

Source: Kristine Fenning.

A family/child's progress may be guided and influenced by new variables introduced or if a specific step is skipped, not achieved, or achieved simultaneously. If, for example, recommended adaptations to the environment were not made, then failure to follow through would be a discussion point prompting discussion between those involved. If a child had not made measurable progress over a long period of time despite a number of accommodations made to an environment (e.g., interesting materials added to extend the child's learning based on observations made), the family may wish to inquire how further assessment might be obtained to better understand how to support their child. What should be apparent is the flexible nature of this process and how it is guided by observation, vigilant monitoring of the child's progress and interactive relationships, ongoing team discussions, and the provision/creation of a responsive, inclusive curriculum and environment.

Demonstrating an appreciative inquiry approach, a responsive, inclusive mindset and dedication to the process should lay the foundation for positive relationships, minimizing delays in process or miscommunication. Working collaboratively with paraprofessionals or resource professionals and families is key. With collaboration and interprofessional education, much good can be achieved.

THEORIES UNDERPINNING THE EARLY INTERVENTION AND IDENTIFICATION PROCESS

Early intervention and identification display foundations in theories that support their validity in social services and human services occupations, particularly the paraprofessionals and team members who may be involved in a child's learning journey. A variety of **constructivist frameworks** indicate the importance of understanding how children interact with their environment as well as the role that adults play as facilitators in a child's learning processes. Examples of sociocultural theories posed by Rogoff, Baker-Sennett, Lacasa, and Coldsmith and those discussed in earlier chapters highlight the importance of relationships in young children's socioemotional development. Piaget's and Vygotsky's theories of development (among many others) and other ecological theories emphasizing influences and factors such as a child's familiar environments, different settings, and the broader ecology also inform the various early intervention and identification practices. These theories and many others confirm for us that engagement in the observational cycle (not limited to just early intervention and identification) is integral to providing the resources, materials, and supports necessary to create environments that are rich with inquiry, reflective of and responsive to diversity, and transformative in nature.

UNDERSTANDING EARLY INTERVENTION AS A SYSTEM

Early intervention is a multilayered and multifaceted system providing services to children and families. The types of agencies and professionals providing services may vary depending on how services are offered within different communities. Within each layer, there is a multitude of services, perhaps from different professions or systems that interrelate with one another. Some examples of who or what might compose that aspect are provided in Exhibit 7.3.

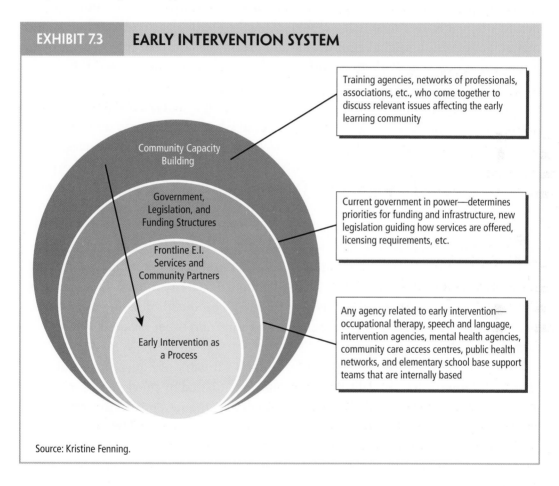

EXHIBIT 7.3 — **EARLY INTERVENTION SYSTEM**

Training agencies, networks of professionals, associations, etc., who come together to discuss relevant issues affecting the early learning community

Community Capacity Building

Government, Legislation, and Funding Structures

Frontline E.I. Services and Community Partners

Early Intervention as a Process

Current government in power—determines priorities for funding and infrastructure, new legislation guiding how services are offered, licensing requirements, etc.

Any agency related to early intervention—occupational therapy, speech and language, intervention agencies, mental health agencies, community care access centres, public health networks, and elementary school base support teams that are internally based

Source: Kristine Fenning.

Using Exhibit 7.3 to guide our examination of the many components of early intervention as a system and a concept, we can see that the dynamics of each layer within the early intervention system can change at any time, which then has an impact on other aspects of the system and, most inevitably, the process and delivery of services. Variations in the set-up and delivery of early intervention services are a result of a number of variables, such as the ministry providing services, the service delivery model, funding streams, the organizational mandate, and the service catchment area. Let's take a look at a couple of examples of early intervention processes.

Our first example is the Ontario Ministry of Education. Here, support services are varied depending upon whether the child is enrolled in an elementary classroom, an early childhood setting, or perhaps a kindergarten, for example. Common to Ontario elementary settings, when a child has been identified by either a parent or an educator as requiring extra supports in the classroom, a complex process begins. For some, the process might begin at the parent–teacher interview or reporting period where it is identified that a child is struggling with a particular skill or subject matter. For others, it might begin with inquiry from the family or the child regarding a concern or question. Perhaps for others, it begins with ongoing observations or reports made by the educator or teacher, and through day-to-day dialogue and documentation by the child, family, and education team, it is determined a child needs extra supports and services. For most, the special education resource teacher, with the support of the teacher and principal, would continue the process by investigating internally the availability of other consultative or direct services, supports, specialists, or specialist teams, some of which are specific to the classroom, school, or board. This might also include the preparation of an Individual Education Plan (IEP) with additional observation and/or assessment, or perhaps participation in an **Identification, Placement, and Review Committee (IPRC)** process. Each of these processes is comprehensive in nature, requiring a number of steps and the involvement of the family, child, and other team members. For more information on these processes, please read further in this chapter and go online for documents and links pertaining to school board processes, report writing, and other processes identified above.

The child-care community within the Ontario Ministry of Education is our second example of service delivery variations. Precipitated by previous observation, documentation, reflective and collaborative dialogue, inquiry, evaluation, or even assessment by the child's team, a family or educator (with approval from the family) might connect with a designated agency for additional support from a resource professional for a child or group of children. This support might come in the form of

- a consultative model, whereby the resource professional visits a setting and provides consultation to the program, child, and/or staff regarding a variety of practices
- a direct model, whereby a resource professional is a full-time staff member in the room with the children and early childhood educator to support inclusive practices

- another direct model, whereby the intensive resource professional provides contracted one-on-one support for a defined and limited length of time to set in process goals and objectives for the child and/or program

THE ROLE OF THE RESOURCE PROFESSIONAL

The **resource educator/early interventionist/resource professional** (among other titles) is often involved with a child, family, and early childhood team when further supports and services are being sought. This professional's role has expanded significantly. Take a look at Exhibit 7.4 to see the vast knowledge and skills required by current resource professionals to do their role effectively with children and families. Educators collaborate with these resource professionals and parents closely to

EXHIBIT 7.4	THE RESOURCE PROFESSIONAL: CREATING COMMUNITIES OF INCLUSIVE PRACTICE AND LEARNERS

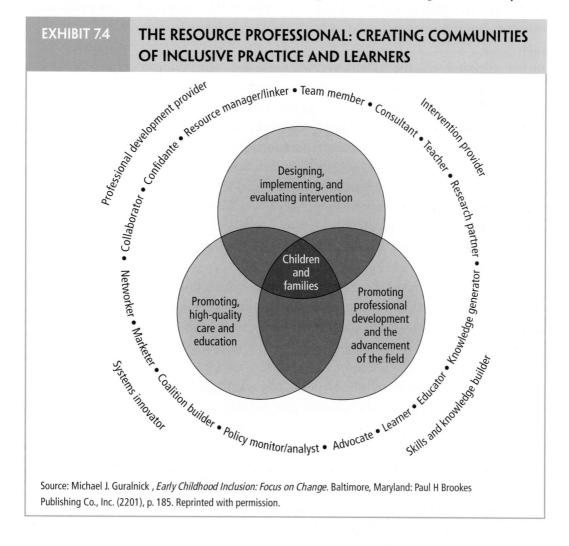

Source: Michael J. Guralnick , *Early Childhood Inclusion: Focus on Change.* Baltimore, Maryland: Paul H Brookes Publishing Co., Inc. (2201), p. 185. Reprinted with permission.

support a best practices and responsive, inclusive approach for their own setting. It can be very overwhelming for a family if a multitude of professionals are working with a child at the same or at different times; therefore, a coordinated team approach is crucial. Understanding the complexities of the resource role is important and requires individuals with unique skill sets. For every child and family, the process is unique and individualized, which may have benefits as well as challenges, depending on the individuals, circumstances, and settings.

At the heart of the diagram in Exhibit 7.4 are common processes by which we conduct our practice and the steps we follow when engaged in early intervention and identification, when ensuring quality environments are being maintained, and specifically when working with a resource professional to support a child. As a process, early intervention and identification can be defined as when a team documents, observes, and/or assesses a child's strengths, skills to be further developed, and interests, all within the context of the child's natural learning and home environments. Together with the resource professional, the team will have conversations to debrief observations, screenings, and/or assessment outcomes, and the influences, reasons, or causes that may have had an impact on those outcomes. The team may generate collaborative **reports**, **family support plans**, possible **referrals**, and individual plans that could involve the preparation of goals and objectives, curriculum changes, environmental design changes, accommodations, and teaching strategy changes. For example, a child's achievement of a skill may be affected by external factors such as lack of exposure to practise the skill, cultural variations (some of which include background, abilities, family values and priorities, and language), and the child's interests. Each of these reasons could facilitate a different approach or plan. The process also involves *identifying* concerns experienced by children early and *intervening* in ways that are supportive to the child, family, and team, thus facilitating a proactive and responsive approach to supporting the success of all involved. The sooner we are able to provide a child with services and supports, the sooner we can assist the child in developing the skills and knowledge needed to achieve his or her full potential.

Throughout the early childhood field, long waiting lists for public services and assessments, large caseloads for current professionals in the field, and perhaps not enough early intervention specialists or professionals to meet the changing needs of children and families are only some of the reasons why we want to identify a child early. Also having an impact on the ability to access services are the high costs of private **developmental assessments** or **psychoeducational assessments**, which may limit a family's ability to access these assessments if one or both of the parents are not privy to benefits within their workplace.

The issues of accessibility within large urban centres or rural areas also impede access to services. In the cold of winter, a parent might find it difficult to take several means of transportation in a large city in order to get to the service her or his child needs. The same goes for families in rural northern areas where services are almost always located in a city a considerable distance away.

Service accessibility is taken for granted for many, but for others it remains a real challenge. All the more reason to begin early the early identification and intervention process for *all* children.

EARLY INTERVENTION, IDENTIFICATION, AND INTERPROFESSIONAL EDUCATION

Recent trends indicate increased emphasis on **interprofessional education** and the interaction of various disciplines to support early intervention and identification and the success of children and families in the early learning sector. This approach emphasizes the sharing of knowledge while supporting family-centred and child-centred practices. Research indicates that interprofessional education facilitates increased collaboration between professionals, ministries, and systems to improve service delivery. This collaboration improves outcomes for children and families, and reduces duplication or the lack of coordinated delivery of services. The medical profession is an example of a profession that has recognized the need for sharing discipline expertise in a team approach. Nursing, doctoral, and schools in various parts of Canada, such as the Early Childhood Advanced Studies Program at Humber College, use this model to improve transition to practice and to enhance quality in their professional practice.

In the early learning profession, many have recognized the need for interprofessional interactions and have invited the participation of community organizations that assist in supporting children and families. With the dynamics of children and families continuing to change, we are sometimes presented with complex situations that are beyond our resources or expertise. Extending invitations for community members (beyond the early learning profession) to provide other discipline expertise or services is advantageous. The rise of mental health concerns in young children is a current example. Seen often in the narrow context as demonstrating attention-getting behaviour (e.g., aggression, swearing), school-age children with mental health needs are often overlooked because educators miss observing the "whole" child and considering the multitude of influences upon children. By enlisting knowledge and expertise from other professionals in other disciplines (e.g., physiotherapists, social workers, public health workers, pediatricians), we are better equipped to support the children and families in our programs. Understanding each of their roles and how they might work together to support a child and family is equally as important. Reaching out to the community for their expertise builds capacity in any organization, which in turn provides better services to families. This collaboration also increases our knowledge of community services, empowering us to become even better at assisting future families in our care.

Before looking at the various steps or processes involved in early identification and intervention, let us first focus on health and wellness checks. This practice is one of the most important daily fundamentals that help early childhood professionals observe and identify the possible factors affecting the children within our classrooms.

CHILDREN'S HEALTH AND WELL-BEING

One of the ways an educator observes the well-being of children is to look for physical health and disposition in a health and wellness check when each child arrives in the morning. According to Ontario provincial legislation, a daily log must be kept of the health, safety and well-being of all enrolled children in a program.

Age fotostock

Educators are active observers. They are attuned to the growth and development of each child in their care. For example, observations relating to a child's health (e.g., ear infection, contagious disease) and welfare (e.g., bumps, bruises, changes in behaviour) are noted and communicated to the supervisor immediately. The morning health check is part of a centre's policies and procedures, and includes the process for reporting child abuse.

REPORTING CHILD ABUSE

As part of the early identification and intervention process, if educators suspect child abuse or neglect, by law they must report their findings immediately. Educators are legally bound to report these findings to the Children's Aid Society (CAS). According to Ontario's *Child and Family Services Act*, the responsibility to act is in keeping with the best interest, protection, and well-being of children (see Exhibit 7.5). The format used to report abuse or neglect is not important; the main point is that the suspected

EXHIBIT 7.5	CHILD ABUSE AND THE DUTY TO REPORT

Under the Child and Family Services Act:

> Professionals and officials have the same duty as the rest of the public
> to report their suspicion that a child is or may be in need of protection.
> However, the Act recognizes that people working closely with children
> have a special awareness of the signs of child abuse and neglect, and
> a particular responsibility to report their suspicions. Any professional or
> official who fails to report a suspicion is liable on conviction to a fine of
> up to $1,000, if they obtained the information in the course of their pro-
> fessional or official duties. [CFSA s.72 (4), (6.2)]. (p. 4)

This would include but would not be limited to the following professionals:

- health care professionals, including physicians, nurses, dentists, pharmacists and psychologists
- teachers and school principals
- social workers and family counsellors
- religious leaders, including priests, rabbis and members of the clergy
- operators or employees of child care programs or centres
- youth and recreation workers (not volunteers)
- peace officers and coroners
- child and youth service providers and employees of these service providers
- any other person who performs professional or official duties with respect to a child (p. 5)

Source: Ontario Ministry of Youth Services. *Reporting Child Abuse and Neglect: It's Your Duty.* Copyright Queen's Printer for Ontario 2012. Reproduced with permission.

abuse or neglect is documented as objectively as possible, separating feelings, interpretations, judgments, and conclusions from the actual description of the perceived
abuse or neglect. When documenting, remember that your description or observation must be accompanied by the following:

- date and time
- location
- your name and position
- your actions: what you said and did

- your description, documentation, and comments written in pen or typed on a computer
- your signature and the date of your report

As this may become a document used in a court of law, remember not to make *any* changes to the original paper document, such as strikeovers, pen marks made on top of pencil marks, or whiteouts. No changes, deletions, or additions to the original can be made when reporting electronically. Early childhood professionals play an important role in the early identification of possible cases of abuse or neglect. Refer to the school or centre's policies and procedures for child abuse, and make yourself aware of your responsibility to children under the appropriate provincial ministry and the Department of Justice Canada. The Department of Justice website (n.d.) lists the types of abuse and neglect as well as the most current initiatives being undertaken on behalf of Canada's children.

No matter where you practise in the world, be informed about your role and the processes involved in reporting suspected abuse. This process can be intimidating for a variety of factors too lengthy to cover in this chapter, but the fact remains that it is incumbent on the person who suspects abuse to act upon it. Search the Internet for further information about reporting child abuse as it relates to your province or territory.

FAMILY-CENTRED APPROACH AND EARLY INTERVENTION

Let us immerse ourselves in the family-centred approach and philosophy so that we can begin to appreciate the many responsibilities and joys of this approach. Appreciating family-centred practices is vital to understanding the unique relationships entered into by families, their child with special needs, and the professionals involved.

Similar to the terms *inclusion* and *responsiveness*, the term *family-centredness* is multifaceted: it is a concept, a process, and, at its very core, an attitude and a very specific way of being. It is a personal choice. What do we mean? The choice is one that you have as an educator to either continue your practice in ways that you see fit or to evolve your practice, putting families, children, and community at the heart of everything that you do. Family-centred practice or service requires a commitment from its participants to weave its core tenets throughout all aspects of a program or setting: educators, environment, policies, and vision.

> Family-centred service recognizes that each family is unique; that the family is the constant in the child's life; and that they are the experts on the child's abilities and needs. The family works with service providers to make informed decisions about the services and supports the child and family receives. In family-centred service, the strengths and needs of all family members are considered. (Law et al., 2003a, p. 2)

Family-centred service has been documented for quite some time. According to Corks (2004), it seems to have begun "in the 1950s, when psychologist Carl Rogers started to discuss giving control to the client as opposed to the service provider. In the 1960s, this approach was expanded to embrace the client and his or her family, and the theory of family-centred care was born. Since then, the concepts of family-centred care and family-centred service have been studied and advanced" (p. 1) by numerous experts, agencies, educational institutions, and organizations.

Family-centred practices continue to have a strong foundation in the early childhood profession within Canada and abroad. What is most interesting is that different settings will have adopted different perspectives and viewpoints regarding the tenets of this approach in order to develop what they feel best reflects the children and families in their programs. Ongoing discussions between parents and educators concerning this approach may have or will need to have taken place in numerous aspects of practice, some of which might include the following:

- how decisions are made
- how to support, collaborate with, and communicate with families (for example, determining roles, behaviour)
- how families want to be involved and how their strengths are utilized in the program
- how resources and new knowledge will be shared and created
- how current observation and assessment methodologies recognize or value family diversity and input. Discussions can also consider how families and children can be involved in deciding how the documentation is to be used.

Ongoing discussions between families and children, centres, schools, or service organizations are vital to provide for smooth transitions from one room, program, or service to another. Additionally, care must be taken to ensure that supports provided in the earlier settings are transferred to the new setting, as noted in Exhibit 7.6.

EXHIBIT 7.6 **EARLY INTERVENTION AND FRAGMENTATION OF SERVICES**

"With children transitioning from the early years to school age, this partnership [home and school] is critical. Currently, when children reach school age the supports that they have been receiving in community settings may be lost due to a lack of integration or they compete with the time spent in school and services being delivered in schools. Ideally, schools will provide comparable services, but many families have found it beneficial to keep their children out of kindergarten in order to continue intensive support programs in other settings."

Source: Underwood, K., & Langford, R. (2011). *Children with Special Educational Needs in Early Childhood.* Toronto, ON: Atkinson Centre for Society and Child Development, OISE/University of Toronto.

Transitions within an early childhood context most often mean a child moving from one room to another, from before- and after-school programs to elementary school, or from one program to another. Lost in the discussion of the child is the parent or family. As shown in Exhibit 7.7, transitions can be more traumatic for parents than children when parents are not included in the initial discussions, asked

EXHIBIT 7.7 **TRANSITION ISSUES**

"The major difficulty for families whose children enter kindergarten is establishing new support networks. Early intervention agencies often have in their mandate to provide treatment to the child, as well as support for the parent (Janus, 2001). In contrast, schools tend to look to parents for support of the school's educational efforts. Parents of children with special needs in elementary school identify four major problems: lack of communication with the school, lack of participation in decisions about their child's education, not feeling welcome in schools, and lack of knowledge on their child's progress (Wolery, 1999). Facing the unknown, together with the loss of established support networks, may contribute to the degree to which these parents take an active role in facilitating the exchange of information between the early intervention services and elementary school." (p. 634)

Source: "Starting Kindergarten: Transition Issues for Children with Special Needs." Magdalena Janus, Jessica Lefort, Ruth Cameron, & Lauren Kopechanski. McMaster University. *Canadian Journal of Education, 30*, 3 (2007): 628–648.

for their thoughts and feelings, or included on the team. Research on the topic of transition focuses primarily on the child, with emphasis on children "getting ready" for kindergarten and the practical issues involved. Less research, however, is found on how parents and families are affected by transitions, particularly parents or the family of a child with special needs.

Families and children have different strengths, needs, desires, and values, resulting in the creation of unique strategies and processes being used to support transitioning from one school or program to another. If a particular transition is more complex in nature, for example, from a segregated to an inclusive setting, then the process may also have an impact on other family members, prompting the need for further discussions, strategies, and supports for the whole family. Studies show that more stress can be experienced by parents of children with special needs owing to having to make other additional sacrifices or decisions that affect them.

FOUNDATIONS OF FAMILY CENTREDNESS: BUILDING RELATIONSHIPS

Taking the time to reflect upon these and other elements of family-centred practice both individually and as a team (which includes families) is necessary for sustained growth and improvement. Take a moment to think about your own professional practice. What are your strengths? What do you need to improve upon? What steps will you take, and how will you evaluate your progress?

> Being thoughtful about the quality of our relationships and showing generosity in our dealings with others are essential components of being effective in life and work. Our personal and professional relationships elicit from us the depth of our capacity to care about others and our ability to be open to their needs. Relationships will challenge the range of our emotions, our ability to persevere with others, and our tolerance for interpersonal chaos. (Roper, 2002)

EARLY IDENTIFICATION AND INTERVENTION: SHARING PERSONAL AND SENSITIVE INFORMATION

As professionals working with families, we have to remember the social imbalance of our relationships. Professionals know far more about their families than the families know about them. Consider that when you might have their life in a folder or on your laptop, and they know virtually nothing about you other than your name and that of your agency. Sharing the personal side of you is important for families to connect with you. From personal sharing you can move forward to build on common, mutual ground, having the parent more comfortable with the give-and-take relationship. What would make the relationship more equitable, interesting, and even fun? When you enter a relationship with parents or families, you share mutual information. Build a relationship, and then, slowly, trust will grow.

Parents who are active participants in the relationship-based, family-centred approach are more apt to develop and recognize their strengths and thus build capacity within their own family. A common outcome is families who demonstrate strong psychological and emotional well-being or health, increased confidence and **self-advocacy** qualities, and the knowledge or resourcefulness needed to locate important supports for their children.

To support your work with families as well as your efforts to reflect upon and improve your own practice, the CanChild Centre for Disability Research at McMaster University developed some very useful reflective checklists for families, service providers, and organizations to use in this regard. One of these checklists is provided in Exhibit 7.8. Each question in that exhibit prompts you to think about your own strengths and needs regarding family-centred services and practices. Each question could easily be transformed into goals for further development and improvement.

Sharing personal or sensitive information with parents about their child can be an emotional experience for both the educator and the parents; it can make everyone involved feel very vulnerable. It is never easy for a parent to hear that their child is having difficulties or is displaying concerning behaviour in the classroom; no parents want to hear that their child is struggling. Sharing the information can be just as uneasy for educators as they attempt to anticipate and empathize about how the parent might feel about or react to the information about to be shared. Have you ever experienced hearing information that made you feel uncomfortable?

Building relationships is fundamental to strong network building in the field of early childhood. When working with families and children with special needs, the consistency, trust, and sustainability of people, agencies, and expectations are very important. Trust is key in establishing relationships, and that is never more important than for a family or child who is vulnerable. Families need to know that when they attend meetings or arrive at the school, they will meet someone familiar. Families thrive on the knowledge that they and their child are cared for personally as well as professionally. Developing those trusting relationships makes all the difference.

EXHIBIT 7.8	FAMILY-CENTRED SERVICE: A CHECKLIST FOR SERVICE PROVIDERS

Do you ...	For more information, refer to FCS Sheet ...
... know how to work with families in a family-centred way?	#1 What is family-centred service?
... talk to your colleagues and the families you work with about what family-centred service means to them?	#2 Myths about family-centred service
... understand the research on family-centred service and use this evidence to advocate for the use of family-centred approaches?	#3 How does family-centred service make a difference?
... discuss family-centred service with your colleagues and support each other in being family-centred?	#4 Becoming more family-centred
... offer families a choice of location and time to meet and schedule appointments that work best for them?	#5 10 things you can do to be family-centred
... ask parents about their strengths and resources, including the people they find supportive and their own skills?	#6 Identifying and building on parent and family strengths and resources
... ask families if they would like to connect with another family and provide resources to do so?	#7 Parent-to-parent support
... listen to what families tell you, believe them, and trust in them?	#8 Effective communication in family-centred service
... describe families in the same respectful way, whether or not they are recent?	#9 Using respectful behaviours and language
... ask parents how involved they want to be in the planning and delivery of their child's services? Do you respect their decision?	#10 Working together: from providing information to working in partnership

(continued)

Do you …	For more information, refer to FCS Sheet …	
… negotiate solutions with families when there is a difference of opinion?	#11	Negotiation: dealing effectively with differences
… present and explain all options to the family to allow them to make decisions?	#12	Making decisions together: how to decide what is best
… collaborate in goal setting with the child, the family, and others (such as pre-school or school personnel)?	#13	Setting goals together
… help parents identify and navigate through the "systems" when they are advo-cating for their child?	#14	Advocacy: how to get the best for your child
… develop an action plan that outlines what tasks need to be done, who will do them, and timelines?	#15	Getting the most from appointments and meetings
… communicate openly and frequently with parents about things that are hap-pening at school?	#16	Fostering family-centred service in the school
… help families prepare for the first formal appointment or assessment by giving them a list of questions to consider?	#17	Family-centred strategies for waiting lists

Source: Law, M., Rosenbaum, P., King, G., King, S., Burke-Gaffney, J., Moning-Szkut, T., Kertoy, M., Pollock, N., Viscardis, L., & Teplicky, R. (2003). Fact Sheet #18: *Are We Really Family-Centred? Checklists for Families, Service Providers, and Organizations.* CanChild Centre for Childhood Disability Research (www.canchild.ca), McMaster University: Hamilton, ON.

FAMILY-CENTRED CONVERSATIONS: FINDING THE RIGHT TIME

When in your early childhood setting, take some time to observe the current conversations taking place with families about their children. What are you hearing? Where are these conversations taking place? Is it at times convenient for the parent, or is the parent in a rush to get out the door? Most conversations with families are currently taking place at pick-up or drop-off time right near the entranceway to the room. As parents are coming to sign their children in or out, many educators are seeing this as a prime time to "catch" the parent to share some important information. Considering this strategy, would that information catch them off guard because of the spontaneity? How would parents feel having private information shared in front of many other people coming in and out of the room? Would the parent have been prepared to receive the information and be able to think about it in a thoughtful way? It is no wonder, then, that we may often see parents feeling frustrated or angry; they were not given the consideration to be able to talk about their child in a meaningful way. What happens then? They worry and wonder and worry some more. Let us make an effort not to place families in those situations.

Knowing that this sharing process may involve sensitive information from time to time, it is important to think about *how* we will communicate the information and where we might have these very personal conversations. We start first by beginning the observation or early intervention and identification dialogue with families as part of their intake process when they enter a new centre. Parents can then begin to develop a "language of learning" that enables them to see these conversations as beneficial to the developmental success of their child.

As we continue on our teaching and learning journey with families, and as we share ongoing observations and information about children, there are a number of things we can do to keep our language respectful, positive, culturally appropriate, and meaningful. Let us think back to what we discussed in earlier chapters regarding writing and communicating information on paper for the intended audience. Previously we discussed the importance of seeing children as children and documenting our observations of their actions and behaviours in a respectful way.

Communicating verbally with parents is no different; they deserve the same level of respect and thoughtfulness when we are discussing information about their child and their family. Take care not to label and judge, be open-minded and culturally sensitive, and actively listen to what they are sharing. Other things to keep in mind when conversing with families about sensitive information include the following:

- maintaining an emotionally safe environment—taking the time to build rapport and trust
- using culturally appropriate communication—ask for feedback from the family on your communication style. Do they feel comfortable with what you are saying?
- assuming ownership for the information you share and respecting the differences in opinion that parents may have when sharing what they see, perceive, and understand

- using "I" messages, taking care to actively listen and pay attention to your verbal and nonverbal cues—do they match?
- always maintaining confidentiality, never sharing information about other children or a child with someone else (without their permission)
- posing thoughtful questions that encourage sharing by parents and enabling them to share their values, priorities, and wishes for their child. Let them lead!
- ensuring that the setting is appropriate for a conversation—find somewhere where there is privacy. Bring in some water and snacks if at the end of a day.
- ensuring that timing is fine and that a meeting time has been scheduled for their convenience
- asking parents in advance if there are things they would like to talk about
- ensuring that any observations or documentation has been shared ahead of time so that the parents have time to reflect on it as well
- sharing knowledge and educating one another
- letting parents know that you are appreciative of their time

Can you think of other considerations? Be sure to see the further research and resources on communication available online.

Always remember that parents are our partners in the process of early identification and intervention. Taking care of other members of our team is an integral part of collaboration. Give families the opportunity to be participating partners.

Courtesy of Scotia Plaza Child Care Centre

SPECIAL NEEDS: A MULTIFACETED TERM

In early childhood education in Canada, the term *special needs* is generally understood to refer to a child who has been diagnosed with an exceptionality. Depending on the province or territory, the definition of what constitutes a "special need" varies. How special needs are defined is determined by a number of factors, some of which include treatment eligibility, services, developmental functioning, funding, community infrastructure, the degree of need, and the number of developmental domains affected. Having special needs means that a child could be born with a medical condition such as a visual impairment or a loss of hearing or have sustained a severe injury that has permanently affected the child's growth and development. A special need could also be emotional or behavioural concerns, a history of abuse or neglect, or a risk factor, such as fetal alcohol syndrome, which is due to parental substance abuse. The definition of "special needs" is not exclusive to diagnosed special needs; it also includes children without identified or diagnosed needs. A special need could refer to those whose English is a second language; those who require extra supports, such as equipment, visuals, or orthotics; children with mental health challenges; and those who may benefit from specialized services or careful monitoring. Special needs may also be short term in nature (perhaps a child with a broken leg who needs assistance with mobility) or lifelong (e.g., a child diagnosed with **autism**). Depending on where you practise, the term may have a very broad definition or a direct focus. If the focus is direct with a narrow definition, often it may be due to ministry funding requirements stating that for eligibility purposes, a child must have a need with a specific diagnosis.

TEAMS: COLLABORATING AND CREATING

In the field of early childhood, the concept of teams and team building has to be more than words. In working with families and children, particularly children who have special needs or extra support needs, teams internal to a school or centre are augmented by those external to it. This collaborative approach is an important part of the efforts made by all on behalf of children and families. Coordination of these efforts is facilitated by team members who know the family, supports and services required, and appropriate professionals in the community. Organization and communication within the teams at a school or centre as well as with and between other disciplines and professional teams is of vital importance to get things right—to reflect the needs and desires of the family. If a child has complex special needs, it is possible to have as few as one or as many as ten or more different professionals or agencies involved. There may be different types of team structures, and each team may present with different challenges (further information on team structures is available online). Depending on these factors, specifically the familiarity and collaboration of the professionals with each other and their organizations, successful progress can be made to assist the child and the family.

What does it mean to work within an effective team? It means building a team vision or mission and determining people's philosophies, developing relationships and shared understandings of meanings, and understanding the purpose of gathering or meeting together. When provided with the opportunity to engage in the process as collaborative partners, parents are further empowered as the primary decision makers for their children and are seen as key partners in the early intervention process and during the process of individualized instruction. Parents and families who have a stronger role in early learning teams build advocacy skills that can be transferred to future advocacy scenarios requiring their leadership and support of their children. These advocacy skills can also be applied to efforts to attain higher-quality care and services for all children and families. Team building within a school or early childhood setting should represent a conscientious approach to include all the involved members, provide opportunities for appreciative inquiry and to investigate and learn together. Including parents and families adds to a community voice.

Taking our own advice, we researched sources external to the early childhood and business sectors for notions of team and team building. One of these sources is the article entitled "Making the Team: Teams, Teamwork, and Teambuilding" (Larsen, 2010). One of the author's suggestions is to "create an environment where all project team members actively contribute to the results. People can become demotivated or demoralized when their only contribution is to attend meetings as functional representatives, without actively contributing to the project or taking away personal achievements for the experience" (p. 43). According to Larsen, "a project team is more than a group of talented professionals. It is an interdependent unit, empowered with understanding, accountabilities and mutual support that permit it to achieve goals—both organizational and personal—more efficiently and successfully than a mere group of individuals could accomplish on its own" (p. 41).

Courtesy of Scotia Plaza Child Care Centre

Adding to Larsen's view, Wilde (2010) states in his article "Personalities into Teams" that "diversity within a team is important in achieving an effective team. In the long run teams do better when they are composed of people with the widest possible range of personalities, even though it takes longer for such psychologically diverse teams to achieve smooth communications and good cooperation" (p. 22).

These and other articles and books found on the subject of teams are often those relating to business or higher education. What can education learn from other disciplines regarding teams?

Logue (2006) wrote of the **action research** carried out by a team of teachers working together as researchers to investigate the question of multi-age groupings. The teachers demonstrated their understanding of the importance of observation in research. They raised questions concerning the hypothesis that age-segregated groups may be negatively contributing to social issues. The key point of this article was not only their action research but also their work as a team. This teamwork is a good example of what happens when early childhood professionals, schools, agencies, or child-care organizations empower themselves and make use of each member's skills and knowledge, thus increasing the potential of any one of the team members alone. When working as a team, the workload is shared, ideas are exchanged concerning what is possible, or a new space is created, thus building capacity within the team and community. We will explore the concept of community capacity building in Chapter 8.

ASSESSMENT

Assessment is part of an inquiry-based and evaluation-based early intervention system. Together, assessment and evaluation can provide the insight needed to lead toward goals, objectives, and the targeting of specific skills to be further developed, or outcomes.

Assessment is a word used to describe appraisal, judgment, review, measurement, and evaluation. The word has been used interchangeably with *observation* as a catchword for all types of assessment, such as authentic, screening, and diagnostic assessment; as another word for *monitoring*; and as an appraisal strategy employed by any educator who may be grading or evaluating papers of some kind. "*Assessment* and *evaluation* are terms that have often been used interchangeably. Policy differentiates them in order to ensure that diagnostic and formative assessments are given as much of a profile as summative assessment or evaluation. Too often, evaluation—the assigning of a value or grade—has been the focus of assessment, evaluation, and reporting discourse" (Ontario Ministry of Education, 2008, p. 1-i).

Authentic assessment is a term meaning flexible ways of collecting informal data (skills and knowledge) that is culturally sensitive, developmentally and educationally appropriate, and taken from a natural environment. Authentic methods can include the observation methods discussed in earlier chapters, as they are used to measure program change as well as the progress of the child to understand the context of a child's learning in settings familiar to the child. Beyond an understanding of child development, it is important to consider the authenticity of assessment administration by reviewing implementation strategies to ensure they are diverse and comprehensive in approach and to marry the assessment measure to curriculum expectations. The use of the term *authentic assessment* has become widespread in Canada but had its origins in the United States, where authentic assessment became the popular alternative to the practice of testing as the sole means to discover what children knew or understood.

How are assessment choices made to measure, quantify, or otherwise evaluate the children of each country? Let's take a look at two philosophical approaches to assessment: one from the Ontario Ministry of Education Full-Day Early Learning–Kindergarten Program and the other from New Zealand's *Te Whāriki* approach. We begin with the Full-Day Early Learning–Kindergarten Program. This program, using a play-based approach, is premised on the concept of interconnectedness shown in Exhibit 7.9.

EXHIBIT 7.9   **THE FULL-DAY EARLY LEARNING–KINDERGARTEN PROGRAM**

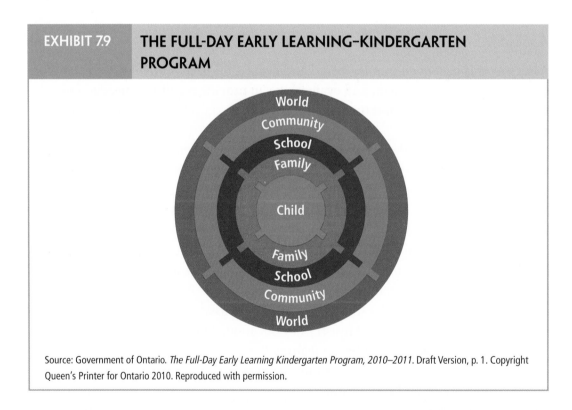

Source: Government of Ontario. *The Full-Day Early Learning Kindergarten Program, 2010–2011.* Draft Version, p. 1. Copyright Queen's Printer for Ontario 2010. Reproduced with permission.

This program is based on the belief that children should be given the time, space, and opportunities they need to not only adjust to school but also demonstrate their learning in different ways. "To allow for the range of influences that may affect a child's learning at any given time, Early Learning–Kindergarten teams should assess the child's learning on an ongoing basis in the context of everyday experiences, using a variety of strategies and tools" (Ontario Ministry of Education, 2010–2011, p. 29). This principle emulates the true nature of authentic assessment, as it prompts educators to think about capturing learning in a variety of ways in natural settings.

Turning our attention now to New Zealand, their philosophy is situated in the exemplar of empowerment—*Whakaman*—that effective assessment practices "should enhance [children's] sense of themselves as capable people and competent learners" (New Zealand Ministry of Education, 1996, p. 30). Their philosophy and practice speak to the very real notion that evaluation influences a child's understanding of self. Put in that context, evaluation or assessment is a highly enlightening experience. It is more than a set of practices, and it is more than how a nation may measure itself; it is about the role assessment plays in highlighting what is valued. The *Te Whāriki* principles reflect a sociocultural approach to learning, and their approach to assessment strongly reflects *Te Whāriki* philosophy, as noted in Exhibit 7.10.

EXHIBIT 7.10	SOCIOCULTURAL APPROACHES TO ASSESSMENT

"Sociocultural approaches to assessment:

- include the children's viewpoint when possible;
- take account of the powerful influence of assessments on children's sense of themselves as learners;
- ensure that assessments of children's learning within a Màori context are situated within a Màori pedagogical framework;
- recognise that assessment is one of the features of a learning community: it influences the quality of children's engagement in learning."

Source: *Kei Tua o te Pae*, p. 4. Copyright Crown, Ministry of Education, New Zealand, 2004.

Cultural beliefs, personal values, accessibility, and exposure to experiences are some of the factors that influence a professional's beliefs about assessment.

Assessment refers not only to personal or professional values and practice; it would be fair to say that nation-states use assessment much the same way that France did in the early 1900s when Alfred Binet devised tests for the French government to determine which children were not capable of achieving in the regular classroom. All children were being considered for public classrooms, and the French government wanted to segregate those who were trainable and those who were educable. Those tests were later studied by Jean Piaget, who was interested not so much in how children obtained the right answers to the tests but why they were consistently getting wrong answers in the same kinds of ways. He wanted to understand how children learn and how the brain digests information. Piaget took a very quantitative approach to developing his theories, and based on his observations, he changed the perception of how children construct their world.

Even after all we know about children has been studied and researched and become public domain, tests, assessments, and evaluations are still being used to the disadvantage of some children. "Via survey research, psychologists reported that 42.96% of the more than 7000 children they assessed would be considered 'untestable' if they had to solely rely on traditional assessment instruments to determine eligibility. This is particularly concerning because more than 90% of the children considered 'untestable' were determined eligible once authentic and curriculum-based methods were applied" (Keilty et al., 2009, p. 245). This illustrates that not every child fits every assessment tool, or vice versa, and not every tool will be appropriate for children and families with whom you work. The implications of this statement are that we need to think carefully about a number of things relating to the assessment process, some of which include the strengths and weaknesses of the assessment tools we choose to evaluate young children, how we plan to use them, and whether using more than one tool might capture a child in a more holistic way.

Assessment is a term that, when used loosely or understood poorly, contributes to misinformation and misunderstanding. When confronted with, for example, "Melissa's assessment" or "we've assessed your child," ask for clarification. Some valid questions might be: Can you tell me more about what assessment tool was used? Under what conditions did the assessment take place? Who made the decision to assess? How was that decision made and why? Were the parents involved in the assessment process? Did they understand what permissions meant and why the assessments were planned? Did the child understand what they were participating in? What these questions tell us is that we have a very important responsibility toward the well-being of children and their families.

THREE STAGES OF ASSESSMENT

We introduced earlier in this chapter the three general stages of assessment: screening, functional, and diagnostic. The functional assessments are discussed later in this chapter, while diagnostic assessment tools are beyond the scope of this text; however, later in this chapter, the importance of the screening tool and its function are examined as several types of screening tools are used in schools and early childhood centres throughout Canada.

ASSESSMENT TOOL TERMS OR JARGON

Before proceeding further, it is necessary to establish a basic acquaintance with the complex world of assessment. What are some of the terms or jargon associated with the topic of assessment tools? First, the kinds of assessments conducted in early childhood settings tend to be those that are criterion referenced. What does that mean? **Criterion-referenced assessment tools** are those assessment tools that measure a child's progress against a **fixed standard** rather than comparing them with the skills or knowledge of others. A fixed standard is an item or competency that is typical for children of that age group to perform, such as tying shoelaces, running without falling, or following a two-step, related direction. If a child can accomplish these skills independently, that competency or fixed standard is checked off as being achieved. If the child is unable to achieve that task, then a different kind of scoring is noted to indicate that the child has yet to accomplish that competency. The educator or resource professional records the observations in the assessment tool: "*Yes*, the child has achieved that skill," or "*No*, the child has yet to achieve that skill." If the person using the screening tool (like the Nipissing District Developmental Screen in Exhibit 7.11) records many "no" responses in an area where most children of this age can accomplish these skills, then it *may* require further conversation with the team to determine if a skill has simply not been attained or whether it might infer a possible delay. If this is the case, further discussion within the team regarding these results is necessary.

Every assessment tool has its own terminology; each one contains terms that are specific to that particular assessment. For example, one assessment tool may refer to areas of child development as domains or sectors. To add to the confusion, each assessment tool contains different terms to describe the areas of child development; these areas are represented in very distinct ways with terms such as *belonging, receptive language, fine motor adaptive*, and *auditory attention*. Terms used for scoring items within assessment tools are also different. Strategies used for assessments do not always provide the context necessary to understand a child's culture, values, family beliefs, or accessibility to materials and things. For some populations, the children may not even have a word in their language for the picture they are asked to identify. With these examples of variations between assessment tools and issues fundamental to this topic, it should be clear that the assessment process is a highly complex enterprise best guided by skilled and knowledgeable professionals trained in the use of the assessment tool.

Child's Name: _____

Birthdate: _____ Today's Date: _____

The Nipissing District Developmental Screen is a checklist designed to help monitor your child's development.

Y N BY **EIGHTEEN MONTHS** OF AGE, DOES YOUR CHILD:

O O 1 Identify pictures in a book? *("show me the baby")**

O O 2 Use a variety of familiar gestures?
          (waving, pushing, giving, reaching up)*

O O 3 Follow directions using "on" and "under"?
          ("put the cup on the table")*

O O 4 Make at least four different consonant sounds? *(b, n, d, h, g, w)**

O O 5 Point to at least three different body parts when asked?
          ("where is your nose?")*

O O 6 Say 20 or more words? *(words do not have to be clear)*

O O 7 Hold a cup to drink? ****

O O 8 Pick up and eat finger food?

O O 9 Help with dressing by putting out arms and legs? ****

O O 10 Walk up a few stairs holding your hand?

O O 11 Walk alone?

O O 12 Squat to pick up a toy and stand back up without falling?

O O 13 Push and pull toys or other objects while walking forward? *A*

O O 14 Stack three or more blocks?

O O 15 Show affection towards people, pets, or toys?

O O 16 Point to show you something?

O O 17 Look at you when you are talking
           or playing together?

18
MONTHS
English

A

* Examples provided are only suggestions.
  You may use similar examples from your family experience.
** Item may not be common to all cultures.

The following **activities for your child** will help you play your part in your child's development.

I feel safe and secure when I know what is expected of me. You can help me with this by following routines and setting limits. Praise my good behaviour.

I like toys that I can pull apart and put back together—large building blocks, containers with lids, or plastic links. Talk to me about what I am doing using words like "push" and "pull".

I'm not too little to play with large crayons. Let's scribble and talk about our art work.

Don't be afraid to let me see what I can do with my body. I need to practise climbing, swinging, jumping, running, going up and down stairs, and going down slides. Stay close to me so I don't get hurt.

Play some of my favourite music. Encourage me to move to the music by swaying my arms, moving slowly, marching to the music, hopping, clapping my hands, tapping my legs. Let's have fun doing actions while listening to the music.

Let me play with balls of different sizes. Take some of the air out of a beach ball. Watch me kick, throw, and try to catch it.

I want to do things just like you. Let me have toys so I can pretend to have tea parties, dress up, and play mommy or daddy.

I like new toys, so find the local toy lending library or play groups in our community.

I am learning new words every day. Put pictures of people or objects in a bag and say "1, 2, 3, what do we see?" and pull a picture from the bag.

Pretend to talk to me on the phone or encourage me to call someone.

Help me to notice familiar sounds such as birds chirping, car or truck motors, airplanes, dogs barking, sirens, or splashing water. Imitate the noise you hear and see if I will imitate you. Encourage me by smiling and clapping.

I like simple puzzles with two to four pieces and shape-sorters with simple shapes. Encourage me to match the pieces by taking turns with me.

I enjoy exploring the world, but I need to know that you are close by. I may cry when you leave me with others, so give me a hug and tell me you will be back.

I may get ear infections. Talk to my doctor about signs and symptoms.

WHO ADMINISTERS ASSESSMENTS?

Depending on the screening tool, educators, some paraprofessionals, or parents may conduct the assessment. However, functional assessment tools are usually administered by a specifically trained professional, such as a resource professional. A diagnostic assessment can be conducted only by a highly trained, specialized professional, such as an audiologist, a psychologist, a doctor, or a speech pathologist. Additional references to functional assessment tools are outlined in this chapter as part of a further process of inquiry and the building of a holistic picture of a child's strengths and skills to be developed. Further information on the various paraprofessionals who might support early childhood, children, and families is available online.

SCREENING TOOLS

The *primary purpose* of a screening tool is to guide educators in identifying areas in a child's development that potentially may indicate a concern or delay in that area. From that information, a family in discussion with an educator may conclude that further investigation is needed and, as a consequence, indicate that the child *may* need a referral for a further assessment.

Another reason for using a screening tool is to target what services, supports, or people are required to meet the needs of the referred children. For example, if a particular area has a **prevalence** and **incidence** of fetal alcohol syndrome in babies, then health services would be most in demand. Depending on geography, accessibility could be a problematic issue within a large urban or small rural city. These problematic issues could include not enough diagnostic services or support personnel to meet the demands of the population; an inadequate tax base to support the hiring of professionals, doctors, or supports needed for a population; or a rapidly growing community without the funding and recognition as an area requiring services or supports.

Screening tools are used in familiar settings and are typically completed informally through observation during normal, daily experiences. Generally speaking, learning experiences are not set up or contrived to achieve a specific skill but rather are observed during the normal course of the day. The screening tool chosen should be appropriate for use with the child, the family, and those administering the screen.

A screening tool does *not* diagnose, nor does it provide a clear overview of all the necessary skills in all developmental areas. The results from screening tools should not be the sole source used for planning an individualized program for a child with special needs.

COMMONLY USED SCREENING TOOLS IN CANADA

Two commonly used Canadian screening tools are the Nipissing District Developmental Screen (NDDS), which was compiled in North Bay, Ontario (see Exhibit 7.11) and the Ages and Stages Questionnaires (ASQ), originating in the United States. The NDDS is a good example of a criterion-referenced tool where groupings of age-related behaviours can be checked by the parent and educator as a "yes" or "no." The Ages and Stages Questionnaires come in the form of two different screening measures. The latest version of the scale, the ASQ-3, is intended to measure a number of developmental domains whereby the parent and educator can discuss and check off skills expected to be performed at a particular age as "yes," "sometimes," or "not yet." One version of the Ages and Stages Questionnaires, Social-Emotional (ASQ: SE-2), is aimed at monitoring the socioemotional behaviours of young children using different rating criteria.

The ASQ-3 is available in English, Korean, Spanish, and French. For more information on this screening measure, please visit the Ages and Stages website (www.agesandstages.com). These and the following screening tools and reference guides are discussed further online:

- The Brigance Infant and Toddler Screen (Brigance & Page Glascoe, 2002)
- Diagnostic Inventory for Screening Children (DISC)/DPS (Mainland, 2001)
- Rourke Baby Record (Rourke, Rourke, & Leduc, 2009).
- The Battelle Developmental Inventory, 2nd edition (Newborg, 2004)
- Early Development Instrument (EDI) (Janus, Brinkman, et al., 2007)
- Infant Toddler Sensory Profile (Dunn, 1999)
- The Carolina Curriculum for Infants and Toddlers with Special Needs (CCITSN), 3rd Edition (Johnson-Martin, Attermeier, & Hacker, 2004)

The Ontario Best Start On Track Guide (www.beststart.org/OnTrack_English/8-screeningtools.html) offers professionals a comprehensive description of a variety of recommended assessment tools, as well as a practical guide to assist in understanding the process of screening and assessment.

"It is important to thoughtfully examine tools," such as those in the above list, "in order to choose ones that are most appropriate for the purpose for which they are being used, as well as for the individual needs of the children and families served by programs. For example, many norm-referenced assessment tools have not included in their norming population children who are culturally and linguistically diverse" (Yates et al., 2008, p. 6). Be sure to also search the Internet for other screening tools relevant to your practice.

FUNCTIONAL ASSESSMENT TOOLS: HOW ARE THEY INITIATED?

Functional assessment tools are often initiated by the resource professional, who, with the parents and educators, uses the child's portfolio documents as well as new information from the developmental assessment tool in order to understand the "whole" child. These tools may be introduced after a screening process has highlighted "red flags" warranting further investigation of specific domains of a child's development. In some circumstances, informal observations will have led to the developmental assessment process, bypassing the screening process altogether. Each level of assessment has its own merits; it is up to the parents, the educators, and the resource professional(s) to determine the best way to collect information on each child. Educators are also encouraged to consult with the child in the process with parent permission.

During the process of collection, the types of methods and procedures may vary; therefore, it is important to look at which one will best represent the child. Some developmental tools do not permit flexibility in administration, which can influence the results gained from a child; in fact, these tools may paint a picture of a child with more "skills yet to be developed" than normally what would have been gathered if the child had been observed in his or her own natural and familiar learning environments.

Go online to learn more about the many tools available to the early intervention and early childhood community.

THE ROLE OF THE EARLY CHILDHOOD PROFESSIONAL IN THE ASSESSMENT PROCESS

The role of the early childhood professional in the screening and functional assessment process is a very important one. Ongoing observations, input, and feedback from the educator, parent, resource professional, and other members of the team can inform and produce a multitude of outcomes and information. Just collecting and organizing the information while communicating and sharing with the family and other professionals is a job in itself. Yet, this time-intensive role is important as it provides ongoing insights needed to respond to a child's strengths, needs, and interests, and to parent priorities and concerns arising from the process. Communicating adjustments to any aspects of practice, such as behaviour guidance, the curriculum, the environment, or the team, is part of the process. What also is created through this process is a collective knowledge of the child that can support appropriate referrals to other agencies and perhaps a diagnostic assessment (which would be done by a **psychologist, psychiatrist, or developmental pediatrician**). Clearly, assessment refers to all aspects of this practice rather than just a specific assessment tool or practice.

Family-centred practice reminds us that parents have the sole decision on how to act upon the information they have gained from the process. In conjunction with the resource professionals we are working with, it is our role as educators to provide the family with the necessary tools to make informed decisions; we are not expected to, nor should we, decide the directions we should take with a child. The sooner parents are informed as to the benefits of this process, the sooner they are able to receive the supports they need.

WHAT IS AN INDIVIDUALIZED PLAN?

One of the many outcomes of the assessment process, formal or informal, will be the creation or preparation of a plan of action for the child and her or his family. This plan can be simplistic or complex in its approach and will be an outcome of the collaborative efforts of the child (where possible), the professionals and team members involved (interprofessional and/or specific to the early learning setting), and the family. **IEPs (Individual Education Plans)**, **IPPs (Individual Program Plans)**, and **ITPs (Individual Training/Teaching Plans)** are some of the more common acronyms that represent the names of specific plans of action for the child.

There are variations to these plans; for example, according to the Ontario Ministry of Education, IEPs detail the strengths and needs of a child according to the curriculum aspects of the specified grade as well as those identified **accommodations** and **modifications** necessary to support the attainment of skills, among other things. If you are an educator in Ontario's full-day kindergarten, it is important to understand what an IEP is and is not as well as to understand the terms *accommodation* and *modification*. Accommodation involves the provision of adaptations that support children in attaining the grade level they are in, whereas modifications infer changes made to curriculum when a child is not at the same level or attaining the same grade level as his/her peers.

These plans in other settings may include other components, such as priority **goals** and **objectives**, implementation considerations and the breakdown of the skills to be achieved (**task analysis**—the breakdown of skills into a step-by-step process, identifying **prerequisite skills**), the roles and responsibilities of those involved in the implementation (which, again, may involve an interprofessional component), a documentation process to measure progress, and, of course, an evaluation component.

These plans typically involve a combination of skills to be further developed as well as description of the child's current strengths and interests. A child's strengths and interests are used to respond with an appropriate learning experience that would further facilitate the child's development in a particular area. For example, if a child loved robots, an educator would use that interest in creating experiences for the child which would simultaneously work on a focused area of need.

These learning experiences, techniques, and materials, regardless of what they might entail, are responsive and inclusive in nature and are intended for implementation in the child's natural setting (home and/or school) in very natural ways. If implemented appropriately, the learning that takes place should be fun and enjoyable for the child and peers, without the child realizing that certain skills are being targeted for development.

For additional learning in this aspect of practice, think about consulting with your setting or community regarding individualized plans and terminology associated with the planning process.

Part of the IPP process also involves a plan for the family because the child cannot be looked at in isolation. Directed by the family, and with assistance from a resource professional or educator if requested, an appropriate **Individual Family Support Plan (IFSP)** can be created. These plans would revolve around the family and would contain an evaluation timeline, breakdowns of roles and responsibilities established with input from other community and/or centre team members, service timelines for all involved, and next steps for service. Incorporating both the home and early learning environments, the IFSP might also outline a child's current strengths and skills to be developed but would go beyond supports for the child to include the supports necessary for the entire family. The collection of authentic input and assessment data for these IFSPs requires time; therefore, the evaluation timeline for these plans is typically every six months or upon request by the family or member of the team. "Participants also identified time as necessary to build a trusting relationship with a family and to acquire, through experience, proficiency in child development and authentic assessment methods" (Keilty et al., 2009, p. 254).

INDIVIDUALIZED STRATEGIES AND PROGRAMS

Early childhood programs are inclusive and responsive to the strengths and abilities of all children. If a young child has been diagnosed as having special needs, that child is entitled to special supports, strategies, and plans to meet his or her needs. An Individual Program Plan (IPP) is an individualized written plan of action that is guided by observations and input from the family, teachers, resource professionals, educators, and other professionals. After team discussions, ideas and strategies are formalized into an action plan that focuses on one or more areas of the child's development, aiming to maximize a child's optimal growth and development. This plan helps coordinate the efforts of parents and professionals and assists in the creation and development of adaptations that are responsive to the child. Whatever the focus, the learning experiences for the child should not differ from others but should complement whatever is set up in the environment for the other children.

Similar to the IEP,

> IPP goals and objectives should be addressed through a variety of instructional procedures appropriate for young children. Wherever possible, instruction on IPP goals and objectives is embedded within activities and taught across environments. Many opportunities should be provided for children to acquire, practice and generalize skills through ongoing activities and routines. Opportunities should also be provided for child initiated learning, particularly in the context of play. The amount of direct teaching and adult-imposed structure varies according to the nature of the goal or objective and the individual needs of children. (Alberta Education, 2006, p. 13)

Alberta has recently updated its IPP templates. For more information, visit the Alberta Ministry of Education IPP Templates website.

These inclusionary practices ensure the child is fully included in daily routines and experiences while developing in the areas indicated in the IPP. According to Donna Lero (2010) of the Division for Early Childhood of the Council for Exceptional Children and the National Association for the Education of Young Children, the defining features of early childhood inclusion encompass access, participation, and supports (Division for Early Childhood and National Association for the Education of Young Children, 2009). Furthermore, in her article she states the following:

> Early childhood programs that are effective in including children with special needs require a mix of resources and supports within the centre (e.g., an accessible environment with specialized equipment and materials as needed; staff who are knowledgeable and committed to inclusion, who are given time to plan and participate in the development of the individual program plans (IPPs) with community specialists and who form an effective team; and support and leadership provided by the program director) and supports provided to the program by specialists and therapists in the community, and through funding to reduce adult-child ratios with staff who have specialized training. (Lero, 2010, p. 25)

OBSERVATION AND ASSESSMENT: INFORMING ADAPTATIONS

As childhood professionals, we are fortunate to have the opportunity every day to learn from, learn with, and educate young children—this is a privilege that we cannot take lightly. We have an important responsibility: educating a very vulnerable population. As educators, we can have a profound effect on young children and their development.

Throughout this text, we have learned the importance of collaborating with colleagues and professionals, with children and families, and with our community so that we might plan the most optimal learning communities possible. We realize now that observation is important for many reasons: it provides us with information and the tools we need to be responsive and inclusive educators. More specifically, it provides insight into a child's strengths, needs, or skills to be developed; the child's interests; the child's learning styles and preferences; the family; and the sociocultural context in which they live. All of this can inform our next steps; what materials, toys, and equipment are reflective of the children in our classroom; where it is best to place materials; and perhaps what teaching strategies and adaptations are going to be most effective to assist a variety of children. At times, adaptations may be made for an individual child to enable her or him to achieve skills with assistance or independently. The adaptations we create, however, can be beneficial to many children. Take a look at the examples of creative adaptations online. Many of those adaptations were informed by full participation in the observation cycle and appreciative inquiry process, and were the result of collaboration among the child, educators, and family.

All the information we have discussed in this and other chapters—observations, portfolios, IPPs, IEPs, and various forms of assessment—can inform the adaptations we design for all children. Adaptations are one way we can respond to children to include them within the classroom through the adjustments we make in our interactions, in the physical environment, and in the materials and experiences provided for children in the classroom. Adaptations can be defined as changes or alterations we make to increase the success of a child in achieving skills in a task independently or with assistance. Increasing the accessibility, responsiveness, inclusivity, and universality of all elements within our professional practice to increase the success of children and their families is our ultimate goal.

EVALUATION: SUMMATIVE AND FORMATIVE

The intent of observation is to uncover the realm of children's everyday experiences, learning, and development. Observation asks the questions "What will I discover today?" "What will it mean?" Evaluation asks questions such as "What did I/the children learn?" and "Was it meaningful? How does what I have learned inform my practice? How does evaluation support learning?"

When using the term *evaluation*, the same ambiguity arises as when we looked at the term *assessment*; these two terms are used interchangeably depending on which province, region, or country is using them. Reflection and evaluation essentially coexist as each leads its participants through a very valuable and meaningful learning process about any aspect of practice.

In the article "Reflection—The Key to Evaluation," Elaine Ferguson (2004) states,

> Evaluation begins, proceeds, concludes and starts over again with reflection. We begin by reflecting upon why we are evaluating and what we will evaluate. We use reflection to collect information on what is being accomplished. We reflect upon the information collected, share our reflections with others and distinguish what we have learned about what we did. These new learnings and affirmations of previous learnings are used to develop new insights that will help us identify how we are going to use what we've learned. (pp. 17–18)

The effect of evaluation is that it brings meaning and clarity to knowledge or experiences. In that context, it is a supportive activity. In that context, "What happened?" is a question of interest. Whether a teacher or a team is evaluating a child's progress or the impact of change to families in our centres and schools, those involved from the beginning should be involved at the evaluation stage as well. Why? When reflecting and evaluating where our journey began, we need to see how our knowledge and experience were gained and then determine where we are now. Evaluation speaks to the original questions, what the answers could be, and what decisions, based on the reflective cycle of observation and all it includes, will be made.

Is it necessary to wait weeks and months before an evaluation takes place? No, it is not because there is variation in the times and types of evaluations that can take place. Ideally, there are two types of evaluative processes: formative and summative. Within this formative and summative framework, evaluation is broken down even further.

Formative evaluation refers to an evaluation that is ongoing. This type of evaluation is informal, is used at any point starting soon after a child is admitted into the program, and includes reference to families, educators, and other professionals; the collaborative efforts of the team to compile information for individualized instruction; and implementation.

In the document *Growing Success*, the Ontario Ministry of Education (2008) explains assessment feedback as differing from evaluation:

> Assessment is the process of gathering information from a variety of sources (including assignments, day-to-day observations, conversations or conferences, demonstrations, projects, performances, and tests) that accurately reflects how well a student is achieving the curriculum expectations in a subject/course. As part of assessment, teachers provide students with descriptive feedback that guides their efforts towards improvement. Evaluation refers to the process of judging the quality of student work on the basis of established criteria, and assigning a value to represent that quality. (p. 1-i)

Although grossly understated, this process serves to point out that formative evaluation can be done at any point for reasons identified by any members of the team. Through discussion and reflection, the team can make changes as the process evolves. Throughout this process, **monitoring** occurs. "Monitoring early learning through documentation is based on the gathering of layers of information to provide rich and rigorous evidence about children's early learning and development. It is not the measurement of discrete skills, out of context with the children's daily lived lives. Young children show their understanding by doing, showing, representing and telling" (Pascal n.d., p. 23). Monitoring could refer to the tracking of a child's progress during the implementation of an IEP, the daily monitoring of a child's emotional health, or monitoring the transition of a family from one agency to another. Using the cycle of observation itself as an example, let us consider some key junctures where monitoring would occur:

- *Initial observations and decisions.* Are the types of records appropriate for the kind of information that is being sought?
- *Appreciative inquiry.* What are the best questions to ask? When? Why?
- *Compiling information.* Who would be documenting, and for how long would observations continue or stop being collected?
- *Reflection and discussion.* Who would be included, and what are the key points of discussion?
- *Planning.* Who will guide the planning, and who will implement the planning?
- *Organization of resources.* What kinds of materials, space, and adaptations have been suggested?
- *Implementation.* Where, when, and how will the daily, inclusive strategies be monitored? Who will be responsible?
- *Evaluation.* When will the summative evaluation be concluded?

Different from formative evaluation, **summative evaluation** is perceived as being a more formal type of evaluation. A summative evaluation takes place at the end of a timeline, when the process has come full circle. The summative evaluation summarizes the process. This type of evaluation

- involves all the people vital to the process
- takes place at an appointed interval: semi-annually, yearly, or monthly
- is done at key junctures—has the child demonstrated the skills targeted by the IPP?
- provides accountability for the process

This process of evaluation does measure more than is at first apparent. It could also measure

- the impact of the **affective** and physical environment
- practices that represent centre philosophy
- skills and knowledge of educators and caregivers
- involvement of all concerned—team functioning
- quality programs in the community

Elaine Ferguson (2004) states that "reflection allows us to review what we've done, know why we did it and incorporate new ideas into our practice. We can do something with what we've learned and enhance what we already know. The quality of our practice is affected and we become active agents in our growth and development" (p. 18).

A quality program is recognized as such by the commitment, caring, and dedication of educators and families working together. Through the observation and documentation of a child's growth and learning, communication and relationships thrive, benefiting all concerned. Another view to evaluating the learning of young children is expressed well in the article "One Teacher, 20 Preschoolers, and a Goldfish: Environmental Awareness, Emergent Curriculum, and Documentation" by Lewin-Benham (2006). This insightful article demonstrates how four-year-olds and their teacher, Mrs. Putnam, first created a documentation panel. This article demonstrates how documentation, including observations and audio recordings, can be used along with the children's interest to facilitate learning. What this article, like play-based learning and emergent curriculum, tells us is that a finished documentation panel should convey what started the experience, how it developed and why, and its outcome—in another word, evaluation. The children and the teacher observed and documented their research about goldfish and environmental awareness; they also evaluated the process leading to their conclusions, and because they are children, the process generated more questions! We began this section with some basic questions about evaluation, and we hope we have left you with your own questions about the subject.

SUMMARY

As new play-based learning and curriculum emerge, it is important to look with the early identification and early intervention lens to what is needed by and provided to any child with special needs or children who require extra supports and/or services. Some of the main topics covered this chapter that support this process include family-centred practice, early identification and early intervention in the early learning and care profession, assessment, and the role of the resource professional. The core focus of the chapter illustrates the complexities of early identification and intervention within a responsive, inquiry-based cycle of observation, but also stresses the ways that children and families are supported in the community.

CHAPTER 8

REFLECTIVE AND TRANSFORMATIVE: OBSERVER AS LEADER

Auremar/Shutterstock.com

OVERVIEW

We have come full circle, exploring the many facets of observation and pedagogical documentation, including the exploration of numerous methodologies and the important role educators play in making children's learning visible. That said, we also emphasize the importance of observing and documenting to understand and appreciate the child within the context of his or her environment. Viewing the environment as co-educator, we can begin to understand, assess, and appreciate what contributes to healthy and responsive interactions as well as delineate what is necessary to prepare quality inclusive environments reflective of the diversity of its learners. Analyzing and assessing the environment is an important focus for this chapter.

We also acknowledge the changing landscape of early childhood education and the role of the educator in early childhood. We realize that "through pedagogical documentation, the roles in education are shifting; what it means to be a learner and an educator are being transformed. Students and teachers alike are demonstrating ownership of and engaging in teaching and learning. Consequently, pedagogical documentation is a vehicle for learning that bridges understanding of children and adults" (Ontario Ministry of Education, 2012, p. 4). Educators must then look to new ways of doing things and to new roles to further support this transition.

Some of these new roles include the observer as pedagogical leader, mentor, and community capacity builder. "There is argument that we cannot expect educators to create a community of learners among children if they do not have a comparable community to nourish their own growth (Grossman, Wineburg, & Woolworth, 2001)" (Brown & Inglis, 2013, p. 14). Educators also have an important role to play in research, whether through involvement in research specific to a setting or community or involvement in longitudinal research over time. It is through research that capacity within early childhood settings, observation, and new ways of documenting can flourish. Staying ahead of and in tune with observational trends, particularly those relating to the relationship between pedagogical documentation and social media is key to understanding how we might continue to collaborate with children, families, and communities. We finish this chapter with a look into educator development and portfolio preparation. The profession expects and children deserve knowledgeable educators who are committed to lifelong learning. As educators within the early childhood community, we have much to celebrate and look forward to!

FOCUS QUESTIONS

1. What does the term *environment* mean?
2. Which aspects of the environment are important to observe and why?
3. What is community capacity building and what is its relevance to observation and documentation?
4. Why are observation and appreciative inquiry so important to pedagogical leadership and mentorship?
5. Why might it be necessary to continue to explore new pedagogical documentation methods and trends?
6. Professional development and e-portfolios for educators have become an expectation of the profession. Why? What impact do they have on our practice?

THE ENVIRONMENT DEFINED

Throughout this text, we've taken many opportunities to introduce aspects of the learning environment in order to prepare for this in-depth examination of the dimensions that compose a quality learning environment for children. When we take a moment to pause, reflect, and observe, what appears more clearly to us is the intimate relationship occurring between the children and their surroundings. We envision this relationship with the environment moving beyond the traditional views of just the physical space, for it also encompasses the ambiance, the "feeling," and the overall atmosphere of the environment. We use observation, documentation, and assessment to assist us in understanding and appreciating this subtle but complex "relationship" between a child and the environment because it provides insight into how children are influenced by their environment and how it might influence their functioning and interactions with others within their learning space. We present the environment as a co-educator and co-play partner in the early childhood setting, for it holds a significant role in the co-education process. Preparing environments for children is a very important responsibility.

RESPONSIVE RELATIONSHIPS AND THE SOCIOEMOTIONAL/ PSYCHOLOGICAL TONE OF AN ENVIRONMENT

From within the womb, to a child's first breath, and all the way to the end of life, we each have an intrinsic desire to feel needed,

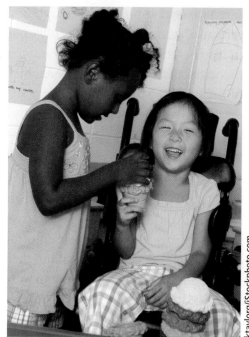

ktaylorg/iStockphoto.com

omgimages/iStockphoto.com

szefei/iStockphoto.com

cared for, and connected to people and aspects of our surroundings. We know that care and learning are inextricably linked—one cannot function without the other. In his *Hierarchy of Physical, Emotional, and Intellectual Needs*, Abraham Maslow theorized that people are involved in an ongoing process of **self-actualizing**. One of the ways in which this is made possible is through the building of trusting and responsive relationships. Consistently being available emotionally and physically to children regardless of their age empowers them to take risks, to try new things, and to immerse themselves as secure, attached participants in a learning community.

> Deep, caring, enduring relationships between children and educators provide predictability and secure attachment in children's lives. Forming warm and responsive relationships with children typically means respecting their emotional rhythms, listening carefully to their conversations, taking their suggestions for problem solving seriously, and following their lead in curriculum planning. Flexible educators respond to children's interests, passions, and strengths; engage children in multiple forms of communication, creativity, and expression; and encourage joint endeavours where children and adults learn and play together. (Early Childhood Research and Development Team, 2008, p. 11)

For families and practitioners alike, creating a **child-centred environment** that is inclusive of the variations in abilities, learning approaches, and diversity of individual children within a group is important. Brain development, **self-regulation**, and **resiliency** are examples of children's socioemotional health that can be affected by the psychological and emotional tone of their surroundings. We know then, that there are added benefits of a relationship-based environment, for it supports early brain development, it enhances the ability of children to self-regulate, and it is integral to the adjustment to a group experience. How we design environments for learning can have lifelong consequences upon a child's quality of life; we must therefore look at a variety of ways to approach this process.

Let us use, as an example, children who are new to a program never having been in group care or any other early childhood environment. They stand by the door having just been dropped off by their parent, tears streaming down their face, and not having developed the security or trust in their environment or teachers to feel that their needs will be met. It is integral, then, for educators to respond to situations like this in order for children to develop the connections and attachments necessary for their health and well-being. Jean Clinton, in her publication within the *Think, Feel, Act* series entitled *The Power of Positive Adult-Child Relationships: Connection Is the Key* (2013), states that "children learn best in an environment that acknowledges this interconnectivity and thus focuses on both emotional and cognitive development. There is now an explosion of knowledge that tells us that healthy development cannot happen without good relationships between children and the important people in their lives, both within the family and outside of it" (pp. 5–6). When we respond to children in a consistent way, and when we frame our interactions and involvement with families within a relationship-based environment approach, the combined approaches contribute significantly to the success of the emotional and intellectual learning or adjustment for a child or children:

> Stated simply, relationships are the "active ingredients" of the environment's influence on healthy human development. They incorporate the qualities that best promote competence and well-being—individualized responsiveness, mutual action-and-interaction, and an emotional connection to another human being, be it a parent, peer, grandparent, aunt, uncle, neighbour, teacher, coach, or any other person who has an important impact on the child's early development. Relationships engage children in the human community in ways that help them define who they are, what they can become, and how and why they are important to other people. (National Scientific Council on the Developing Child, 2004, p. 1)

A final consideration that falls within the relationship dimension of the early learning environment is the sociocultural approach introduced in earlier chapters. *The Early Years Framework for Australia* (2009) and *Te Whāriki* (1996), the framework developed by New Zealand, both support this element of quality:

> There is growing recognition of the need to develop and expand measures in the area of cultural competence as a facet of quality in early care and education. Cultural awareness, ethnic and racial socialization strategies, and culturally responsive pedagogy are constructs that have been identified as necessary to the measurement of quality environments and practices involving culture. Global characteristics of child care quality, such as provider-child interactions, appropriate responsiveness, authentic knowledge about families, capacity to support multiple cultures, and characteristics of the caregiving environment, are important to assess regardless of culture. Measurement strategies and procedures are needed to ensure that these characteristics are assessed in a culturally responsive manner. (Forry, Vick, & Halle, 2009, p. 3)

To develop your own culturally responsive and inclusive pedagogy and to ensure equity in your observation and assessment approaches, begin reflecting upon what you believe and value, as well as your feelings toward different aspects of your practice. What might you be curious about? What are the learners (child, family, educator, students, etc.) in your classroom curious about? Knowing how we affect our interactions with others, as well as how what we believe and feel influences the design and creation of learning communities for children and their families, is necessary. Your choice to enter into the early childhood profession signifies your desire to include children and respond to their needs—this is at the

Juanmonino/iStockphoto.com

very heart of our teaching. Establishing a process whereby we can engage in ongoing self-reflection is an important aspect of the observation cycle. As inferred by the cycle of observation, reflecting on all elements of practice is necessary, but we cannot begin to appreciate the significance of our learning if we do not understand ourselves. By adding thoughtfulness and meaning to our thinking and actions, we can progress forward in the development of our own pedagogy of observation, assessment, and documentation.

There is no doubt that social inclusion is an important aspect of this approach because all children want to feel respected and included alongside their peers in an environment that enables them to develop and expand their identity, whether it be gender, ability, culture, or other aspects of their being. Reflecting on your childhood and your stages of development, was feeling included also an important part of your self-identity and your ability to self-regulate and be resilient?

Resiliency and self-regulation in young children has been a topic of concern for early childhood professionals and mental health professionals for a number of years and continues to be of significant concern even today. The health and well-being of children—socially, mentally, cognitively—are a priority for all those who educate or work with young children. Helping children develop an awareness of who they are, their strengths and abilities, how they relate and work with others, and how they deal with conflict or barriers is of particular importance. Take, for example, the following analogy:

> Young people are like trees. They come in various shapes and sizes and grow up in most parts of the world. Families can be thought of as the soil and water at the base of trees. Schools, neighbourhoods, communities and society at large can be compared to the sun, rainfall, insects, birds and animals. The different characteristics of trees, qualities of soils and weather conditions (such as the amount of sun and rainfall) can affect the health and growth of trees. In a similar way, the varying traits of young people, and the characteristics of their families and environments, can positively or negatively affect young people's health and growth. Trees go through developmental stages as they mature from young saplings to full grown specimens. Children also go through developmental stages on their way to adulthood, and what happens to them at various stages of development can affect their outcomes. Resilient children and youth grow, branch out and flower when systems supporting their healthy development (such as well-functioning families and environments) work together. Such young people are more likely to withstand and overcome challenges, learn from them, and develop and succeed in healthy ways. (Barankin & Khanlou, 2007, p. 14)

In this respect, we must not take our role and influence upon young children lightly. Documenting children's actions and behaviours, and observing our environment can give us significant insight into how we might support their building of self-regulation and resilience. How we act and respond, what we prepare, and how we design our environments or learning communities for children require us to be diligent in our observation and reflective processes! More information on assessment measures for resiliency and emotional well-being is available online.

THE PHYSICAL ENVIRONMENT

Regardless of philosophy or demographics, the physical design of a program or environment both indoors and outdoors can be structured in a way to support the participation of all children in a quality learning community experience. Like other aspects of the environment identified in the cycle of observation, we can achieve further understanding of the impact of the physicality of a space by engaging in each step within the cycle as well as reflecting upon our findings throughout the process. "The physical elements of a learning environment help to create a psychological climate of ambiance. Whether the message is overt or symbolic the physical environment communicates information about the kinds of behaviors and performances expected of children" (Crowther, 2006, p. 98).

Children have the right to learning spaces and experiences that expand all areas of their development through active play–based and child-centred learning, essentially creating their own learning story each and every moment of the day. Space allotment for children may vary according to where the early childhood setting is located; however, we know that there must be adequate space to accommodate individual variations in development, such as children who might use equipment to support their learning (e.g., wheelchairs, **standers**, **orthotics**). Consideration given to the way that equipment and furniture are positioned can have significant implications for accessibility as well as for the actions and behaviours of the children in the setting. Balancing louder and quieter areas of the room is one of the features to consider that might influence a child's ability to sustain his or her attention at an experience.

xefstock/iStockphoto.com

The overuse of wall space by educators for purposes such as artwork, bulletin boards, and pictures is a frequent oversight when looking at one's environment. When you look around your environment, what do you see on the walls? Are materials at eye level? Do the visuals reflect children's learning and participation in the room? How stimulating or over-stimulating are the materials on the wall? Children in your classroom may require different levels of sensory stimulation to optimize their learning and engagement with others. Having too much on the walls may prompt children to feel distracted and overwhelmed. Too little may prompt children to not "see" themselves or connect with their learning environment or peers.

Stable and predictable schedules and routines that can be supported through the use of **social stories** and **visual schedules** will assist children in building trust and security. You can see by the photograph of the visual schedule in Exhibit 8.1 that

EXHIBIT 8.1   VISUAL SCHEDULE

Kristine Fenning.

children are able to see and then understand visually what is coming next. By the design of this schedule—through the placement of Velcro on the backs of the laminated pictures—children are able to participate in the scheduling of their day by removing and reorganizing what comes first, second, and so on, making this visual schedule very interactive. Through this type of participation, children may begin to develop an awareness or recognition of their need for different things, such as sleep, food, and physical activity. Visual schedules can be developed using various visual schedule apps, such as Choiceworks, or by interacting with a program known as **Boardmaker**. Other settings have been known to develop schedules through the use of pictographs, hand-drawn pictures, or actual photos of different routines and parts of the day. Community Living Toronto has designed a site called **ConnectABILITY**, where professionals and parents can access tools and supports they can use to support children and youth with special needs in different aspects of the home or program. One aspect of their site is a Visuals Engine, which offers tools for educators to create various types of visuals that they can then print for their classroom. Social stories and visual schedules can be a helpful strategy to reduce the anxiety often experienced by children when they are unsure of what is going to happen next, or if a change is about to occur in their day-to-day experiences that they have never experienced before. Use of visuals should begin with photos of the real objects, and as children become more attuned to abstract visuals, a schedule like the one in Exhibit 8.1 can be understood.

As you look about your own classroom environment, does everything have a purpose for being there? Is your environment accessible enough for children to foster their independence and thus develop control and decision-making skills? Listen to the pulse of your own learning community to hear the inner workings of children's play; through this process, you may find yourself looking at numerous other elements of classroom design you had never thought of before. If you also look forward to some of the environmental tools discussed later in this chapter, you will see that each introduces a number of other elements that are necessary to consider when designing a physical space. Lighting, the selection of culturally and developmentally responsive materials and **universally designed** learning materials geared to children's interests and abilities, the use of natural elements, the use of open-ended and closed-ended materials, a balance between small-group and large-group experiences, the adapting of materials and experiences to meet individual needs and abilities within a group, ratios and number of children at different learning spaces, health and safety considerations, and numerous other inclusive qualities are just some of the many environmental aspects we must consider. These and other provisions and qualities of a physical environment

> create the context for children's learning and relationships. A flexible learning environment supports the holistic way children learn. Physical activity enhances brain development, coordination and social skills as well as motor skills and helps children to build confidence in their own abilities and learn to enjoy being active. Exploration of the natural environment helps children to develop an appreciation of the natural world, an awareness of the impact of human activity on the environment and to begin to think of ways in which they can contribute to a sustainable future. (Australian Government, Department of Education, Employment and Workplace Relations, 2010, p. 57)*

As we revisit the concept of pedagogical documentation, eliciting feedback from children and families is just as integral to this evaluation and reflection process. When children and families are involved in the selection of materials and experiences in the room, as well as in the layout and design of their classroom and wall spaces, children are more apt to become engaged, extend their own learning and understanding of self-assessment, and perhaps become more confident in taking risks and trying new things. Furthermore, when children see their contributions to their environment, there is a sense of pride and a feeling of community because they are able to evolve their identity and see themselves and their families in the environment (e.g., through photos and artwork at children's level).

*Australian Government, Department of Education, Employment and Workplace Relations, 2010, p. 57.

The physical environment also requires us to look at the quality of the outdoor learning environment.

> Outdoor places where children play can be important social places, not just for children and young people, but also for parents, carers and the wider community. They should be places where children and young people can enjoy spending time, be physically active, interact with their natural surroundings, experience change and continuity, take risks in an environment where they feel safe and, of course, play—alone or with others—in a wide variety of ways. (Shackell, Butler, Doyle, & Ball, 2008, p. 8)

Now "ask any adult to recall their best play memories. These were almost always outside—often in natural surroundings—with friends; exciting, social, creative experiences often high in anticipation. Ask the same adults if their children can play in the same way today and silence falls" (Shackell et al., 2008, p. 13). With increased exposure to video games, computers, the Internet, and numerous other stresses facing parents who are raising children in today's society, the time spent by children outdoors is becoming less and less. Merge these factors with the statistics and research highlighting the increase in obesity in young children around the world and there is reason for concern. Focusing our attention and observations on creating natural outdoor play environments that encompass responsive and inclusive elements is therefore extremely necessary. The health and well-being of children in our community and in our care require us to take action.

Sacha Cabezas/Sally Wylie

Sacha Cabezas/Sally Wylie

Sacha Cabezas/Sally Wylie

Providing a healthy and safe outdoor play space that will attract and engage children in active and sensory-based play experiences is an important investment we need to make. One such approach is the introduction of **natural design** and **loose parts** elements into the indoor and outdoor learning environments. Take a look at Exhibit 8.2,

EXHIBIT 8.2   **NATURAL MATERIALS AND LOOSE PARTS**

Kristine Fenning

Kristine Fenning

Kristine Fenning/Hawkins Exhibit, Seneca College

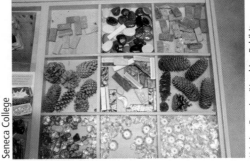

Kristine Fenning/Hawkins Exhibit, Seneca College

Above we find a number of loose parts, natural and manufactured, prepared for young children to use in ways of their choosing. Below we see educators and teachers engaged in a professional development day preparing a creation with some of the loose parts offered to them for exploration. Why might it be important for educators to play and experiment?

Reggio Summer Intensive, Acorn School/Kristine Fenning

If you offered these materials to children in your setting, what do you think they would do with them?

Source: Kristine Fenning, with thanks to the Hawkins Exhibit and the Reggio Inspired Summer Intensive

which portrays a number of natural elements and loose parts made available to children. What do you think might occur if these materials were provided as a provocation to three- to four-year-old children in your early childhood setting?

Please go online for literature and additional resources exploring creative approaches to indoor and outdoor play spaces for children, much of which highlights the return to natural landscape elements such as water and land features, varying surfaces for accessibility, spaces for social togetherness, and the development of community.

Let's turn our attention now to environmental assessments and frameworks that further assist us in preparing quality inclusive and responsive environments for children, educators, families, and the community.

EARLY CHILDHOOD FRAMEWORKS AND ENVIRONMENTAL ASSESSMENTS: BEGINNING WITH A QUESTION

Caregivers and educators can use a multitude of methods to gather information on the status of responsiveness and inclusiveness in their relationships and early childhood environment. Observation methods like those mentioned in earlier chapters, including learning stories, self-made checklists, rating scales, narratives, and anecdotes, are just some of the many ways information can be gathered as a team to reflect upon and implement action or change. Environmental assessment measures and community early childhood frameworks of practice can add additional knowledge and learning to our professional practice, and subsequently support the creation of quality learning environments. To understand and discern what might be the best approach for a particular setting, we begin with a question. If you recall back in Chapter 2, we laid the foundation for forming questions about children and our practice that can begin our inquiry. Using a simple reflective questioning methodology that prompts educators to consider different environmental dimensions and reflect upon what they see using an appreciative inquiry approach is a great place to start.

Questions and questioning are a sound pedagogical approach used in many early childhood frameworks around the world. These frameworks, on their own or in conjunction with observations and assessment tools, give us significant insights into and understanding of how we might continue to provide quality early childhood environments.

An example of the *Te Whāriki* reflective questioning approach is provided in Exhibit 8.3 to illustrate how the simple phrasing of questions and subsequent reflection can elicit volumes of information and insight into what is taking place for children within a specific type of early childhood environment.

EXHIBIT 8.3   *TE WHĀRIKI* FRAMEWORK AND REFLECTIVE APPROACH EXAMPLE

Goal: Children and their families experience an environment where they know that they have a place.

Questions for Reflection

Examples

- How is knowledge about children collected and shared among adults who work with them, and does this provide sufficient information for those who need it?
- What arrangements are made for personal space and personal belongings, and are these suitable for the children, the adults, and the setting?
- How does the programme ensure that all children are receiving attention and affection and that children will always have familiar adults who know about them? How well are these goals achieved?
- What are the procedures for individual welcomes and farewells and for settling in new children?
- How, and to what extent, is it possible to allow for children's attachment to particular people and things?
- What aspects of the environment help children feel that this is a place where they belong?

Source: *Te Whariki*, p. 58, Copyright © Crown, Ministry of Education, New Zealand, 1996.

Other reports, frameworks, and research findings within and outside Canada have their own suggestions regarding how environments should be designed for young children, such as Ontario's *Early learning for Every Child Today: A Framework for Ontario Early Childhood Settings* (the Ontario Early Learning Framework), *Think, Feel, Act: Lessons from Research about Young Children*, and *How Does Learning Happen? Ontario's Pedagogy for the Early Years*, and Australia's *Belonging, Being and Becoming: The Early Years Learning Framework*. We have frequently referred to Ontario's Early Learning Framework throughout this text, as there are a number of aspects of this document that not only assist us in understanding what constitutes a quality early childhood environment, but also allow us to connect to principles that support children's learning and development in a responsive and inclusive way.

"*Early Learning for Every Child Today* complements, rather than replaces, specific curricular and pedagogical approaches, early identification protocols and regulated requirements now in place in Ontario early childhood settings. It also provides direction for programs that do not have an explicit curriculum or consistent pedagogical approach. It features a continuum of developmental skills and a shared language that will support early childhood practitioners and caregivers as they work together across early childhood settings."

Source: Ontario Ministry of Children and Youth Services, Best Start Expert Panel on Early Learning. (2007, January). *Early learning for every child today: A framework for Ontario early childhood settings.* Retrieved from http://www .cfcollaborative.ca/wp-content/uploads/2010/10/ELECT.pdf

British Columbia's Early Learning Framework is another example of a framework that assists and guides educators, children, families, and the community in designing quality early childhood environments.

"The British Columbia Early Learning Framework strives to guide early childhood educators and adults who work with children and families—and families themselves—to reflect on children's enormous capacity for learning in the early years. The Framework is designed to support the development of tools needed to stimulate learning and create learning environments that build on each child's unique potential. At the same time, the Framework recognizes the individual, social, cultural, and linguistic identities of B.C.'s children and families. Acknowledging the richness of these identities and providing the tools to support diversity is an essential element of the Framework."

Source: From *Understanding the British Columbia Early Learning Framework: From Theory to Practice*, British Columbia Ministry of Education. Copyright © Province of British Columbia. All rights reserved.

Each of these frameworks prompts educators to begin with an appreciative questioning process. Applying these to your professional practice, which framework guides you? What questions might you pose based on these guidelines?

Questions can also be derived from the use of environmental assessment tools and measures. Let's take a look.

ENVIRONMENTAL ASSESSMENT TOOLS AND MEASURES

There is no one universal tool that is available to professionals to observe and assess all the environmental components that contribute to a meaningful "learning community" for children. Instead, a number of informal and formal tools are available to practitioners to aid their analysis of their learning community's strengths and needs. As you continue your research exploring these and other environmental assessment tools, be sure to consider pedagogical principles and inclusive values so that your measure meets the needs of your learners.

A number of formal assessment tools have been developed by **stakeholders** and agencies in different cities, provinces, and states which reflect the geographical and cultural aspects of their community. Assessment measures like the ones below may be necessary to pattern and gain insights into the context of an environment, so as to assess its strengths and areas for improvement. Some of these environmental assessments include:

- the SpeciaLink Child Care Inclusion Practices Profile and Principles Scale (Lero, 2004)
- the SpeciaLink Early Childhood Inclusion Quality Scale (Hope Irwin, 2009)
- the Infant Toddler Early Childhood Environment Rating Scale (Harms, Clifford, & Cryer, 2006), the Early Childhood Environment Rating Scale (Harms, Cryer, & Clifford, 2004), and the School Age Early Childhood Rating Scale (Harms, Vineberg Jacobs, & Romano White, 1995)
- the Family Child Care Environment Rating Scale (Harms, Cryer, & Clifford, 2007)
- the Early Learning and Care Assessment for Quality Improvement, available for infant, toddler, preschool, playground, nutrition, and school age (Toronto Children's Services, 2014)
- NAEYC Accreditation Criteria for Physical Environments: Standard 9 (NAEYC, 2005)
- the Classroom Assessment Scoring System for Infants (Hamre, Laporo, Pianta, & Locasale-Crouch, 2014), the Classroom Assessment Scoring System for Toddlers (Hamre, Laporo, Pianta, & Locasale-Crouch, 2012), the Classroom Assessment Scoring System for Pre-K (Hamre, Laporo, Pianta, & Locasale-Crouch, 2008b), the Classroom Assessment Scoring System for K-3 (Hamre, Laporo, Pianta, & Locasale-Crouch, 2008a). Each of these assessments measures the quality of interactions between the educator and the child, and is not philosophy specific.
- the Rating Observation Scale for Inspiring Environments (ROSIE) measuring the aesthetics of an early childhood environment (Deviney, Duncan, Harris, Rody, & Rosenberry, 2010)
- the Arnett Caregiver Interaction Scale (Arnett, 1989). This scale measures the quality of interactions between the educator and the child.

- Australia's Draft National Quality Standard Assessment and Rating Instrument (Australian Government, Department of Education, Employment and Workplace Relations, 2010)

This list is not exhaustive; it is only a short list of the many comprehensive tools out there. Note that some of the measurements identified are standardized, while others are not. Each environmental assessment will have a different focus; it is the responsibility of the educator to use, create, and/or combine assessment tools with other frameworks to get the information she or he is looking for. Engage in inquiry to research some of the environmental tools listed. What are the similarities and differences? What assessment tool reflects pedagogical principles and approaches? Are there tools that invite reflection from children, families, educators, and the community? What quality assurance or licensing assessment mechanism is used in your community to license or guide the creation of your early childhood setting? What aspects of each tool resonate with your setting's philosophy? What other tools have you come across in your research that also look at the aspect of environmental design? Weblinks and further information on environmental assessments are available online.

ENVIRONMENTAL ASSESSMENT: STAKEHOLDER CONTRIBUTIONS

Throughout our examination of the environment, we discussed repeatedly the importance of including the voices of children, families, and educators in the observation and documentation processes. We now turn our attention to the importance of including the community in our environmental scan or assessment.

We begin this examination on a broader scale with the following questions:

- Who could potentially be a stakeholder and thus have opportunity for observation of, influence on, and input into the creation of these environments? How can they influence what takes place?
- What environmental elements or designs would we request their perspectives on? Where do we start? What aspects of quality and environmental design might we obtain their support with?
- How do we know what is "right" for our own early childhood settings?

These questions are important to many people; their relevance moves beyond the boundaries of an early childhood setting, its staff, children, and families.

In Exhibit 8.4, we can see the various players who may at times influence or provide input into the design or environmental elements that make up a learning community. We see that governmental regulations and policymakers (province or

EXHIBIT 8.4 **STAKEHOLDER POSSIBILITIES**

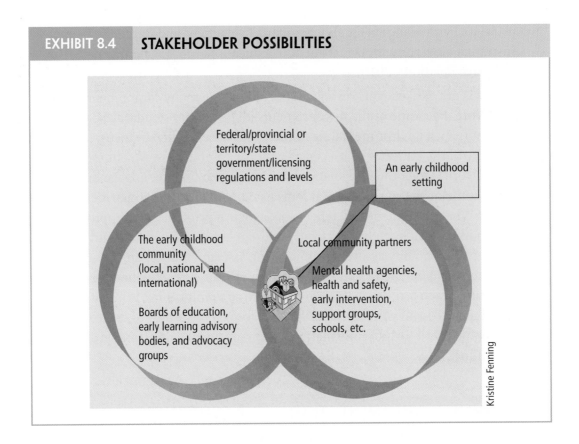

Federal/provincial or territory/state government/licensing regulations and levels

An early childhood setting

The early childhood community (local, national, and international)

Boards of education, early learning advisory bodies, and advocacy groups

Local community partners

Mental health agencies, health and safety, early intervention, support groups, schools, etc.

Kristine Fenning

territory wide) as well as local or municipal licensing bodies require us to develop, implement, and/or evaluate specific environmental elements or standards mandatory for settings within their jurisdiction. For example, "in the 2004 Speech from the Throne the Government of Canada, the Liberals announced that it would work with the provinces and territories to put in place a national system of early learning and child care based on four key principles" known as QUAD: quality, universality, accessibility, and developmental programming (Cool, 2007, "Bilateral Agreements," para. 1). These principles still hold value today.

If you were to ask families in your community if they look for quality in learning environments and surroundings for their children, 100 percent of families would say yes. Created using research and input from stakeholders and policymakers, these QUAD principles relate to the Ontario Early Learning Framework, to the *How Does Learning Happen? Ontario's Pedagogy for the Early Years*, and to elements of responsive and inclusive philosophies. Keep in mind that quality is determined by a number of factors and may vary from province to province and region to region.

The QUAD principles are defined as follows:

- *"Quality*—evidence-based, high quality practices relating to programs for children, training and supports for early childhood educators and child care providers, and provincial/territorial regulation and monitoring.
- *Universally inclusive*—open to all children, without discrimination.
- *Accessible*—available and affordable for those who choose to use it.
- *Developmental*—focused on enhancing early childhood learning opportunities and the developmental component of ELCC [early learning and child care] programs and services."

Source: Adapted from http://www2.parl.gc.ca/content/LOP/ResearchPublications/prb0420-e.htm PRB 04-20E *Child Care in Canada: The Federal Role.* Prepared by Julie Cool, Political and Social Affairs Division, Parliamentary Information and Research Service, Library of Parliament. Revised 16 April 2007.

Despite frequent leadership and political changes in government infrastructure and funding, these principles are just one example of how external policies or forces might cause early childhood professionals and programs to reframe how they define quality and environmental design.

One example illustrating the design and creation of a quality assessment measure that reflects collaboration with external stakeholders is the Early Learning and Care Assessment for Quality Improvement measure prepared by Toronto Children's Services. Developed as separate measures for infant, toddler, preschool, and school-age programs, these measures aim to identify the following:

"[S]ix key elements [...] are essential for a high-quality child care program, including:

1. Sound management practices
2. Training, experience and stability of caregivers
3. Group size: ratio of children to caregivers
4. Family involvement in the program
5. Health and safety standards of the physical facility
6. Program content and development." (p. 2)

Source: Toronto Children's Services. (2014). *Early Learning and Care Assessment for Quality Improvement,* Infant Measure. Used with permission.

Exhibit 8.5 highlights from the *Early Learning and Care Assessment for Quality Improvement* an excerpt of environmental components being evaluated for an infant program. Measures and environmental assessment tools like this have been developed for good reason, and it is the responsibility of educators to know about, understand, and access a variety of these tools, perspectives, materials and research to inform the best approach for their setting and the children and families within it. What licensing measures for the environment are used in your geographical area?

The College of Early Childhood Educators in Ontario is another regulatory body that requires educators to prepare learning environments for children that are responsive and inclusive to all learners. For example, in Standard III of the Code of Ethics and Standards of Practice document, the college expects licensed educators to provide safe, healthy, and supportive learning environments. Educators are held accountable to the profession and broader public to "support children in culturally, linguistically and developmentally sensitive ways and provide caring, stimulating and respectful opportunities for learning and care that are welcoming to children and their families, within an inclusive, well planned and structured environment" (College of Early Childhood Educators, 2011, p. 17).

It is easy to detect the "value-added" benefits when other stakeholder groups and community partners collaborate with our early childhood professionals, families, and children in creating learning communities and assessment measurements that "fit" and reflect community participants. According to Martha Friendly and Jane Beach (2005), the benefit of collaboration is that "it makes it possible to involve community members, parents and children in the issues of program delivery that are most important for them—staffing, facility design

Toronto Children's Services, Early Learning and Caro Assessment for Quality Improvement 2014

Assessment|Infant

	Does Not Meet Expectations ① or ②	Meets Expectations ③	Exceeds Expectations ④ or ⑤	Score
3. Learning Experiences	☐ Learning experiences offered are not developmentally appropriate ☐ Learning experiences do not promote choice for children ☐ There is no current documentation which demonstrates that observations of children are used in the development of learning experiences	☐ Evidence of opportunities to discuss developmental progress with families ☐ Standardized Developmental Screening tool is completed for all children	☐ Photo documentation of learning experiences available ☐ Enrichment program, in addition to regular program, is included monthly ☐ Activity resources accessible for families ☐ Portfolios regarding each child's development are accessible to families	1 2 3 4 5

Source: Toronto Children's Services, (2014) *Early Learning and Care Assessment for Quality Improvement*, p. 4. Used with permission.

and programming—to ensure responsive programming. Above the level of the individual program, community members and parents can be involved with setting priorities, planning and quality assurance for a locally managed system" (p. 2). It is safe to say that any community member or stakeholder wants children to be as successful as possible in life, and as indicated in the Early Development Index (EDI), there are meaningful decisions to be made by increasing community members' and stakeholders' knowledge and participation in understanding how to support children's readiness to learn and grow to their utmost potential. The Bernard Van Leer Foundation is one organization that has provoked its readership to think larger scale regarding the access to physical spaces in cities for children. In the November 2014 article entitled "Small Children, Big Cities," Lisa Karsten was interviewed saying she has observed that "children used to be seen as resilient, whereas today they are primarily seen as vulnerable" (Cary, 2014, p. 5). This speaks volumes about the need for stakeholders to think about the physical design of community natural outdoor space in order to challenge children to take risks and explore their environments independently without constraints, allowing them to build resiliency. Lisa Karsten also states that it is important to observe and document the changing landscape of childhood within the context of family life and lifestyles so that cities can improve physical environments to prompt more children to connect to the outdoors. The cycle of observation supports this level of examination by educators, families, children, and stakeholders to create the best possible experiences for children within their natural environments.

ENVIRONMENTAL ASSESSMENT, PEDAGOGY, AND CONTEXT: VOICES OF CHILDREN AND ADULTS

We know the importance of beginning an inquiry with a question, for it leads us to many new discoveries about our practice. We also understand that use of any of the assessment tools mentioned earlier yields valuable information about environmental design, use, materials, interactions, and other areas. We finish this environmental component by bringing you back to the voices of children and adults. No matter what approach is taken to collect information about an early childhood environment, nothing is more important than ensuring that all voices, observations, and pedagogical documentation collected and shared by all members within an early childhood environment are heard and respected. In doing this, quality is enhanced in our curriculum, our materials, our interactions, and our environment.

COMMUNITY CAPACITY BUILDING: EDUCATING AND PREPARING FOR FUTURE EARLY CHILDHOOD OBSERVERS

Quality in our environments is also enhanced through community **capacity building**. In previous chapters we have alluded to the community and the importance of building capacity within our classrooms, agencies, and schools, and within this chapter, we build on that from an appreciative inquiry lens of educator as leader, mentor, researcher, and team member. If the capacity of an early childhood community is to build upon its strengths, resources, and possibilities, it needs to rely on innovative, constructive, and inclusive partnerships. Building partnerships facilitates the development of social connections between people and invests in the social capital of its people. **Social capital** is the result of ongoing community building and interacting with others within a social network of teams and professionals, which can support the sustainability of learning, the increase in resources, and overall positive functioning of a community. It requires interactions premised on learning and reflection so as "to develop an intellectual community to share expertise and conversations that go beyond discussing the typical daily routines, scheduling, staffing, and regulations" (Johanson & Kuh, 2013, p. 1).

> Community building focuses on developing and strengthening social networks in a community to support families' emotional, social, and economic needs. One of its objectives is to create an environment that fosters members' participation in issues of community concerns. Equally important is the creation of local leaders who can partner with external institutions to enhance the well-being of the community (Hirota, Brown, & Martin, 1996). (Austin, 2005, p. 106)

Given the numerous examples of capacity building in a variety of different organizations, agencies, and businesses, further questions remain:

- What can community capacity building offer early childhood education?
- How is this concept relevant to communities across Canada: rural and urban?

Community capacity building is similar to the intended vision and goals of interprofessional education and interdisciplinary collaboration within the early childhood profession and numerous other professions.

With issues such as childhood obesity as a concern regarding the health of our children and families, it becomes more and more a pressing challenge to collaborate with all health, education, sports and recreation, and government and corporate sectors seeking ways in which to mobilize strategies for resolution. These stakeholders are getting the message out with major conferences, webinars, multimedia advertising, and a high-profile focus within schools. On the Pan-Canadian Public Health Network website, they discuss a variety of community-based programming and community capacity-building initiatives (see Exhibit 8.6).

INTERPROFESSIONAL COLLABORATION

Many early childhood communities, such as those in Toronto, have enlisted the participation of community partners to develop community capacity. This has been achieved through professional networking and new approaches to skill development and through interprofessional collaboration between ministries, systems, professions, teams, and families, essentially creating a whole professional development system to support knowledge building in the community.

Reaching and supporting healthy weight in children requires collaboration from a number of community stakeholders, including participation from the federal, provincial, and territorial governments. In the *Towards a Healthier Canada—2013 Progress Report*, some of the initiatives discussed to promote healthy weight were the following:

Join the Wellness Movement

"Join the Wellness Movement is an ongoing social marketing initiative of the New Brunswick Wellness Strategy. It encourages community groups, schools and workplaces to make a commitment to a healthier lifestyle and register it at wellnessnb.ca."

The Northwest Territories Active After-School Program

"The Northwest Territories Active After-School Program provides funding to schools and community-based organizations to engage inactive or underactive school-aged children and youth during the after-school time period. The program builds on existing activities or supports creating new ones. It encourages children and youth who are already highly active to participate in after school activities as youth leaders and peer-to-peer role models."

Why is interprofessional collaboration important to early childhood? It is important for a number of reasons. "Interprofessional collaboration gives professionals the opportunity to learn with, from, and about each other, building mutual respect as well as shared knowledge and decision making in the best interests of parents. This collaboration has been linked to greater provider satisfaction, leading us to enhanced recruitment and retention and improved patient safety and outcomes (Health Canada, 2013)" (Pimento & Kernested, 2014, p. 19). Families and children bring with them a multitude of strengths and offerings to our learning environment, and we

IS_ImageSource/iStockphoto.com

know that every family will also face challenges and happy events in their life that will change dynamics in their family—whether it be divorce, same-sex marriage, the death of a loved one, the birth of a sibling, trauma of some kind, diagnosis of a special need … the list goes on. Educators are not expected to know how to work with families in all these situations, nor are they expected to know how to handle these situations. When we observe these types of situations taking place, and we collaborate with families and other professionals, everyone benefits.

THE OBSERVER AS PEDAGOGICAL LEADER

Appreciative inquiry is a concept and practice that is a part of all topics in this text. Pedagogical leadership has its own unique set of questions beginning with the most fundamental inquiry: what does it mean? In the online article "Pedagogical Leadership," authors Coughlin and Baird (2013) define pedagogical leadership by simply stating,

> Pedagogy can be defined as the understanding of how learning takes place and the philosophy and practice that supports that understanding of learning. Essentially it is the study of the teaching and learning process. Leadership is often defined as the act of leading or guiding individuals or groups. If we are to combine these two we are offered the notion of pedagogical leadership as leading or guiding the study of the teaching and learning process. (p. 1)

As shown in Exhibit 8.7, central to leadership is developing relationships and trust with people involved while learning everything possible about a project, situation,

EXHIBIT 8.7	LEADERSHIP IN TEACHING AND LEARNING: SHARING PORTFOLIO STRATEGIES

Reggio Summer Intensive, Acorn School/Kristine Fenning

Evidenced by this photo, central to leadership is the development of relationships and trust with others while learning everything possible about a project, situation, or endeavour.

or endeavour. In this photo, led by Dr. Diane Kashin and Louise Jupp, educators and teachers are engaged in dialogue about their teaching and learning experiences in regards to developing learning stories and portfolios for children within their classrooms. In this dialogue educators question, problem-solve, and share the way in which these pieces are created, how they involve the families, and how they fit pedagogical documentation into everyday practice considering the multifaceted roles they must fulfill during the course of the day.

What are some other ideas about what leadership does? Sciarra and Dorsey (2002), in their text *Leaders and Supervisors in Child Care Programs*, state that "the principles that the leader of any group must follow are pretty basic:

- Gather information
- Assess the situation
- Figure out what has to be done
- Decide what role you can play to add the most value
- Lay out a sequence of steps to get started" (p. 109)

Leadership can arise from administrative positions such as managers of agencies, supervisors of centres, or directors of large organizations or companies, as they have the authority and community profile and connections. Managers can lead within their organizations, schools, and colleges and universities in ways that help their collective profession maintain and raise standards of practice.

Leadership evolves and influences over time. Every province in Canada had those early pioneers who developed standards of practice and worked with great perseverance to establish early childhood as a profession. Their work continues through this generation of educators and will continue to influence future early childhood professionals. As those early leaders clearly showed us, we cannot assume leadership; it must be demonstrated. So where do we see evidence of leadership today?

Partly as a result of the immediacy of electronic communication and social networks, we do have leaders, but present-day leadership may not be as obvious as the more traditional model of one person standing in front leading others. The notion of leadership is changing to reflect a more interconnective leadership and reality. A less egocentric and more collaborative style of leadership fits well into the changing paradigm of community building, interprofessional relationships and services, and responsive, inclusive practices in early childhood. With discussion of change, leadership can facilitate finding new spaces and constructing new paradigms with community partnerships. Leaders who understand that reality are those who have the capacity to self-regulate in the face of change and challenge and the ability to negotiate diversity and differences, adopt new forms of social capital and organization, and find new ways to enact leadership (Dempster & Lizzio, 2007).

Can leadership be demonstrated without the benefit of institutions, agencies, or schools? Educators, parents, resource professionals, and many other members of an early learning community hold the potential to lead and guide others. Leadership does not have to stem from the "top"; leadership can come from within oneself because it is not restricted by gender, culture, language, ability, or any other aspect of a person. Many of us likely know several educators and parents who started out simply with a "passion" for advocating for a child with special needs and, through their experiences and struggles, took a leadership role in advocating for all children and their families, not just their own child. Such is the example of Georgina Rayner, who is a parent advocate. She is on several boards of directors of agencies such as Aspergers Ontario and the Centre for ADHD Awareness, Canada (CADDAC). Another example is provided in Exhibit 8.8. In this exhibit, students within the Advanced Studies in Special Needs Post Graduate Certificate at Humber College are conversing about leadership and community advocacy projects that support children with special needs and their families. Evidenced by the photo, beginning with one voice, merged with another voice, and again with more voices, increased collaboration can create positive change; anyone can be a leader!

| EXHIBIT 8.8 | PRESERVICE RESOURCE PROFESSIONALS AND LEADERSHIP |

Reggio Summer Intensive, Acorn School/Kristine Fenning

Students here are dialoguing, reflecting, and giving a voice to issues they have faced in the early intervention system that affect children with diverse needs and their families.

What are some other questions leadership asks?

- If the population is increasingly diverse ethnically, socially, and culturally, is there such a thing as culturally relevant leadership?
- Has gender identity predetermined that women in early childhood education will occupy many positions of management but few positions of leadership?

Pedagogical leadership within the early childhood profession can also be demonstrated in a number of ways and mediums. Pedagogical leadership as it relates to observation has prompted trends in pedagogical documentation resulting in a number of new trends in observation, as discussed in earlier chapters. Diane Kashin and Louise Jupp (2013) capture some of these trends as they describe the changing definition of a pedagogical leader:

> Now a pedagogical leader can disseminate information through social media platforms like Facebook, Twitter, and Pinterest. Kagan and Bowman (1997) also suggest that pedagogical leadership is linked to:
>
> - How you believe children learn best
> - Your program philosophy, goals and everyday practices
>
> Being a pedagogical leader is value laden. How you lead reflects your underlying philosophy. If you believe as we do that children learn best in a social construct that is collaborative, reciprocal and respectful then you too will recognize teachers learn best that way as well! ("What Is a Pedagogical Leader?" para. 2)

OBSERVER AS MENTOR: THE IMPORTANT ROLE OF MENTORSHIP

Mentoring is one of many leadership approaches in early childhood aimed at building capacity and quality in early childhood settings, overall professional practice, and, in this text, capacity and sustainability for observation and pedagogical documentation. According to Wong and Waniganayake (2013), "mentoring is a facilitated process involving two or more individuals that have a shared interest in professional learning and development.... It has been shown to boost teachers' professional confidence, identity and their willingness to participate in professional learning" (p. 163).

Traditional and historical approaches to mentoring typically involved persons in higher authority such as supervisors or directors mentoring and guiding their staff. While it is still important for supervisors and directors to provide this leadership role, mentoring can occur between any two people for any particular purpose. Viewing mentoring from an appreciative lens, its intention is to lend a voice and feedback mechanism to two or more people desiring to build knowledge and skill, share in teaching and learning with and from one another, and co-construct new knowledge together. Each participant in the mentoring relationship may hold knowledge and expertise they wish to share with the other. Long term or short term in nature, this proactive, educational, and reflective approach assists those who participate to build capacity for positive change in professional practice. It requires a number of skills to be present in the person who desires to mentor someone else, including having the ability to self-reflect, collaborate with others as a team member, take risks, appreciate and respect the perspectives of others, and be open to change.

Reggio Summer Intensive, Acorn School/Kristine Fenning

"Often success is forged in the workplace by the existence of a local mentor or pedagogical leader who has a vision for the capacity building of staff, and willingness to support the growth and the implementation of ideas (Carter & Curtis, 2010). The mentor acts as someone to encourage, to exchange ideas with, to assist in deciphering and contextualizing information and to 'risk take' alongside (Peterson, 2000)." (p. 13)

Source: Brown, A., & Inglis, S. (March, 2013). So what happens after the event? Exploring the realisation of professional development with early childhood educators. *Australasian Journal of Early Childhood*, 38(1), 11–15.

Whether you are a preservice educator about to embark upon your first position or a seasoned educator in the profession for quite some time, it is important to engage in mentoring practices that support observation, reflection, and pedagogical documentation. It is through this supportive team approach that innovative ideas and approaches are generated, the voices of everyone are reflected, and quality environments are created.

OBSERVER AS LIFELONG LEARNER: THE IMPORTANCE OF PROFESSIONAL DEVELOPMENT

Over the last five to ten years, significant changes have occurred in the early childhood profession, one of which has been increased emphasis on having well-trained, knowledgeable, responsive, and inclusive educators working in early childhood settings. The College of Early Childhood Educators (CECE), advocacy groups, the **Association of Early Childhood Educators of Ontario (AECEO)**, and changes to the *Early Childhood Educators Act* all place value and emphasis on continuous professional learning for educators. With the royal assent of the *Child Care Modernization Act* recently renamed as the **Child Care and Early Years Act,** 2014, registered educators in Ontario are now expected to engage in a continuous professional learning program in order to maintain their registration with the College of Early Childhood Educators (CECE, 2014b). "Continuous professional learning refers to the systematic and intentional maintenance and expansion of the knowledge, skills, and ethical values and behaviours necessary to ensure ongoing quality professional practice throughout an early childhood educator's career" (CECE, 2014a, p. 1).

It is a professional and ethical responsibility of registered early childhood educators to engage in professional development and lifelong learning. Children and families deserve to have educators who are competent, qualified, reflective, and creative leaders committed to providing the best possible learning environments for children. Learning does not stop at the point in which we obtain our diploma or degree in early childhood education or teaching. In fact, a new learning journey begins when we start our professional practice.

"Reflective practitioners integrate theoretical frameworks, research findings and their own daily experiences to guide their interactions with young children and their families. Reflective practitioners figure out how the children in their program think, learn, and make sense of the world. They know what the children are currently capable of doing and what next steps are possible. Responsive adults help to focus children's observations, use language that describes events and ask questions that provoke children's thinking. Thus, curriculum is meaningful when there are clear matches between a child's current knowledge and interests and the opportunities provided." (p. 19)

Source: Ontario Ministry of Children and Youth Services, Best Start Expert Panel on Early Learning. (2007, January). *Early learning for every child today: A framework for Ontario early childhood settings.* Retrieved from http://www .cfcollaborative.ca/wp-content/uploads/2010/10/ELECT.pdf

---

Reflecting back on previous chapters, we are reminded of the importance of questioning, inquiry, and evaluation of our own professional practice, including reflection upon ourselves as professional educators so that we might meet the needs of our children, families, and communities. In addition to engaging in professional development or formal learning opportunities, building capacity for learning can also be achieved by providing training to others, sharing your knowledge, and co-constructing new knowledge together. The following photo illustrates educators coming together for professional development purposes, engaging in conversation to examine how they might document children's learning. It is through this process that they begin to inquire and question the environment, materials, and space through a child's perspective. In the photo, Helen, a kindergarten teacher and lifelong learner, documents her exploration of light through photo narratives on her cellphone while tweeting her learning through vines and text to colleagues who are part of an online community of educators interested in pedagogical documentation with young children through the use of social media. This social media connection allows her to engage her families and children in co-creating, co-documenting, co-leading, and co-learning together in real time. Be sure to visit some of the suggested blogs and Twitter feeds provided online demonstrating the leadership of teachers and educators like Helen.

Reggio Summer Intensive, Acorn School/Kristine Fenning

PEDAGOGICAL DOCUMENTATION AND EDUCATOR E-PORTFOLIOS

Chapter 6 introduced us to the use of e-portfolios in early childhood education as a way in which to document children's learning in a digital way. We can apply that discussion directly to our new discussion here on educator e-portfolios. The use of e-portfolios for educator development provides an excellent forum for teacher reflection and self-evaluation of one's growth and development, goal setting, and demonstration of learning. Tying e-portfolios to our previous discussion on educator professional development, they are a way in which educators can store, discuss, and share their teaching and learning journey with their superiors, families, or other educators.

> Early childhood teachers believe in constructing knowledge and experiential learning. One major advantage of creating an e-portfolio is that … you are learning to construct your portfolio by putting into practice skills and abilities using technology and the Internet. You are also learning the technological skills that the profession now agrees are important to teaching. Many of the skills that you acquire can be passed on to children. You can teach them to gather information, research topics, access data, and create reports using today's tools: the computer and the Internet. (Lowe Friedman, 2012, p. 114)

E-PORTFOLIO DESIGN AND CONSIDERATIONS

If embarking upon e-portfolio creation for the first time, be assured that any one of the e-portfolio websites mentioned in Chapter 6 possesses tutorials that will walk you through the set-up of a site. Many will say to consult with children when embarking on this process, as they often possess the computer literacy skills required to navigate different tool-bars and computer language. They have much to teach us!

Most postsecondary institutions that have an early childhood program prepare preservice educators with e-portfolios

that outline their acquired knowledge, skills, and attitudes relating to the profession for future use in interviews with employers. If you are a seasoned educator about to embark on this journey, we recommend that you consult with various preservice educator portfolio websites to assist you in determining your presentation design, how to organize your artifacts, and how best to feature key knowledge you wish to profile. An advantage of the electronic nature of this portfolio is that educators can populate their site with videos of their professional practice, including their work with children, interactions and classroom design, curriculum examples aligned with the Ontario Early Learning Framework, and much more! Once begun, educators will be amazed by what they have accomplished over time to evolve their skills. Like children's e-portfolios, consideration of confidentiality and ethics is a necessary step in e-portfolio creation. Examples of sites that feature educator e-portfolios are provided online.

OBSERVER AS RESEARCHER

The early childhood profession is changing at a rapid pace; this means a core responsibility of current and future educators is to stay abreast of requirements and changing expectations in the profession, as well as to look at ways to lead the profession. To do this well, it is important for educators not only to participate in professional development and maintain professional e-portfolios, but also to think about engaging in research opportunities to further inform their practice, as well as to contribute their own publications back to the profession. A primary example of this is the emerging trend of social media use as a pedagogical documentation approach, a topic we will explore a little later. Without professionals in the field exploring and developing innovative ways to approach their practice as well as to meet the changing needs of children and families, we may not be as equipped as we think to provide quality early childhood environments. Let's take a look at the role of educator-observer with **longitudinal studies** and ethnographic research.

THE EDUCATOR-OBSERVER: LONGITUDINAL STUDIES AND ETHNOGRAPHIC RESEARCH

In Chapter 1 we introduced you to the role of the educator with ethnographic research and its relevance to longitudinal studies. There may be opportunities in your career path to work interprofessionally or within the profession on research relating to early childhood education. Longitudinal studies, research conducted over an extended period of time, are used to confirm the relevance of a particular practice, explore the merits of government policy, or examine issues such as childhood obesity, low infant birth rates, or the impact of funding on certain early childhood programs.

Gathering longitudinal data is one of the various ways economic rationale for public spending on child-care programming is determined. For example, "validation of the human capital approach is heavily influenced by U.S. longitudinal studies showing sustained benefits from early interventions for children from disadvantaged homes. Based on these findings, respected economists, such as Nobel Prize winner James Heckman, concluded that scarce public resources would best be used for at-risk communities" (Mustard & McCuaig, 2011, para. 2).

Decades of research go into the investigation of theories and policies before human resources capital is dedicated. Policymakers, economists, government officials, and early childhood professionals must take into account multiple variables and factors during a specific time frame to put forward their case.

To illustrate the complexity of this kind of research, check out the three most referenced longitudinal studies on the impact of preschool education on children from disadvantaged backgrounds. "Ypsilanti's Perry Preschool [initiated in 1962], the Abecedarian study in North Carolina [1972] and the Chicago Child-Parent Centers [1967] have tracked their original cohorts for up to four decades. Each study was unique, but all provided a group program emphasizing parent involvement and the development of children's literacy skills." (McCuaig, 2013, p. 1). See McCuaig (2013) for a thorough discussion of these longitudinal studies.

It is difficult to replicate these types of studies in Canada as Canadian populations are diverse. Yet, Salazar and Palkhivala (2009), in their discussion of the Nurse-Family Partnership (NFP) Pilot Study in Canada, looked to other countries to see if similar programs helped families to become more economically independent and fostered safer communities. Before the NFP program was introduced at McMaster University in Hamilton, Ontario, they looked at how the program had an impact on families and children in England, Holland, Germany, and the United States.

OBSERVATION AND PEDAGOGICAL DOCUMENTATION TRENDS

Pedagogical documentation methodologies combined with emerging technologies will continue to expand and transform the way we observe and learn about and with children, families, and early childhood environments. Many educators around the world are now experimenting with blogs, Twitter, Instagram, and Pinterest as a way to connect with others. These are just four examples of social media applications amid many that are enabling children, families, and educators to document and share their learning, thus making their learning visible, communicating about resources and research they have prepared or discovered, and co-constructing new knowledge with others by inviting new perspectives. Rapid changes in technology continue to spur development of new apps and ways in which to document, and when we reflect upon their relevance to pedagogical principles, their value becomes increasingly evident. As we discuss each application below, we remind you to think about ethics and technology once again, revisiting the content in Chapters 4 and 6, as it is important to think about ensuring confidentiality, respecting children and families, and being aware of how information is accessed and used. Marlina Oliveira from Richland Academy in Richmond Hill, Ontario, describes the role of social media in leadership:

> Social media is the new medium for sharing information. Articles, research, images, notifications of events, and much more can be distributed and reviewed instantly with your team. Material can be collected and shared daily; by the hour, the minute, the second. In a Reggio inspired learning environment, the teacher is seen as a co-learner and researcher. Having current, relevant, authentic and useable information available and accessible for teaching and learning is a huge benefit to their work, to their classroom, to the children and the learning community. As a pedagogical leader, I see my role as supporting and encouraging on-going learning and professional development of my team to keep them current, engaged and inspired.

While personally engaging with social media, I ultimately have the opportunity to connect to others and to extend those relationships to form a professional learning network. (qtd. in Kashin, 2013, "On the Relationship between Social Media and Leadership")*

Pedagogical documentation and professional learning networks enabled by technology are not solely for Reggio-inspired environments, for they apply to any philosophy and all settings that are interested in transforming their observational practices. Examples of these forums and networks are available online. This is not to say that hard-copy pedagogical documentation methods have gone by the wayside, but rather that children, families, educators, and the community can transform these hard-copy artifacts into digital form for future and ongoing review.

BLOGS

Blogs are online forums on websites that house ongoing commentaries and information on topics of interest to registered members or anonymous visitors. There can be one or more blogs on these sites depending on the purpose and intention of the site. Blogs are a viable option for keeping historical entries of classroom projects, individual accomplishments, videos and vines of excerpts recorded by children and adults reflecting learning taking place, special memories, and much more. The Diigo Group blog is one example of a blog where various teaching practices are shared. This particular site is not password protected; however, there are a number of blogging sites, such as the Leading with Technology blog in Exhibit 8.9, in which educators and families could use this additional protective feature when sharing information.

| EXHIBIT 8.9 | LEADING WITH TECHNOLOGY |

In the May 2014 Diigo Group blog Leading with Technology, Mauri Dufour shared the following example with colleagues:

> Here are some examples of ways my students have enhanced their learning experience with an iPad this year. We have been able to go paperless using the app Showbie. With Showbie, I the teacher was able to send out customized lessons to students to work on and they could send me back the work in progress or finished product. The students would use the iPad to make short videos to document learning and they would

(continued)

*Courtesy of author, Dr. Diane Kashin

use other apps like Pic Collage and Educareations to produce work documentation and upload to their Showbie digital portfolio. The best part of Showbie as a teacher is that I could leave voice notes, send the individual students a text and even upload supplemental materials for students. I could do all of this from my own iPad. For the students having one place to store their work was powerful for them to see their learning progression and depth of knowledge they have gained this year. The simple answer to what can my iPad do is: the iPad can only do what you want it to. If you limit the way you implement it, then you will limit the things it can do. If you go beyond just using apps, then you open a whole new door to what the iPad will provide as a learning tool. (para. 2)

Source: Dufour, Mauri. "Leading with Technology." Forum. Diigo Group. May 2014. Retrieved from https://www.diigo.com/bookmark/https%3A%2F%2Fleadingwithtechnology.wordpress.com?gname=ecetech. Used with permission of author, Mauri Dufour.

In this same forum, other educators discuss how they share and text group developments and learning via other apps such as Remind. A wealth of resources are available on this site. Classroom blogs with password protection could be developed as a forum in which families, children, and educators could contribute and document their learning.

WIKIS

Educause Learning Initiative (2005) describes a wiki as follows:

> A wiki is a web page that can be viewed and modified by anybody with a web browser and access to the Internet. This means that any visitor to the wiki can change its content if they desire.… Wikis permit asynchronous communication and group collaboration across the Internet. Variously described as a composition system, a discussion medium, a repository, a mail system, and a tool for collaboration, wikis provide users with both author and editor privileges; the overall organization of contributions can be edited as well as the content itself. (p. 1)

This editing attribute is what makes wikis different from blogs, which do not allow users to edit the content produced by other users. What might be some of the pros and cons of editing content prepared by others? How might wikis be used to support observational practices?

TWITTER

Twitter is another way in which educators, children, and their families are sharing the learning of children through the use of a tablet, iPad, iPhone, or other communication device. Twitter allows for the sharing of learning in real time, subsequently allowing the recipient to share in the inquiry and perhaps reciprocate a question or query immediately. Tweeting is not limited to educators, for children and families can also tweet out new inquiries, experiences, learning, and threads of information of interest to their preferred contacts. To find threads of interest, users can simply communicate via specific hashtags or do a search with key terms they feel describe their pedagogical beliefs about documentation and how children learn. Educators are able to add a short text in a timely fashion for parents about their child's learning, and can support their thread of conversation with video vines, where children provide the video vine capturing their learning taking place for the benefit of their parent(s). Essentially, a trail or history can be created, scaffolding topics of interest or points of learning for children, and allowing for ongoing review of past learning. There are many examples in Canada and around the world whereby Twitter has been interconnected with a password-protected blog or website for the purposes of sharing and co-creating pedagogical documentation. Please go online to see some of the many examples available.

These social media tools are transforming the way many educators can document, considering the complexities and business of the educator role. These tools allow educators to search the history of their pins, tweets, blogs, and so forth, for evidence of children's learning to support portfolio development, report cards, or term evaluations.

Users of social media must make important ethical decisions and considerations when choosing to document in this way. In addition to the ethical and confidentiality considerations outlined in earlier chapters, it is also important to think about and be reminded of

- ensuring that policies and guidelines are in place for appropriate use of these technologically enabled methodologies. This includes verifying with your quality assurance or licensing services and agencies to ensure that the appropriate steps have been taken
- excluding identifiers such as names of children or centres/schools in mass communications sent out to families. Typically, group communications would involve discussion of group projects.
- giving credit to the author of information being shared, pinned, or tweeted
- knowing how to link your content with online communities of practice
- using passwords for blogs and wikis

- obtaining parental written consent to use photos and information about their children in social media, and informing parents about what they are signing
- being aware of the implications of information being available on the Internet even with password protection

Can you think of any other considerations?

INSTAGRAM

Visual documentation methods are synonymous with this particular social media website. Instagram has taken educators and those in the early childhood community to a new level, permitting the sharing and use of visual documentation methods and environmental design amid other topics related to early childhood that have been prepared by children, families, and educators around the world. Not recommended as an individual documentation forum representing confidential portfolio artifacts, Instagram does allow users to post photos and videos (less than 15 seconds) as well as examples and exhibits of documentation to inspire others. This site is helpful in assisting users to build and create environments, explore new curriculum ideas, network with others who have similar philosophies, and follow only the subjects of interest to them. If we reflect back to our section on the role of the educator-observer in building capacity for observation and pedagogical documentation, this particular online forum does just that. Users also have the ability to set parameters allowing only specific users to be able to follow their posts. More information regarding the application of Instagram to pedagogical documentation is available online.

SUMMARY

As expectations change within the profession concerning observation and documentation, so too must educators evolve and transform their practice to be able to adequately prepare quality learning environments. Topics covered in this chapter, such as the psychological and physical environment, leadership, mentorship, professional development, e-portfolios for educators, social media documentation trends, and educator as researcher, all reveal just how important the role of the educator as observer really is.

Each of these topics also leads us to realize the importance of educator as leader and mentor, for it is through collaboration with others (children, families, educators, and community) that we are able to meet the needs of our learners. The time is now to create, co-construct, and build with others the supports and information we need to be able to pave the way for new and innovative pedagogical documentation methods. We hope that with this text, you will be able to seize this opportunity as an educator-observer, and lead the early childhood profession toward many new and wonderful opportunities!

GLOSSARY

ABC analysis (p. 155)
A type of documentation that records a sequence of related events over time.

abscissa (p. 212)
The horizontal axis of a graph.

accommodate (p. 121)
To bring into agreement, for example, adapt new information to previous knowledge.

accommodations (p. 325)
Resources or adaptations that can support a child or individual to fully participate and/or attain the same grade level as his or her peers.

action research (p. 315)
A collaborative and reflective inquiry process assumed by a community or team of individuals who actively research, plan, and implement solutions to solve real problems and/or improve practice.

advocate (pp. 22, 248)
Someone who amplifies a client's voice, gives support, and pursues objectives according to instruction while empowering the client to self-advocacy.

affective (p. 331)
Refers to the expression of feelings or emotions.

analogue (p. 156)
Something similar in function or comparable with another; a model.

anecdotal record (p. 138)
A narrative form of observation, a word picture, a description so clearly written that when read, the image of what is seen and heard immediately comes to mind. Anecdotal records capture spontaneous behaviour as it occurs.

antecedent (p. 155)
Occurring before, prior to, preceding.

appreciative inquiry (p. 6)
The practice of asking questions to enlist members of an organization in a collaborative conversation concerning positive change. In this active dialogue, participants have the opportunity to query the positives of their current organizational climate; envision what they want their organization or environment to be like in the future; share their hopes, values, and desires; design and break down the steps needed to achieve their vision; and then implement their ideas to facilitate growth in that direction. Relating to the cycle of observation, appreciative inquiry prompts observers to query their practice and engage in processes that will assist them in achieving positive change.

artifacts (p. 33)
Objects that are representative of a culture and are made by a human being, typically an item of cultural or historical interest.

assessment portfolio (p. 275)
A collection of documentation in hard-copy or digital form that show a child's growth or change over time; it may help in the process of self-evaluation and goal setting, identify areas of focus, or track development of one domain or more.

Association of Early Childhood Educators of Ontario (AECEO) (p. 362)
A nonprofit professional organization committed to advocating, supporting, and promoting the early childhood profession. This is demonstrated through the provision of professional development, research, and actions that support capacity building in the community.

at-a-glance records (p. 155)
Point-form notes typically recorded by teachers; intended to be read quickly.

audio recording (p. 169)
A way of recording sound waves, such as spoken voice, singing, instrumental music, or sound effects.

aural (p. 169)
Referring to hearing or concerning the ear.

authentic assessment (pp. 267, 315)
An assessment that is connected to practical, pragmatic, real-world skills to demonstrate performance and understanding.

autism (p. 313)
A lifelong neurological and developmental disorder that may affect one's ability to develop relationships, communicate with others, and function intellectually.

behaviour (p. 155)
Anything that can be seen, measured, or counted.

behaviour tallying (p. 209)
Counting a specific behaviour or monitoring the frequency of a behaviour and adding it up.

best practices (p. 38)
Based on or originating from evidence-based research and outcomes, these are ideal practices suggested by the early learning and care profession or other agencies or licensing bodies.

biases (p. 127)
Preconceived ideas or attitudes (personal or philosophical) that affect objectivity; prejudice.

Boardmaker (pp. 228, 341)
Computer software composed of a picture-based electronic library that can be manipulated and printed to create a variety of communication or print visuals to assist any individual with aspects of their learning, communication, and understanding. Examples of print visuals include schedules, transitions, and pictures for a picture exchange system.

capacity building (p. 354)
Refers to all stakeholders within a community network who are working collaboratively to provide support, resources, services, and opportunities

to strengthen all members and promote their success within their community.

caveat (p. 32)
A warning or specification of conditions that must be considered before taking action.

central tendency error (p. 127)
A judgment error that evaluates all children the same way, regardless of their individual characteristics.

checklist (p. 195)
A type of record providing a list of items that, if present, are marked or checked off.

Child Care and Early Years Act **(p. 362)**
Previously known as Bill 10 and newly known as the *Child Care and Early Years Act* (2014), this act replaces the *Day Nurseries Act*, an act that oversees and governs child care in Ontario.

child-centred environment (p. 336)
An environment adapted to meet the interests, strengths, and needs of children.

child-sensitive (p. 16)
Attitudes, awareness, and practices that demonstrate care and sensitivity to the uniqueness of each child and his or her family and culture in a group setting.

closed methods (p. 191)
Records or methods used for targeted behaviours.

Code of Ethics (p. 78)
Guidelines for responsible behaviour; principles and practices that guide the moral and ethical conduct of professionals in a field or discipline.

coding scheme (p. 197)
A design or diagram using a specific symbol to represent an idea, for example, colour coding to chart various activities.

cognition (p. 119)
The process of knowing; thinking; reasoning.

ConnectABILITY (p. 341)
A resource website developed by Community Living Toronto, designed to offer a plethora of research, resources, and strategies appropriate to support individuals with special needs, professionals who support those who have special needs, or parents of children who have special needs.

consequence (p. 155)
Relation of an effect to its cause; a natural or necessary result.

constructivist framework (p. 296)
Based in cognitive and humanistic theory, constructivism is a framework that proposes that the learner, along with the educator or teacher, is an active co-constructor of knowledge, ideas, and information.

contextual information (p. 141)
Relevant information from the environment that directly or indirectly influences the behaviour of a child; information that helps explain or give meaning to a child's behaviour.

continuum (p. 205)
A continuous line of reference.

contrived observation (p. 146)
Observation that is prearranged for a specific purpose in a formal or informal setting.

criterion-referenced assessment tools (p. 319)
Fixed standards used to evaluate an individual's performance; points of reference used when an individual is assessed against himself or herself rather than compared to the performance of others.

cultural bias (p. 129)
The action of interpreting what one sees by the values, beliefs, and principles attributed to one's own culture.

culturally responsive (p. 129)
The act of being respectful toward others and using and incorporating knowledge of another's culture, beliefs, values, and approaches to learning to be both responsive and inclusive.

cycle of observation (p. 49)
An ongoing and interactive reflective cycle of observation, including interpretation and appreciative inquiry, team participation and discussion, planning, and evaluation. This cycle outlines for the observer the many interactive components and steps of the observation process.

descriptor (p. 97)
A word or phrase that characterizes an idea or item; the adjectives used to rate the items of a rating scale continuum.

developmental assessments (p. 300)
Diagnostic or informal assessments meant to ascertain an individual's current level of functioning in all domains of development.

developmental pediatrician (p. 324)
A medically trained physician with the credentials to diagnose special needs or attend to special needs or extra-support concerns for individuals.

dexterity (p. 30)
Skilled physical movement or ease of use, typically relating to the hands.

diagnostic (p. 294)
Concerned with the diagnosis of a special need or illness.

diagnostic assessment (p. 294)
Assesses what the learner already knows and/or the nature of difficulties that the learner might have. It typically focuses on a specific developmental area.

didactic (p. 242)
Meant to intentionally teach, guide, or instruct.

direct quotation (p. 95)
When exact words have been used in another source and are supported with quotation marks to indicate the exact phrasing selected.

disequilibrium (p. 15)
Unstable, unbalanced, or lacking stability.

display or showcase portfolio (p. 272)
A digital or hard-copy portfolio that showcases end-of-year/semester

accomplishments (according to an educator) or children's/students' perspectives of their best or most important work; also a means to communicate with others a child's current interests in a particular topic.

diversity (p. 1)
A reference to a range of categories, such as those of culture, religion, ethnicity, abilities, or beliefs.

documentation panel (p. 166)
A panel that displays the ideas and feelings of a child or group of children through artwork, photographs, and text.

domain (p. 30)
A sphere of activity or function; psychology; area (of development), for example, cognitive, gross motor.

duration (p. 193)
The time frame within which an action occurs; how long something lasts.

early childhood professionals (p. 5)
Dedicated and credentialed early childhood professionals providing care, education, and responsive, inclusive learning experiences in a variety of early learning settings for children from birth to 12 years. These professionals are trained to promote the health and well-being of children; encourage learning; create responsive, inclusive learning environments; and connect and liase with families, professionals, and community stakeholders for the benefit of children.

early intervention/early identification (p. 288)
A system or set of social and educational services and supports aimed to provide referrals, supports, and resources for children with extra-support or special needs and their families.

eclectic approach (p. 38)
A method of selecting what seem to be the best practices from various philosophies or programs.

ecological approach (p. 221)
An approach for understanding a child's development in terms of the environment, which includes family, neighbourhood, or community.

emergent/emergent curriculum (p. 7)
A form of curriculum development where educators follow the children's leads by observing their interests, skills, areas for improvement, and family and community cultures, and then reflect, document, and plan accordingly.

emotional intelligence (p. 39)
Often associated with highly sociable, communicative, and motivated individuals who are able to easily identify with the needs and desires of others. Individuals with this type of intelligence are able to manage the dynamics of relationships effortlessly, are self-reflective individuals and very aware of how their emotions affect others, and are able to maintain composure and self-regulate their emotions easily in changing circumstances.

e-portfolio (p. 275)
An electronic portfolio that contains a purposefully selected collection of documentation over time; similar to a traditional portfolio but presented electronically.

ethnographic research (p. 41)
A type of research that is similar perhaps to *longitudinal studies* in that it falls under the broad umbrella of qualitative research, which means that the research or outcomes from one study are not applied to any other studies.

evaluation (p. 124)
To examine and judge carefully; appraise.

expanded observation (p. 145)
Multiple observations of one child from different settings, during different times, or with other educators and, as a result, will include multiple examples of behaviour.

expectancy or logical error (p. 128)
An assumption made about two seemingly related behaviours, without a base from direct observation.

family support plans (p. 300)
A written plan created in collaboration with a family outlining resources, services, goals and objectives, and roles assumed by family and/or professionals. This plan may vary according to the agency or centre in terms of content and format.

family tree (p. 229)
A diagram (sometimes in the form of a symbolic tree with branches detailing names of relatives) outlining the ancestry, connections, and relationships between people within multiple generations of a family.

fixed standard (p. 319)
A rule, principle, or measure established by an authority that is accepted without deviation.

formal settings (p. 40)
Settings for observation that are structured for a specific purpose, such as testing or research.

formative evaluation (p. 329)
Evaluation that can be done at any point for reasons identified by any members of the team. Through discussion and reflection, the team can make changes as the process evolves.

frequency (p. 193)
The number of times a specific incident occurs.

functional assessment (p. 294)
Assesses a child's competence against specific criteria. In principle, no account is taken of how other children have performed on the assessment.

generic (p. 38)
Relating to or descriptive of an entire group or class; universal.

goals (p. 325)
A generalized statement of intended change in direction, ability, knowledge, or outcomes. They are usually composed of a number of objectives that support movement toward and attainment of the intended goals.

guide (p. 31)
To direct the way with the implication being that those following will benefit.

High/Scope (p. 38)
A curriculum model based on a constructivist approach originating from David Weikart. Through hands-on experiences and exposure to materials in interest centres around the classroom, children have the opportunity to direct and scaffold their own learning. In this model, adults and children are seen as partners in learning. Through a plan-do-review cycle, children have the opportunity to plan their day, implement their plan, and then actively review and discuss their learning and ideas with their trained educators/teachers.

holistic (wholistic) (p. 41)
Information gathered and integrated from as many sources as possible, encompassing every aspect of a belief or approach.

Identification, Placement, and Review Committee (IPRC) (p. 298)
A committee of people from a school or school board created to support children with diagnosed special needs and their families. This committee acts to make decisions regarding the identification (categorization) of special needs, as well as an appropriate placement for a child as per the Ontario Ministry of Education requirements.

incidence (p. 322)
The frequency, rate, or number of times something happens or occurs.

inclusion (p. 14)
An attitude, a process, and a concept that accepts, respects, and embraces the individuality of any person regardless of ability, race, class, gender, language, ethnicity, age, sexual orientation, family, beliefs, or values. It is about "feeling" like a part of a group, being "connected" to others in some way, and having the same opportunities and decisions as everyone else.

inclusive (p. 14)
The belief and practice of according full participation of all children regardless of abilities, gender, ethnicity, or beliefs in all aspects of the children's day.

Individual Education Plan (IEP) (p. 325)
A document outlining a child's strengths, interests, and skills to be developed (needs) in each developmental domain; may include other things such as goals, adaptations and/or accommodations required, an evaluation date, and who is responsible for implementation.

Individual Family Support Plan (IFSP) (p. 326)
Every organization and community will have variations on what is included in this plan, when it is written, who writes it, roles assumed, and how it is implemented. Commonly, this is a family-centred written plan of action developed for children and their families and outlines the following: the strengths of a child and family,

their goals and priorities, services and supports currently being received or required, and what roles are being assumed by each member. This plan also outlines directions of service, as well as expected outcomes and timelines.

Individual Program Plan (IPP) (p. 325)
A written plan capturing the strengths, skills to be developed, and interests of an individual. Its content is collaboratively developed by those who work directly with the individual (i.e., parent, educator, outside professionals) and will change and evolve as the individual changes and evolves. This plan is in constant development, with new skills being added as others are achieved. It is an ideal document for discussing an individual's growth and progress with a team and is used to inform planning and/or adaptations for an individual within a classroom.

Individual Training/Teaching Plan (ITP) (p. 325)
An alternative name for an action plan for a child, outlining items as specified in an IEP.

inference (p. 124)
An opinion based on given data or assumptions; judgment.

informal settings (p. 41)
Settings for observation that are familiar and known to a child, such as a private home daycare or a group daycare setting.

interpretations (p. 121)
Subjective responses to what is observed; personal or professional judgments or beliefs.

interprofessional education (p. 301)
Professionals from different and the same disciplines working within their realm of practice in a mutually trusting and collaborative way to educate and learn from other members of the team about their profession and role, for the betterment of their practice as well as for a client (i.e., child and family).

interrater reliability (p. 128)
The degree to which persons who are evaluating a particular behaviour or competency agree that the results are reliable; a method of controlling bias.

interview (p. 232)
A face-to-face meeting, usually within a formal context for a specific purpose.

intrinsic (p. 23)
Belonging to the nature of a thing; inherent; from within.

introspection (p. 40)
To look into or within at one's thoughts or feelings.

key feature (p. 139)
An integral or central part or component of something.

labelling (p. 115)
To attach a term or phrase to a person or thing that classifies or characterizes him, her, or it.

learning stories (p. 179)
A narrative approach incorporating the feelings, actions, strengths, needs, and interests of a child or group of children.

leniency error (p. 127)
A common judgmental bias that occurs when the observer is overly generous when rating children.

Livescribe pen (p. 171)
A paper-based computing platform consisting of a digital pen, digital paper, software applications, and developer tools. Central to the Livescribe platform is the smartpen, a ballpoint pen with an embedded computer and digital audio recorder. It records what it writes for later uploading to a computer and synchronizes those notes with any audio it has recorded.

longitudinal studies (pp. 365, 41)
Observational studies consisting of research over extended periods of time.

loose parts (p. 343)
A concept and theory proposed in the 1970s by Simon Nicholson and gaining steady recognition in the profession. Loose parts consist of open-ended natural or manufactured materials (e.g., stones, sticks, logs, cones, fabrics, cardboard), which can be manipulated, used, or combined creatively. These materials allow for "possibility thinking" and play opportunities full of wonder and creativity.

mapping (p. 232)
A graphic representation (map or visual drawing) detailing the context of the environment and movements of a child/group of children.

microcosm (p. 18)
A small representational system with the characteristics of a larger system; a little world.

modifications (p. 325)
Alterations or changes. Specific to education, modifications involve changing the level of academic performance and achievement expected from a student, resulting in the student attaining learning outcomes not within the same grade level or prescribed curriculum as his or her peers. This term is different from accommodations.

monitor (p. 10)
To check or test a process in a systematic fashion.

monitoring (p. 330)
Periodic assessment of a person or event to inform the state of compliance with an expectation, objective, or outcome.

Montessori school (p. 38)
A school or program employing the principles and teachings of Maria Montessori, known as the first female physician in Italy. Montessori believed and taught that children learn at their own pace, learn through discovery, and need to employ all five senses to understand the world around them.

multifaceted (p. 75)
Having many facets or aspects; combining a variety of features, parts, or perspectives.

narrative (pp. 89)
The describing or telling of an event involving characters and setting; a story.

natural design (p. 343)
Environmental design which incorporates natural materials and natural elements in an indoor or outdoor play space.

natural observation (p. 146)
Observation that is recorded as it happens within a familiar environment.

norms (p. 32)
A set of scores that represent the distribution of test performance in the norm group; a standard against which others are measured.

objective (p. 325)
An end that can be reasonably achieved within an expected time frame and with available resources.

observation cycle (p. 49)
See *cycle of observation*.

observation room (p. 66)
A specially designed room adjacent to the classroom, usually equipped with a one-way glass used for observing children.

observational drift (p. 128)
A common error made by teachers when observing a targeted behaviour with an ambiguous definition, for example, sharing.

occupational standards (p. 64)
Standards in Canada that have been developed to define acceptable professional behaviour and the knowledge required for a particular occupation.

open methods (p. 136)
Records or methods used for unanticipated behaviours.

operant conditioning (p. 156)
Often associated with the works of B.F. Skinner and Ivan Pavlov, it is a form of behaviour modification whereby through the use of positive or negative reinforcement, a behaviour can be either increased or decreased under the same conditions or circumstances.

ordinate (p. 212)
The vertical axis of a graph.

orthotics (p. 340)
Braces, pads, and/or splints designed and created specifically to provide assistance, support, and strength for parts of the body, particularly the foot and ankle.

palmar grasp (p. 30)
A grasp whereby the tool or utensil lies across the palm of the hand with fingers curled around it, and the arm, rather than the wrist, moves the tool.

paradigm shift (p. 180)
To have a sudden change in perception, a change in a point of view, of how you see a set of assumptions, concepts, values, and practices that constitutes a way of viewing reality.

paraphrasing (p. 95)
To say the same thing but in other words; a restatement; to give meaning in another form.

paraprofessional (p. 294)
A trained person who works under the guidance of a more qualified professional in that field.

participation chart (p. 190)
A method in chart form of recording the participation of children engaged in the environment, noting the areas where they play, their playmates, duration of time, and any other pertinent information. Can be organized to record the participation of one child or a group of children.

patterning (p. 142)
Determining the repetition or recurrence of behaviour. Common behaviours of individuals can be easily patterned through the integration of information gathered from various observation tools, looking for common or similar actions or skills.

patterns (p. 64)
Observable reoccurring behaviours that become predictable or sequential skill development that follows a particular model or relationship.

pedagogical documentation (p. 2)
An inquiry into individual or group learning that involves the collection of artifacts, audio/visual images, artwork or notes, and the process of collaborative reflection to understand and support more deeply the learning that evolved from this process. This process makes not only the children's learning visible but also that of the perspectives of the documenter.

It serves as meaning-making; a democratic process rather than a managerial assessment.

pedagogical practices (p. 236)
Practices that provide multiple opportunities for students to engage in intellectually challenging and real-world learning experiences; educator practices that are child focused with learning activities that may reflect a particular philosophy.

pedagogy (p. 1)
The art or practice of a profession of teaching or instruction.

perception (p. 147)
An intuitive judgment often implying subtle personal bias; insight.

photography (p. 161)
Using a picture (hard copy or digital) originating from a camera as part of observation and documentation.

pincer grasp (p. 30)
A grasp whereby small objects are picked up using the thumb and forefinger.

pictorial representations (p. 227)
Visual images that are drawn, painted, or photographed, used to represent an idea.

play-based curriculum (p. 7)
A form of curriculum and learning based on the child's play interests and competencies, with its methodology reflected in journaling, documentation, and an educator's reflective practices.

play deprivation (p. 23)
The notion that not playing may deprive children of experiences that are regarded as essential to human development, with possible long-term emotional and social effects.

play therapist (p. 146)
A therapist or consultant who specializes in working with children in a play-based environment to assist with their social, emotional, or communicative development.

Pledge of Confidentiality (p. 83)
A written declaration indicating that whoever signs the pledge understands that the information that is shared within an early learning and care setting will not be discussed, revealed, or transmitted outside the setting in any way without the expressed consent of the supervisor or person in charge.

pluralistic (p. 39)
The idea that there is more than one method, philosophy, or pedagogy.

portfolio (p. 130)
A purposeful collection of work that conveys relevant information about a child; a collection and a dynamic process that reflects the individuality of the child through artwork, photographs, and text.

pragmatics (p. 102)
Dealing with events sensibly and realistically in a way that is based on practical rather than theoretical considerations; practical.

predisposition (p. 58)
The act of predisposing or the state of being predisposed; previous inclination, tendency, or propensity; predilection, such as a predisposition to anger.

prerequisite skills (pp. 198, 325)
Skills that are required as a prior condition for other skills to develop.

prevalence (p. 322)
The quality or condition of being prevalent; superior strength, force, or influence, such as the prevalence of a virtue, a fashion, or a disease.

profile (pp. 185, 220)
A method of documentation that focuses on a specific, targeted area of child development, allowing the observer to record behaviours of a child that are typically demonstrated within that developmental area.

prosocial behaviour (p. 291)
Positive, commonly valued social behaviours, such as helping.

provocations (pp. 34, 145)
Inspired by Reggio Emilia, provocations are materials or experiences that educators set out to provoke children's thinking.

psychiatrist (p. 324)
A physician with additional medical training and experience in the diagnosis, prevention, and treatment of mental disorders.

psychoeducational assessments (p. 300)
This is a process involving three steps: the gathering of background and

educational history from an individual's teachers and/or parent(s); a battery of educational and psychological diagnostic assessment tests for the individual; and a diagnosis or outcome-reporting component. Conducted by a qualified psychologist, each step of the process analyzes and estimates an individual's cognitive or academic adaptive behaviour and attention abilities and challenges. The outcome is a psychoeducational report that may provide a diagnosis as well as recommendations concerning an individual's learning challenges and abilities and the supports he or she requires, all of which pertain directly to an individual's educational plan.

psychologist (p. 324)
An individual holding a doctoral degree in psychology who is qualified to support the mental health of others through the provision of research, therapy, and diagnosis.

qualitative research (p. 41)
Research designed to reveal a target audience's range of behaviour and the perceptions that drive it with reference to specific topics or issues. It uses in-depth studies of small groups of people to guide and support the construction of hypotheses. The results of qualitative research are descriptive rather than predictive.

rating scale (p. 205)
A method of documentation that records behaviours targeted in advance and provides a continuum against which to judge the behaviour by degree or frequency.

reciprocal (p. 16)
Mutual; corresponding to each other as being equivalent or complementary.

referral (p. 300)
To send or direct someone to a treatment/program or service.

Reggio Emilia (pp. 33, 161)
An educational philosophy started by Loris Malaguzzi and the parents of the villages around Reggio Emilia in Italy after World War II. It is an approach to early childhood education emphasizing children's symbolic representations (including drawing, sculpture, dramatic play, and writing), documentation of the children's experiences in long-term projects, and extensive involvement of parents and the community. It is child centred and directed, taking the philosophy that learning must make sense to the student to be effective and meaningful.

reinforcement (p. 156)
Consequences that increase the likelihood that a certain behaviour will occur again; in behavioural theory, any response that follows a behaviour that encourages repetition of that behaviour.

reliability (p. 208)
The extent to which a test is consistent in measuring over time what it is designed to measure.

reports (p. 300)

Word-processed written documents that may take many forms in early childhood education. Some of these reports may involve the summarization of research, observations, and conclusions made, and others may discuss services in place for a child, program planning, and licensing requirements to name a few.

resiliency (p. 336)

The ability to recover quickly from illness, change, or misfortune; buoyancy. In psychology, resilience is the positive capacity of people to cope with stress and adversity. This coping may result in the individual "bouncing back" to a previous state of normal functioning.

resource educator/early interventionist/resource professionals (p. 299)

Professionals who provide services, materials, equipment, facilities, or personnel to meet the needs of children, families, and the communities they serve.

responsive (p. 14)

The act of responding with respect and intention to another's requests, needs, or situations; a pedagogy grounded in educators displaying sensitivity and responsiveness to others.

rhetorical (p. 26)

An adjective used to describe, for example, a question that is asked for effect or to make a statement rather than inform; expressed in terms designed to impress or persuade.

running record (p. 151)

A series of chronological observations represented in minutes, hours, days, or weeks. This open-ended approach to collecting information on a child over time requires dedicated observation, time and considerable commitment. A running record generally focuses on a child throughout the day, recording samples of behaviour from morning until the child leaves the centre.

scaffolding (p. 17)

A concept developed by Soviet psychologist and social constructivist Lev Vygotsky, who stated that an adult will scaffold, or put in place a form of assistance, whereby a child gradually develops the ability to do certain tasks without help. Vygotsky's often-quoted definition of zone of proximal development presents scaffolding as the distance between the actual developmental level, as determined by independent problem solving, and the level of potential development, as determined through problem solving under adult guidance or in collaboration with more capable peers.

screening (p. 294)

The first stage of a multipurpose assessment process that identifies possible areas in a child's development that may need extra support. The screening process indicates if a child may need a referral or further assessment.

self-actualizing (p. 336)

The motivation to realize one's own maximum potential and possibilities.

The term is used in various psychology theories, such as Abraham Maslow's hierarchy of needs. In that context, self-actualization is the final level of psychological development that can be achieved when all other basic needs are met.

self-advocacy (p. 308)
The process of taking action for oneself to share one's views.

self-rectifying (p. 54)
To set right; correct. To correct by calculation or adjustment.

self-regulation (p. 336)
The ability to control or adapt one's own behaviour and/or emotions according to the context, goals, or expectations of a situation or person.

semantics (p. 102)
The study of the meaning of language; the relationship between words (symbols) and what they refer to, and how these meanings influence behaviour and attitudes.

severity bias (p. 127)
The strict or severe treatment of a child by a teacher who is predisposed by a sometimes inexplicable dislike for that child.

social capital (p. 354)
A sociological concept used in economics, organizational behaviour, political science, public health, and the social sciences in general to refer to connections within and between social networks.

social construct theories (p. 20)
Sociological theories that involve looking at ways social phenomena are created. These theories focus on human choices rather than laws resulting from divine will or nature. A major focus of social constructionism is to uncover ways in which individuals and groups participate in the construction of their perceived social reality, including what it means from one generation to the next.

social story (pp. 178, 340)
A simple description of an everyday social situation written from a child's perspective. The stories can help a child prepare for upcoming changes in routine or learn appropriate social interactions. The notion is that the child rehearses the story ahead of time, with an adult. The child can use the story to guide his or her behaviour.

sociogram (p. 229)
A graphic representation of the social structures and links that a person or group of people have with others.

sociometry (p. 229)
The qualitative state of interpersonal relationships in populations.

specimen record (p. 155)
Detailed observations taken over a period of time and used for research purposes.

stakeholder (p. 348)
A person, group, or organization that has direct or indirect stake in an

organization because it can affect or be affected by the organization's actions, objectives, and policies.

standardized assessments (p. 267)
An assessment that has reliability and validity and that specifies how the assessment is administered, which materials are used, and how it is scored/evaluated.

standers (p. 340)
Assistive devices aimed to support an individual physically to be able to stand. This metal and Velcro-strapped piece of equipment might also have a table attached to it.

summary report (p. 103)
A report that presents the substance or general idea in brief form; summarizing; condensed; the compilation of the pertinent factors of an educator's notes that is shared with the child's family.

summative evaluation (pp. 206, 331)
A process that concerns final evaluation to ask if the project or program met its goals. It occurs at the end of a learning or instructional experience, such as a class or a program, and may include a variety of activities.

targeted behaviours (p. 191)
Behaviours that are preselected by the observer.

task analysis (p. 325)
A systematic identification of the fundamental elements of what needs to be done or accomplished; an examination of knowledge and skills required for a

particular task in which all the elements of the activity are defined, including knowledge requirements, skills, materials, sequencing, number of steps, resources, safety issues, related procedures, and training.

tenet (p. 78)
A principle, belief, or doctrine generally held to be true by a person or especially by members of an organization, movement, or profession.

total communication (p. 165)
An approach using as many kinds of communication as necessary for a child to understand an idea or concept, for example, sign language, hearing aids, pictures.

tourist curriculum (p. 127)
An approach marked by trivializing diversity, such as by organizing activities only around holidays or food. This curriculum disconnects cultural diversity from daily classroom life by bringing it up only on special occasions and then having nothing further to do with the culture.

transformation (p. 20)
A process of profound and radical change that orients a person or organization in a new direction; a basic change in character or structure that bears little resemblance to the past configuration.

universally designed (p. 342)
Refers to broad-spectrum ideas meant to produce buildings, products, and environments that are inherently

accessible to people with or without disabilities; a barrier-free building design usable by all people, to the greatest extent possible, without the need for adaptation or specialized design.

unobtrusive (p. 69)
Blending with the environment so as not to stand out; inconspicuous.

validity (p. 208)
Capable of being justified or supported; the degree to which something measures what it claims to measure.

video diaries (p. 41)
A form of video recording, a personal view of how the subject of the diary views the world, capturing an unrehearsed, on-the-spot reaction of thoughts and feelings.

video recording (p. 172)
An electronic capture of both the audio and visual aspects of what is seen and heard.

visual schedule (p. 340)
A set of pictures that communicates a series of activities or the steps of a specific activity. It is meant to help children manage the daily events in their lives by using photographs, pictures, written words, or physical objects that help clarify expectations for the child.

webbing (pp. 182, 258)
A tool used with an emergent curriculum approach to create a tentative plan where possibilities are explored such as an interest, material, or idea and developed with the input of the children.

working/developmental portfolio (p. 272)
A growing and changing hard-copy or digital portfolio aimed to house information, observations, and a variety of artifacts prepared (by a family, child, or educator) representing a child's growth and development.

REFERENCES

Abramson, S. (2008). *Voices of practitioners: Co-inquiry meetings for facilitated pro-fessional interchange.* Washington, DC: National Association for the Education of Young Children. Retrieved from http://www.naeyc.org/files/naeyc/file/vop/Voices_Abramson_Co-Inquiry.pdf

Affiliated Children and Youth Services. (2010). *Implementing Ontario's Early Learning Framework, trainer and mentor manual* (1st ed. rev.). Hamilton, ON: Author.

Affiliated Services for Children and Youth. (n.d.). *For goodness sake.* Retrieved from https://ascy.ca/goodness-sake/

Agbenyega, J. (2009). The Australian Early Development Index, who does it measure: Piaget or Vygotsky's child? *Australasian Journal of Early Childhood, 34*(2), 31–38.

Alat, K. (2002). Traumatic events and children: How early childhood educators can help. *Childhood Education, 10*(1), 2–7.

Alberta Children and Youth Initiative, Government of Alberta. (2006, March). *Guidelines for supporting successful transitions for children and youth. Children and Youth In Transition: An Alberta Children and Youth Initiative.* Retrieved from http://www.assembly.ab.ca/lao/library/egovdocs/2006/alac/158807.pdf

Alberta Education. (2006). *Standards for the provision of early childhood special edu-cation.* Edmonton, AB: Alberta Education. Retrieved from https://education.alberta.ca/media/452316/ecs_specialedstds2006.pdf

Alberta Education, Early Learning Branch. (2009). *Working with young children who are learning English as a new language.* Edmonton, AB: Government of Alberta. Retrieved from http://education.alberta.ca/media/1093791/earlylearning.pdf

Allen, K. E., & Marotz, L. R. (2003). *Developmental profiles: Pre-birth through twelve* (4th ed.). Belmont, CA: Thomson Nelson.

Andrews, K. (2008, May). *Family centred practices in children's services.* Retrieved from http://www.gowrie-melbourne.com.au

Ashton, J., Woodrow, C., Johnston, C., Wangmann, J., Singh L., & James, T. (2008). Partnerships in learning: Linking early childhood services, families and schools for optimal development. *Australian Journal of Early Childhood, 33*(2), 10–16.

Atkinson, K. (2012). Pedagogical narration: What's it all about? *The Early Childhood Educator,* 3–7.

Austin, S. (2005). Community-building principles: Implications for professional development. *Child Welfare, 84*(2), 106–122.

Australian Government, Department of Education, Employment and Workplace Relations. (2010, November). *Draft Assessment and Rating Instrument: National Quality Standard for Early Childhood Education and Care and School Age Care.* Retrieved from http://apollo.hutchins.tas.edu.au/community/asc/Resources%20 for%20Parents/National%20Quality%20Standards/Assessment%20and%20 Rating%20Instrument.pdf

Australian Government, Department of Education, Employment and Workplace Relations for the Council of Australian Governments. (2009). *Belonging, being and becoming: The Early Years Learning Framework for Australia.* Retrieved from https://docs.education.gov.au/system/files/doc/other/belonging_being _and_becoming_the_early_years_learning_framework_for_australia.pdf

Autism Ontario. (2006). *Red flags for autism.* Retrieved from http://www.autismontario .com

Bailey, M. (2007). *Digital learning stories: Empowering students' representations and reflections.* Retrieved from http://education.ed.pacificu.edu/bailey/resources/ papers/Lstories/whatare.html

Ball, J. (2006). *Cultural safety in practice with children, families and communities.* School of Child and Youth Care, University of Victoria. Retrieved from http:// www.ecdip.org/docs/pdf/Cultural%20Safety%20Poster.pdf

Barankin, T., & Khanlou, N. (2007). *Growing up resilient: Ways to build resilience in children and youth.* Retrieved from http://www.camh.net/Publications/ Resources_for_Professionals/Growing_Resilient/index.html

Barrett, H. C. (2010, September). Electronic portfolios—a chapter in *Educational Technology*; an encyclopedia to be published by ABC-CLIO, 2001. Retrieved from http://electronicportfolios.com/portfolios/encyclopediaentry.htm

Bates, C. C. (2014, September). Digital portfolios: Using technology to involve families. *Young Children, 69*(4), 56–57.

Beaty, J. (2006). *Observing development of the young child.* Upper Saddle River, NJ: Prentice Hall.

Benjamin, A. C. (1994). Observations in early childhood classrooms: Advice from the field. *Young Children, 49*(6), 14–20.

Bentzen, W. R. (2009). *Seeing young children: A guide to observing and recording behaviour* (6th ed.). Belmont, CA: Delmar.

Bertrand, J. (2008). *Understanding, managing, and leading: Early childhood programs in Canada.* Toronto, ON: Thomson Nelson.

Billman, A. C., & Sherman, J. (2003). *Observation and participation in early child settings: A practicum guide* (2nd ed.). Boston, MA: Allyn & Bacon.

Boardman, M. (2007). I know how much this child has learned. I have proof! *Australian Journal of Early Childhood, 32*(3), 59–66.

Boise, P. (2010). *Go Green Rating Scale for early childhood settings.* St. Paul, MN: Redleaf Press.

Bouvier, R. (2010). Good community schools are sites of educational activism. *Our Schools/Our Selves, 19*(4), 169–184.

Bowers, F. B. (2008). Developing a child assessment plan: An integral part of program quality. *Exchange: The Early Childhood Leaders Magazine, 184,* 51–57.

Bowie, B. H. (2010). Emotion regulation related to children's future externalizing and internalizing behaviors. *Journal of Child and Adolescent Psychiatric Nursing, 23*(2), 74–83.

Bowne, M., Cutler, K., DeBates, D., Gilkerson, D., & Stremmel, A. (2010, June). Pedogogical documentation and collaborative dialogue as tools of inquiry for pre-service teachers in early childhood education: An exploratory narrative. *Journal of the Scholarship of Teaching and Learning, 10*(2), 48–59.

Bradley, J., & Kibera, P. (2006). Culture and the promotion of inclusion in child care. *Young Children, 61*(1), 34–38.

Briody, J., & McGarry, K. (2005). Using social stories to ease children's transitions. *Young Children, 60*(5), 38–42.

British Columbia Ministry of Education. (2009). *Understanding the British Columbia Early Learning Framework: From theory to practice.* Retrieved from http://www.bced.gov.bc.ca/early_learning/pdfs/from_theory_to_practice.pdf

Broadhead, P. (2006). Developing an understanding of young children's learning through play: The place of observation, interaction and reflection. *British Educational Research Journal, 32*(2), 191–207.

Bronstein, L. R. (2002). Index of interdisciplinary collaboration. *Social Work Research, 26*(2), 113–123.

Brotherson, M. J., Summers, J. A., Naig, L. A., Kyzar, K., Friend, A., Epley, P., … Turn-bull, A. P. (2010). Partnership patterns: Addressing emotional needs in early intervention. *Topics in Early Childhood Special Education, 30*(1), 32–45.

Brown, A., & Inglis, S. (March, 2013). So what happens after the event? Exploring the realisation of professional development with early childhood educators. *Australasian Journal of Early Childhood, 38*(1), 11–15.

Brown, W. H., Odom, S. L., & Halcombe, A. (1996). Observational assessment of young children's social behaviour with peers. *Early Childhood Research Quarterly, 11*(1), 19–40.

Browne, K. W., & Gordon, A. M. (2009). *To teach well: An early childhood practicum guide.* Upper Saddle River, NJ: Pearson Education.

Bullard, J. (2010). *Creating environments for learning: Birth to age eight.* Upper Saddle River, NJ: Pearson Education.

Burke, A. (2012, Fall). Empowering children's voices through the narrative of drawings. *Morning Watch: Educational and Social Analysis, 40*(1–2). Retrieved from http://www.mun.ca/educ/faculty/mwatch/mwatch_sped13/Burke.pdf

Buysse, V., & Wesley, P. (2004). *Consultation in early childhood settings.* Baltimore, MD: Paul H. Brookes.

Buysse, V., Welsey, P., & Skinner, D. (1999). Community development approaches for early intervention. *Topics in Early Childhood Special Education, 19*(4), 236–243.

Bzock, K. R., League, R., & Brown, V. L. (2003). *Receptive-Expressive Emergent Language Test (REEL-3).* Austin, TX: PRO-ED.

Canadian Child Care Federation. (2000). *A self-assessment checklist based on National Statement of Quality Early Learning and Child Care.* Retrieved from http://www.cccf-fcsge.ca/practice/assessment/self-reflection.pdf

Canadian Child Care Federation. (2006). The child's right to be heard. *Interaction, 20*(3). Retrieved from http://www.cccf-fcsge.ca/pdf/Interaction-focus.pdf

Canadian Child Care Federation. (2010, November). *Supporting and encouraging children's right to be heard* (Resource Sheet No. 8). Retrieved from http://www.cccf-fcsge.ca/pdf/81_en.pdf

Canadian Child Care Federation. (2011). *Code of ethics.* Retrieved from http://staff.oxfordkids.ca/wp-content/uploads/2013/09/Code-of-Ethics-Attachment-to-Personnal-Handbook1.pdf

Canadian Child Care Federation. (2012). *About CCCF.* Retrieved from http://www.cccf-fcsge.ca/about/

Canadian Coalition for the Rights of Children. (2009). *Promoting children's rights in Canada.* Retrieved from http://rightsofchildren.ca/

Canadian Council on Learning. (2010). *State of learning in Canada: A year in review.* Ottawa, ON: Author. Retrieved from http://www.ccl-cca.ca/pdfs/SOLR/2010/SOLR-2010-Report-FINAL-E.pdf

Canadian Heritage. (2009, March). *Rights of children.* Retrieved from http://www.pch.gc.ca/pgm/pdp-hrp/canada/enfnt-eng.cfm

Canadian Partnership for Children's Health and Environment. (2010). *Advancing environmental health in child care settings: A checklist for child care practitioners and public health inspectors.* Toronto, ON: Author. Retrieved from http://www.healthyenvironmentforkids

Capone, A., Oren, T., & Neisworth, J. T. (2004). *Childmate: A guide to appraising quality child care.* New York, NY: Delmare Cengage Learning.

Carl, B. (2007, December). *Child Caregiver Interaction Scale* (Doctoral dissertation). Retrieved from http://www.dspace.lib.iup.edu:8080/dspace/bitstream/2069/53/1/Barbara

Carlisle, R. P. (2009). *Encyclopedia of play in today's society* (Vol. 1). Thousand Oaks, CA: Sage.

Carr, M., & Lee, W. (2012). *Learning stories: Constructing learner identities in early education.* Thousand Oaks, CA: Sage.

Cartwright, C. A., & Cartwright, P. G. (1984). *Developing observation skills.* New York, NY: McGraw-Hill.

Cary, J. (2014, November). Small children, big cities. *Early Childhood Matters, 123.* The Hague, The Netherlands: Bernard van Leer Foundation. Retrieved from http://www.bernardvanleer.org/English/Home/Publications/Browse_by_topic .html?ps_page=1&getTopic=104#.VITskNyTTy8

Caspe, M., Seltzer, A., Lorenzo Kennedy, J., Cappio, M., & DeLorenzo, C. (2013, July). Engaging families in the child assessment process. *Young Children, 4*(7), 8–14.

Catapano, S. (2005). Teacher professional development through children's project work. *Early Childhood Education Journal, 32*(4), 261–267.

Centre for Adult English Language Acquisition. (2001). *Helping adult English language learners transition into other educational programs.* Retrieved from http://www.cal.org/caela/esl_resources/

Centre for Canadian Language Benchmarks. (2010, March). *Canadian Language Benchmark Test.* Retrieved from http://www.language.ca

Chandler, K. (2008). *Families and practitioners: Collaborating to support cultural identity in young children* (Canadian Child Care Federation Resource Sheet No. 9). Retrieved from http://www.cccf-fcsge.ca/wp-content/uploads/RS_91-e.pdf

Chen, D. W., Nimmo, J., & Fraser, R. (2009). Becoming a culturally responsive educator: A tool to support reflection by teachers embarking on the anti-bias journey. *Multicultural Perspectives, 11*(2), 101–106.

Child and Family Services Act, R.S.O. 1990, c. C. 11.

Child Care Human Resources Sector Council. (2010, March). *Occupational standards for early childhood educators.* Retrieved from http://www.ccsc-cssge.ca/sites/default/files/uploads/ECE-Post-Secondary-docs/OSECE_2010_EN.pdf

Child Care Human Resources Sector Council. (2011). *Identifying ongoing professional development needs using the occupational standards for ECE's.* Retrieved from http://www.youtube.com/user/ChildCareHRCouncil#p/u/3/pQvd-BDTN3o

Child language acquisition. (1998). In *Concise Oxford companion to the English language.* Retrieved from http://www.oxfordreference.com/views/ENTRY .html?subview=Main&entry=t29.e246

Child Rights Information Network. (2011). *Convention on the Rights of the Child.* Retrieved from http://www.crin.org/themes/ViewTheme.asp?id=2

Chorney, D. W. (2006). Teacher development and the role of reflection. *Physical and Health Education Journal, 72*(3), 22–25.

City of Vancouver. (1993). *Childcare design guidelines.* Retrieved from http://vancouver .ca/files/cov/child-design-guidelines.pdf

Claxton, G., & Carr, C. (2004). A framework for teaching learning: The dynamics of disposition. *Early Years, 24*(1), 87–97.

Clinton, J. (2013). *The power of positive adult-child relationships: Connection is the key.* Toronto: ON: Queen's Printer for Ontario. Retrieved from http://www.edu .gov.on.ca/childcare/clinton.pdf

Cohen, N. J., Kiefer, H., & Pape, B. (2004). *Handle with care: Strategies for promoting the mental health of young children in community-based child care.* Retrieved from http://www.cmha.ca/data/1/rec_docs/156_handle_with_care

Coleman, D. (1995). *The nature of emotional intelligence.* New York, NY: Bantam Books.

College of Early Childhood Educators. (2011, February). *Code of ethics and standards of practice: Recognizing and honouring our profession.* Retrieved from https:// www.college-ece.ca/en/Documents/Code_Ethic_English_Web_August_2013.pdf

College of Early Childhood Educators. (2014a, September). *Reflective practice and self-directed learning.* Retrieved from http://www.college-ece.ca/en/Members/ Documents/Reflective%20Practice%20and%20Self-Directed%20Learning%20 Booklet%20September%201%202014.pdf

College of Early Childhood Educators. (2014b, December 9). *Child Care Modernization Act, 2014.* Retrieved from http://www.college-ece.ca/en/Public/ News/Pages/Child-Care-Modernization-Act,-2014-(Bill-10)-.aspx

Cool, J. (2007). *Child care in Canada: The federal role.* Retrieved from http://www .parl.gc.ca/content/lop/researchpublications/prb0420-e.htm

Cooperrider, D. L., Whitney, D., & Stavros, J. M. (2008). *Appreciative inquiry handbook: For leaders of change* (2nd ed.). San Francisco, CA: Berrett-Koehler.

Corks, I. (2004, Summer). The case for family-centred service: A best-practice approach for special needs children. *Paediatrics: Rehab & Community Care Medicine.* Retrieved from http://www.canchild.ca/en/ourresearch/resources/ RCCM_Smr04_CanChild.pdf

County of Wellington. (2009). *County of Wellington child care operating criteria.* Retrieved from http://www.wellington.ca/document_download.aspx?id=3271

Coughlin, A. M., & Baird, L. (2013). *Pedagogical leadership.* Retrieved from http://www.edu.gov.on.ca/childcare/Baird_Coughlin.pdf

Cox-Suárez, S. (2010). Show me again what I can do: Documentation and self-determination for students with social challenges. *Theory Into Practice, 49,* 21–28.

Craft, A., & Paige-Smith, A. (2007, December). *Developing reflective practice in the early years.* Berkshire, UK: Open University Press, McGraw-Hill Education EMEA.

Crowther, I. (2006). *Inclusion in early childhood settings: Children with special needs in Canada.* Toronto, ON: Pearson Education Canada.

Cryer, D. (2003). Defining program quality. In D. Cryer & R. Clifford (Eds.), *Early childhood education and care in the U.S.A.* (pp. 31–46). Baltimore, MD: Paul H. Brookes.

Curtis, D. (2006). No ordinary moments: Using observations with toddlers to invite further engagement. *Child Care Exchange, 3*(6), 36–40.

Curtis, D. (2008). Seeing children. *Child Care Exchange, 307*(6), 38–42.

Dahlberg, G., Moss, P., & Pence, A. (2007). *Beyond quality in early childhood education and care: Language of evaluation* (2nd ed.). London, England: Routledge.

Davis, E. L., Levine, L. J., Lench, H. C., & Quas, J. A. (2010). Metacognitive emotion regulation: Children's awareness that changing thoughts and goals can alleviate negative emotions. *Emotion, 10*(4), 498–510.

Dempster, N., & Lizzio, A. (2007). Student leadership: Necessary research. *Australian Journal of Education, 51*(3), 276–285.

Department of Justice Canada. (n.d.). *Child abuse: A fact sheet from the Department of Justice Canada.* Retrieved from http://www.justice.gc.ca/eng/pi/fv-vf/facts-info/child-enf.html

Derman-Sparks, L., & Edwards, J. O. (2010). *Anti-bias education for young children and ourselves.* Washington, DC: National Association for the Education of Young Children.

Devereux Early Childhood Assessment Program. (n.d.). *Enhancing social emotional development.* Retrieved from http://www.kaplanco.com/media/DECA_Manual.pdf

Devereux Early Childhood Initiative. (2007). *The Devereux Early Childhood Assessment for Infants and Toddlers (DECA-I/T).* Retrieved from http://www.devereux.org/site/PageServer?pagename=deci_index

Devereaux Early Childhood Initiative. (2009). *Devereux Early Childhood Assessment for Infants and Toddlers. Reflective checklist for connecting with families.*

Retrieved from http://www.centerforresilientchildren.org/wp-content/uploads/DECA-IT-ReproduciblePlanningForms.pdf

Dickinson, P., Lothian, S., & Jonz, M. B. (2007, March). Sharing responsibility for our children: How one community is making its vision for children a reality. *Young Children, 62*(3) 49–55.

Dinnebeil, L. A., Hale, L., & Rule, S. (1999). Early intervention program practices that support collaboration. *Topics in Early Childhood Special Education, 19*(4), 225–235.

Division for Early Childhood and National Association for the Education of Young Children. (2009). *Early childhood inclusion: A summary.* Chapel Hill, NC: University of North Carolina, FPG Child Development Institute. Retrieved from http://www.naeyc.org/files/naeyc/file/positions/DEC_NAEYC_ECSummary_A.pdf

Dodge, E. P., Dulik, B. N., & Kulhanek, J. A. (n.d.). *Clouds come from New Hampshire: Confronting the challenge of philosophical change in early childhood programs.* Retrieved from http://ceep.crc.uiuc.edu/pubs/katzsym/dulik.pdf

Dufour, M. (2015, February 23). Writing for the world to see [Blog post]. Retrieved from Leading with Technology blog: https://www.diigo.com/bookmark/https%3A%2F%2Fleadingwithtechnology.wordpress.com?gname=ecetech

Dunn, W. (1999). *Sensory Profile Caregiver Questionnaire-SPCQ.* San Antonio, TX: Psychological Corporation.

Earl, L. (2003). *Assessment as learning: Using classroom assessment to maximize student learning.* Thousand Oaks, CA: Corwin Press.

Early Childhood Research and Development Team, Early Childhood Centre, University of New Brunswick. (2007). *Early learning and child care: English curriculum framework for New Brunswick, 2007.* Fredericton, NB: Family and Community Services. Retrieved from http://eyeonkids.ca/docs/files/nb_early_learning_framework%5B1%5D.pdf

Early Childhood Research and Development Team, Early Childhood Centre, University of New Brunswick. (2008, March 31). *New Brunswick curriculum framework for early learning and child care.* Fredericton, NB: Department of Social Development. Retrieved from http://www.gnb.ca/0000/ECHDPE/curriculum-e.asp

Educause Learning Initiative. (2005, July). *7 things you should know about wikis.* Retrieved from https://net.educause.edu/ir/library/pdf/ELI7004.pdf

Edwards, C. P. (2002). Three approaches from Europe: Waldorf, Montessori, and Reggio Emilia. *Early Childhood Research and Practice, 4*(1). Retrieved from http://ecrp.uiuc.edu/v4n1/edwards.html

Elliott, M. J. (2000). Project approach: Celebrating human dimensions of learning. In *Issues in early childhood education: Curriculum, teacher education, and dissemination of information. Proceedings of the Lilian Katz Symposium.* Champaign, IL, November 5–7, 2000. Retrieved from http://ceep.crc.uiuc.edu/pubs/katzsym/elliott.pdf

Ferguson, E. (2004). Reflection—the key to evaluation. *Interaction, 17*(4), 17–18.

Ferns, C., & Friendly, M. (2014). *The state of early childhood education and care in Canada 2012.* Toronto, ON: Moving Childcare Forward Project. Retrieved from http://childcarecanada.org/sites/default/files/StateofECEC2012.pdf

Ford, D. Y. (2010). Culturally responsive classrooms: Affirming culturally different gifted students. *Multicultural Issues, 33*(1), 50–54.

Forman, G. (1999). Instant video revisiting: The video camera as a "Tool of the Mind" for young children. *Early Childhood Research and Practice, 1*(2), 1–6. Retrieved from http://ecrp.uiuc.edu/v1n2/forman.html

Forman, G. (2010). Documentation and accountability: The shift from numbers to indexed narratives. *Theory Into Practice, 49,* 29–35.

Forman, G., & Hall, E. (2005). Wondering with children: The importance of observation in early education. *Early Childhood Research and Practice, 7*(2). Retrieved from http://ecrp.uiuc.edu/v7n2/index.html

Forman, G. E. (2010). Reading the intentionality of young children. *Early Childhood Research & Practice, 12*(1). Retrieved from http://ecrp.uiuc.edu/v12n1/forman.html

Forry, N., Vick, J., & Halle, T. (2009). *Evaluating, developing, and enhancing domain-specific measures of child care quality.* Retrieved from http://www.childtrends.org/Files//Child_Trends-2009_5_21_RB_MeasureChildCare.pdf

Fraser, S. (2012). *Authentic childhood: Experiencing Reggio Emilia in the classroom* (3rd ed.). Toronto, ON: Nelson Education.

Free Play Network. (n.d.). *PLACES for PLAY: Exhibition.* Retrieved from http://www.freeplaynetwork.org.uk/playlink/exhibition/index.html

Friedman, D. L. (2004). When teachers participate, reflect and choose change. *Young Children, 5*(6), 64–70.

Friendly, M., & Beach, J. (2005). *Elements of a high quality early learning and child care system* (Quality by Design Working Document). Toronto, ON: Childcare Resource and Research Unit, University of Toronto. Retrieved from http://www.childcarequality.ca/wdocs/QbD_Elements.pdf

Friendly, M., & Prabhu, N. (2010, January). *Can early childhood education and care help keep Canada's promise of respect for diversity?* (Occasional Paper No. 23).

Toronto, ON: Childcare Resource and Research Unit, University of Toronto. Retrieved from http://www.childcarecanada.org/sites/default/files/crru_op23 _diversity.pdf

Froebel, F. (2005). *The education of man* (Vol. 5). (W. N. Hailmann, Trans.). Belmont, CA: Dover. (Original work published 1887)

Gandini, L., & Goldhaber, J. (2001). Two reflections about documentation. In L. Gandini & C. Edwards (Eds.), *Bambini: The Italian approach to infant-toddler care* (pp. 124–145). New York, NY: Teachers College Press.

Gee, J. P. (2008). A sociocultural perspective on opportunity to learn. In P. A. Moss, D. C. Pullin, P. Gee, E. H. Haertel, & L. Jones Young (Eds.), *Assessment, equity, and opportunity to learn* (pp. 76–108). New York, NY: Cambridge University Press.

Gennarelli, C. (2004). Communicating with families: Children lead the way. *Young Children, 59,* 98–99.

Gestwicki, C. (2011). *Developmentally appropriate practice* (4th ed.). Delmar, NY: Thomson.

Gestwicki, C., & Bertrand. J. (2008). *The essentials of early childhood education* (3rd Canadian ed.). Toronto, ON: Thomson Nelson.

Gilman, S. (2009). "Social stories": Pathways to inclusion. *English Quarterly, 39*(2), 33–45.

Gjems, L. (2001, December). What explanations matter: A study of co-construction of explanations between teachers and children in everyday conversations in kinder-garten. *European Early Childhood Education Research Journal, 19*(4), 501–513.

Gonzalez-Mena, J. (2008). *Diversity in early care and education: Honoring differences* (5th ed.). New York, NY: McGraw-Hill.

Good, L. (2005–2006). Snap it up: Using digital photography in early childhood education. *Childhood Education: Infancy through Early Adolescence, 82*(2), 79–85.

Goode, T. D. (2009a). *Promoting cultural and linguistic competency: Self-assessment checklist for personnel providing services and supports in early interven-tion and early childhood settings.* Washington, DC: National Center for Cultural Competence, Georgetown University Center for Child and Human Development, University Center for Excellence in Developmental Disabilities Education, Research & Service.

Goode, T. D. (2009b). *The self assessment checklist for personnel providing services and supports in early intervention and early childhood settings.* Washington, DC: National Center for Cultural Competence, Georgetown University Center for Child and Human Development, University Center for Excellence in Developmental

Disabilities Education, Research & Service. Retrieved from http://www11
.georgetown.edu/research/gucchd/nccc/documents/Checklist.CSHN.doc.pdf

Gordon, A. M., & Williams Browne, K. (2007). *Beginning essentials in early childhood education.* Clifton Park, NY: Thomson Nelson.

Gotzke, C., & Sample Gosse, H. (2007). *Introduction to language 25–36 months— understanding and using more words and sentence types.* Retrieved from http://www.theroadmap.ualberta.ca/understandings

Government of British Columbia. (2007). *British Columbia Early Learning Framework.* Victoria, BC: Ministry of Education; Ministry of Health; Ministry of Children and Family Development, Queen's Printer for British Columbia. Retrieved from http://www2.gov.bc.ca/gov/DownloadAsset?assetId =245C9B82FFF94171BB61818A53F0674A&filename=early_learning _framework.pdf

Government of Saskatchewan, Early Learning and Child Care Branch, Ministry of Education. (2009, May). *Creating early learning environments.* Retrieved from http://www.education.gov.sk.ca/Default.aspx?DN=4de38060-953f-4922-9b9b -1d3bec94400d

Halfon, N., Russ, S., Oberklaid, F., Bertrand, J., & Eisen-stadt, N. (2009, May). *An international comparison of early childhood initiatives: From services to systems* (Vol. 111). Retrieved from http://www.healthychild.ucla.edu/PUBLICATIONS/ Halfon_intl_comparison_early_child_init_svcs_to_sys_FINAL.pdf

Hall, N. S., & Rhomberg, V. (1995). *The affective curriculum: Teaching the anti-bias approach to young children.* Scarborough, ON: Nelson Canada.

Hallam, R., Fouts, H., Bargreen, K., & Caudle, L. (2009). Quality from a toddler's perspective: A bottom-up examination of classroom experiences. *Early Childhood Research & Practice, 11*(2), 1–16.

Harcourt, D., & Sargeant, J. (2011, September). The challenges of conducting ethical research with children. *Education Inquiry, 2*(3), 421–436.

Harms, T., Clifford, R. M., & Cryer, D. (2004). *Early Childhood Environment Rating Scale–Revised.* New York, NY: Teachers College Press. Retrieved from http://ers.fpg.unc.edu/early-childhood-environment-rating-scale-ecers-r

Harms, T., Cryer, D., & Clifford, R. M. (2006). *The Infant Toddler Early Childhood Environment Rating Scale.* New York, NY: Teachers College Press. Retrieved from http://ers.fpg.unc.edu/node/82

Harms, T., Cryer, D., & Clifford, R. M. (2007). *The Family Child Care Environment Rating Scale.* New York, NY: Teachers College Press. Retrieved from http://ers.fpg .unc.edu/family-child-care-environment-rating-scale-revised-edition-fccers-r

Harms, T., Vineberg Jacobs, E., & Romano White, D. (1995). *The School Age Early Childhood Rating Scale.* New York, NY: Teachers College Press. Retrieved from http://ers.fpg.unc.edu/school-age-care-environment -rating-scale-sacers

Haugen, K. (2005, January/February). Learning materials for children of all abilities: Begin with universal design. *Child Care Exchange, 161,* 45–48.

Helm, J. H., Beneke, S., & Steinheimer, K. (2007). *Windows on learning: Documenting young children's work* (2nd ed.). New York, NY: Teachers College Press.

Henshon, S. E. (2006). The evolution of creativity, giftedness, and multiple intelligences: An interview with Ellen Winner and Howard Gardner. *Roeper Review, 28*(4). Retrieved from http://find.galegroup.com

Hertzman, C. (1998). The case for child development as a determinant of health across the life course. *Canadian Journal of Public Health, 89*(Suppl.), S14–S19.

Hewes, J. (2006, November). *Let the children play: Nature's answer to early learning.* Montreal, QC: Early Childhood Learning Knowledge Centre, Canadian Council on Learning. Retrieved from http://www.ccl-cca.ca/pdfs/ECLKC/ lessons/Learningth-roughPlay_LinL.pdf

Hope-Irwin, S. (2009). *The SpeciaLink Early Childhood Inclusion Quality Scale.* Sydney, NS: Breton Books. Retrieved from http://www.specialinkcanada.org/ about/rating%20scales.html

Houston, L., Worthington, R., & Harrop, P. (2006, March). *Design guidance for play spaces.* Retrieved from http://www.forestry.gov.uk/pdf/fce-design-guidance-for -play-spaces.pdf/$FILE/fce-design-guidance-for-play-spaces.pdf

Hughes, E. (2005). Linking past to present to create an image of the child. *Theory into Practice, 46*(1), 48–56.

Human Resources and Skill Development Canada. (n.d.). *Writing tip sheet.* Retrieved from http://www.nald.ca/library/learning/hrsdc/essential_skills/writing_tip _sheet/writing_tip_sheet.pdf

Hunt, A., Nason, P. N., & Whitty, P. (2000). Documentation as a forum and showcase in an education faculty. In *Issues in early childhood education: Curriculum, teacher education, and dissemination of information. Proceedings of the Lilian Katz Symposium.* Champaign, IL, November 5–7, 2000. Retrieved from http:// ceep.crc.uiuc.edu/pubs/katzsym/hunt.pdf

Hunt, P., Soto, G., Maier, J., Liboiron, L., & Bae, S. (2004). Collaborative teaming to support preschoolers with severe disabilities who are placed in general education early childhood programs. *Topics in Early Childhood Special Education, 24*(3), 123–142.

Hyland, N. E. (2010). Social justice in early childhood classrooms: What the research tells us. *Young Children, 65*(1), 82–90.

Jablon, J. R., Dobro, A. L., & Dichtelmiller, M. L. (2007). *The power of observation for birth through eight.* Washington, DC: National Association for the Education of Young Children.

Jackson, S., Pretti-Frontczak, K., Harjusola-Webb, S., & Grish, J. (2009, October). Responsive to intervention: Implications for early childhood professionals. *Language Speech & Hearing Services in Schools, 40*(4), 424–434.

Janus, M., Brinkman, S., Duku, E., Hertzman, C., Santos, R., Sayers, M., … Walsh, C. (2007). *The Early Development Instrument: A population-based measure for communities. A handbook on development, properties, and use.* Hamilton, ON: Offord Centre for Child Studies, McMaster University. Retrieved from http://www.rch.org.au/emplibrary/australianedi/2007_12_FINALEDIHANDBOOK.pdf

Janus, M., Kopechanski, L., Cameron, R., & Hughes, D. (2008). In transition: Experiences of parents of children with special needs at school entry. *Early Childhood Education Journal, 35,* 479–485.

Janus, M., Lefort, J., Cameron, R., & Kopechanski, L. (2007). Starting kindergarten: Transition issues for children with special needs. *Canadian Journal of Education, 30*(3), 628–648. Retrieved from http://asq.org/education/why-quality/overview.html

Johanson, S., & Kuh, L. (2013, November). Critical friends groups in an early childhood setting: Building a culture of collaboration. *Voices of Practitioners, 8*(2), 1–16. Retrieved from https://www.naeyc.org/files/naeyc/file/Voices/Voices_Johanson_v8n2.pdf

Kaiser, B., & Rasminsky, J. S. (1996). The volcano at the day-care centre. *Interaction, 9*(4), 12–15.

Kashin, D. (2013, April 11). Leading the Reggio way: A profile of a pedagogical leader [Blog post]. Retrieved from Technology Rich Inquiry Based Research blog: https://tecribresearch.wordpress.com/2013/04/11/leading-the-reggio-way-a-profile-of-a-pedagogical-leader/

Kashin, D., & Jupp, L. (2013). Documentation and assessment: The power of a learning story [Blog post]. Retrieved from Technology Rich Inquiry Based Research blog: https://tecribresearch.wordpress.com/2013/04/24/documentation-and-assessment-the-power-of-a-learning-story-10/

Katz, L. G. (2005). *The developmental states of teachers.* Retrieved from http://ceep.crc.uiuc.edu/pubs/katz-dev-stages.html

Keilty, B., LaRocco, D. J., & Bankler Cassell, F. (2009). Early interventionists' reports of authentic assessment methods through focus group research. *Topics in Early Childhood Special Education, 28*(4), 244–256.

Kennedy, A., & Stonehouse, A. (2012). *Victorian Early Years Learning and Development Framework: Practice principle guide.* Melbourne, Australia: State of Victoria (Department of Education and Early Childhood Development). Retrieved from http://www.education.vic.gov.au/Documents/childhood/providers/edcare/pracfamily.pdf

Keyes, C. R. (2000). Parent-teacher partnerships: A theoretical approach for teachers. In *Issues in early childhood education: Curriculum, teacher education, and dissemination of information. Proceedings of the Lilian Katz Symposium.* Champaign, IL, November 5–7, 2000. Retrieved from http://ceep.crc.uiuc.edu/pubs/katzsym/keyes.pdf

King, G., King, S., Law, M., Kertoy, M., Rosenbaum, P., & Hurley, P. (2002). *Family-centred service in Ontario: A "bestpractice" approach for children with disabilities and their families.* Retrieved from http://www.canchild.ca/en/canchildresources/resources/FCSinbriefNov2002.pdf

Kirk, S. A., Gallagher, J. J., & Anastasiow, N. J. (2003). *Educating exceptional children* (10th ed.). Boston, MA: Houghton Mifflin.

Larsen, E. R. (2010). *Making the team: Teams, teamwork, and teambuilding.* Retrieved from http://findarticles.com/p/articles/mi_qa5350/is_201006/ai_n54366116/pg_6/

Laverick, D. M. (2008). Starting school: Welcoming young children and families into early school experiences. *Early Childhood Education Journal, 35,* 321–326.

Law, M., Rosenbaum, P., King, G. S., Burke-Gaffney, J., MoningSzkut, T., Kertoy, M., … Teplicky, R. (2003a). *What is family-centred service?* (Fact Sheet No. 1). Hamilton, ON: CanChild Centre for Disability Research, McMaster University.

Law, M., Rosenbaum, P., King, G. S., Burke-Gaffney, J., MoningSzkut, T., Kertoy, M., … Teplicky, R. (2003b). *Are we really family-centred? Checklists for families, service providers, and organizations* (Fact Sheet No. 18). Hamilton, ON: CanChild Centre for Disability Research, McMaster University.

Lero, D. (2004). *The SpeciaLink Child Care Inclusion Practices Profile and Principles Scale.* Sydney, NS: Breton Books. Retrieved from http://www.specialinkcanada.org/about/rating%20scales.html

Lero, D. S. (2010, February). *Assessing inclusion quality in early learning and child care in Canada with the SpeciaLink Child Care Inclusion Practices Profile and Principles Scale. A report prepared for the Canadian Council on Learning.* Retrieved from http://www.specialinkcanada.org

Lewin-Benham, A. (2006). One teacher, 20 preschoolers, and a goldfish: Environmental awareness, emergent curriculum, and documentation. *Young Children, 61*(2), 28–34.

Liebovich, B. J. (2000). Children's self-assessment. In *Issues in early childhood education: Curriculum, teacher education, and dissemination of information. Proceedings of the Lilian Katz Symposium.* Champaign, IL, November 5–7, 2000. Retrieved from http://ceep.crc.uiuc.edu/pubs/katzsym/liebovich.pdf

Lindgren, A. -L. (2012, November). Ethical issues in pedagogical documentation: Representations of children through digital technology. *International Journal of Early Childhood, 44*(3), 327–340.

Logue, M. E. (2006). Teachers observe to learn: Differences in social behavior of toddlers and preschoolers in same-age and multiage groupings. *Young Children, 61*(3), 70–76.

Lowe Friedman, D. (2012). *Creating and presenting an early childhood education portfolio: A reflective approach.* Belmont, CA: Wadsworth Cengage Learning.

Luckenbill, J. (2012, March). Getting the picture: Using the digital camera as a tool to support reflective practice and responsive care. *Young Children, 67*(2), 28–36.

MacDonald, B. (2006, November/December). Observation—the path to documentation. *Exchange, 172,* 45–49.

Maclean, D. C. (2006). Learning to see … seeing to learn: The role of observation in early childhood development. *Child Care Exchange, 3*(6), 42.

Maione, L., & Mirenda, P. (2006). Effects of video modeling and video feedback on peer-directed social language skills of a child with autism. *Journal of Positive Behaviour Interventions, 8*(2), 106–118.

Maloch, B., & Horsey, M. (2013). Living inquiry. *The Reading Teacher, 66*(6), 475–485.

Marshall, H. (2001). Cultural influences on the development of self-concept: Updating our thinking. *Young Children, 56*(6), 19–25.

Mastrangelo, S. (2009). Harnessing the power of play: Opportunities for children with autism spectrum disorders. *Teaching Exceptional Children, 42*(1), 34–44. Retrieved from http://www.lianalowenstein.com/power_of_play.pdf

Mathers, S., Linskey, F., Seddon, J., & Sylva, K. (2007). Using quality rating scales for professional development: Experiences from the UK. *International Journal of Early Years Education, 15*(3), 261–274.

McArthur Butterfield, P., Martin, C. A., & Pratt Prairie, A. (2004). *Emotional connections: How relationships guide early learning.* Washington, DC: National Centre for Infants, Toddlers and Families.

McCain, N. M., Mustard, J. F., & McCuaig, K. (2011). *Early years study 3: Making decisions, taking action.* Toronto, ON: Margaret & Wallace McCain Family Foundation. Retrieved from http://eys3.ca/media/uploads/report-pdfs -en/i_xii_eys3_fm_2nd_ed.pdf

McCain, M. N., Mustard, J. F., & Shanker, S. (2007). *Early years study 2: Putting science into action.* Toronto, ON: Council for Early Childhood Development. Retrieved from http://www.councilecd.ca/cecd/home.nsf/7F1BCE63A330D017 852572AA00625B79/$file/Early_Years_2_rev.pdf

McCuaig, K. (2013, November 11). *Early childhood development as economic development.* Paper presented at the Third Nordic Conference, Oslo, Norway. Retrieved from http://www.oise.utoronto.ca/atkinson/UserFiles/File/ Presentations/McCuaig_Nordic_Conference_.pdf

McFarland, L., Saunders, R., & Allen, S. (2009). Reflective practice and self evaluation in learning positive guidance: Experiences of early childhood practicum students. *Early Childhood Education Journal, 26,* 505–511.

McKinlay, L., & Ross, H. (2008). *You and others: Reflective practice for group effectiveness in human services.* Toronto, ON: Pearson Education Canada.

McNaughton, K., & Drenz, C. (2007). The Construction Site Project: Transforming early childhood teacher practice. *Theory into Practice, 46*(1), 65–73.

Meeting the needs of refugee families. (2007, March 15). *SWIS News & Notes, 18.* Retrieved from http://wiki.settlementatwork.org/wiki/SWIS_News_and _Notes_Newsletter

Mills, H., & O'Keefe, T. (2010, Spring). Collaborative inquiry: From kidwatching to responsive teaching. *Association for Childhood Education International, 169,* 1–100.

Mistrett, S., & Ruffino, A. G. (2006). *Universal design for play guidelines.* Retrieved from http://letsplay.buffalo.edu/UD/UDP%20Guidelines.pdf

Mitchell, L. M. (2007). Using technology in Reggio Emilia–inspired programs. *Theory into Practice, 46*(1), 32–39.

Moore, G. T., Sugiyama, T., & O'Donnell, L. (2003). *Children's Physical Environments Rating Scale.* Sydney, Australia: Environment, Behaviour and Society Research Group, University of Sydney. Retrieved from http://sydney.edu.au/architecture/ documents/staff/garymoore/112.pdf

Moss, P. (2011, February). *Early childhood policy, provisions and practice: Critical questions about care and education.* Symposium conducted at Ryerson University, Toronto, Ontario.

Naparstek, A. J., & Dooley, D. (1997). Community building, in R. L. Edwards, ed-in-chief, *Encyclopaedia of social work* (19th ed., 1997 Suppl., pp. 77–89). Washington, DC: National Association of Social Workers/NASW Press.

National Association for the Education of Young Children. (2005). *NAEYC accreditation criteria for physical environments: Standard 9.* Retrieved from http://www.naeyc.org/torch

National Association for the Education of Young Children. (2009). *Developmentally appropriate practice in early childhood programs serving children from birth through age 8* [Position Statement]. Retrieved from http://www.naeyc.org/files/naeyc/file/positions/PSDAP.pdf

National Association for the Education of Young Children. (2014). *12 principles of child development and learning that inform practice.* Retrieved from http://www.naeyc.org/dap/12-principles-of-child-development

National Association for the Education of Young Children & National Association of Early Childhood Specialists in State Departments of Education. (2004). Where we stand on curriculum, assessment, and program evaluation. *Young Children, 59,* 51–53.

National Scientific Council on the Developing Child, Center on the Developing Child. (2004). *Young children develop in an environment of relationships* (Working Paper No. 1). Cambridge, MA: Harvard University. Retrieved from http://www.developingchild.net

National Scientific Council on the Developing Child, Center on the Developing Child. (2007). *The timing and quality of early experiences combine to shape brain architecture* (Working Paper No. 5). Cambridge, MA: Harvard University. Retrieved from http://www.developingchild.net

National Scientific Council on the Developing Child, Center on the Developing Child. (2008). *Mental health problems in early childhood can impair learning and behavior for life* (Working Paper No. 6). Cambridge, MA: Harvard University. Retrieved from http://www.developingchild.net

Nebraska Department of Education. (2005). *Nebraska early learning guidelines for ages 3 to 5: A resource to support young children's development and learning.* Lincoln: Nebraska Department of Education. Retrieved from http://www.education.ne.gov/OEC/pubs/ELG/3_5_English.pdf

New Zealand Ministry of Education. (1996). *Te Whāriki: He Whāriki Mātauranga mō ngā Mokopuna o Aotearoa. Early childhood curriculum.* Wellington, New Zealand: Learning Media Limited. Retrieved from http://www.educate.ece.govt.nz/~/media/Educate/Files/Reference%20Downloads/whariki.pdf

Niguidula, D. (2005). Documenting learning with digital portfolios. *Educational Leadership, 63*(3), 44–47.

Nilsen, B. (2014). *Week by week: Plans for documenting children's development* (6th ed.). Belmont, CA: Wadsworth Cengage Learning.

Nipissing District Developmental Screen Intellectual Property Association. (2011). *Nipissing District Developmental Screen: 18 month checklist.* North Bay, ON: Author.

Nissen, H., & Hawkins, C. J. (2010). Promoting cultural competence in the preschool classroom. *Childhood Education, 86*(4), 255–259.

O'Connor, A., & Diggins, C. (2002). *On reflection: Reflective practice for early childhood educators.* Lower Hutt, New Zealand: Open Mind.

Odom, S. L. (2003). A unified theory of practice in early intervention/early childhood special education. *Journal of Special Education, 37*(3), 164–173.

Ontario College of Teachers. (2015). *Ethical standards.* Retrieved from http://www.oct.ca/public/professional-standards/ethical-standards

Ontario Ministry of Children and Youth Services. (2010). *Reporting child abuse and neglect: It's your duty.* Retrieved from http://www.children.gov.on.ca/htdocs/English/topics/childrensaid/reportingabuse/abuseandneglect/abuseandneglect.aspx

Ontario Ministry of Children and Youth Services, Best Start Expert Panel on Early Learning. (2007, January). *Early learning for every child today: A framework for Ontario early childhood settings.* Retrieved from http://www.cfcollaborative.ca/wp-content/uploads/2010/10/ELECT.pdf

Ontario Ministry of Education. (2000). *The Individual Education Plan process.* Retrieved from http://www.edu.gov.on.ca/eng/general/elemsec/speced/individu.html

Ontario Ministry of Education. (2002). *Ontario Curriculum Unit Planner: Assessment strategies companion.* Toronto, ON: Queen's Printer for Ontario.

Ontario Ministry of Education. (2004). *The Individual Education Plan (IEP): A resource guide.* Retrieved from http://www.edu.gov.on.ca/eng/general/elemsec/speced/guide/resource/iepresguid.pdf

Ontario Ministry of Education. (2005). *Many roots, many voices: Supporting English language learners in every classroom. A practical guide for Ontario educators.* Toronto, ON: Queen's Printer for Ontario. Retrieved from http://www.edu.gov.on.ca/eng/document/manyroots/manyroots.pdf

Ontario Ministry of Education. (2006). *The revised kindergarten report.* Retrieved from http://www.edu.gov.on.ca/eng/curriculum/elementary/kindergarten.html

Ontario Ministry of Education. (2008). *Growing success: Assessment, evaluation and reporting: Improving student learning.* Toronto, ON: Queen's Printer for Ontario.

Retrieved from https://faculty.nipissingu.ca/douglasg/EDUC4315/Resources/GrowingSuccessAssessmentevaluationandreportingimprovingstudentlearning.pdf

Ontario Ministry of Education. (2010–2011). *The Full-Day Early Learning–Kindergarten Program draft version.* Retrieved from http://www.edu.gov.on.ca/eng/curriculum/elementary/kindergarten_english_june3.pdf

Ontario Ministry of Education. (2012, October). Pedagogical documentation: Leading learning in the early years and beyond. *Capacity Building Series K–2. Secretariat Special Edition, 30,* 1–8.

Ontario Ministry of Education. (2013). *Think, Feel, Act: Lessons from Research about Young Children.* Retrieved from http://www.edu.gov.on.ca/childcare/document.html

Ontario Ministry of Education. (2014). *How does learning happen? Ontario's pedagogy for the early years.* Retrieved from http://www.edu.gov.on.ca/childcare/HowLearningHappens.pdf

Ontario Ministry of Education. (2015). *An introduction to special education in Ontario.* Retrieved from http://www.edu.gov.on.ca/eng/general/elemsec/speced/ontario.html

Paige-Smith, A., & Craft, A. (Eds.). (2007). *Developing reflective practice in the early years.* Berkshire, England: Open University Press, McGraw-Hill.

Pan-Canadian Public Health Network. (2013). *Towards a healthier Canada—2013 progress report advancing the federal/provincial/territorial framework on healthy weights.* Retrieved from http://www.phn-rsp.ca/thcpr-vcpsre-2013/index-eng.php

Pascal, C. E. (n.d.). *Every child every opportunity: Curriculum and pedagogy for the early learning program. A compendium report to "With our best future in mind: Implementing early learning in Ontario."* Retrieved from http://www.pcfk.on.ca/PDFs/Research_Ken/Every%20Child%20Every%20Opportunity.pdf

Pascal, C. E. (2009). *With our best future in mind: Implementing early learning in Ontario. Report to the Premier by the Special Advisor on Early Learning, Canadian Council on Learning.* Retrieved from http://www.opha.on.ca/our_voice/consultations/docs/PascalReport-recommendations-27Jan10.pdf

Pearson, R. (2006). Respecting culture in our schools and classrooms. *Child & Family, 9*(2), 37.

Pelo, A. (2006, November/December). Growing a culture of inquiry: Observation as professional development. *Child Care Exchange, 172,* 50–53.

Pence, A. (2006). Seeking the other 99 languages of ECE: A keynote address by Alan Pence. *Interaction, 20*(3), 28–29.

Perry, B., Dockett, S., & Harley, E. (2007). Learning stories and children's powerful mathematics. *Early Childhood Research and Practice, 9*(7). Retrieved from http://ecrp.uiuc.edu/v9n2/perry.html

Pimento, B., & Kernested, D. (2010). *Healthy foundations in early childhood settings* (4th ed.). Toronto, ON: Nelson Education.

Pimento, B., & Kernested, D. (2014). *Healthy foundations in early childhood settings* (5th ed.). Toronto, ON: Nelson Education.

Public Health Agency of Canada. (2012). *Childhood and adolescence.* Retrieved from http://www.phac-aspc.gc.ca/dca-dea/allchildren_touslesenfants/rights -index-eng.php

Puckett, M., & Black, J. (2000). *Authentic assessment of the young child: Celebrating development and learning* (2nd ed.). Upper Saddle River, NJ: Merrill.

Reading, S., & Richie, C. (2007). Documenting changes in communication behaviours using a structured observation system. *Child Language Teaching and Therapy, 23*(2), 181–200.

Reeves, S., Goldman, J., & Oandasan, I. (2007). Key factors in planning and implementing interprofessional education in health care settings. *Journal of Allied Health, 36*(4), 231–235.

Rivkin, M. S. (1995). *The great outdoors: Restoring children's right to play outside.* Washington, DC: National Association for the Education of Young Children.

Roper, L. (2002, Summer). Relationships: The critical ties that bind professionals. *New Directions for Student Services, 98*, 11–26.

Rourke, L., Rourke, J., & Leduc, D. (2009, August). *Rourke Baby Record: Evidence-based infant/child health maintenance.* Retrieved from http://www .rourkebabyrecord.ca

Rowan, C. (2011). *Exploring the possibilities of learning stories as a meaningful approach to early childhood education in Nunavik* (Master's thesis). University of Victoria, BC. Retrieved from https://dspace.library.uvic.ca/bitstream/ handle/1828/3483/Rowan_Marycaroline_2011-1.pdf?sequence=1

Ryan, K. (2006). Learning stories. *JIGSAW, 41,* 25–26.

Ryan, S., & Grieshaber, S. (2004). It's more than child development: Critical theories, research, and teaching young children. *Young Children, 59*(6), 44–52.

Salend, S. J. (2008). *Creating inclusive classrooms: Effective and reflective practices* (6th ed.). Columbus, OH: Merrill/Prentice Hall.

Salend, S. J. (2009). Technology-based classroom assessments: Alternatives to testing. *Teaching Exceptional Children, 41*(6), 49–58.

Sansosti, F. J. (2009). Teaching social behavior to children with autism spectrum disorders using social stories: Implications for school-based practice. *Best of the Journal of Speech-Language Pathology & Applied Behavior Analysis, 4,*170–179.

Salazar, S., & Palkhivala, A. (2009, January). The Nurse-Family Partnership Pilot Study in Canada. *Early Childhood Learning Knowledge Centre Bulletin on Program Evaluation, 4*(1), 3–4.

Schön, D. A. (1983). *The reflective practitioner: How professionals think in action.* New York: Basic Books.

Schuster, D., & Leland, C. (2008). Considering context: Encouraging students to consider the content of an observation can invite further inquiry. *Science and Children, 45*(6), 22–24.

Sciarra, J., & Dorsey, A. (2002). *Leaders and supervisors in child care programs.* Belmont, CA: Wadsworth Cengage Learning.

Seitz, H. (2008, March). The power of documentation in the early childhood classroom. *Young Children, 63*(2), 88–93.

Seitz, H., & Bartholomew C. (2008). Powerful portfolios for young children. *Early Childhood Education Journal, 36,* 63–68.

Services and Supports to Promote the Social Inclusion of Persons with Developmental Disabilities Act, 2008, S.O. 2008, c. 14.

Shackell, A., Butler, N., Doyle, P., & Ball, D. (2008). *Design for Play: A guide to creating successful play spaces.* Retrieved from http://www.playengland.org.uk/resources/design-for-play

Sheridan, S. M. (2004, September). *Family-school partnerships: Creating essential connections for student success.* Keynote presented at the Resource Teacher: Learning and Behaviour Conference, Christchurch, New Zealand. Retrieved from http://digitalcommons.unl.edu/cgi/viewcontent.cgi?article=1017&context=cyfsposters

Shriver, C. (2014, Winter). E-portfolios. *Independent School, 73*(2), 70.

Skouge, J. R., Kelly, M., Roberts, K. D., Leade, D. W., & Stodden, R. A. (2007). Technologies for self-determination for youth with developmental disabilities. *Education and Training in Developmental Disabilities, 42,* 475–482.

Snow, K. (2010). *People first language.* Retrieved from http://www.disabilityisnatural.com

Sosna, T., & Mastergeorge, A. (2005, December). *The Infant, Preschool, Family Mental Health Initiative: Compendium of screening tools for early childhood social-emotional development.* Retrieved from http://www.cibhs.org/sites/main/

files/file-attachments/the_infant_preschool_family_mental_health_initiative
_compendium_of_screening_tools_for_early_childhood_social-emotional
_deve.pdf

Sugiyama, T., & Moore, G. T. (2005). Content and construct validity of the Early
Childhood Physical Environment Rating Scale (ECPERS). In *Proceedings of
the 36th Annual Conference of the Environmental Design Research Association*.
Retrieved from http://sydney.edu.au/architecture/documents/ebs/EDRA_2005
_pub_paper.pdf

Tarr, P. (2011). Reflections and shadows. *Canadian Children, 36*(2), 11–16.

Teaford, P., Wheat, J., & Baker, T. (2010). *Checklist items from HELP®: 3-6*. Palo Alto,
CA: VORT Corporation.

Thompson, J. R., Meadan, H., Fansler, K. W., Alber, S. B., & Balogh, P. A. (2007).
Family assessment portfolios: A new way to jumpstart family/school collaboration. *Teaching Exceptional Children, 39*(6), 19–25.

Tingstrom, D. H., Wilczynski, S. M., & Scattone, D. (2006). Increasing
appropriate social interactions of children with autism spectrum disorders
using social stories. *Focus on Autism & Other Developmental Disabilities,
21*(4), 211–222.

Toomey, J., & Adams, L. A. (1995, Fall). The naturalistic observation of children with
autism: Evidence for intersubjectivity. *New Directions for Child and Adolescent
Development, 1995*(69), 75–89.

Toronto Children's Services. (2014). *Early learning and care assessment for quality
improvement*. Retrieved from http://www1.toronto.ca/City%20Of%20Toronto/
Children's%20Services/Files/pdf/O/Operating%20criteria/oc_introduction.pdf

Toronto Preschool Speech & Language Services. (n.d.). *Communication
Checklist*. Retrieved from http://www1.toronto.ca/wps/portal/
contentonly?vgnextoid=7c4c45d26137a410VgnVCM10000071d60f89RCRD

Toronto Public Health. (n.d.). *Early identification in Toronto: Toronto red flags guide.
A reference guide for working with young children*. Toronto, ON: Author.

Turner, T., & Gray Wilson, D. (2010). Reflections on documentation: A discussion
with thought leaders from Reggio Emilia. *Theory into Practice, 49*(1), 5–13.

Underwood, K., & Langford, R. (2011). *Children with special educational needs
in early childhood*. Toronto, ON: Atkinson Centre for Society and Child
Development, OISE/University of Toronto.

United Nations General Assembly. (1989, November). *The United Nations
Convention on the Rights of the Child*. Retrieved from http://www.unicef.org/
crc/files/Rights_overview.pdf

Universal Design for Play Project, University at Buffalo. (2005). *Universal Design for Play Tool*. Retrieved from http://letsplay.buffalo.edu/UD/FINAL%20final%20 Tool%207.pdf

Valentino, L. (2004). *Handle with care* (3rd ed.). Toronto, ON: Thomson Nelson.

VanderVen, K. (2000). New perspectives on theory-to-practice: Implications for transforming teacher education and child outcomes. In *Issues in early childhood education: Curriculum, teacher education, and dissemination of information. Proceedings of the Lilian Katz Symposium.* Champaign, IL, November 5–7, 2000. Retrieved from http://ceep.crc.uiuc.edu/pubs/katzsym/vanderven.pdf

Velez Laski, E. (2013, July). Portfolio picks: An approach for developing children's metacognition. *Young Children, 68*(3), 38–43. Retrieved from http://www .bclearninglab.bc.edu/downloads/Laski_YC2013.pdf

Warash, B, Curtis, R., Hursh, D., & Tucci, V. (2008). Skinner meets Piaget on the Reggio playground: Practical synthesis of applied behaviour analysis and developmentally appropriate practice orientations. *Journal of Research in Childhood Education, 22*(4), 441–453.

Webster, M., Belanger, J., & Conant F. (2002). You can't draw on air: Stretches and sketches. *Canadian Children, 27*(2), 4–11.

Wein, C. A. (2013). *Making learning visible through pedagogical documentation.* Toronto, ON: Queen's Printer for Ontario. Retrieved from http://www.edu.gov .on.ca/childcare/Wien.pdf

Wellhousen, K., & Giles, R. M. (2005/2006). Building literacy opportunities into children's block play: What every teacher should know. *Childhood Education, 82*(2), 75.

Wesley, P. W., Buysse, V., & Skinner, D. (2001). Early interventionists' perspectives on professional comfort as consultants. *Journal of Early Intervention, 24*(2), 112–128.

Wiggins, G. (2006). *Healthier testing made easy: The idea of authentic assessment: Tests don't just measure absorption of facts. They teach what we value.* Retrieved from http://www.edutopia.org/healthier-testing-made-easy

Wilde, D. (2010). Personalities into teams. *Mechanical Engineering, 132*(2), 22–25.

Williams, S. T. (2008, October). *Mental health screening and assessment tools for children.* Retrieved from http://humanservices.ucdavis.edu/academy/pdf/ final2mentalhealthlitreview.pdf

Wilson, K. (2006). To speak, participate and decide: The child's right to be heard. *Interaction, 20*(3), 30–33.

Wilson, L. (2014). *Partnerships: Families and communities in early childhood.* Toronto, ON: Nelson.

Winter, S. (1999). *The Early Childhood Inclusion Model: A program for all children.* Olney, MD: Association for Childhood Education International.

Wong, D., & Waniganayake, M. (2013). Mentoring as a leadership development strategy in early childhood education. In E. Hujala, M. Waniganayake, & J. Rodd (Eds.), *Researching leadership in early childhood education* (pp. 163–180). Tampere, Finland: Tampere University Press.

Wozniak, N. M. (2012). Enhancing inquiry, evidence-based reflection, and integrative learning with the lifelong eportfolio process: The implementation of integrative eportfolios at Stony Brook University. *Journal of Educational Technology Systems, 41*(3), 209–230. doi:10.2190/ET.41.3.b

Wright, R. J. (2010). *Multifaceted assessment for early childhood education.* Thousand Oaks, CA: Sage.

Yates, T., Ostrosky, M. M., Cheatham, G. A., Fettig, A., LaShorage Shaffer, & Milagros Santos, R. (2008). *Research synthesis on screening and assessing social-emotional competence.* Retrieved from http://csefel.vanderbilt.edu/documents/rs_screening_assessment.pdf

Yu, G.S. (2008). Documentation: Ideas and applications from the Reggio Emilia approach. *Teaching Artist Journal, 6*(2), 126–134.

Zachary, L. (2009). Make mentoring work for you: Ten strategies for success. *T+D Magazine, 63*(12), 76–77.

Zhang, M., Lundeberg, M., & Eberhardt, J. (2010). Seeing what you normally don't see. *Phi Delta Kappan, 91*(6), 60–66.

Zuniga, R., & Fischer, J. M. (2010). Emotional intelligence and attitudes toward people with disabilities: A comparison between two cultures. *Journal of Applied Rehabilitation Counseling, 31*(1), 12–18.

INDEX

Note: **Bold** page numbers
indicate glossary terms.

A

ABC analysis, 137, **155**–161
adapting, 158–159
and behaviourists, 156
and curriculum develop-
ment, 159–161
format, 157–158
purpose, 155
unique feature, 155–156
Abecedarian study, 365–366
abscissas, **212**
acceptance, of diversity, 21
accessibility issues, 278, 301,
340, 342–343, 350–351
accommodate, **121**
accommodations, **325**
action research, **315**
adaptations
of ABC analysis, 158–159
of anecdotal records,
146–149
of behaviour tallying and
charting, 214
of checklists, 203–204
of communication in early
childhood, 98–99
environmental, 13
observation in making, 13,
64, 328
of participation charts,
217–219
of profiles, 222–226
of rating scales, 207
video recordings, 175

adjectives, 100
adverbs, 100
advocate role, **22, 248**
affective environment, **331**
Affiliated Services for
Children Youth
(Hamilton Ontario), 291
Ages and Stages
Questionnaires, 32–33,
201–202, 323
Alberta Education, 284, 327
analogue, **156**
anecdotal records, 137,
138–151. *See also*
ABC analysis; running
records
adapting, 146–149
format, 139–142, 147
interpretations, 141,
142–146
perceptions and cultural
inferences, 147, 149–151
purpose, 138–139
unique feature, 138–139
antecedents, **155**
ABC analysis, 155–156, 160
behaviourism, 156
appreciative inquiry, **6,** 239–241
anecdotal records, 139,
147–148
behaviour tallying and
charting, 209–210
of directors and
supervisors, 73, 74
early intervention/early
identification,
288–291, 296

observation and, 5–8,
32–33, 57–58, 74, 81–82,
242–246
observer as pedagogical
leader, 357–360
pedagogical framework,
240–241
process, 239–241
and reflection, 255–258
of responsive, inclusive
educators, 14–16, 34
rights of the child, 75–76,
81–82
Arnett Caregiver Interaction
Scale, 348
artifacts, **33,** 263, 272
Ashton, J., 17–18
assessment
administration, 322
authentic, 267, 271–278,
315–316
criterion-referenced, 319
developmental, 300
diagnostic, 294, 318, 322–323
early intervention/early
identification, 294, 300,
315–332
environmental, 345–354
functional, 294, 318, 324
psychoeducational, 300
screening, 294, 318,
319–323
sociocultural approaches,
316–317
standardized, 267,
317–318, 319
three stages, 294, 318–324

assessment portfolios, **275**

Association of Early Childhood Educators of Ontario (AECEO), **361**–362

at-a-glance records, **155**

Atkinson, K., 146

attachment, 50

audio/digital recordings, 95, 137, **169**–172

    format, 170–171

    and portfolios of children, 172

    purpose, 170

    unique feature, 170

aural world, **169**

authentic assessment, **267**, 271–278, **315**–316

autism, 207, **313**

B

Baird, L., 357

"Band-Aid" approach to learning, 291

Barankin, T., 339

Battelle Developmental Inventory, 323

Beach, Jane, 352–354

Beaty, J., 12

behaviourists, 39–40, 156

behaviours, **155**

    ABC analysis, 155–156, 160

    changes in, 27–28

    defining in pedagogical documentation, 110–111, 113–114

    designing an observational tool, 194–195

domains of child development, 30–32, 118–121

    duration, 193–194

    frequency, 193–194

    observing, 69–70

    specific learning experience or event (closed recording). *See* closed methods (recording)

    unanticipated (open recording). *See* open methods (recording)

    variables affecting, 116–118

behaviour tallying and charting, **209**–214

    adapting, 214

    conventional graphs, 212–213

    format, 210–212

    interpreting information, 213–214

    purpose, 209

    textbook/internet examples, 213

    unique feature, 209–210

Belanger, Jessica, 58, 59

belonging, 20–21, 28

Belonging, Being, and Becoming (Australian Department of Education), 50, 109, 346

Bertrand, J., 36

best practices, **38**

bias, 89, 124–130

    areas of, 126–127

    awareness of, 124–127, 129–130, 151

    cultural, 129

    defined, **127**

    forms of, 127–128

    perceptions and, 129–130

Binet, Alfred, 317–318

blogs, 367–368

Boardmaker system, **228, 341**

Boardman, Margot, 164

Bowne, M., 260

Brigance Infant and Toddler Screen, 323

British Columbia Early Learning Framework, 53–54, 59, 60, 347

Bronfenbrenner, Urie, 236

Browne, Kathryn Williams, 49, 63

Bruner, Jerome, 17–18

Bullard, J., 174

C

Cameron, Ruth, 306

Canadian Child Care Federation (CCCF), 76, 77, 78–79

Canadian Council on Learning, 41

Canadian Language and Literacy Research Network, 102, 103

CanChild Centre for Disability Research (McMaster University), 308, 310

capacity building, 64–65, **354**–363

Capone, A., 18

Carolina Curriculum for Infants and Toddlers with Special Needs (CCITSN), 323

Carr, Margaret, 37, 179, 185

Cartwright, C. A., 110, 111

Cartwright, P. G., 110, 111

Catapano, S., 46

caveat, **32,** 255

central tendency error, **127**–128

characteristics

  labels and, 114–116

  in pedagogical documentation, 113–116

checklists, **195**–205

  adapting, 203–204

  with anecdotal section, 149

  commercial examples, 201–203

  design considerations, 200–201

  developmental sequence of skills, 198–199

  format, 196–198

  interpreting information, 204–205

  knowledge of children within group, 199–200

  purpose, 195

  reflecting upon information, 204–205

  unique feature, 195

child abuse reporting, 302–304

Child Care and Early Years Act, 362

Child Care Modernization Act, **362**

child-centred environment, **336**–337, 340

child development. *See also* early intervention/early identification

  areas of, 30, 31

domains of, 30–32, 118–121

ecological approach, 221, 236

frameworks, 16, 17–18, 20, 26–33, 38, 53–54, 283–284, 296

framing observations about, 26–33, 45

norms and developmental guidelines, 32–33, 198–199

observing growth and development of children, 9

play in early learning cycle, 53–54

portfolios, 267

principles of, 28–30

profiles, 222, 223–224, 228

rates of, 32

rating scales, 207

socioemotional development, 31, 120, 173–178, 296, 335–339

Childhood Autism Rating Scale (CARS2), 207

Child-Parent Centers (Chicago), 365–366

children

  communication by, 46, 111

  expectations for, 13

  immigrant, 21–22

  methods for observing, 66–68

  in problem solving process, 73

  rights of, 75–76, 81–82

  roles in portfolio development, 268–270

with special needs. *See* children with special needs

  views of, 76

  well-being, safety, and health, 62–63, 302–312

Children's Aid Society, 302–304

children with special needs. *See also* early intervention/early identification

  accessibility issues, 278, 301, 340, 342–343, 350–351

  checklists, 201–202

  person-first approach, 116

  photographs, 165

  special needs as concept, 288, 312–313

  total communication, 165

  video recordings, 177–178

child-sensitive approach, **16**

Child Study Movement, 40

Choiceworks, 341

Classroom Assessment Scoring System for Infants/Toddlers/ Pre-K/K-3, 348

classroom environment, 339–342

Clifford, Richard M., 207

Clinton, Jean, 336–337

closed methods (recording), 134, 189–234

  behaviour tallying and charting, 209–214

  checklists, 195–205

  defined, **191**

  making decisions, 192–195

  mapping, 50, 232–234

  participation charts, 190, 215–220

closed methods (recording)
(*Continued*)
    pictorial representations,
       227–229
    profiles, 185, 220–227
    rating scales, 205–209
    sociograms, 50, 229–232
Code of Ethics, 76–79
    CECE Code of Ethics and
       Standards of Practice, 78
coding scheme, **197**
cognition, 31, **119**–120
    portfolios in supporting
       metacognition, 280–282
co-inquiry, in cycle of obser-
    vation, 248, 250–251
collaboration
    in cycle of observation, 248,
       250–251
    in early intervention/early
       identification programs,
       291, 293–296, 300,
       313–315
    in environmental
       assessment, 352–354
    of families and educators,
       16–22, 27–28
    interprofessional, 355–357
    in pedagogical leadership,
       357–360
    roles in portfolio
       development, 268–270,
       276–277
College of Early Childhood
    Educators (CECE,
    Ontario), 77, 78, 292,
    352, 361–362
communication. *See also*
    cultural and
    linguistic diversity

adapting in early childhood,
    98–99
children with special
    needs, 165
in family-centred approach,
    307–312
nonverbal, 46, 111, 224,
    226, 228, 311–312
observation combined
    with, 24, 74
in pedagogical
    documentation process,
    93, 98–99, 101
sharing information with
    colleagues, 74
sharing information with
    parents, 19, 25, 307–312
speech and language
    development, 31, 120,
    283–284
video recordings, 172–179
by young children,
    46, 111
community building, 64–65,
    354–363
cycle of observation as,
    246–247
in early intervention/early
    identification
    programs, 291
interprofessional collabora-
    tion, 355–357
observer as lifelong learner,
    361–363
observer as mentor,
    360–361
observer as pedagogical
    leader, 357–360
observer as researcher,
    364–365

in pedagogical documenta-
    tion, 90–91, 93–98
social capital, 354–355
Community Living
    Toronto, 341
computer technology
    electronic communication
       methods, 358–359
    e-portfolios/digital
       portfolios, 176, 186,
       275–280, 363–370
    pedagogical documentation
       trends, 366–370
    voice-to-text software, 171,
       278–280
Conant, Faith, 58, 59
conditioning, 40, 156
confidentiality, 83, 85
ConnectABILITY, **341**
consent, 83–86, 166–167
consequences, **155**
    ABC analysis, 155–156, 160
    behaviourism, 156
constructivist frameworks, 16,
    17–18, 20, 38, **296**
contextual information, **141**
    in appreciative inquiry, 7–8
    for checklists, 199–200
    in environmental
       assessment, 354
continuum, **205**
contrived observations, **146**
Convention on the Rights
    of the Child (United
    Nations), 75–76, 81–82
Coughlin, A. M., 357
Craft, Anna, 249
criterion-referenced
    assessment tools, **319**
Cryer, Debby, 207

cultural and linguistic diversity, 18, 19–22, 32–33, 103, 106–108, 147, 149–151, 229, 283–284, 316–317, 337–338

cultural bias, **129**

cultural inferences, in anecdotal records, 147, 149–151

culturally responsive, **129**

cultural sensitivity, 150

curriculum, 36

ABC analysis and development of, 159–161

play-based, 7, 288, 340

video captures, 175

Cutler, K., 260

cycle of observation, 36, **49**–61, 242–258. *See also* pedagogical documentation; portfolios

anecdotal records, 139

appreciative inquiry approach, 57–58

co-inquiry, 248, 250–251

collaboration, 248, 250–251

as community building, 246–247

community response, 248

components, 51, 52

early intervention/early identification, 288–291

guiding words, 55–56

holistic approach, 41, 50–51

as interactive process, 54–59

key words, 55

mutual education, 251–253

overview, 52

pedagogical questions, 58–59, 60

questions of self-reflection, 59–61

reflection, 51, 56, 195

reflective educator role, 253–258

as transformational process, 249

variations, 52–54, 242–246

cycle of planning, 52–53

D

Dahlberg, G., 235–236

DeBates, D., 260

descriptors, **97**–98, 99–101, 125, 192–193

development. *See* child development

developmental assessments, **300**

developmental pediatricians, **324**–325

developmental portfolio. *See* working/developmental portfolios

Dewey, John, 40, 250

dexterity, **30**

diagnostic assessment, **294**, 318, 322–323

Diagnostic Inventory for Screening Children (DISC)/DPS, 323

dialogue

cycle of observation as transformational process, 249

between home and school, 17–18

recording in pedagogical documentation, 95

diaries, 155

video, 41

didactic approach, **242**

Diigo Group, 367–368

directors and supervisors

in observation process, 73, 74

roles in portfolio development, 270–271

direct quotations, **95**

disability. *See* children with special needs; early intervention/early identification

disequilibrium, **15**

display or showcase portfolios, **272,** 273–274

diversity, **1**

cultural and linguistic, 18, 19–22, 32–33, 103, 106–108, 147, 149–151, 229, 283–284, 316–317, 337–338

cultural inferences in anecdotal records, 147, 149–151

cultural sensitivity, 150

of developmental guidelines, 32–33

family, 18–22

respecting, 21

of skills, 32, 33

documentation
  of child development,
    31–32
  of children at play, 22–26
  ethical and legal issues,
    83–85
  fundamental questions,
    57–70
  office files, 85
  pedagogical. *See* pedagog-
    ical documentation
  process of, 14
  recording methods, 63–64
  roles and forms, 58, 59.
    See also closed methods
    (recording); open
    methods (recording)
  value of, 14
  as visible listening, 49
documentation panels, **166**
domains of child develop-
    ment, **30**–32, 118–121
Draft National Quality
    Standard Assessment
    and Rating Instrument
    (Australia), 349
Dragon Naturally Speaking
    software, 171
Dufour, M., 367–368
duration, **193**–194

E

Early Childhood Environment
    Rating Scale, 348
early childhood professionals,
    5–6
  as advocates for children,
    21–22, 248
  appreciative inquiry, 6–8

e-portfolios, 363–370
family diversity, 18–22
image of the child, 5–6
inclusive, 14–16, 34
interprofessional
    collaboration, 355–357
interprofessional education,
    301–302
observation by. *See*
    observation
occupational standards, 64,
    65, 282–284
partnership with families,
    16–22, 27–28
professional development,
    63, 301–302, 361–365
reflective educators, 253–258
resource educators/
    early interventionists/
    resource professionals,
    299–302
responsive, 14–16, 34,
    335–339
role in portfolio
    creation, 268
role of observation, 45
self-reflection, 59–61, 63,
    253–258
shared responsibility for
    pedagogical documenta-
    tion, 90–91
sharing information with
    parents, 19, 25,
    307–312
specialists, 324–325
video recordings of,
    174–175
Early Development
    Instrument (EDI),
    323, 353

early intervention/early
    identification,
    287–332. *See also*
    children with special
    needs
  appreciative inquiry,
    288–291, 296
  assessment, 294, 300,
    315–332
  child abuse reporting,
    302–304
  collaborative approach,
    291, 293–296, 300,
    313–315
  cycle of observation,
    288–291
  defined, **288, 293**
  early intervention as
    system, 297–299
  family-centred approach,
    304–312
  individualized
    plans, 279, 298,
    325–326, 327
  interprofessional education,
    301–302
  nature of, 293
  observation in supporting,
    10, 288–302
  process description,
    293–296
  resource professional role,
    299–302
  special needs as concept,
    288, 312–313
  theories underpinning, 296
early interventionist. *See*
    resource educator/early
    interventionist/resource
    professionals

Early Learning and Care Assessment for Quality Improvement (Toronto Children's Services), 348, 351–353

Early Learning for Every Child Today (ELECT), 28–29, 256–257, 346–347, 362

Early Years Framework (Australia), 337

eclectic approach, **38**

ecological approach, **221,** 236

ecomaps, 50, 230–232

Educa, 186

educators. *See* early childhood professionals

Educause Learning Initiative, 368

emergent/emergent curriculum, **7**

Emergent framework, 179–180

emotional intelligence, **39**

emotions
    affective environment, 331
    observing, 13
    socioemotional development, 31, 120, 173–178, 296, 335–339

environment, **335**–354.
    See also environmental assessment
    checklists, 197–198, 200
    early childhood frameworks, 20, 296, 337–338, 345–347
    inclusive, 14–16
    observing, 13, 64

in pedagogical documentation, 117–118
    physical, 339–345
    responsive relationships, **14**–16, 34, 335–339
    socioemotional/psychological, 335–339
    video recordings, 175

environmental assessment, 345–354
    early childhood frameworks, 345–347
    pedagogy and context, 354
    stakeholder contributions, 348, 349–354
    tools and measures, 347–349

e-portfolios, 186, **275**–280
    accessibility issues, 278
    design and considerations, 275–276, 364
    of early childhood education professionals, 363–370
    e-portfolio websites, 275–276, 364
    school-wide, 281
    video recordings, 176
    voice-to-text software, 171, 278–280

equipment. *See also* computer technology; technology
    observing use of, 11

ethics
    bias, 124–130
    code of ethics and standards of practice, 76–79
    confidentiality, 83, 85
    consent, 83–86, 166–167

observation process, 57–58, 75–76, 79–82
    pedagogical documentation, 80, 82–83, 94
    of photo documentation, 166, 168–169
    rights of children, 75–76, 81–82
    of social media, 168

ethnographic research, **41,** 365–366

evaluation, **124,** 328–332
    anecdotal interpretations, 146
    formative, 329–330
    summative, 206, 331–332

everyday events, as challenge to observation, 72

expanded observation, **145**–146

expectancy or logical error, **128**

F

families. *See also* family-centred approach
    ABC analysis model, 156
    confidentiality issues, 83, 85
    consent issues, 83–86, 166–167
    in discovery process, 12
    diversity of, 18–22
    in early intervention/early identification programs, 294–296
    e-portfolios, 276–277
    in holistic approach, 50–51

families (*Continued*)
   parent and family literacy
      teams, 250–251
   partnership with educators,
      16–22, 27–28
   in problem solving
      process, 73
   roles in portfolio develop-
      ment, 268–270,
      276–277
   sharing information with
      parents, 19, 25, 307–312
   video recordings, 176
family-centred approach, 17,
   304–312
   checklist for service pro-
      viders, 309–310
   decision-making role of
      parents, 325
   personal and sensitive infor-
      mation, 307–310, 311
   relationship-building, 307
   timing of communication,
      310–312
   transition issues, 305–307
Family Child Care
   Environment Rating
   Scale, 348
family support plans, **300**
family tree, **229**
Ferguson, Elaine, 329, 331
Filippini, Tiziana, 11–12
fine motor development, 30,
   31, 119
fixed standard, **319**
For Goodness Sake
   Program, 291
formal settings, **40**–41
Forman, George, 174, 175, 252
formative evaluation, **329**–330

France, 317–318
Fraser, S., 6, 13
frequency, **193**–194
Freud, Sigmund, 40
Friendly, Martha, 21, 352–354
Froebel, Friedrich, 22–23
functional assessment, **294,**
   318, 324

G

Gambetti, Amilia, 16
Gardner, Howard, 39
generic nature of
      observation, **38**
Gesell, Arnold, 32, 40
Gestwicki, Carol, 36, 52–53
Gilkerson, D., 260
goals, **325**
Goleman, Daniel, 39
Gonzalez Mena, Janet, 24, 45,
   124, 129, 251–252
Good, Linda, 162–163
Gordon, Ann Miles, 49, 63
Gosse, Heather Sample, 103
Gotzke, Carrie, 103
Gray Wilson, D., 11–12, 137
gross motor development,
   31, 119
groups
   checklists, 199–200
   new children in, 47–48,
      49, 68
   observing, 10–11, 25–26
   running records, 153–154
Growing Success (Ontario
   Ministry of
   Education), 330
guardians. *See* families;
   family-centred approach

guides, **31**–32
Guralnick, Michael J., 299

H

Hall, N. S., 126
Harms, Thelma, 207
Hawaii Early Learning
   Profile, 202
health of children, 62–63,
   302–312
Heckman, James, 365
High/Scope, **38**
holistic approach, **41,** 50–51
Horsey, M., 14
How Does Learning Happen?
   (Ontario Ministry of
   Education), 20, 28–29,
   280, 282, 283, 346
Hughes, E., 60–61

I

Identification, Placement,
   and Review Committee
   (IPRC), **298**
identity, observation and,
   80–82
IEPs (Individual Education
   Plans), 279, 298,
   325–326, 327
IFSPs (Individual Family
   Support Plans), **326**
immigrant children, 21–22
incidence, **322**
inclusion, **14**–16
inclusive educators,
   14–16, 34
Individual Education Plans
   (IEPs), 279, 298,
   325–326, 327

Individual Family Support Plans (IFSPs), **326**

Individual Program Plans (IPPs), **325**–327

Individual Training/Teaching Plans (ITPs), **325**

Infant Toddler Early Childhood Environment Rating Scale, 348

Infant Toddler Sensory Profile, 323

inference, 113–116, 118, **124**
   in anecdotal records, 147, 149–151

informal settings, **41**

inquiry-based process
   in inclusive/responsive approach, 15–16
   pedagogical documentation in, 36–37
   students as inquirers, 14

Instagram, 370

interactive process
   cycle of observation as, 54–59
   observing interactions, 10

internal conditions, in pedagogical documentation, 112–113, 114

interpretations, **121**
   of anecdotal records, 141, 142–146
   of behaviour tallying and charting, 213–214
   of checklists, 204–205
   nature of, 121–122
   of participation charts, 219–220
   of rating scales, 208–209
   variations within, 123–124
   writing, 122–123

interprofessional education, **301**–302, 355–357

interrater reliability, **128**

intervention, early. *See* early intervention/early identification

interview, **232**

intrinsic process, **23**

introspection, 39–**40**

IPPs (Individual Program Plans), **325**–327

IPRC (Identification, Placement, and Review Committee), **298**

Ireton, Harold, 6

Itard, Jean-Marc-Gaspard, 39, 138

ITPs (Individual Training/ Teaching Plans), **325**

J

Janus, Magdalena, 306

Jupp, Louise, 181, 358, 360

K

Kagan, Jerome, 39

Karsten, Lisa, 353–354

Kashin, Diane, 181, 358, 360

Katz, Lilian G., 41, 253

Kennedy, A., 17

Kernested, D., 62, 64–65, 356

key feature, **139**

Khanlou, N., 339

Kinderloop, 186

Kopechanski, Lauren, 306

L

labelling, **115**

labels, 114–116

Langford, R., 306

language. *See* communication; cultural and linguistic diversity; speech and language development

Lansdown, G., 76

learning communities, 347–348

learning stories, 110, 137, **179**–186
   format, 182–186
   nature of, 179–180
   objectivity, 184–185
   purpose, 180–181
   technology-enabled, 185–186
   unique feature, 181–182

learning styles, 39, 328

Lee, W., 37, 179, 185

Lefort, Jessica, 306

leniency error, **127**

levels of observation, 44–46
   personal, 44–45
   professional, 45–46

Lewin-Benham, A., 331–332

Lindgren, A.-L., 169, 177

listening, in observation process, 48–49

Livescribe pen, **171**

location of observation, 69

logical error, **128**

longitudinal studies, **41, 365**–366

loose parts, **343**–345

Luckenbill, J., 163

M

Maloch, B., 14

Many Roots/Many Voices (Ontario Ministry of Education), 284

Maori, 179–180

mapping, 50, **232**–234

Maslow, Abraham, 336

materials

observing use of, 11

pedagogical documentation, 91, 92, 94–95

mentorship, 360–361

microcosm, **18**

Miller, Melinda, 256

MindTap, 151, 169, 232, 234

misperception, as challenge to observation, 72

modifications, **325**

monitor, **10**

monitoring, **330**

Montessori school, **38**

Moss, Peter, 57–58, 235–236

multifaceted observation, **75**

multiple intelligences, 39

mutual education, in cycle of observation, 251–253

N

narrative, **89, 151**. *See also* running records

National Association for the Education of Young Children (NAEYC), 29, 30, 327, 348

National Scientific Council on the Developing Child, 337

natural design, **343**–345

natural observations, **146**–147

NDDS (Nipissing District Developmental Screen), 201–202, 319, 320–321, 323

Neisworth, J. T., 18

New Zealand

learning stories, 37, 179, 185, 186

Te Whāriki, 30, 179–180, 316, 317, 337, 345–346

Nipissing District Developmental Screen (NDDS), 201–202, 319, 320–321, 323

nonverbal communication, 46, 111, 224, 226, 228, 311–312

norms, **32**–33

nouns, 100

Nurse-Family Partnership (NFP) Pilot Study, 366

O

objectives, **325**

objectivity, in learning stories, 184–185

observation, 33–39. *See also* appreciative inquiry; documentation; pedagogical documentation

audio/digital recordings, 169–170

behaviours, 69–70

benefits of, 73

biases in, 2, 89, 124–130

challenges to effective, 70–75

of children, 22–26, 50, 66–68

cycle of. *See* cycle of observation

defined, 98

in different philosophies, 38–39

in early intervention/early identification programs, 291–302

ethical issues, 57–58, 75–76, 79–82

expanded, 145–146

as feedback to children, 24–25

framing observations about child development, 26–33, 45

holistic approach, 41, 50–51

identity and, 80–82

levels, 44–46

location, 69

in making adaptations, 13, 64, 328

modes, 66–68

new child in group, 47–48, 49, 68

of whom (subjects of observation), 68

participatory mode, 66–68, 94

problem solving and teamwork, 71, 72–75

reasons for observing young children, 9–14, 61–65

in research, 39–41

and responsive, inclusive educator, 14–16

rights of children, 75–76, 81–82

spectator mode, 66, 67–68, 94

in supporting early intervention/early identification, 10, 288–302

systematic process, 46–49

timing, 68–69, 70–71, 73, 116–117

observational drift, **128**

observational plans, 292–293

observational tools, 194–195

observation cycle. *See* cycle of observation

observation room, **66**

occupational standards, **64,** 65, 282–284

Oliveira, Marlina, 366–367

Ontario Best Start on Track Guide, 323

Ontario College of Teachers, 77, 78

Ontario Early Learning Framework (OELF), 28–29, 179–180, 186, 254, 280, 346–347, 364

Ontario Ministry of Children and Youth Services, 28, 60, 256–257, 266, 302–304, 347, 362

Ontario Ministry of Education, 7, 15, 18, 20, 28–29, 34–35, 247, 280, 282, 283, 293, 298–299, 316–317, 325, 330, 334, 336–337, 346

open methods (recording), 134, 135–187
ABC analysis, 137, 155–161
anecdotal records, 137, 138–151
audio/digital recordings, 95, 137, 169–172
defined, **136**
learning stories, 110, 137, 179–186
photographs and text, 137, 161–169

running records, 137, 151–155

video recordings, 137, 172–179

operant conditioning, **156**

ordinates, **212**

Oren, T., 18

organization, lack of, 71

orthotics, **340**

outdoor environment, 343–345

P

Paige-Smith, Alice, 249

paired observations, 135–136

palmar grasp, **30**

Pan-Canadian Public Health Network, 355, 356

paradigm shift, **180**–181

paraphrasing, **95**

paraprofessional, **294**

parents. *See* families; family-centred approach

participation charts, **190,** 215–220
adapting, 217–219
format, 190, 216–217
interpreting information, 219–220
purpose, 215
reflecting upon information, 219–220
unique feature, 215

participatory mode, 66–68, 94

patterning, **142**

patterns, **64**

Pavlov, Ivan, 156

Pearson, Robin, 21, 22

pedagogical documentation, **2,** 87–131. *See also* cycle of observation
adapting communication style, 98–99
audio/digital recordings in, 170
bias, 89, 124–130
characteristics, 113–116
child development domains, 30–32, 118–121
community building, 90–91, 93–98
defining behaviour, 110–111, 113–114
descriptive language, 97–98, 99–101, 125, 192–193
documenting process, 92–93
educator e-portfolios, 363–370
essential information, 94
ethical issues, 80, 82–83, 94
in inquiry-based process, 36–37
internal conditions, 112–113, 114
interpreting observations, 89, 121–124
labels, 114–116
learning stories, 180
learning to document, 103–110
mapping, 234
materials, 91, 92, 94–95
meaning of, 36–37
nature of, 34
observation and, 33–39
photographs in, 166–169

pedagogical documentation
(*Continued*)
portfolios, 130–131
pragmatics, 102
recording dialogue, 95
reflective educators,
253–258
rough notes and rewriting,
95–96, 103–106,
107–108
self-evaluation, 108–110
semantics, 101–102
shared responsibility, 90–91
subjects, 94
teacher-observer
guidelines, 93–98
teacher-observer role,
98–102
translation issues, 106–108
trends, 366–370
variables affecting
behaviour, 116–118
variety of recording
methods, 63–64,
103–110
vocabulary
development, 101
webbing, 182, 258–262
writing with confidence, 106
pedagogical frameworks,
240–241
pedagogical leadership,
357–360
pedagogical practices, 235–**236**
pedagogical questions,
58–59, 60
pedagogy, **1**, 36
and environment, 354
observation in
developing, 13

Pence, Allan, 38, 235–236
perceptions, 129–130, **147,**
149–151
Perry Preschool, 365–366
personality types, 39
personal level of observation,
44–45
person-first approach, 116
philosophy of setting, 71–72
photographs/photography,
137, **161**–169
children with special
needs, 165
digital technology, 164–165
and documentation
panels, 166
format, 163
and other documentation
methods, 165–166
and pedagogical documen-
tation, 166–169
pictorial combinations,
164–165
purpose, 162
unique feature, 162–163
physical environment,
339–345
classroom, 339–342
outdoor, 343–345
Piaget, Jean, 39–40, 138, 155,
296, 318
pictorial representations,
227–229
Pimento, B., 62, 64–65, 356
pincer grasp, **30**
Pinterest, 183
play
in early learning cycle, 53–54
in emergent or play-based
curriculum, 7, 22–23

importance of, 22–23
observation of children
during, 22–26, 50
play-based curriculum, **7,**
288, 340
play deprivation, **23**
play therapist, **146**
Pledge of Confidentiality, **83**
pluralistic society, **39**
portfolios, **130**–131, 262–284
artifacts, 33, 263, 272
assessment portfolios, 275
audio/digital recordings
in, 172
child roles, 268–270
contents, 131, 172
director and supervisor
roles, 270–271
display or showcase portfolios, 272, 273–274
educator roles, 268
e-portfolios/digital portfolios, 186, 275–280, 281,
363–370
family roles, 268–270,
276–277
learning stories, 185–186
metacognition of children,
280–282
pedagogical frameworks,
282–284
preparation stages and content, 264–267
professional standards,
282–284
purpose of developing, 130
video recordings, 176
working/developmental
portfolios, 272–275
Prabhu, Nina, 21

pragmatics, **102**

predisposition, **58**

prerequisite skills, **198**–199, **325**

prevalence, **322**

problem solving, in observation process, 71, 72–75

process. *See also* inquiry-based process

defined, 46

documenting, 92–93. *See also* documentation; pedagogical documentation

observation as interactive, 54–59

systematic process of observation, 46–49

professional development importance, 63, 361–363

interprofessional education, 301–302, 355–357

observer as researcher, 364–365

professional level of observation, 45–46

profiles, **185, 220**–227

adapting, 222–226

format, 221–222, 223–224, 225, 228

purpose, 220

reflecting upon information, 226–227

unique feature, 220–221

prosocial behaviour, **291**

provocations, **34, 145**

psychiatrists, **324**–325

psychoeducational assessments, **300**

psychologists, **324**–325

QUAD (quality, universality, accessibility, and developmental programming), 350–351

qualitative research, **41**

questions

cycle of observation, 57–61

in documentation process, 57–70, 93, 255

in environmental assessment, 345–354

pedagogical, 58–59, 60

portfolio preparation process, 264–267

rhetorical, 25–26

self-reflection, 59–61

why, how, who, when, where, and what, 61–70, 93

Rating Observation Scale for Inspiring Environments (ROSIE), 348

rating scales, **205**–209

adapting, 207

commercial examples, 206–207, 208

design considerations, 208

in early childhood, 207

format, 205–206

interpreting information, 208–209

purpose, 205

unique feature, 205

reciprocal approach, **16**

recordings. *See* audio/digital recordings; video recordings

referrals, **300**

reflection, 253–258. *See also* appreciative inquiry

creating time for, 254–255

and cycle of observation, 51, 56, 139, 195

importance for educators, 253–254

on information in checklists, 204–205

on information in participation charts, 219–220

on information in profiles, 226–227

self-evaluation of pedagogical documentation, 108–110

self-reflection questions, 59–61

webbing, 258–262

Reggio Emilia philosophy, 11–12, **33**–34, 38, 60–61, **161,** 179–180, 250, 367

reinforcement, **156**

reliability, **208**

interrater, **128**

reports, **300**

research

on early childhood, 39–41

ethnographic, 41, 365–366

longitudinal, 41, 365–366

on observation process, 75, 364–365

resiliency, **336,** 338–339

resource educator/early interventionist/resource professionals, **299**–302
respect, for diversity, 21
responsive educators, **14**–16, 34, 335–339
rhetorical questions, 25–**26**
Rhomberg, V., 126
rights of children, 75–76, 81–82
Rodari, Gianni, 137
Rogers, Carl, 305
Rourke Baby Record, 323
routines, 117
Rowan, C., 180
running records, 137, **151**–155
    diaries, 41, 155
    format, 151–154
    purpose, 151
    unique feature, 151

S

safety of children, 62–63, 302–312
scaffolding, **17**, 23
Schön, D. A., 15
School Age Early Childhood Rating Scale, 348
screening, **294**, 318, 319–323
self-actualizing, **336**
self-advocacy, **308**
self-help, 31, 119
self-rectifying, **54**–55
self-reflection, 59–61, 63
self-regulation, **336**, 338–339
semantics, 101–**102**
severity bias, **127**
showcase portfolios, **272**, 273–274

Shriver, C., 281
skills
    developmental sequence on checklists, 198–199
    diversity of, 32, 33
    domains of child development, 30–32, 118–121
    observing variability of, 11–12
Skinner, B. F., 40, 156
social capital, **354**–355
social construct theories, **20**, 38
social media, 168, 177, 358, 367–370
social stories, **178**, 340–341
sociocultural assessment, 316–317
sociocultural theory, 179, 337–338
socioemotional development, 31, 120, 296
    socioemotional/psychological environment, 335–339
    video recordings and, 173–178
socioemotional/psychological tone, 335–339
sociograms, 50, **229**–232
sociometry, **229**
SpeciaLink Child Care Inclusion Practices Profile and Principles Scale, 348
SpeciaLink Early Childhood Inclusion Quality Scale, 348

special needs. *See* children with special needs; early intervention/early identification
specimen records, **155**
spectator mode, 66, 67–68, 94
speech and language development, 31, 120, 283–284
spirituality of children, 50
stakeholders, **348**, 349–354
standardized assessments, **267**, 317–318, 319
standers, **340**
State of Learning in Canada (Canadian Council on Learning), 41
Stonehouse, A., 17
Storypark, 186
Stremmel, A., 260
student-educators, 85–86, 221
summary reports, **103**
summative evaluation, **206**, 331–332
supervisors. *See* directors and supervisors

T

targeted behaviours, **191**
Tarr, Pat, 14
task analysis, **325**
teachers. *See* early childhood professionals
teamwork. *See also* collaboration
    early intervention/early identification, 313–315
    lack of, 71
    problem solving and, 71, 72–75

technology. *See also* audio/digital recordings; computer technology; video recordings

digital photography, 164–165

ethical issues, 80

learning stories, 185–186

Technology Rich Inquiry Based Research, 183

temperament, observing variability of, 11–12

tenet, **78**

Terman, Lewis, 40

Te Whāriki (Maori philosophy), 30, 179–180, 316, 317, 337, 345–346

Think, Feel, Act (Ontario Ministry of Education), 7, 247, 336–337

"third space" (Gonzalez-Mena), 251–252

timing

of communication with families, 310–312

of observation, 68–69, 70–71, 73, 116–117

Toronto Children's Services, 348, 351–353

total communication, **165**

tourist curriculum, **127**

transformation, **20**

in cycle of observation, 249

translation, in pedagogical documentation, 106–108

trust, 307–312, 340–341

Turner, T., 11–12, 137

Twitter, 369–370

U

Underwood, K., 306

unfamiliarity, as challenge to observation, 72

United Nations General Assembly, Convention on the Rights of the Child, 75–76, 81–82

universally designed (learning materials), **342**

unobtrusive observation, **69**

V

validity, **208**

verbs, 100

video diaries, **41**

video recordings, 137, **172**–179

adapting, 175

effectiveness, 178–179

format, 176–177

purpose, 172–174

and socioemotional development, 173–178

unique features, 174–176

visual communication. *See also* photographs/photography; video recordings

children with special needs, 165

visual schedules, **340**–341

vocabulary development, in pedagogical documentation, 101

voice recordings. *See* audio/digital recordings

voice-to-text software, 171, 278–280

Vygotsky, Lev, 17–18, 296

W

watching, in observation process, 48–49

Watson, John B., 40, 156

webbing, **182, 258**–262

emergent documentation, 260

nature of, 258–260

"thinking and wondering," 260–262

Webster, Marilyn, 58, 59

well-being of children, 62–63, 302–312

wikis, 368

Wilson, L., 49

working/developmental portfolios, **272**–275

Working with Young Children Who Are Learning English as a New Language, 284